CW01647431

BUSINESS CYCLES

This abridgement has been reviewed and approved by the Schumpeter Committee of Harvard University.

BUSINESS CYCLES

A Theoretical, Historical and Statistical Analysis of the Capitalist Process

Joseph A. Schumpeter

ABRIDGED, WITH AN INTRODUCTION BY,
Rendigs Fels

PORCUPINE PRESS

First edition 1939
First abridged edition 1964
(New York: McGraw-Hill Inc., 1964)

© Copyright 1964 by McGraw-Hill, Inc.
All rights reserved. This book, or parts thereof, may not be reproduced in any form without permission of the publishers.

Reprinted 1989 by
Porcupine Press, Inc.
Philadelphia PA 19107
By arrangement with McGraw Hill Inc.

Library of Congress Cataloging-in-Publication Data

Schumpeter, Joseph Alois, 1883-1950.
Business cycles.

Reprint. Originally published: New York: McGraw Hill, 1964.
Includes bibliographical references and index.
1. Business cycles. 2. Economics. 3. Economic history. I. Fels, Rendigs, 1917- . II. Title.
HB3711.S392 1989 338.5'42 86-8183
ISBN 0-87991-263-4 (pbk.)

Manufactured in the United States of America

TABLE OF CONTENTS

TABLE OF CONTENTS (Continued)

CHAPTER V

CHAPTER VI

CHAPTER VII

CHAPTER VIII

TABLE OF CONTENTS (Continued)

CHAPTER IX

EDITOR'S INTRODUCTION

> "The younger generation of economists should look upon this book merely as something to shoot at and start from—as a motivated program for further research."—Joseph A. Schumpeter, Preface to *Business Cycles*, 1939 edition, p. v.

Schumpeter had bad luck with *Business Cycles.*[1] The most ambitious work of the trilogy setting forth "the Schumpeterian system," it has attracted less attention than his *Theory of Economic Development*[2] or his *Capitalism, Socialism, and Democracy.*[3] It is true that a reference to *Business Cycles* can occasionally be found in a footnote, but the text to which the footnote is appended rarely contains a discriminating discussion of its ideas. Clemence and Doody accorded it its proper place in *The Schumpeterian System,* but they preferred defending their former teacher against criticism to paying him the higher compliment of building on his work.[4]

The publication date of *Business Cycles* proved singularly unfortunate. Had it appeared three years before Keynes's *General Theory* sent economists scurrying off in other directions instead of three years' afterwards, it would have gained from the enormous interest everyone had in business cycles in 1933 and might have been accorded a reception second only to that later received by the *General Theory* itself.[5] Instead, it appeared just as the outbreak of World War II raised economic problems to which Keynes's tools, but not Schumpeter's, could be readily adapted. But *Business Cycles* lost almost as much from appearing six years too soon as from appearing six years too late. Given a different title, it might in 1945 have profited from the growing interest in economic devlopment, for its theme is as much how the present industrial nations developed as the themes indicated by its title and subtitle. Modern scholars can hardly be blamed if they turn for Schumpeter's ideas on the subject that currently fascinates them to a book called *The Theory of Economic Development* rather than to a book called *Business Cycles.*

They might have done so even if the titles had been reversed;

they might well prefer the shorter, more finished account to the longer, less polished one. The kind of fault that contributed to the success of Keynes's *General Theory* added to the neglect of Schumpeter's *Business Cycles.* Both would have been better books had their authors spent another year improving them. Whereas the shortcomings of the *General Theory* stimulated other economists to lay bare and refine and apply the model half-concealed in it, incidentally making Keynesians of them, the similar need to clarify and improve and use the Schumpeterian model repelled them. There are no Schumpeterians. One need not take issue with Schumpeter's criticism of Marshall for lavishing too much time on the eight editions of the *Principles* to hold that he himself made the opposite error.[6]

Though a quarter of a century has elapsed since the first edition of *Business Cycles,* the opportunities it opened up for further research remain largely unexploited. The chief exception is Schumpeter's own *Capitalism, Socialism, and Democracy.* Much has been published on innovation and entrepreneurship, usually with a nod in Schumpeter's direction but no more. Even a work like Yusif A. Sayigh's *Entrepreneurs of Lebanon,* which ostensibly takes Schumpeter's concepts as its starting point, actually deals with entrepreneurs as people—their education, religion, opinions, even the number of their children—to the neglect of what was central to Schumpeter's analysis, innovating activity and its impact.[7]

At the time *Business Cycles* was written, work on Kuznets cycles—the long swings of fifteen to twenty years—was still at an early stage. Since then a large amount of statistical and a small amount of analytical work has gone forward. Those who have made the principal efforts to explain Kuznets cycles, Matthews and Abramovitz, have not seen fit to draw on Schumpeter's work but have resorted to an incomplete and essentially aggregative tool, the capital-stock adjustment principle.[8] (It is ironic that a generation of economists that regards disaggregation as a shining virtue has underestimated the theory of such a staunch opponent of aggregation as Schumpeter. In our heart of hearts, we prefer the aggregates of Keynes, Harrod, Domar, etc.; despite Walras's earlier and better claim to a general theory, we permitted Keynes to take over the term, Schumpeter's objections notwithstanding. Our cant about disaggregation means only that we have guilty consciences.) Yet Schumpeter's concept of recession could be exceedingly helpful in interpreting the 1870s, a period which raises a problem ignored by Matthews and Abramovitz in the works cited in the footnote above. Their most telling evidence for the existence of Kuznets cycles consists of two circumstances, swings in the rate of growth of real GNP that average fifteen to twenty years, and the recurrence of deep depressions at similar intervals—there was one in the 1870s, one in the 1890s, there would (or might) have been one in the 1910s but for World War I, and there was one in the 1930s. Including 1873-78 in the category of deep depressions at first sight seems reasonable enough, since it is generally considered not only the longest but also one of the worst business contractions on record. But Abramovitz shows a "tentative" peak in the rate of growth of real GNP, after eliminating the effects of business cycles, which he dates 1874.25.[9] This means that the average annual rate of growth between the complete business cycle with peaks in 1869 and 1873 and the complete business cycle with peaks in 1873 and 1882 was higher than for neighboring pairs of cycles—in fact it was the highest on record for any successive pairs of cycles, in spite of the fact that the contraction included in the 1873-82 period is rated a deep depression, whereas the contraction phase of the preceding cycle was very mild. Thus the statistical finding about the rate of growth of real GNP collides with the judgment that 1873-78 was a deep depression; furthermore, it plays hob with Abramovitz's analysis of the way Kuznets cycles unfold, in which deep depressions and troughs in growth rates go together. How can the paradox of a rapid rate of growth in a period encompassing deep depression be resolved? Schumpeter's concept of recession could illuminate it: previous innovation must have made possible a great increase in output that imposed hardship—symptoms of depression—on all parts of the economy unable to adapt to the new conditions. Not that one can turn to Schumpeter's own account of the 1870s for a ready-made explanation of the facts Matthews and Abramovitz have wrestled with; it is rather that today's economists are missing an opportunity to build on Schumpeter's work.

The importance of a book is judged by what it leads to. By this test, it is doubtful if Schumpeter's *Business Cycles* would merit rescue from the limbo of "out of print." The first reason for the present edition lies in the conviction that it can yet stimulate significant research. Why an *abridged* edition? Ordinarily,

I deplore abridgements, but in the present case there is every reason to believe that a shorter version will prove more useful, especially since the longer one will always be available in libraries. Eliminating digressions and the less valuable parts of the original two volumes, which ran to more than a thousand pages, will enable the reader, I hope, to spend his time more profitably. Having myself spent a great deal of labor trying to master the original edition, I have nothing but sympathy for economists who felt that it was not worth the effort.

In the work of abridgement, my first concern has been to preserve a complete statement of the theory, since less thorough accounts are readily available elsewhere. This has meant retaining most of Chapters II, III, and IV and parts of Chapters I and V. Even in Chapters II-IV, however, I have not hesitated to cut footnotes, paragraphs, and whole pages where the discussion seemed to go pretty far afield, as well as deleting superfluous sentences and phrases. Although I hope that what remains is somewhat more readable than the original, it is still hard going, and I would have liked to add as an appendix a summary of Schumpeter's theory that I prepared for my own use many years ago. But it seemed better to save the space for Schumpeter's own words. Besides, an excellent summary of Schumpeter's theory is already available in Clemence and Doody's *The Schumpeterian System*.[10]

My second concern was to retain a full account of the interpretation of the cyclical history of one country, in preference to partial accounts of the three countries that Schumpeter discussed at length. The nature of the theory, which includes a Kondratieff cycle sixty years in duration, calls for a long sweep of history. That the country chosen should be the United States rather than England or Germany reflects more than the national origins of editor and publisher. The United States was the country Schumpeter devoted most attention to and, particularly in the discussion of the 1930s, is the one that best illustrates the working of his model.

The decisions to keep fairly complete accounts of the theory and of its application to one country dictated omitting virtually all the statistical analysis (Chapters VIII-XIII and a long section of Chapter XIV of the original edition). One of the reviews that appeared not long after the 1939 edition was published criticized it for not having a serviceable statistical technique.

The criticism was just, and omitting the statistical chapters may be deemed no great loss. Perhaps it would have been desirable to have cut them heavily, retaining the parts most useful for throwing light on the implications of the theory, but the abridged edition is quite long enough as it is.

I have regularly deleted references to sources of information. Since Schumpeter's sources are now obsolescent, if not obsolete, very few readers would be interested in them.

Schumpeter's style ran not only to frequent digressions, which I have tried to eliminate, but also to surplus words, to stating what is already implied, to burdening the reader with phrases that distract his attention. In such a sentence as, "*It is surely not too much to ask economists to realize that* behavior in human societies differs from behavior in animal societies or in physical systems. . . ." (p. 1046 of the 1939 edition), I have deleted the italicized words without using dots to so indicate. Occasionally it was convenient to alter the punctuation. I have generally resisted the temptation to substitute a word or two of my own, even where doing so could have saved a good deal of space, on grounds that my words would have to be in square brackets which would distract the reader; but I have, on rare occasions, taken the liberty of rearranging Schumpeter's own words. To give an extreme example, a passage on p. 31 of the first edition reads, "We cannot enter here into the epistemological problem of the relation between 'theory' and 'facts.' But it must be emphasized that what will be said in this chapter and those following is, in part, nothing but a generalized formulation of some of the facts presented later. Therefore the term *verification* does not accurately describe that relation." Wanting to omit the first sentence, I transposed a few words from it to the last, which in this edition reads, "Therefore, the term *verification* does not accurately describe the relation between 'theory' and 'facts.' "

There are severe limits to what an editor may properly do. I wish Schumpeter were still alive to do the rewriting the book cries out for. Since that is not possible, McGraw-Hill is to be commended for deciding on its own initiative to publish an abridged edition.

RENDIGS FELS

Vanderbilt University

FOOTNOTES TO EDITOR'S INTRODUCTION

[1] The full citation is Joseph A. Schumpeter, *Business Cycles: A Theoretical, Historical, and Statistical Analysis of the Capitalist Process*, 1st edition (New York and London: McGraw-Hill Book Company, Inc., 1939).

Schumpeter, an Austrian economist who spent the last eighteen years of his life at Harvard, was born in 1883 and died in 1950. For an account of his life see the "Memorial" by Arthur Smithies in the *American Economic Review*, September 1950, pp. 628-45.

[2] *The Theory of Economic Development; an Inquiry into Profits, Capital, Credit, Interst, and the Business Cycle*, translated from the German by Redvers Opie (Cambridge, Mass.: Harvard University Press, 1934).

[3] 3d edition (New York: Harper & Brothers Publishers, 1950).

[4] Richard V. Clemence and Francis S. Doody, *The Schumpeterian System* (Cambridge, Mass.: Addison-Wesley Press, 1950).

[5] John M. Keynes, *The General Theory of Employment, Interest, and Money* (New York: Harcourt, Brace and Company, 1936).

[6] Alfred Marshall, *Principles of Economics*, 8th edition (London: Macmillan and Co., Limited, 1922).

[7] *Entrepreneurs of Lebanon; The Role of the Business Leader in a Developing Economy* (Cambridge, Mass.: Harvard University Press, 1962).

[8] R.C.O. Matthews, *The Business Cycle* (Chicago: University of Chicago Press, 1959), Ch. 12; Moses Abramovitz, "The Nature and Significance of Kuznets Cycles," *Economic Development and Cultural Change*, April 1961, pp. 225-48.

[9] Moses Abramovitz, Statement in United States Congress, Joint Economic Committee, *Employment, Growth, and Price Levels, Hearings* (86th Congress, 1st Session), Part II (Washington: Government Printing Office, 1959), p. 434.

[10] *Op cit.*, pp. 7-21.

Chapter I

INTRODUCTORY

Among the factors which determine any given business situation there are some which act from within and some which act from without the economic sphere. Economic consideration can fully account for the former only; the latter must be accepted as data and all we can do about them in economic analysis is to explain their effects on economic life. Hence we arrive at the very important concept of factors acting from without (let us call them External Factors), which it stands to reason we must try to abstract from when working out an explanation of the causation of economic fluctuations properly so called, that is, of those economic changes which are inherent in the working of the economic organism itself.[1]

The best examples of what we mean by an external factor are offered by such events as the great Tokyo earthquake, the virtue of which from our standpoint consists in the fact that no one has thought of attributing responsibility for them to our industrial system. Whenever a disturbance is the product of social

[1] The effects of these external factors will be called the ***external irregularities*** of our material, as distinguished from its ***internal irregularities***, to be defined later.

processes, the difficult question arises whether it is not as much a consequence as a cause of economic events and situations and hence whether we are within our rights if we speak of it as "acting from without the economic sphere." In a deeper sense, the answer is undoubtedly in the negative. But for our purpose it is yet permissible to draw a line between the phenomena directly incident to the working *of* the economic system and the phenomena produced by other social agencies acting *on* the economic system, however obviously this action may be conditioned by economic situations or propelled by economic aim or class interest. In a sense, therefore, we may within the limited range of our investigation look upon wars, danger of war, revolutions, and social unrest as external factors. Changes in the tariff policy of a country or in its system of taxation, measures of social betterment, and government regulations of all kinds we include in the same class. After all, there is probably little that could be objected to in our recognition of the fact that it would not help us much, for instance in an analysis of the problems of foreign exchange, to deal indiscriminately with cases in which exchanges are determined by commercial factors alone and cases in which they are "pegged" as the French exchange was during the war. And this is all that our distinction amounts to so far. But for obvious reasons it is less easy to carry out the distinction in other cases, and great care—carried even to the extent of hairsplitting—is required in order to do justice to the endless variety of the social patterns we encounter.

Variations of crops due to natural causes, such as weather conditions or plagues, raise a problem only because of the difficulty of separating them from variations due to other causes. But for this, we could class them with the effects of earthquakes. Gold discoveries also could be listed in the same category as far as they may be considered, from the standpoint of the business organism, to be chance events. But it is a fact that variations in the *total* supply of gold often come about in response to business situations and in exactly the same way as variations in the supply of any other commodity. The variations in the *monetary* supply of gold are never conditioned by chance discoveries alone. Hence we have here a case of mixed character not always easy to interpret.

This, however, raises the question of discoveries of new countries and of what is readily seen to be for our purposes similar in character and effect, inventions. Both create new possibilities and are no doubt among the most important causes of economic and social change. But are they external factors in our sense? Our answers will best be given by way of examples. If we scrutinize the motives and methods of Columbus's venture, we find that it would be by no means absurd to call it a business venture. In this case it would be just as much an element of the business situation as is any other enterprise. But if we refuse to do this, the discovery of America does not thereby become an external factor, for it was not directly relevant to the course of the economic process at all. It acquired relevance only as and when the new possibilities were turned into commercial and industrial reality, and then the individual acts of realization and not the possibilities themselves are what concern us. Those acts, the formation of companies for the exploitation of the new opportunities, the setting of the new countries, the exports into and the imports from them, are part of the economic process, as they are part of economic history, and not outside of it. Again, the invention of, say, the Montgolfier balloon was not an external factor of the business situation of its time; it was, indeed, no factor at all. The same is true of all inventions as such, witness the inventions of the antique world and the middle ages which for centuries failed to affect the current of life. As soon, however, as an invention is put into business practice, we have a process which arises from, and is an element of, the economic life of its time, and not something that acts on it from without. In no case, therefore, is invention an external factor.

We sometimes read that in the nineteenth century the opening up of new countries was the background on which economic evolution achieved what it did. In a sense this statement is true. But if the inference is that this circumstance was an external factor, that is, something distinct from that very economic evolution and independently acting upon it, then the statement ceases to be true: our vision of the evolution of capitalism must precisely include the opening up of new countries as one of its elements and as a result of the same process which also produced all the other economic features of that epoch. Among them is the mechanization of industry. Again, we read a statement made by a high authority in our field, to the effect that it is not "capitalistic enterprise" *but* technological progress (invention, machinery) which accounts for the rate of increase in total output during the nineteenth century. Obviously it is not a matter of indifference whether we accept the theory underlying that statement, namely that the mechanization of industry was a phenomenon distinct from "capitalistic enterprise" and independently influencing it—a phenomenon which could and would have come about in substantially the same way whatever the social organization—or whether we hold as we do (in this respect entirely agreeing with Marx) that technological progress was of the very essence of capitalistic enterprise and hence cannot be divorced from it.

We need not stay to explain why, for any country, business fluctuations in another country should be looked upon as external factors. But to treat in this way variations in the number and age distribution of populations is less easy to justify. Migrations in particular are so obviously conditioned by business fluctuations that no description of the mechanism of cycles can claim to be complete without including them, and including them—at least some of them—as internal factors. However, as we shall not deal with this group of problems in this volume—although the writer is alive to the seriousness of this breach in our wall—it will be convenient to consider migration over the frontiers of the territories to which our statistics refer, provisionally, as an external factor, while migration within those territories, which it would be imposible so to consider, will be noticed but incidentally. Changes in numbers and age distributions due to other causes than migration sometimes are in fact external factors or consequences of external factors, such as wars.[1]

Finally, we have had examples (changes in tariff policy, taxation, and so on) of what we may term changes in the institutional framework. They range from fundamental social reconstruction, such as occurred in Russia after 1917, down to changes of detail in social behavior or habits, such as keeping one's liquid resources in the form of a demand deposit rather than in the

[1] Readers will see that our arrangements about the element of population are partly motivated by factual propositions and partly by considerations of expository convenience arising out of the purposes of this book. It is not, of course, held that those arrangements would be satisfactory outside of these purposes or that the subject of population has no claim to other treatment than is given to it here. Work done by Dr. A. Lösch, Bevölkerungswellen und Wechsellagen, 1936, has even shaken the writer's conviction, which used to be strong, that changes in population have no place among the causal factors of economic cycles.

form of cash at home or contracting collectively rather than individually. It is entirely immaterial whether or not such changes are embodied in, or recognized by, legislation. In any case they alter the rules of the economic game and hence the significance of indices and the systematic relations of the elements which form the economic world. In some cases, however, they so directly act by means of business behavior that it may become difficult to recognize them as external factors. Change of practice by the Federal Reserve System or by any Central Bank in Europe may be itself an act of business behavior and an element of the mechanism of cycles, as well as an external factor; and so may collective measures taken by the business world itself. Every such case must be treated on its merits, and decision may be difficult indeed. Our distinction must be kept in mind even in such cases, but it works with increasing difficulty the more frequent they become. This is but a consequence of the fact that our economic system is not a pure one but in full transition toward something else, and, therefore, not always describable in terms of a logically consistent analytic model.

Now, it is obvious that the external factors of economic change are so numerous and important that if we beheld a complete list of them we might be set wondering whether there was anything left in business fluctuations to be accounted for in other ways. This impression is much intensified by the fact that the impact of external factors would of itself account for wavelike alternation of states of prosperity and of depression, both because some disturbances occur at almost regular intervals and because most of them induce a process of adaptation in the system which will produce the picture of a wavelike oscillation in every individual case.

In fact, it would be possible to write, without any glaring absurdity, a history of business fluctuations exclusively in terms of external factors, and such a history would probably miss a smaller amount of relevant fact than one which attempts to do without them. Consequently, a theory of business fluctuations to the effect that they are caused by external factors would not lack verifying evidence; indeed, it might be the first to suggest itself to an unprejudiced mind.

There are instances covering considerable stretches of our material, in which effects of external factors entirely overshadow everything else, either in the behavior of individual elements of business situations or in the behavior of business situations as a whole. The fall of greenback prices during the greenback "deflation" after 1866, which even the prosperity of 1872 was powerless to reverse (although it did arrest it) is an instance of the first class. The whole course of economic events from 1914 to about 1920 may be cited as an instance of the second. There is no perfectly satisfactory remedy for this. We shall, indeed, exclude from the facts on which we are to base fundamental conclusions, material which is obviously vitiated by such things as the World War, "wild" inflations, and so on. This is the reason why we shall deal with postwar cycles separately and try, as far as possible, to work out fundamentals from prewar material, although sources of facts and figures flow much more freely since 1919 than they did before 1914. We cannot, however, go very far in this direction without losing too much of our material. But the influence of external factors is never absent. And never are they of such a nature that we could dispose of them according to the schema of, say, a pendulum continually exposed to numerous small and independent shocks. The power of the economic machine is great enough to hold its own to an astonishing degree, even as it shows its working in the worst material and the most faultily constructed indices. But it never works entirely true to design, although at some times more so than at others. Seven conclusions of great, if sinister, importance follow from this.

In the first place, it is absurd to think that we can derive the contour lines of our phenomena from statistical material only. All that we could ever prove from it is that no regular contour lines exist. We must put our trust in bold and unsafe mental experiments or else give up all hope. Here also we strike one of the fundamental difficulties about economic forecasting—one which goes far to explain and even to excuse some of the failures of predictions to come true. At almost any point of time statistical contour lines bear uncomfortable resemblance to the skyline of a city after an earthquake. Hence it is as unreasonable to expect the economist to forecast correctly what will actually happen as it would be to expect a doctor to prognosticate when his patient will be the victim of a railroad accident and how this will affect his state of health.

Second, it is important to keep in mind that what we know from experience is not the working of capitalism as such, but of a distorted capitalism which is covered with the scars of past injuries inflicted on its organism. This is true not only of the way in which our business organism functions but also of its structure. The very fundaments of the industrial organisms of all nations have been politically shaped. Everywhere we find industries which would not exist at all but for protection, subsidies, and other political stimuli, and others which are overgrown or otherwise in an unhealthy state because of them, such as the beet-sugar industry in Europe and shipbuilding all over the world. Such industries are assets of doubtful value, in any case a source of weakness and often the immediate cause of breakdowns or depressive symptoms. This type of economic waste and maladjustment may well be more important than any other.

Third, in some cases we may gather enough information about the nature, range and duration of a big disturbance to know more or less precisely which of our figures are vitiated by it. Then we can either drop these items or try to correct them —as we sometimes do, for instance, in the case of prices during an inflation. But whether we do this or something else or nothing at all, it is always of the utmost importance for us to be thoroughly masters of the economic history of the time, the country or the industry, sometimes even of the individual firm in question, before we draw any inference at all from the behavior of time series. We cannot stress this point sufficiently. General history (social, political, and cultural), economic history, and more particularly industrial history are not only indispensable but really the most important contributors to the understanding of our problem. All other materials and methods, statistical and theoretical, are only subservient to them and worse than useless without them.

Chapter II

EQUILIBRIUM AND THE THEORETICAL NORM OF ECONOMIC QUANTITIES

A. The Meaning of a Model.—Much can be done by the mere survey of those facts which we designate by the expression *business situation* and by the common-sense discussion of them. To make headway beyond this, it is obviously necessary to collect more facts and to find more elaborate statistical methods. We must go as far as possible into the past—because we have no other means of observing a large number of units of fluctuation —and hence historical research must be of paramount importance even for dealing with the most practical of contemporaneous problems.

But in any such discussion of economic fact we run up against a wall which blocks the road toward precise answers to many of our questions. We must now try, with a view to acquiring a more powerful apparatus of analysis to refine upon our common-sense methods exactly as we must try to increase our stock of facts and to improve upon our statistical methods. That is what we propose to do in this chapter and the two that follow.

Surely this is the most natural thing to do. But since well-known controversies have arisen about it, the following remarks are submitted in explanation and defense.

1. If we present certain concepts and propositions at the outset and in a connected argument, this is partly a mere matter of expository convenience. Other concepts and propositions will follow later, as the need for them arises. But this method of exposition carries the danger of a misunderstanding. It will seem to many readers as though the facts introduced later had no other role to fill than that of verifying a preexisting thoery. What will be said in this chapter and those following is, in part, nothing but generalized formulation of some of the facts presented later. Therefore, the term *verification* does not accurately describe the relation between "thory" and "facts." A much wider claim than it implies must be made and is here made for the direct study of historical and statistical fact.

2. Some of our refinements upon common sense are logically anterior to the facts we wish to study and must be introduced first, because our factual discussions would be impossible without them. What we mean differs from what students of economic cycles usually understand by a "theory." Many even of those who do not look upon theory as "babble," are in the habit of identifying it with explanatory hypotheses. And it is reckless or dilettantist hypothesis making which is responsible for both the discredit into which theory has fallen and the contrast which for some students exists between factual (or "realistic" or "empirical") and theoretic work. But the framing of hypotheses, although sometimes as necessary in our science as it is in all others, is neither the sole nor the main function of a theory in the sense in which it is synonymous with "analytic apparatus." If we are to speak about price levels and to devise methods of measuring them, we must know what a price level is. If we are to observe demand, we must have a precise concept of its elasticity. No hypotheses enter into such concepts, which simply embody methods of description and measurement, nor into the propositions defining their relations (so-called *theorems*), and yet their framing is the chief task of theory, in economics as elsewhere. This is what we mean by *tools of analysis*. Obviously, we must have them before we take hold of the material we wish to measure and to understand. A set of such analytic tools, if framed to deal with phenomena which form a distinct process, we call a *model* or *schema* of this process.

3. Some workers in our field not only neglect the task to which we are about to turn, but take pride in doing so. They

justify this by the claim that they are applying to social facts the methods of the physical sciences. They entirely overlook the role of theory in physics, which is precisely the kind of arsenal of tools we have in mind. However right, therefore, it may sometimes be to enter solemn protests against preconceived ideas, speculation, and metaphysics, no argument of weight can be gained from the physical analogy for the view that the right way to go about our task is to assemble statistics, to treat them by formal methods, and to present the results as the solution of a problem. The illusion underlying this view may be further exposed by an instance of what we may term Nonsense Induction. In every crisis or depression we observe that commodities become unsalable. If on the strength of this we say, "People produce too much, hence they are, from time to time, unable to sell what they produce," we are saying something for which there is really no warrant in the factual finding itself. Yet we have to make statements of this kind. If we do so on the finding alone, we are performing an operation void of sense, although it may be clothed in terms that look exact.

4. Statistical and historical facts have, on the one hand, much more important roles to play in the building of our knowledge of a phenomenon than to verify a theory drawn from other sources. They induce the theoretical work and determine its pattern. But, on the other hand, they cannot be said to fill quite satisfactorily the function that theorists usually assign to them—the function of verification. For there is, along with Nonsense Induction, such a thing as Spurious Verification. Starting from the common-sense impression that the interest rate is an important factor in business situations, we may jump to the conclusion that it is the causal factor responsible for booms and slumps. In fact, almost always a low rate of interest precedes a boom and a high rate of interest a slump. If this were enough to establish causal connection, this proposition would be one of the safest of our science. Yet, it is wrong and could be proved to be so, even if no statistical fact ever contradicted it. Nor is this all. Even if the proposition were correct, statistics could not prove it to be so, for it stands to reason that the behavior of our time series could also be explained by another relation or on grounds perfectly free from causal implication—for instance, on the ground that every boom must be preceded by a state of things which we recognize as being the reverse

to "booming," that in such nonbooming situations there is little demand for money and, therefore, a low rate of interest. Hence prosperous business would always be preceded by low interest, even if this had nothing to do with bringing it about or if it were an obstacle to it.

No statistical finding can ever either prove or disprove a proposition which we have reason to believe by virtue of simpler and more fundamental facts. It cannot prove such a proposition, because one and the same behavior of a time series can analytically be accounted for in an indefinite number of ways. It cannot disprove the proposition, because a very real relation may be so overlaid by other influences acting on the statistical material under study as to become entirely lost in the numerical picture, without thereby losing its importance for our understanding of the case. It follows that the claim usually made for statistical induction and verification must be qualified. Material exposed to so many disturbances as ours is, does not fulfill the logical requirements of the process of induction.

B. The Fundamental Question.—When we behold one of the familiar graphs of economic time series, we undoubtedly have the impression of an "irregular regularity" of fluctuations. Our first and foremost task is to measure them and to describe their mechanism. It is primarily for this purpose that we shall now try to provide the analytic tools or a schema or model. But our mind will never be content with this. However much wisdom there may be in the warnings against premature questions about causes,[1] they will always be asked until they are answered. Moreover, our mind will never be at rest until we have assembled in one model causes, mechanisms, and effects, and can show how it works. And in this sense the question of causation is the Fundamental Question, although it is neither the only one nor the first to be asked.

Now if we do ask this question quite generally about all the fluctuations, crises, booms, depressions that have ever been ob-

[1] There is, of course, a strong argument against using that questionable term at all. We shall speak of causes in a common-sense way, which, it is believed, is not subject to epistemological indictment. If a definition be thought desirable, we may say that we mean by causes of a phenomenon a set of circumstances without which it would not present itself. We might define them as "necessary and sufficient conditions," but the greater precision only opens up new difficulties.

served, the only answer is that there is no single cause or prime mover which acounts for them. Nor is there even any set of causes which account for all of them equally well. For each one is a historic individual and never like any other, either in the way it comes about or in the picture it presents. To get at the causation of each we must analyze the facts of each and its individual background. Any answer in terms of a single cause is sure to be wrong.

But an entirely different question emerges behind this one. If we succeed in describing the economic system by means of a general schema embodying certain properties of it, there is obviously much practical utility in asking the question whether the system, as thus depicted, will *by its own working* produce booms or crises or depressions, and, if so, under what circumstances. Similarly, there is no sense in looking for a single reason why men die, for there is obviously a great variety of reasons. But there is both sense and interest in the question whether and why death would come about, in the absence of lesions, by virtue of the working of the human organism or the cells of which it consists. This is the truly fascinating problem, although it hardly ever enters into the ordinary mental operations of medical practice, which are always concerned with one or another of the innumerable patterns of the actual occurrence of death.

Having formulated the question as we wish it to be understood, we have to admit that the answer may still be negative. External factors certainly account for much in economic fluctuations, and they might even account for everything. This would amount to a theory of the cycle which may be very simply stated: a crisis or depression occurs whenever there is an unfavorable event of sufficient importance. We cannot dismiss this view a priori. Moreover, it derives some support from traditional economics. Where economic life is not treated as stationary, it is, by the best authorities, treated as a process of organic growth which simply adapts itself to changing data. Barring the waves which can easily be shown to result from the properties of the adaptive mechanism, this does not point to any internal cause of cycles. Some have frankly held the cycle to be a "sham" or a random fluctuation.[1]

[1] Any of these views may be right, of course, while it is certain that some supporters of the contrary view are guilty of faulty reasoning or have otherwise failed to establish the claim they make for the cycle as

No doubt, the testimony of facts might be such as to make the existence or absence of a cyclical component inherent in the economic process a practical certainty. But atually they do not speak with a certain voice—especially because prima-facie adequate external factors are always with us—and however we may treat them by formal methods, they leave the Fundamental Question unanswered. Nothing remains, therefore, but to construct a model of the economic process and to see how it works in the study of time series. It also follows that in doing so we cannot take for granted that there is a cyclical movement inherent in the economic process, as we could if this were an indubitable fact of economic experience.

C. The Stationary Flow.—The analytic treatment of the facts of autonomous change in a closed domain begins conveniently with the model of an unchanging economic process which flows on at constant rates in time and merely reproduces itself.[1] Obviously, such a model will present the fundamental

---

a distinct phenomenon. In part, also, final decision will simply rest on fertility in results and satisfactory fit to facts. Just here, however, it is important to emphasize that even straight negation of the existence of the cycle may mean very different things. Mr. Carl Snyder, for example, seems to mean no more than that the importance of the business cycle, taken by itself, has often been exaggerated—which is quite true. Professor Irving Fisher, in *Econometrica*, October 1933, p. 338, however, says that "the motion of the business cycle as a single simple self-generating cycle" is a myth. We quite agree, as the reader will see, that the business cycle does not consist of a single wavelike movement and that it is not "simple." It is very difficult to say whether the passage quoted means more than that. Other authors, again, when they deny the existence of the cycle, mean only to deny exact periodicity in the sense of constancy of period. In any case, in order to deny anything we have expressly or by implication claimed so far, it would be necessary to deny that business is sometimes good and sometimes bad.

[1] The nonprofessional reader will find this section, and perhaps others, difficult to absorb. And so it is, although the writer has simplified to the point of risking incorrectness of statement. The professional reader, in turn, will take offense at this simplification. In particular, he will find that some tools used by the writer are antiquated and that in many points recent progress of analysis has not been sufficiently taken into account. This will be done in another book which, in a wider frame, will among other things overhaul the purely theoretic parts of the present argument. Here, no other course seemed open to the writer than the one he has taken.

The first two tools we have just introduced—the idea of the closed

facts and relations of economic life in their simplest form, and it is hardly possible to bring them out satisfactorily without it. Implicitly and in a rudimentary form it has, therefore, always been present in the minds of absolutely all economists of all schools at all times, although most of them were not aware of it. Some even displayed hostility to it as soon as it was rigorously defined and made to stand out in all the gauntness of its abstractions. This was attempted by the physiocrats and definitely achieved by Leon Walras. The Marshallian structure is based upon the same conception, which it is important to emphasize in view of the fact that Marshall did not like it and almost made it disappear from the surface of his exposition.

The commonsense of this tool of analysis may be formulated as follows: first, if we deal with, say, the organism of a dog, the interpretation of what we observe divides readily into two branches. We may be interested in the processes of life going on in the dog, such as the circulation of the blood, its relation to the digestive mechanism, and so on. But however completely we master all their details, and however satisfactorily we succeed in linking them up with each other, this will not help us to describe or understand how such things as dogs have come to exist at all. Obviously, we have here a different process before us, involving different facts and concepts such as selection or mutation or, generally, evolution. In the case of biological organisms nobody takes offense at the distinction. There is nothing artificial or unreal about it and it comes naturally to us; the facts indeed impose it on us.

Second, our distinction is by no means foreign to the ways of thinking of practical business. Every businessman realizes that running his plant in the customary way, going through all the

---

domain and the stationary process—although absolutely necessary for straight thinking, already call for apologies. The first, while unexceptionable in itself, becomes very doubtful when applied to countries linked to each other and the rest of the world by a multitude of economic relations, of which we shall take but the most superficial account. This is a very serious imperfection, not only because we relegate to the realm of disturbing factors what is part of the real process of economic change, but also because the most urgent task in the field of the theory of international trade is obviously its reconstruction from the standpoint of the theory of cycles. The second tool meets with objections even from specialists. We want it in order to bring out, by contrast, the contours of the phenomena of economic evolution.

motions of daily business routine, is one thing and that setting up the plant or changing its setup is another. He approaches these tasks with attitudes which differ characteristically from each other. There would be no object in trying to fuse into one schema the things to be done and the behavioristic types encountered in the two cases, merely because "real life" hardly ever presents one of them without the other, or because the real world is always "dynamic." The answer to any unwillingness to accept our distinction on the score of its being too theoretical is simply that everybody actually works with it, both in practical life and in analysis, although in a subconscious and inexact way—and that it is just as well to put logical definiteness into this universal practice. We shall see, moreover, that this is one of the most important means of understanding the mechanism of the business cycle.

D. Equilibrium and the Theoretical Norm.—For our present argument we may thus visualize an economic process which merely reproduces itself at constant rates: a given population, not changing in either numbers or age distribution, organized for purposes of consumption in households and for purposes of production and trade in firms, lives and works in an unchanging physical and social (institutional) environment. The tastes (wants) of households are given and do not change. The ways of production and usances of commerce are optimal from the standpoint of the firms' interest and with respect to existing horizons and possibilities, hence do not change either, unless some datum changes or some chance event intrudes upon this world.

Technological data may be expressed, for every firm, by a function which links quantities of facts, such as labor, services of natural agents and means of production that are themselves produced ("intermediate products": raw material, equipment, and so on) to the quantity of the product which it is possible to produce by each of the infinite number of ways in which they can be combined for this productive task, technological practice and the whole environment being what they are. This function, known as the production function, tells us all we need to know for purposes of economic analysis about the technological processes of production. Production, in the sense relevant to economics, is nothing but combining quantities of factors, and it is, for economic purposes, exhaustively described by such a combination (productive combination). While the production function itself, in the case of a stationary economy, is a datum and invariant in form, the actual combinations of factors, as measured, for example, by coefficients of production, are among the variables of the problem, and must be determined by economic considerations. If these coefficients were all fixed, that is, if in order to produce, say, a bushel of wheat it were necessary to combine land, labor, seed, fertilizers, and so on, in given and unalterable proportions, there would be no economic problem of production beyond deciding whether to produce the bushel or not. If, however, there is some freedom of choice between combinations, which means that it is possible to produce the bushel of wheat either with, say, a certain quantity of land and a certain quantity of labor or with more land and less labor or less land and more labor, other factors remaining constant, then the economic problem emerges in the shape of considerations about costs and values. This is what is usually referred to as Substitutability of Factors. Inasmuch as that freedom of choice is not absolute and substitution is possible only according to certain rules and within certain limits, the production function which embodies these rules and limits may be looked upon as a condition or constraint imposed by the technological horizon and the structure of the economic environment on economic decision or on the maxima of economic advantage or profitableness which economic decision strives to attain. So far as substitution is not possible at all, analytic difficulties arise which need not detain us here.

But another point calls for notice. If all factors were infinitely divisible, the production function would be continuous and we could move about on it by infinitesimal steps. Many factors, however, are not infinitely divisible but available only in such large minimum units—think, for example, of a railroad track or even a steel plant—that product responds to addition of a unit not by a small variation but by a jump, which means that the production function is discontinuous in such points. Such factors we call *lumpy*. Now in the presence of a lumpy factor it will very often happen that production below a certain quantity of output will entirely have to do without that factor. An instance is the small-scale production of the artisan type, in which it would not pay to use costly machinery. In this case, mere increase in output within the technological horizon of the producers and along one and the same production function may spell change in what is usually referred to by the ill-defined term Method of Production. The same effect may be brought about by change in the relative prices of factors: an increase in wages may induce agriculture to proceed from intensive to extensive methods of cultivation, or industry to replace labor by machinery which may involve complete change of technological processes or principles. Yet both classes of cases may come about within one and the same production function.

In view of much that is to follow, it is to distinguish those classes of cases from others—which could also be described as changes in method of production but which do imply changes in the production function. The criterion is whether or not the change occurs within the given horizon of businessmen. Or, to put it in another way, whether or not firms would have from the outset adopted the method which they actually adopt when their output has increased sufficiently, had the output been at that figure from the outset, or whether or not firms would have adopted production by, say, machinery from the outset, had wages also stood at their higher figure from the outset. In general, though not universally, this is equivalent to saying that we move on an invariant production function as long as variations in the quantity of product either can be decomposed into infinitesimal steps *or cannot be so decomposed exclusively because of lumpiness in factors.*

No other than ordinary routine work has to be done in this stationary society, either by workmen or managers. Beyond this there is, in fact, no managerial function—nothing that calls for the special type of activity which we associate with the entrepreneur. Nothing is foreseen but repetition of orders and operations, and this foresight is ideally borne out by events.[1] The productive process is entirely "synchronized," which means that there is no waiting for the results of production, all of which

[1] The reader may pause for a moment to reflect on the nature of such statements. Is it not useful to distinguish, for the sake of clarity, phenomena which would present themselves under such assumptions from those which are contingent upon failure of a foreseen course of events to come true? And is the above statement really quite so unrealistic as it sounds? Why should the businessman be surprised when his foresight fails, if there were not a great mass of routine things which actually do conform to expectation?

present and replace themselves at the moment they are wanted according to a plan to which everything is perfectly adapted. Everything is financed by current receipts. When dealing with the pure logic of the process, it is convenient to exclude savings —unless we define savings so as to cover replacement—since the man who saves obviously does something either to change his economic situation or to provide for a change in it which he foresees; and these cases violate, if we take the strictest view, the assumptions defining the stationary process. The income stream, constant if we neglect such things as seasonal variation, consists of wages—payments for productive and consumptive services rendered by human beings, managers included—and rents—payments for services of natural agents. There may be monopoly gains, but they must be entirely consumed either by the monopolists themselves or by some agency which takes them away from the monopolists, for otherwise they would change the stationary flow. As far as monopoly gains are due to the peculiar quality of some factor or to a monopolistic organization of those who own the factor, these gains will simply appear as wages or rents and may be entered into the appropriate category. If there are appliances, which are themselves products but infinitely durable ones, we may also list the return from them under the Marshallian title *quasi-rent*. But no other cases of quasi-rent would exist in so perfectly balanced a state of things. Readers who hold any theory of interest according to which that phenomenon would be present also in a perfectly stationary state (which the writer does not believe) are free to insert here also interest as a payment for the productive service which the particular theory chosen holds to be responsible for it.

Such a process would turn out, year after year, the same kinds, qualities, and quantities of consumers' and producers' goods; every firm would employ the same kind and quantities of productive goods and services; finally, all these goods would be bought and sold at the same prices year after year. Yet all these prices and quantities are "variables" in the sense that they are not uniquely determined by extra-economic constraint but may, ordinarily, vary within wide limits imposed by the physical and social environment. If in the stationary state they do not vary as they could within those limits, this is a purely economic fact which is to be accounted for by purely economic reasoning. We know from experience what kind of relations subsist between prices and quantities, by virtue of which they influence each other. This we express by saying that prices and quantities of all goods and services are *interdependent* and form a *system*.

The first and foremost task of economic analysis is to explore the properties of that system. The method of doing this is analogous to the method known in mechanics as the method of virtual displacements. What we want to learn before anything else is whether or not the relations known to subsist between the elements of the system are, together with the data, sufficient to determine these elements, prices and quantities, uniquely. For our system is logically selfcontained only if this is the case: we can be sure that we understand the nature of economic phenomena only if it is possible to deduce prices and quantities from the data by means of those relations and to prove that no other set of prices and physical quantities is compatible with both the data and the relations. The proof that this is so is the magna charta of economic theory as an autonomous science, assuring us that its subject matter is a cosmos and not a chaos. It is the rationale of the idea of variables that do not vary, the justification of the schema of a stationary economic process. The values of prices and quantities which are the only ones, the data being what they are in each case, to satisfy those relations, we call *equilibrium values*. The state of the system which obtains if all prices and quantities take their equilibrium values we call the *state of equilibrium*.[1] Should there

[1] Friction may keep stationary an economic process that is not in equilibrium. This case is of considerable importance for any study of business situations and their changes, particularly for a study of their reactions to any impulse to change. It divides up into the subcase in which there is no equilibrium position and the subcase in which the system displays no tendency to move toward an equilibrium position, which may, nevertheless, be proved to exist. For the rough purposes of our volume, we shall not have to go into this matter except incidentally. Let us, however, settle on a term by which to identify the case, and call it *inactive*. Whenever it obtains, we do not "understand" the particular prices and quantities which exist, in the sense mentioned above. They could, *so far as the relations embodied in our theory are concerned*, just as well be different from what they are. But in all cases in which there is an economic rationale for unchanging prices and quantities (to these we will henceforth confine the term *stationary*), this rationale is afforded by the concept of equilibrium. Hence, in these cases, *stationary flow* and *equilibrium* are analytically equivalent and, describing the same

be more than one set of values of variables satisfying these conditions, we speak of a multiple equilibrium. The terms *stable*, *neuter* (or *indifferent*), and *unstable equilibrium* are self-explanatory. Equilibrium that is unique and stable is, of course, the only perfectly satisfactory case.

So far we have been using the concept of *general* or *Walrasian equilibrium*. It implies that every household and every firm in the domain is, taken by itself, in equilibrium. For the households, this means that, under the existing circumstances, tastes and economic horizon included, no household feels able to improve its situation by transferring any element of its money income from the commodity on which it is actually spent to any other commodity. For the firms this means that, under existing circumstances, technological and commercial knowledge and economic horizon included, no firm feels able to increase its revenue by transferring any element of its monetary resources ("capital") from the factor it is actually spent on, to any other factor. More simply and yet somewhat more generally, all households and all firms must believe that, under the circumstances and considering those elements of their economic situation which it is in their power to change, they cannot improve their position by altering their behavior—that is to say that their pattern of consumption and production is trimmed to perfection. Mathematically, of course, this is expressed by maximum and minimum theorems. Prices and quantities must also fulfill the following conditions if Walrasian equilibrium is to prevail. Every household's and every firm's budget must exactly balance. All quantities of all commodities produced by firms must be bought by households or other firms. All existing factors must be used as far as their owners wish to see them used at the prices they can get, and no demand, effective at those prices, must go unsatisfied. The last condition affords the basis of a rigorous definition of unemployment.

Two more concepts of economic equilibrium we shall designate by the terms *partial* or *Marshallian*, and *aggregative equilibrium*. If general equilibrium prevails, every firm and every industry is individually in equilibrium; but an individual firm

---

mass of facts, have the same empirical basis, the statistical part of which consists primarily in the well-known findings about the great stability in time of the pattern of consumption.

or an individual industry may be in equilibrium while there is no general equilibrium. And for some purposes, an individual industry may be said to be in state of equilibrium while the firms composing it are not. This concept is appropriate to the Marshallian type of analysis, and recommends itself for many purposes by its simplicity and "handiness." But the concept which matters to us and which is the only strictly correct one, is the Walrasian equilibrium.

Whoever works with partial equilibria soon discovers the necessity of an instrument that will enable him to handle processes going on in the system as a whole which escape his "partial" tools. He is then likely to complement his apparatus by a system of relations between social aggregates—such as total output, total income, net total of profits—and to reason on these, together with elements of outstanding importance for the system as a whole—such as quantity of money, rate of interest, and price level. If these elements are so adjusted that there is no tendency to change *arising from their relations to each other*, we may speak of *aggregative equilibrium*. This is the equilibrium concept used, for example, in Mr. Keynes' Treatise on Money. Its usefulness for some purposes we do not deny. But it is obvious that this kind of equilibrium is compatible with most violent disequilibria in every other sense. And these disequilibria will assert themselves by changing the given situation, *including the aggregative quantities themselves*. It is, therefore, misleading to reason on aggregative equilibrium as if it displayed the factors which initiate change and as if disturbance in the economic system as a whole could arise only from those aggregates. Such reasoning is at the bottom of much faulty analysis of business cycles. It keeps analysis on the surface of things and prevents it from penetrating into the industrial processes below, which are what really matters. It invites a mechanistic and formalistic treatment of a few isolated contour lines and attributes to aggregates a life of their own and a causal significance that they do not posses. If we consider what those aggregates are, we understand immediately how easy it is, once this starting point is chosen, to slide off into all the superficialities of monetary theories of cycles. It should, however, be noticed that, for a point of equilibrium, one of the relations subsisting between aggregative quantities may be expressed by what is known as the *equation of exchange* or even in terms of the "quantity theory of money," which is formally correct for such points and only for such points. In fact, it is simply a condition of equlibrium. We shall refer to it as the *monetary ligamen.*

Another distinction may be introduced here which is of special importance in the case of general equilibrium. If the elements of the economic system exactly satisfy all the relations, conditions, or ligamina constitutive of the system, we shall say that the system is *in perfect equilibrium.* If we find that a system, without satisfying ligamina exactly, is as near to perfect equilibrium as it will go, and that it will not move from that position unless some event impinges upon it, we shall say that it is *in imperfect equilibrium.*[1] An equilibrium the imperfection of which consists exclusively in the facts that firms use more factors and keep larger stocks and balances than would be the case if they were organized according to the highest standard of efficiency possible under the circumstances and that there is unemployment of resources from indolence of owners we shall call *sloppy.*

We have not had to make any reference to time since we replaced rates by absolute quantities. But now it is convenient to follow Marshallian tradition and to make use of time in order to define another type of imperfection of equlibrium. What was meant above was the case of a system so circumstanced as never to reach perfect equilibrium. But in other cases we find that, while the system is not constitutionally incapable of reaching perfect equilibrium, changing conditions or disturbing events require adaptations which can be made only in time. In such cases there may be equilibrium as far as rapidly changing elements are concerned and disequilibrium in elements of slower adaptation, such as contracts and equipment. These "momentary" or "provisional" or "short-time" or "tentative"

[1] There are, of course, many reasons for the prevalence of such imperfections besides the fundamental one that no part of the world of real phenomena ever lives up to its conceptual picture. But our distinction is not intended to express the mere fact that schemata never fit reality exactly. This we could dispose of by saying that the theoretical schema of perfect equilibrium is simply our tool by which to express some aspects of what in reality is always but imperfect equilibrium. The distinction is not between schema and reality, but between two schemata designed to take account of differences in factual situations which are not negligible but important and productive of consequences, which deserve separate theoretical treatment.

equilibria may usefully be contrasted with "definitive" or with "long-time" equilibria.

There is some danger in associating a certain *state of the system* with a *lapse of time* during which changes will unavoidably occur that will substitute a set of prices and quantities entirely different from the one which would have satisfied equilibrium conditions before and toward which the system was conceived to be drifting. What matters here, however, is only that Marshallian readers should realize that our concept of perfect Walrasian equilibrium is akin to what Marshallian theory means by the long-time equilibrium, if the conditions thus designated are satisfied for every individual element of the economic system. The values which elements must take to satisfy those conditions, Marshall's Normal Values, we call their Theoretical Norms. And that state of the system in which every element conforms to its theoretical norm, however distant it may be from actual life, is what renders to the theorist the service which to the businessman is rendered by the idea of a normal business situation. Logically purified, the latter concept merges into the former.

E. Complications and Clarifications.—Before going on, we must pause to glance for a moment at our magna charta. Is it satisfactory in every respect, *i.e.*, has it been satisfactorily proved that for each set of data there is a unique set of prices and physical quantities? No; nor is, for that matter, the magna charta of any other science entirely satisfactory, for everywhere a keener spirit of criticism and more powerful tools of observation *and analysis* have destroyed the primitive simplicity and comfortable determinateness of earlier stages. It is, however, possible to prove beyond reasonable doubt and with but unimportant qualifications that there exists a uniquely determined equilibrium state of the economic system in the special case of *perfect competition*. This case is defined by the conditions (*a*) that no seller or buyer is able to influence the price of any commodity or factor by his own action and that there is no concerted action, and (*b*) that there is perfect mobility of commodities and factors all over the economic field (*i.e.*, among all possible uses). Léon Walras has built the relations subsisting between the elements of the economic system into equations, and has shown that they suffice to determine unique values of variables. His proof left much to be desired in technique and details,[1] but later analysis still retains the principle. However, several comments are called for, even in the case of *perfect equilibrium in perfect competition.*

1. The proof, were it even perfectly satisfactory in logic, that, given certain data and certain relations, there is one and only one set of values of the variables that will satisfy the latter and, at the same time, be compatible with the former, does not imply that firms and households will actually behave in such a way as to arrive at that set of values or return to such a set when some disturbance has driven them from it. Yet, we cannot rest content with a mere existence theorem of the former sort. What matters to us is precisely the presence or absence of an actual tendency in the system to move toward a state of equilibrium: if this concept is to be useful as a tool of business-cycle analysis, the economic system must strive to reestablish equilibrium whenever it has been disturbed.

This problem has first been seen by Walras, although some critics do not seem to be aware of the fact. His solution starts from the observation that disequilibrium, which means deviation of at least one price or quantity from equilibrium value, necessarily spells profits or losses to somebody at the spot or spots in which it occurs. And the argument is that this somebody can, under conditions of perfect competition, get out of that loss or fully reap that profit in no other way than by decreasing or increasing the quantity of his commodity. This will drive him toward equilibrium, and if all firms and households simultaneously react in the same manner, it will eventually bring the whole system to equilibrium, *provided that all actions and reactions are performed within the bounds of familiar practice that has evolved from long experience and frequent repetition.* Common sense tells us that this mechanism for establishing or reestablishing equilibrium is not a figment devised as an exer-

[1] It must be admitted that, mathematically, our proof is even now imperfect and becomes convincing only when supplemented, step by step, by economic considerations. The original method of counting equations, showing that they are linearly independent and in the same number as the variables is, of course, inadequate. Considerable progress achieved mainly by Amoroso and Wald has not quite overcome the difficulty. But critics forget (besides the fact that our proof is no worse than many currently used in physics) that the proof does not rest on mathematics alone.

cise in the pure logic of economics but actually operative in the reality around us. Yet it constitutes but a first approximation which stops far short of what we need for an analysis of processes in an incessantly disturbed economic world, and leaves out of account many facts that may be just as important as those it includes and even go far toward producing exactly opposite results.

2. Later on we shall often meet with patterns of reality which require qualification, improvement, or even abandonment of that Walrasian model. Here we will notice a few points that seem particularly relevant to the question of principle. All, or nearly all, of the difficulties we encounter will be seen to be amenable to reduction to the one fact that economic behavior cannot be satisfactorily expressed in terms of the values which our variables assume at any single point of time. For instance, quantity demanded or supplied at any time is not merely a function of the price that prevails at the same time, but also of past and (expected) future values of that price: we are, therefore, driven to include in our functions values of variables which belong to different points of time. Theorems which do this we call *dynamic*.

The simplest case in point arises from technological lags which would in themselves suffice to account for the fact that in practice we never observe any but those provisional or short-time equilibria mentioned above. There are always elements in the setup of a *firm*, as well as in the economic *system*, which for technological reasons cannot be adapted quickly, while others can. Now the importance of this for our present discussion does not lie in the obvious fact that full or perfect equilibrium, since it takes so much time to come about, may fail to come about at all and that, therefore, new disturbances always impinge on an imperfectly equilibriated system. For this fact does not *per se* negative the existence of a tendency toward perfect equilibrium which will assert itself in spite of it and serve to explain many actual processes, even if it never reaches its goal—which is all we want. In order to produce new phenomena and to impair seriously the usefulness of the Walras-Marshall description, reaction to the intermediate situations created by such partial adaptation would have to counteract or to reverse that tendency and to lead away from instead of toward full equilibrium.

This is not in general so: necessity for intermediate adaptation and for reaction to measures of intermediate adaptation alters the paths the system takes and thereby almost unavoidably also the particular set of values which will eventually be reached, but does not in itself bar the way to *some* equilibrium. Technological facts which entail this are data. The perfect equilibrium we can still visualize in this case is relative to them and different from what it would be if they were different. In the general case, however, this is all. We shall meet exceptions, but they must be recognized as such and treated on their merits and with due regard to their particular causes.

3. As an instance which enters into the class of lag effects and which will call for attention at later stages of our analysis, we will mention the cases in which producers' reactions to changes in price do not take effect at all for some time—say, in the case of many agricultural commodities, not until the next harvest—and then all take effect at once. In such cases supply does not work up to equilibrium point by small steps and stop there, but outruns it in one jerk. Price then in turn reacts with a corresponding jerk, and the process repeats itself in the opposite direction. It is theoretically conceivable that it will never stop and that prices and quantities will, without any new disturbance and under conditions of perfect competition, fluctuate indefinitely around equilibrium values without ever hitting them. Whether these fluctuations display increasing or decreasing or constant amplitudes—whether they are *explosive*, *damped* or *stationary* —depends on the constants of the demand and supply functions. This is the Cobweb Problem of recent fame, which first attracted widespread attention in the shape of the so-called Hog Cycle. Just now we will merely notice, first, that it is obviously not the lag alone which produces the phenomenon and, second, that damped fluctuations of this sort are, of course, movements toward equilibrium. Stationary fluctuations would have to take the place of the equilibrium point but would not otherwise affect our argument.

4. Not only the lags envisaged in 2, but any kind of provisional equilibria, however conditioned, may create that difficulty. Ultimate equilibrium will in general depend on the path by which it is reached, *i.e.*, on the whole series of transactions that are usually carried out at varying prices as the situation unfolds. In this sense the outcome is indeterminate. Walras arrived at his unique equilibrium by starting from a *prix crié*

par hazard and allowing people to say what quantities they would be willing to demand and to supply at that price without actually buying or selling until that initial price is—*par tatonnement*—so adjusted as to equate quantity supplied and quantity demanded. Edgeworth for the same purpose admitted "recontracting." But if the tatonnement consists in people's actually buying and selling at the initial price, this will absorb part of the supply and satisfy part of the demand and the equilibrium price for the rest will be different from what the equilibrium price for the whole would have been, which argument can be repeated for any subsequent price that is not yet an equilibrium price. Some equilibrium, however, will be reached: barring the case to be noticed below (6), reaction to the various intermediate situations that arise is corrective and not disruptive. Moreover, experience acquired in dealing with other people and the possibility of profiting in each market period from the lessons taught by the preceding ones, tend to reduce the practical importance of the pattern under consideration and to make results approach those of the Walras-Edgeworth schema. It is incessant change in the data of the situations, rather than the inadequacy of the data of any given situation, which creates what looks like indeterminateness of pricing. We conclude, on the one hand, that we must take account of this pattern when dealing with the process of change which it is our task to analyze in this book and which must be expected to create precisely such situations, and, on the other hand, that it does not paralyze the tendency toward equlibrium.

5. As provisional equilibria may result from causes other than lags, so lags may result from causes other than technological. Friction is an example. The reader may think of costs incident to change of occupation or to any shift from the production of one kind or quality of commodity to the production of another kind or quality, or to the exchange, by means of selling and buying, of one asset for another, or of the resistance to change of some prices or of the difficulty of adapting long-time contracts or of persuading oneself or other people to act, and so on. The presence of friction, will, of course, always entail an equilibrium different from that which would otherwise be reached, as well as slow up progress toward equilibrium. Moreover, if different elements or different sectors of the system work with different amounts of friction, lack of harmony will ensue, the more

slowly and the more quickly adaptable elements getting out of step with each other. The same question arises and the same answer suggests itself as in the case of technological lags. The very existence and length of those periods of adjustment which we shall study later on testify to the importance of the phenomenon.

The effect of friction on the progress of the system toward an equilibrium state is not wholly of that negative kind. Its presence may steady adaptation by making it impossible to react to every disturbance instantaneously and to the full extent it may seem to justify at the moment. Some friction may even be said to be necessary for the economic system to function at all: it is in part due to friction which slows up the adaptation of supply that the equilibrium point is not much more frequently outrun. Just as the physical would would be an uninhabitable chaos if the slightest difference in temperature sufficed to transfer *all* heat instantaneously to the region of the minimum, so the economic world could not function if, for example, the slightest variation in a rate of exchange sufficed to set *all* gold flowing at once.

6. Many cases of frictional resistance to change are frequently referred to as Stickiness or Rigidity. In view of the role these terms play in modern discussions of economic policy and in arguments about business cycles, it is necessary to point out that they are nontechnical and cover many different patterns. And to the difficulty of defining—we might facilitate the task by considering Rigidity as the limiting case of Stickiness—corresponds the difficulty of measuring them. There are, of course, numbers of reasons why some prices should move more slowly or less strongly than others or all of them more slowly or less strongly than other elements of the system, and nothing can be inferred from the statistical fact alone. The latter may even mean no more than that demand and cost conditions are more stable in some sectors than in others, or that a price holds place behind others in the time sequence of events. But there is, nevertheless, a distinct group of facts which has some claim to a name of its own, *viz.*, what we might call willful stickiness. If a price be "regulated" either by public authority or by the individual or group in control of supply, this need not imply that it will move less often or less strongly than it would if its determination were left to the competitive pricing process.

Even if it does, this may be due to friction only, for instance to the friction incident to a public authority's producing a new decision. But it is also possible that the policy of that public authority or that private group is to "stabilize" the price in question. Then we have a phenomenon *sui generis,* to which we shall have to return more than once.

For the moment it is enough, first, to point out that our definition turns on the comparison of the actual behavior of a price with what it would do under perfect competition. While this criterion is extremely difficult to handle, it is not admitted that this constitutes an objection if criteria that are easier to apply lack either precise meaning or relevance. Second, occurrence of stickiness or rigidity in our sense—as distinguished especially from the frictional type—presupposes absence of perfect competition, although this is not in itself sufficient to produce it. A perfectly competitive system cannot display stickiness in that sense, however sluggish it may be to react.

If a value other than the equilibrium value be imposed by public authority upon an element—a price for instance—of a perfectly competitive system otherwise in equilibrium, we have a particular case of imperfection. The system will adapt itself to this condition but, when it has done so, will no longer fulfill all the other conditions of perfect equilibrium. Since inserting a new condition into a determinate system spells overdeterminateness, some other condition has to be dropped. Which one it will be is *quaestio facti,* the individual firm's choice being guided by a principle of minimizing the effects (in terms of money) of the disturbance. If the element which has been made rigid is the price of an original or nonproduced factor of production and if that price is higher than the equilibrium price, the condition violated is that of full employment of resources. For perfect competition this is the only possible case of underemployment of resources in a perfect equilibrium. Of course, since we never meet perfect equilibria in real life, there will in general be many other cases of it even without rigidity and even without friction.

7. Of course we do not attribute omniscience to our firms and households, or any theoretical understanding of the processes in which they play a part, but simply that amount of information and understanding which they actually possess and which varies greatly between different groups. In the case of an undisturbed

stationary process this question is of little moment, everyone having been taught by experience to follow the beacon lights which are relevant to him. Since every decision refers to the future, this implies foresight; and since the fruits of every effort mature in the future, it also implies caring for the future—forethought. The Walrasian men, for instance, keep their durable instruments and their stocks at least intact. It is, hence, no more justifiable to call the systems of Walras and Pareto timeless than to charge them with the absurdity of assuming omniscience. The particular kind and amount of information, understanding, foresight, or forethought is one of the data of the problem on a par with the particular tastes or the particular technological knowledge of any particular people. And for the static theory of the competitive case there is no more reason to bother about the former than there is to bother about the latter. The assumption really made is that people react to existing prices only, and it is from this that trouble arises as soon as we start analysis from a state of disequilibrium or investigate the effects of any disturbance that is more than an isolated interruption of the ordinary routine. It is then that expectation or anticipation enters the picture, to threaten the existence of our equilibrium tendency.

Expectation, however, in many cases materially facilitates both the movement toward, and the preservation of, equilibrium, sometimes to the point of preventing disequilibria that would without it arise from the working of the Walras model. Action upon expectations such as can plausibly be attributed to firms will often tend to smooth out things and to iron out fluctuations that would otherwise occur. The effects of technological lags, for instance, will be reduced if the change has been expected, and the Hog Cycle, as far as it is really due to inability to foresee the mass effect of "improvident" reaction to a favorable fodder-pork ratio, would entirely disappear if the time range of farmers' expectations increased. Speculation of the type described by classical theory—buying in advance of a rise in price that is foreseen, selling in advance of a fall—works the same way. In such cases expectations may open up a shortcut toward a definitive (though possibly different) equilibrium state.

But this not always so. The source of trouble is not adequately described by saying that expectations are uncertain or that they have to be currently revised or that different people form expectations differing in range and reasonableness. Uncertainty of the future course of events gives rise, to be sure, to many phenomena that are very important for any realistic study of business cycles, among them, again, the existence of prolonged periods of adjustment. It is responsible for an important type of social losses and of excess capacity. It will be seen, however, that there is no great difficulty of principle handling this element, and we may dismiss it here. Nor need we feel concern about the fact that action on certain types of expectation may be disruptive and help to drive the system away from equilibrium. These types, instanced by expectations which simply project into the future the actual rate of change of some quantity, will, at various turns of our way, come in to complete the mechanisms of certain phases of economic fluctuations. But although they may often temporarily counteract it, they do not in themselves disprove the existence of an equilibrium tendency or the proposition that at times it prevails in such a way as actually to draw the system toward equilibrium.

The real trouble to the theorist comes from the fact that introducing expected values of his variables changes the whole character of his problem and makes it technically so difficult to handle that he may easily find himself unable to prove an equilibrium tendency which, nevertheless, may exist, or even the existence and stability of the equilibrium position itself. The nature of our difficulty may be illustrated as follows. Suppose that the firms of a competitive industry in the act of deciding what quantities of their product they are to produce take account of the past, present, and expected future values of any economic variables they believe to be relevant, weighting those values by weights that in general rapidly decrease to zero in function of distance from the time of the decision. Those expectations are data and quite arbitrary. Given the kind of people they are—their disposition to react—it is, under acceptable assumptions about consistency and so on, possible to speak of a uniquely determined decision. When it has taken effect, however, the industry and the whole system may, in consequence of it, be farther from settling down to a stationary state just as well as they may be nearer to it. If, now, those firms suddenly began to behave in the Walrasian way, Walrasian equilibrium would be approached in either case; but since *ex hypothesi* they do not do this but, instead, revise their expectations somehow and then again behave according to their disposition to react, they may forever travel away from any state that in any sense could be dubbed equilibrium or else, turning toward it, outrun it and jump back again until doomsday.

But for our practical purposes the predicament vanishes as soon as we realize to what it is due: we have admitted any expectations and we have taken them as given. As for the first, we have ourselves to blame if with such tremendous generality we do not get any results. As for the second, we have emptied the schema of everything that matters. In other words, if we discontinue the practice of treating expectations as if they were ultimate data, and treat them as what they are—variables which it is our task to explain—properly linking them with the business situations that give rise to them, we shall succeed in restricting expectations to those which we actually observe and not only reduce their influence to its proper proportions but also understand how the course of events molds them and at certain times so turns them as to make them work toward equilibrium. For the moment, however, this question must be left open.

In certain cases in which there is no danger of ambiguity we shall speak of correct and incorrect expectations. But in this fragment of a discussion it was not necessary to draw that distinction, which, because of the interdependence between expectations and outcome, is a difficult one at best; since most of what is relevant to us applies equally to all expectations, we need not attach any general meaning to it. It would certainly not do to define correctness of expectation by means of congruent event, or by means of an assumption that correct expectation necessarily works toward equilibrium.

F. Imperfect Competition.—From our discussion of the case of perfect competition we emerge with the result that there is a real tendency toward equilibrium states in a perfectly competitive world. Qualifications and reservations do not materially impair our tool. They rather improve, although they also complicate, it by supplying us with a rich menu card of possible cases, the theory of which comes in usefully at many crossroads of any study of cycles. But many readers who admit this will question whether this is still so when we leave the precincts of the perfectly competitive case. It is necessary to present at least the sketch of an answer, which may be omitted by those who feel convinced already.

The limiting case of pure monopoly is still plain sailing. If one individual or combination of individuals controls either the supply of, or the demand for, some commodity or service, we get a determined price and a determined output of that commodity or service. But even in this case we meet with an element which tends to deprive that determinateness of the stringency it has in the perfectly competitive case. In perfect competition, the individual firm is not only powerless to alter market price, but also under strong compulsion to accept it. The firm cannot charge a higher price without losing all its business. It can, of course, charge a lower price, but will be penalized for doing so by a loss which, considering the absence of surpluses, will in the long run threaten its life. If a monopolist charges a higher or lower price than the one that maximizes his gain, he will also lose but only in the sense that he will, within limits, gain less than he could. Hence he can, if he should choose, go on doing so indefinitely, and there may be reasons for it other than error, indolence, and benevolence. He may have to consider public opinion, he may wish to maximize not immediate gains but gains over time and to "nurse up demand." He may or may not discriminate. Generally, there are many courses of action open to him and many ways in which to react to a disturbance. Each of them, however, yields a determinate result and supplies an equilibrating mechanism.

As long as each monopoly position is surrounded by a sufficiently broad zone of perfect competition, no new difficulty arises about determinateness, even if the system contains a considerable number of them. Every monopoly then presents an isolated maximum problem with respect to given buyers' demand curves and competitively determined factor prices. But difficulties do arise as soon as those monopolies get near enough to one another in such a way as to influence one another's orbits, or, less figuratively speaking, as to make it necessary for each monopolist to shape his policy with regard to the policy of one or more of the others. Let us take at once the limiting case, that in which every commodity and service, every product and factor, is monopolized. The trouble with this case, known as Universal Monopoly, is not in any inability of ours to prove the existence of a case in which determinateness prevails but in our inability to prove that there is any tendency for reality to conform to it. In general such a system would be what we have called inactive. We shall not, however, discuss this but merely notice the three standard instances of imperfect competition: Bilateral Monopoly, Oligopoly, and Monopolistic Competition.

1. We have bilateral monopoly when a monopolist faces a single buyer (monopsonist). If exchange between the two is isolated—both in the sense that they meet just once and never again, and in the sense that for the purpose in hand the economic system consists of the two only—there will, of course, be limits between which the exchange ratio must fall, but no equilibrium exists within this zone, one exchange ratio being as likely as any other. This case has some bearings on situations which actually arise in the course of the phases of business cycles: momentary situations emerge that are very imperfectly understood by the actors on the business stage and often lead to erratic actions more or less conforming to that type. Selling and buying a going concern amidst the excesses of a violent boom may serve as an example. The only thing we can do, even in less extreme instances, is to replace an equilibrium point by an equilibrium zone. It should be observed (see above, Sec E, 4) that under those conditions even perfect competition would not yield determinate results, particularly if parties have no experience with each other and if there are experimental transactions at the beginning of the market. At the other end of the scale of possibilties stands the case of a monopolist and a monopsonist who deal regularly with each other, know from experience all about each other's situation and ways, and desire to arrive at an agreement which will cover the whole period they envisage so that there are no experimental transactions influencing the terms of later ones. We will also let the freedom of choice be limited for both parties by the relations in which they stand to the rest of the system. On these lines we construct the following case: a trade union so strongly organized as to be perfectly safe from the breaking away of members and the intrusion into its field of outsiders, deals with a monopsonist employer. This employer, in turn, is monopolist with respect to his product, which he sells to a perfectly competitive crowd of consumers. All the other factors he buys in competitive markets which he cannot influence by his own action, the industry being too small for

that and also too small to influence the purchasing power of the masses by the wages it pays.

Now in this particularly favorable case we have at least a determined demand curve of the monopsonist employer for the services of labor. This demand curve will shift in the cycle but is exactly known not only to the employer but also to, say, the secretary of the workmen's union. The employer, in turn, knows exactly from long experience with his workmen what the minimum wage rate is that the secretary can accept for each total of man-hours. Neither wants to fight, which means that neither uses the threat of withdrawing the whole supply of labor or of employment. The whole strategy of both parties consists in varying rate and quantity by small steps without trying to bluff. Under these conditions there is a determined wage rate which, together with the associated amount of man-hours, will be most advantageous to the union and another determined rate which, together with the associated amount of man-hours, will be most advantageous to the employer. But those rates will not, in general, be equal. Between them we have again a zone of indeterminateness.

Although some of the highest authorities in the field, particularly Cournot and Wicksell, and many recent writers could be quoted to the contrary, this is the opinion of the majority of students and particularly of Professor Bowley. But it is, of course, true for the general case only and in the absence of any further information. The equilibrating mechanism does not work thus *in vacuo*, but within the specific circumstances of each case. Therefore, that indeterminateness does not necessarily mean that such a system is constitutionally incapable of equilibrium but only that the case divides up into subcases, for each of which the question must be put separately, as in fact it must in the case of straight monopoly as well. Among these subcases there are obviously many determinate ones. If, for instance, it is the practice that the union asks for a rate and the employer simply replies by taking as many man-hours as it is most advantageous for him to take at that rate, determinate equilibrium will obviously be arrived at. Other subcases may be constructed which are indeterminate. Practically more important for our purpose is the fact that, within the process for the analysis of which we are now assembling the analytic tools, situations change so quickly as to make the assumption of perfect knowledge and invariant reaction inadmissible. The characteristics of those changing situations may, however, give us to some extent precisely that information which we need in order to reduce ranges of indeterminateness. But temporary necessity, consciously planned strategy, and fluctuating anticipation of the general course of events acquire a very much wider scope than was assumed in the foregoing analysis. We are then left not only with zones but with shifting zones. Moreover, in many cases the demand and supply curves are not independent of each other.

Whatever their importance, those subcases in which bilateral monopoly yields determined equilibrium may be used to show that perfect equilibrium may, outside of the perfectly competitive case, be compatible with the existence of unemployed resources. For it is clear that the bargain most advantageous to the workman in our example will not, in general, lead to the sale of as many man-hours per workman as each workman would individually be willing to sell at that rate. No man need actually be out of work, of course, but whether some will or not is a secondary matter to be settled between the secretary and the employer, so that it is always possible to characterize the situation by associating with it a certain number of totally unemployed men. It is, in fact, very probable that the rate which will yield the maximum sum total of real wages, the maximum being relative to the value put upon leisure and to length of period envisaged, will generally imply some unemployment. Even if the unemployed have to be kept out of the earnings of their comrades, that wage rate will *ex definitione* remain the most advantageous one. If the unemployed are partly or wholly kept from other sources, the proposition applies a fortiori, but the conditions of the maximum are altered thereby.

2. If supply in a perfect market, *i.e.*, in a market in which there can, owing to perfect homogeneity of the commodity and perfect mobility and indifference of buyers, be only one price, is controlled by firms that are in a position to influence that price by their individual action (oligopoly or, if there are but two of them, duopoly), it is easy to see that we lose the conditions which enforce determinateness of behavior in the perfectly competitive case as well as those which account for such determinateness as there is in the monopoly case. This pattern, implying as it does that all customers will instantly transfer their allegiance from one firm to another on the slightest provoca-

tion, is of very little interest to us, because it is another limiting case which in practice must be rare, if not altogether absent. The obvious thing to do for any firm that finds itself, potentially or actually, in such a situation, is to try to alter it. The typical courses that are, in practice, resorted to in order to effect this, therefore, matter more to us than does the pure logic of oligopoly. They may be roughly grouped under three headings.

First, a firm may attack to kill or cow. This may result in a monopoly situation—which in most cases will be a precarious one requiring endless defensive moves—or in a situation which gives the aggressor more or less complete control, the unconquered positions being insignificant or submitting to his leadership. Since it is poor method to try to cover a wide variety of different patterns by one term and one argument, we should avoid speaking simply of cutthroat competition in all cases of such attacks: the intrusion of a new and superior method of production for instance, an event of particular importance to the subject of this book, identifies a special case which should be treated differently and distinguished from the genuine case in which there is or may be "wasteful" competition, overproduction, overcapacity in a sense to which nothing corresponds in the former, although throats are being actually cut in both. Whatever the nature of the struggle, while it lasts there cannot be an equilibrium, of course. But it will, in general, lead to a state which, though perhaps never fulfilling equilibrium conditions strictly and though often sloppy or lacking in stability, yet suffices for our purpose. This particular type of "equilibrium tendency" issues in a set of equlibrium or quasi-equilibrium values different from that which the system would otherwise reach. Rare, indeed, are the cases in which a campaign of this kind can be embarked upon irrespectively of the general business situation: as a rule, the phase of the cycle will provide us with determining conditions for the outcome. As common experience teaches, everything will turn out differently according as such a struggle occurs in a phase of expansion when demand curves shift upward, or in a phase of contraction when demand curves shift downward. Typically, it occurs in the latter, a fact which is of considerable importance to the picture of the mechanism of business cycles in a society in which big units prevail.

The same applies to the second course open to firms in oligopolistic situations—agreement. Whether this be secret or open, tacit or explicit, complete or restricted to certain regions, products, practices (such as credit to customers), whether it is aimed and arrived at directly or after struggle for shares in the trade, does not affect the principle. The outcome enters in any case into the category of monopoloids. Creation of excess capacity as a war reserve or simply for the sake of its nuisance value is particularly characteristic of this case, for which the cartel is as typical as is the "trust" of the first case. The former is the most likely outcome whenever, on the one hand, nothing can be done to alter the homogeneity of the product and, on the other hand, no firm is, or thinks it is, strong enough to venture on a fight to a finish. This is also a kind of equilibrium tendency, although the resulting set of values will again be different from any of those that would follow from any other course. The quaint metaphor by which Edgeworth illustrates the indeterminateness of oligopoly but serves to show how very likely combination or some understanding is: Nansen and Johansen, the two explorers who are all that is left of the personnel of a polar expedition, wishing to drag their only sledge in different directions may reasonably be assumed not to go on pulling against each other forever. It also serves to show that their final course will not be determined by any automatic result of mere dragging. Dropping metaphor, we must recognize that the monopoly that emerges, were it even much more complete and much more durable than as a rule it can be expected to be, will be a compromise that could, from the standpoint of economic theory, just as well be different. There is an element in the case, the distribution of the profit, which is theoretically indeterminate and has to be settled, say, by fixing cartel quota, in order to supply the missing datum. For us, however, this does not matter.

As a third course, firms may try to do away with the homogeneity of the product or rather to increase that lack of homogeneity which already exists in most cases. Though this course may also be taken for purposes of attack, it is primarily a measure of defense. It merges oligopoly into the third standard instance of imperfect competition—monopolistic competition. Hence, though we need not deny the occasional occurrence of pure oligopoly and though we cannot deny its logical possibility, we are certainly within our rights in denying the practical importance of the question of its determinateness. Two things should be added. First, any indeterminate situations that might arise if "pure" oligopoly actually persisted for some time, must not be confused with that indeterminateness which owes its existence to incessant variation of data that confront a firm in a world full of actual and expected change and are imperfectly known for this very reason. The latter type of indeterminateness has nothing to do with the former. Second, such cases of indeterminateness of the first and genuine kind would also suffice to produce excess capacity, quite independently of the special reasons we have above seen to expect it. This follows from the fact that firms which find themselves in an indeterminate situation can never plan except for a *range* of prices and outputs.

3. The term Monopolistic Competition will be used to connote product differentiation. Each firm in any sector of the system in which monopolistic competition prevails offers products that differ in some way from the products of every other firm in the sector, and thus supplies a special market of its own. This product differentiation must be interpreted with reference to its rationale, the creation of such a special market, hence very broadly: it comprises not only "real" but also "putative" differences, not only differences in the product itself, but also differences in the services incident to supplying it (atmosphere and location of shops included) and every device that enables the buyer to associate the thing he buys with the name of a particular firm. Differences in location and other factors which will induce customers to prefer one firm to another, are of course unavoidable, irrespective of any intention to create them. And there is simply no such thing as a homogeneous motorcar or liver pill.

At first sight it may appear that the case is covered by the theory of monopoly and that the questions of the existence of an equilibrium and of a tendency toward it are disposed of thereby. Some authorities, Mrs. Robinson in particular, seem in fact to be of this opinion. To a certain extent they are right. Creation of a special market may be described as a device to increase the friction that militates against buyers' transferring their allegiance from one firm to another. If this friction be strong enough, it may in the limiting case annihilate, in many other case materially reduce, that interrelation of demands for the products of individual firms which is responsible for the olipolo-listic difficulty, and thus create monopoly situations or, at all events, situations which are acceptable approximations to straight monopoly. The affinity becomes still more marked when we reflect that there is in real life hardly such a thing as absolute monopoly and that at least potential competition is present in most cases. We note, therefore, that one corner of business reality is adequately taken care of by this theory.

In general, however, that is not so. The very essence of monopolistic competition is in the fact that the price at which a quantity can be sold at any time is a function of the behavior both of the firm itself and of all the other firms in the field. We can gain, however, in the direction of competition, some of the ground we thus lose in the direction of monopoly: since in practice almost every firm either actually produces, or at very short notice is able to produce, any of a wide variety of commodities or qualities, some of which are, as a rule, almost perfect substitutes for the products of its competitors, its price and quantity adjustments will not in general differ fundamentally from those that it would have to make under conditions of perfect competition. That is to say, the demand curves for the products of individual firms will, in general and in the long run, display a high elasticity, though not the infinite one of the pure logic of competition. And this, in turn, will enforce approximate realization of the results of perfect competition that follow from it—in particular, differences in the prices of different qualities or types will tend to correspond to the differences in the costs that must be incurred in producing them.

Strictly, this applies only to cases which differ from perfect competition in nothing else but product differentiation. An exception must be allowed in those cases which would, in the absence of product differentiation, be of the type of pure oligopoly. A certain amount of indeterminateness flows from this source. Where potential competition is no more than a remote possibility, this exception may be important for the course of events in the particular industry; but it is hardly ever important enough to interfere substantially with the working of the system as a whole. There are other qualifications. Product differentiation cannot be strictly continuous. Plants and shops cannot be spread continuously over an area. But all this is not overwhelmingly interesting or important.

Two points remain. The one is the great increase in the amount of friction which, as stated above, monopolistic competition will bring about in the system. It will also produce additional sloppiness and, in some sectors, inactivity in our sense and rigidity. Traditionalistic and cooperative forms of behavior will often lead to, and be reenforced by, all that. We must expect our system to function much less promptly and effectively than it otherwise would and everywhere points to be replaced by zones. Moreover, it is not denied that in some professions and in many branches of retail trade, the consequences predicated by some authorities on monopolistic competition may even in the long run prevail: if newcomers flock into the legal profession and fees are being kept up, all lawyers will be underemployed and feel unable to make what they consider a decent living. Acting in a well-known frame of mind, they may well try to mend the case by raising fees. Independent cabmen, retailers of milk, and so on are very likely to behave just like that. Excess capacity and the paradox of prices rising with increase of potential supply then ensue. In interperting the details of a situation, all this must be taken into account, of course, as it always has been. In doing so, we must not forget, nevertheless, that this is but one of many possible forms of behavior and that such pyramids of prices and capacities will, as a rule, be brought down by the capitalist machine itself; into the peaceful pastures of backward retailers the department store and the mail-order house intrude, and disregarding this mechanism is, in matters of application to reality, as serious a mistake as reasoning on the hypothesis of perfect competition would be.

Second, in the short-run situations of an economic world incessantly disturbed by external and internal factors of change, immediate reaction is very different in the case of monopolistic competition from what it would be in the case of perfect competition. The possession of a special market, however precarious, gives scope for short-time strategy, for moves and countermoves which would not otherwise exist. In particular, reaction by decreasing output rather than by decreasing prices may suggest itself as a short-run policy, and if any given situation is expected to be short-lived, construction of a more elaborate plant than can be used to optimum point often becomes advantageous. Excess capacity results from this, rather than from any particular properties of normal equilibrium in monopolistic competition that are held to account for the phenomenon irrespectively of actual or expected change. Again, presence of monopolistic competition not only means a different technique of adjustment characterized by many movements that seem, and sometimes are, erratic, but possibly also a different equilibrium, if indeed any equilibrium be eventually reached. It is worth noticing, however, that unemployment could in this case be due only to imperfections of equilibrium.

On the one hand, then, change that comes from within the system, as well as change that comes from without it, impinges on situations, induces short-time adaptations and produces short-time equilibria, which in many cases conform well to the picture drawn by the authors of the theory of monopolistic competition. On the other hand, new firms producing new commodities or old commodities by new methods will, as a rule, try to behave according to it, for that is the obvious method of exploiting to the full, and of keeping alive, the temporary advantages they enjoy. It will be seen, as our argument unfolds, how important that is for the subject of this book. Knowledge of the mechanism of cyclical situations has, indeed, been improved by that theory.

G. Equilibrium Economics and the Study of Business Fluctuations.—In order to sum up part of the argument of this chapter and to take one further step, we will now return to the question: What is the use, for our purpose, of the analytic apparatus thus imperfectly described? For brevity's sake we will consider the perfectly competitive case only, although there is nothing to prevent us from extending the following remarks to all other cases. We have seen, first of all, that the theory of equilibrium or of the stationary flow, gives us the bare bones of economic logic which, however, abstract or remote from real life it may be, yet renders indispensable service in clearing the ground for rigorous analysis. The best way to convince oneself of the value of this service is to try to define such phenomena as overproduction, excess capacity, unemployment, maladjustment. These terms, as commonly used, do not carry any precise meaning at all, and the fact that they do not, explains the inconclusivenes of much argument that goes under those headings. As soon as we try to find such precise meaning for them and to fit them for the task of identifying definite states of the economic organism, the necessity of falling back on equilibrium relations becomes apparent.

Although, in the second place, every event impinges on an economic world that is already disturbed and in disequilibrium, our understanding of the way in which the economic organism reacts to any given new event is unavoidably based upon our understanding of those equilibrium relations. The time-honored exercises which consist in trying to define by means of a generous allowance of *ceteris paribus*, the consequences of the imposition of a small tax on some commodity or of a small increase in the supply of labor and so on, are nothing but a method of exploring the nature and properties of those equilibrium relations which determine how any given change in data will be absorbed by the economic system and what final results will eventually emerge. Now, what causes fluctuations may either be individual shocks which impinge on the system from outside, or a distinct process of change generated by the system itself, but in both cases the theory of equilibrium supplies us with the simplest code of rules according to which the system will respond. This is what we mean by saying that the theory of equilibrium is a *description of an apparatus of response*. It is no more than a first step toward such a description, but even so it is just as important for the study of fluctuations as is the theory of disturbing events or disturbing processes itself.

Third, the concept of a state of equilibrium, although no such state may ever be realized, is useful and indeed indispensable for purposes of analysis and diagnosis, as a point of reference. Actual states can conveniently be defined by their distance from it. The more rigorous procedure of the theorist does not differ fundamentally from a habit of the layman's mind. During the whole of the postwar period, for instance, individuals and groups frequently argued their case in terms of a comparison of absolute or relative quantities of commodities and of absolute or relative prices or incomes with those values of the same variables which obtained in 1913. Of course, there is no warrant for doing this. All the data of the economic system having changed, there is no reason why prices of agricultural commodities, for instance, should stand now in the same proportion to other prices as they did then. But the idea which underlies that habit also lends itself to a more favorable interpretation. It may imply recognition of the fact that there are equilibrium relations between economic quantities, departure from which creates difficulties and untenable situations, and comparison with which is the obvious method to be followed in order to estimate the nature and extent of actual deviations. If, instead of comparing the actual situation with that equilibrium state which would correspond to its data, people compare it with a past situation that was not an equilibrium state and would, even if it had been, no longer be relevant, they are simply acting on a belief that the situation of 1913 was at any rate more normal than any later one and that it is not too far removed from us to serve as a norm. This may be wrong, but the underlying principle of comparing actual with normal values is not invalidated thereby. One of the services which the business and political worlds can most justifiably expect from the economist consists precisely in devising more satisfactory methods in order to give effect to that principle.

Hence, much more interest and importance than most of us are inclined to admit attach to the endeavors of some statisticians and economists to distill from the statistical material of an economic world which is chronically in a state of disequilibrium, the time sequence of equilibrium values. Perhaps it is true to say that some such idea must be present in the back of the mind of any statistician who calculates trends. He may have no other purpose but to eliminate them in order to make fluctuations stand out more clearly. But fluctuations must be fluctuations around something and, if pressed, he would probably define that something in terms more or less related to our equilibrium concept. The first economist to develop the idea consciously and to go, at least in conception and intention, the whole way, was Henry L. Moore. Throughout his work, summed up in his Synthetic Economics, runs the principle that trends or loci of points, everyone of which indicates the ideal equilibrium value corresponding to the actual value taken by each time variable in the same point of time.

The most important of the uses we shall make of the concept of equilibrium is, fourth, contingent on the existence of a tendency toward equilibrium. We have seen that assertion of it is subject to many qualifications and is not so simple a matter as older generations of theorists have believed. Since factors of change actually impinge on a world that is disturbed already and since, even if they had the opportunity of impinging on a world that was in perfect equilibrium previously, the processes of response would in most cases not directly lead to equilibrium in a simple way, our belief in the existence of an equilibrium tendency, which after every excursion draws the system back toward a new state of equilibrium, will have to stand on trial to the last page of this book, although facts of the most common observation support it much more strongly than does general theory, which quite rightly endeavors to take account of even the most freakish cases. The thing that matters to us, is nevertheless this tendency considered as an actual force, and not the mere existence of ideal equilibrium points of reference. We take our stand on the fact that the values of economic variables fluctuate in the course of business cycles between figures which roughest practical common sense recognizes as abnormally high and figures which it recognizes as abnormally low and that somewhere between these two lie values or ranges of values which that same common sense would recognize as normal. We wish to distinguish definite periods in which the system embarks upon an excursion away from equilibrium and equally definite periods in which it draws toward equilibrium. In order to harness our equilibrium concept to this service, which is fundamental for our analytic technique, we will not postulate the existence of states of equilibrium where none exist, but only where the system is actually moving toward one. When, for instance, existing states are in the act of being disturbed, say, by a war financed by government fiat, or by a "mania" of railroad building, there is very little sense in speaking of an ideal equilibrium coexisting with all that disequilibrium. It seems much more natural to say that while such a factor acts there is no equilibrium at all. When it has ceased to act, and when we observe that readjustment sets in which we interpret as a movement toward equilibrium, then and only then the ideal equilibrium becomes the goal of an economic process, the nature of which can be elucidated by reference to it. Then and only then equilibrium becomes what we have called it before, the "theoretical norm" of the economic variables. Hence, we will, for our purpose, recognize existence of equilibria *only at those discrete points on the time scale at which the system approaches a state which would, if reached, fulfill equilibrium conditions.* And since the system in practice never actually reaches such a state, we shall consider, instead of equilibrium points, ranges within which the system as a whole is more nearly in equilibrium than it is outside of them. Those ranges, which are the operational form to which we shall apply properly modified equilibrium considerations, we call *neighborhoods of equilibrium* (the term must not be understood in its mathematical sense).

Chapter III

HOW THE ECONOMIC SYSTEM GENERATES EVOLUTION

A. Internal Factors of Change.—We start from the picture, sketched in the preceding chapter, of an economic process which merely reproduces at constant rates and is in equilibrium at every point of time. We recall that there are two motives for doing so. We wish to guard effectively against circular reasoning, and to use the relations which link economic quantities in such a process as an "apparatus of response." And we ask the question: What is it that makes that process change in historic time?

One reason why the process changes is obviously that it is acted upon by what we have termed external factors. These we shall now exclude from consideration, recalling once more, however, not only that they are always important and sometimes dominant, and that the *response* of the system to their impact must always be expected to account for a great part of the economic changes we observe, but also that their occurrence may and often does *condition* changes of the kind which we are about to consider. These two things must be kept distinct. By response we mean only what may be termed passive adaptation, *i.e.*, adaptation within the fundamental data of the system. Adaptation may, however, consist in altering some of those data, and such creative response belongs to the class of internal change.

For example, if government demand for any given type of weapon increases, business may adapt itself according to the rules of the game which we (virtually) observe in the stationary process: it may turn out increasing quantities of that type of weapon at increasing costs and prices, which impulse may in turn propagate itself throughout the system according to the same rules. But it may also adapt itself by turning out another type of weapon or by producing the one demanded by a new method. This would be internal change *conditioned* by an external factor.

Factors of change internal to the economic system are changes in tastes, changes in quantity (or quality) of factors of production, changes in methods of supplying commodities. One of the services that our equilibrium system renders consists precisely in assuring us that this classification of internal factors is logically exhaustive, for everything else in the system is deducible from tastes, quantity and distribution of productive resources, and production functions. (Autonomous monetary changes have been included in the class of external factors.) We take up those three factors in turn.

1. We will, throughout, act on the asumption that consumers' initiative in changing their tastes—*i.e.*, in changing that set of our data which general theory comprises in the concepts of "utility functions" or "indifference varieties"—is negligible and that all change in consumers' tates is incident to, and brought about by, producers' action. This requires both justification and qualification.

The fact on which we stand is, of course, common knowledge. Railroads have not emerged because any consumers took the initiative in displaying an effective demand for their service in preference to the services of mail coaches. Nor did the consumers display any such initiative wish to have electric lamps or rayon stockings, or to travel by motorcar or airplane, or to listen to radios, or to chew gum. The great majority of changes in commodities consumed has been forced by producers on consumers who, more often than not, have resisted the change and have had to be educated up by elaborate psychotechnics of advertising. For our purposes, the case is not impaired by the fact that consumers' satisfaction supplies the social meaning for all economic activity, or by the fact that new and unfamiliar commodities have ultimately to be "taken up," or ratified, by consumers and may be said to have been produced with a view to latent consumers' wishes, or on indications other than effective demand. As far as changes in taste go, this is entirely irrelevant to the mechanics of the processes we are to analyze. The fact that the work of "consumers' research" is typically one of criticism of commodities, brands, and qualities may be pointed to in illustration.

But however completely the proposition that changes in consumers' tastes are brought about by the action of producers may fall in with the general opinion on the subject, it is yet not quite true. It is easy to adduce instances of initiative change of consumers' tastes and even to group them around familiar types. Two of them may be mentioned. In every social circle, we observe leaders of fashion, specialists in creating new forms and habits of private life. Again, there are "movements" which may powerfully influence the collection of consumers' goods that is being bought by households—the temperance movement may serve as an example.

We hold, however, that this class of facts is not important enough to matter and that its neglect will not substantially invalidate our picture. Shifts in demand which come about in that way are, besides, no more than different choices between existing commodities, and, if unsupported by a change in real income which they do not in themselves entail, create a situation to which industry can and will passively adapt itself. Whenever we meet exceptions (war demand by governments seems to be the most important of them) nothing prevents us from dealing with such cases on their merits, but we do not include them in our general schema.

This arrangement rests on several assertions of fact and, of course, stands and falls with them. If anyone should hold that changes in taste do arise regularly and systematically from consumers' initiative in the above sense, in such a way that this initiative constitutes one of the main motive powers of economic evolution, he would logically have to deny the validity of our analytic schema.

2. Increase in productive resources might at first sight appear to be the obvious prime mover in the process of internal economic change. Physical environment being taken as constant (opening up of new countries enters into a different category), that increase resolves itself into increase of population and the

increase of the stock of producers' goods. Neither can, of course, be treated as an independent variable; both are at the same time effects of economic changes and conditions of other economic changes. Our reason for listing variations in population among external factors was that there is no unique relation between them and variations in the flow of commodities. Hence, it seemed convenient for our purpose to look upon an increase in population as an environmental change conditioning certain phenomena. Moreover, it could be demonstrated by familiar cases (India and China) that mere increase in population does not *bring about* any of those phenomena which presuppose either a certain density or a certain rate of increase in population except a fall in real income per head. Finally, it occurs so continuously as to be capable of current absorption. Short-time variations in marriage rates are obviously the reflex of business fluctuations and do not cause them.

Similar considerations apply to the increase in the stock of durable producers' goods which would ordinarily follow from the presence in a society of a positive rate of net savings. We will profit by the occasion in order to introduce a few concepts, conventions, and propositions which will be of use later on.

By Saving we mean the earmarking, by a household, of an element of its current receipts—as distinguished from "capital gains"—for the acquisition of titles to income or for the repayment of debt. If a firm does the same thing with an element of its net receipts from the sale of products and services, we shall speak of Accumulation. The distinction between Saving and Accumulation also applies, although it may be difficult to carry out, in cases in which, as in the case of many farmers, "firm" and "household" are one. We confine both concepts to decisions about monetary funds and we neglect, for convenience's sake, any similar decision that may be taken with respect to commodities. Saving and Accumulation will thus be treated as elements of a monetary process: the complementary processes in the world of goods constitute a distinct problem. Where no confusion is to be feared we shall use the word Saving to cover also Accumulation. Dissaving—which includes consumers' spending of "capital gains"—and Decumulation are self-explanatory.[1]

[1] Full justification of the conceptual arrangement adopted cannot be given without going much more thoroughly into the theory of money than is possible in this book, and will, it is hoped, be presented in the

Therefore, Saving (Accumulation included, when required by the context) does *not* mean:

a. The assembling of a sum earmarked for the purpose of buying a durable consumers' good, or of meeting an item of expenditure which cannot be covered by current receipts: "saving" in order to buy a motorcar for nonbusiness use or a house to live in, or "saving up" for holidays is not saving at all in our sense, but merely rearranging consumptive expenditure so as to fit "lumpy" items. Nor does any mere rearrangement of the time shape of one's real income stream necessarily involve saving.

b. Notspending or deferment of spending.[1] The decision on which our definition turns, may, but need not, result in the money leaving the saver's account and eventually reaching some commodity-market later than it would have done if retained in the service of financing consumptive expenditure. It may possibly reach it sooner. In itself the decision to save is not a decision not to spend or to defer spending, and the latter decision may equally well occur with respect to sums which are and remain earmarked

writer's treatise on money. That provision, say, for one's old age, is Saving only if the intention is to live on the revenue from the sum assembled for the purpose, and not if the intention is to spend that sum as well (so that, ideally, there is nothing left on the dying day), sounds not less strange than that it is Saving if one "earmarks" in order to purchase a house for the purpose of letting it, while it is not Saving if the intention is to live in the house. Also, it will be objected that, the defining criterion being an intention, we cannot from observable behavior know whether there is Saving or something else until the intention is carried into effect, and that even then we could not be certain because what we see might still be Temporary Investment (to be defined presently in the text). These and similar objections vanish, however, if the purpose and the logic of our definition are kept in mind. Saving in the sense defined is a distinct phenomenon, playing a role and producing effects different from those produced by the other actions or decisions which it is usual to include in Saving, and much confusion can be averted by distinguishing them clearly. To some extent, the importance of this will become evident as we go on. We include earmarking of elements of income for the purpose of repaying debts. But this will be dealt with separately and is not considered in this section. In fact, it has no place within our present set of assumptions.

[1] The objection to the term deferment is not only that expenditure can be deferred for many reasons which characteristically differ in nature and effect, but that in no case does it express the social meaning of thrift. The saver himself does not defer but definitively renounces expenditure on consumers' goods of the sum saved, while the latter may be spent on consumers' goods by other people without any delay.

for consumptive use or, in the case of a firm, for expenditure in the ordinary run of business. Whether the decision not to spend occurs in these spheres, or in the sphere of saving, it is in any case neither saving nor explainable by saving as such, but a distinct phenomenon calling for a distinct explanation. Nor is Hoarding (to be defined later) synonymous with saving.

The carrying into effect of the decision to acquire titles to income we shall call Investment. In the case of households we shall mainly think of the acquisition of shares and bonds (including mortgages and the like) and of land or buildings, if intended for business purposes. In the case of firms we shall, however, include spending on all kinds of producers' goods beyond replacement. Such acts of expenditure we will designate by the term Real Investment.

Older doctrine has undoubtedly excluded a great mass of facts from its horizon by despising the monetary approach and by linking investment—in particular real investment, still more real investment in plant and equipment—much too closely to saving. Saving and investment, as here defined, are of course distinct events. The former exerts influence of its own independently of investment and the latter can be financed, as we shall see, from sources other than saving. One of them should be mentioned at once. Suppose that somebody who is in the habit of buying a new motorcar every five years, assembles the necessary sum continuously on his checking account. The units of account earmarked for that purpose are not withdrawn from circulation. They "circulate" in the same sense that any others do, only they do so with a longer period (lower "velocity," to be defined later) than others. The modern money market offering the facility, our man may decide to buy, say, treasury certificates as his motorcar fund grows and to sell them when the time has arrived to buy the car. He does save. His behavior toward consumption or his intention to spend on consumers' goods has not changed. Yet he invests. The money leads a sort of double existence, serving all the purposes of a cash item earmarked for a certain purpose and at the same time all the purposes of the borrower. We call this Temporary Investment, and will carefully bear in mind its obvious peculiarities.

Moreover, saving, even if invested, need not issue into real investment as readily as the reasoning of older authors seems to imply. Not only can the saver invest by financing other people's consumption, but his money may serve to finance producers' deficits or to pay debts. Even if it does not, it need not be applied in such a way as to entail increase of the national stock of durable producers' goods, although it is obvious that, inasmuch as increased saving means rates of interest lower than any otherwise would be, there always will be a tendency in that direction. In addition, the reader is welcome to insert here a whole chapter on the innumerable incidents and accidents, errors, frictions, and lags, by which savings may be lost or stopped on their way or misdirected or dissaved again and which will account for imperfect coordination between saving and investment. But any want of coordination which we may observe is not simply due to the absence of an equilibrating mechanism; for, though different acts, saving and investment are interdependent and correspective so as to shape each other.

Saving implying intention to acquire titles to income, the decision to save is taken with reference to given or expected investment opportunities and the prospect of income they offer. Moreover, it can be currently revised as they change: the case of savers is not analogous to that of farmers who have to make decisions which will take effect but one year later and then take effect for all of them simultaneously. In the case in which saving issues in real investment, however, there is a lag between decision to effect the latter and the emergence of the corresponding equipment goods. This lag gives room for the ordinary chapter of accidents to unfold itself but not for a special kind of maladjustment, since the rate of interest is free to react at once. Even if saving, say, becomes a habit and outruns its rationale, maladjustment does not necessarily ensue because, whether savers save rationally or not, their action in any case influences investment opportunity, which in turn tends as much to adapt itself to the amount and the rate of saving as it tends to influence that amount and rate. Of course, there is very little meaning in an application of Marshallian demand and supply curves to this case. They do not illustrate but rather obscure the nature of the relation between saving, investment, and the rate of interest. Since this relation is the net result of the interaction of all the variables of the system, it can be expressed only in terms of the Walrasian apparatus. From the attempt to do so by means of two independent single-value functions of the rate of interest nothing but caricature can result.

Actually, of course, that equilibrating mechanism very often does not work. But sound diagnosis cannot be expected from denying its existence or from setting up such entities as "optimism," "pessimism," "saving instinct," or from simply asserting that people elect to act in such a way that maladjustment will ensue and that saving and investment can each go its own way indefinitely. In order to make headway, we must locate the sources of the trouble. They will be found in the business situations incident to the process of economic change we are about to describe, and link up with notspending and with variations in real investment rather than with saving. At the moment, however, it is desirable, since the ground is so fertile in misconceptions, to make quite sure that the saving-investment mechanism, as such, does not produce anything that could qualify for the role of an explanation of crises or depressions.[1]

For this purpose we will envisage a society, stationary in every respect except in that it displays a positive rate of saving. Production functions are invariant and external disturbances are absent. There is a positive rate of interest. We exclude—but this is only for the sake of convenience and brevity—all investment opportunities except lending to firms (this merely excludes

[1] If given our definitions, the reader should think this obvious, so much the better. If he should think, in particular, that our rigorous distinction between saving and notspending begs the question, this would precisely imply granting the point which the writer wishes to make. There are many economists, however, who do use the simple saving-investment mechanism for the purpose above alluded to, and it is they whom the reader should blame for what the writer agrees are very trivial considerations. It should be observed that, while the argument presented above runs substantially on very familiar lines—it would be possible to quote in support, besides Walras, Mill, Boehm-Bawerk, Hayek, Hansen (for the latter's views see his criticism of Foster and Catchings in Business-cycle Theory, for instance, p. 57)—agreement ceases beyond it. For, barring many individual points which cannot be insisted on since this is no place for a full development of the theory of saving, there is a fundamental difference which must be kept in view: all those authors attribute to saving a role which is denied to it here. And all of them look upon the argument to be presented, or a similar one, as a satisfactory theory of saving, to which not more than a general proviso about frictions and disturbances from outside has to be added in order to make it applicable to the explanation of reality. This is not so, however. For us, the stationary assumptions we are going to make have importance only for the purpose of preliminary clarification and are admitted from the outset to yield an inadequate picture which, taken by itself, could only mislead.

consumers' credit) and assume that saving is the only source of supply of such monetary means as these firms may wish to have in addition to their current receipts (this assumption excludes credit creation: money consists, say, of a fixed number of gold coins which must be actually handed over to effect a transaction). Obviously, this model will display only the effects of saving and investment as such. We start from competitive equilibrium, although extension to the imperfectly competitive case would not present any difficulties. Now, that equilibrium is incessantly disturbed by the flow of new savings which are being offered to the firms. If, however, the system is adapted to the actual rate of savings—an assumption which is not only reasonable under the circumstances of this model, but also much nearer the truth in reality than devotees of oversaving theories are in the habit of admitting—this disturbance will be currently absorbed; for, as long as saving goes on at all, each installment will depress the rate of interest to the extent required to create its own investment opportunity. No other price, either of consumers' or of producers' goods will be affected at this stage. As to consumers' goods, the question whether saving in general reduces their prices is irrelevant here, since in any case they have been produced in quantities, decision about which already took account of that rate of saving. As to producers' goods, the analogous question—*i.e.*, whether investment increases their prices—is irrelevant for the same reason. And the new producers' goods are sure to find their buyers because the previous combination of factors of production is, owing to the fall in rate of interest, no longer optimal and the combination which is optimal now requires an increase in the more durable elements, let us call them machinery, such as will exactly equal the additional savings offered both in value and in cost, which is what we mean by saving creating its own demand. It is readily seen that, in this case, what above has been described as a caricature, works satisfactorily, because we have by our assumptions paralyzed everything else that could vary. The result would, in fact, be a steady growth of the system's industrial outfit by the steady addition to it of new units of plant and machinery, which, however, must be of the same types as those which are already in use or would be in use but for lumpiness, in order to exclude a new and different element which would otherwise intrude.

The fundamental meaning of saving and investment, as interpreted by classical doctrine, stands out clearly and need not detain us. But it is important to notice that since no losses are incurred by producers of consumers' goods owing to the failure of the households to spend their whole income for purposes of consumption, there is no reason for any producer to refuse additional "capital" on the ground that, because of such losses, he wants to contract rather than to expand operations. Nor will there be any "glut" when the products of the new machines reach the markets for the consumers' goods. Prices will now fall but this does not spell losses, because it will necessarily be compensated for by the corresponding fall in costs per unit of finished product. There may be difficulties, of course, such as the impossibility of adjusting old loan contracts quickly, but they belong to the class of frictions. Unless interest falls to zero—and then saving in our sense stops, though, for example, "saving for the rainy day" may continue—this process can go on indefinitely, without of itself creating any problem, along constant production functions. The continuity of the latter is in this case no more serious a restriction than it is in others. It is worth while noticing, however, that such addition to the stock of durable producers' goods can be injurious to the interests of the working class. Whether it is or not depends on the elasticity of substitution between labor and those goods. But this is not relevant to our argument.

If, however, the system is not adapted to the saving actually done, analysis becomes more complicated. We will assume that savers suddenly and unexpectedly take to saving, say, double the sum per unit of time they used to save. It should be observed at once that the violent fluctuations usually associated with thrift are variations in the rate of spending.[1] Our problem is, therefore, little more than an exercise in pure theory, for long time changes

[1] This will become clear later on. Meanwhile, it is useful to insist again on the consequences, for analysis and policy, the confusion between those two things, which are different in nature and in behavior, must have. Most of what writers who are above primitive error attribute to thrift really applies to non-spending—in particular, most of what is true in the talk about "saving financing the losses which it creates" and "saving helping to destroy rather than to increase the stock of society's real capital." Hence, though it is no doubt regrettable that it is impossible to present a definition of saving which will make it less refractory to statistical evaluation, we have no choice. Statistical measurability is no advantage if the measurable thing is devoid of meaning, or carries another meaning.

in the rate of saving come about by truly infinitesimal steps, and although its fluctuations in the business cycle are considerable, owing to the great variability of the profit component, it must be borne in mind that these are a consequence of the cyclical situations, while here we are primarily concerned with the question whether saving would of itself produce depressions. Autonomously, abrupt changes in the rate of saving hardly ever occur. At least, the writer does not know of any instances, outside of the cases of "wild" inflation.

But assuming that such changes do occur, disturbance of the sort which always attends sudden changes in the channels of trade will in most cases ensue. Its precise nature, as well as the ultimate outcome, now depends on a great many variables, and also on other properties of the process and of the system, such as the number and sequence of the steps in the saving-investment process. We will simplify matters by again excluding bank credit and assuming that savers offer their additional savings to firms which, having been in competitive equilibriums at the previous point of time, have no use for them at the previous rate of interest and, at a suitably reduced rate, no other use than to add new units to their existing stock of machinery.

Now it is easy to construct a case in which the sudden withdrawal of the savers' demand from the market of the consumers' goods which they used to buy before their decision to double their rate of saving, causes catastrophe. This withdrawal on the one hand enforces emergency borrowing by the firms which produced those goods that they are now unable to sell and, on the other hand, deters all firms from committing themselves to new real investment. If savers go on after this, we can even, by properly choosing sequences, arrive at the result that all values will after a time asymptotically approach zero.

It is not less easy to construct a case in which there will be no fall at all in prices of consumers' goods because, the additional savings having been offered and accepted and work on the new machines having started before those prices had time to fall, demand from the increase incomes in the machine industries steps into the place of the demand discontinued by savers, so that nothing can happen except possibly a shift within the sphere of consumers' goods. This case is but a paraphrase, in monetary terms, of the idea that saving and investing fundamentally consist in handing one's claims to consumers' good to laborers and other suppliers of productive services in order to set them to work on, say, intermediate products. It does not make any difference whether these services were previously employed or not: saving is not "abortive" if they were previously employed. But then their employment in the machine industry will temporarily reduce the supply of consumers' goods, so that in this case there will be a period during which saving and investment produce an increase in their prices.

The best that can be said for both constructions is that, though they are absurdly overdrawn pictures of possible variants of an impossible case, they nevertheless may serve in the role of magnifying glasses with which to look for otherwise invisible traits of reality. The second is perhaps more apt to bring out fundamental truth that is not obvious to the layman, but for our purpose we are particularly interested in the first. In itself it is trivial, for all it teaches is that a violent change in the rate of saving causes trouble which may go on intensifying itself so that the new rate of saving and the new rate of investment may diverge for a considerable time. But such a violent change, coming about autonomously, yields the only case in which saving could possibly have anything to do with the causation of business depressions in the sense that it could create them by iself. Moreover, these changes would have to recur periodically.

We now return to our argument. We do not, of course, exclude Saving and Accumulation from the internal factors making for economic change; for, unlike variations in population, they certainly are a purely economic phenomenon. But we do exclude them from the fundamental contour lines of our analytic model. This decision may well look strange. To many it may seem to exclude the very essence of the matter.[1] A little reflection will, however, quickly dispel that impression. As soon as we realize the necessity of starting our analysis of economic change from a stationary state in perfect equilibrium, exclusion of savings as a major factor in bringing about that change follows logically, for whatever the definition of saving the reader adopts, it is clear that most of its sources, as well as most of the motives for it, would be absent in a stationary state. If we take up any of the familiar attempts at estimating statistically the amount

[1] The element of saving will, however, be reintroduced and the reader will then be in a position to judge whether or not the position assigned to it does or does not do justice to its actual importance.

of saving done in any country at any time, we see immediately that the bulk of it, whether done within the sphere of business or the sphere of households, flows from revenues or elements of revenues which would not exist at all in a stationary state, namely from profits, or from other incomes created or swelled by previous economic change.

As to motives, it is equally obvious that most of them arise out of situations incident to economic change. It does not matter now, whether we define the stationary state so rigorously as to exclude all saving or not. What matters is the fact that its quantitative importance would be exceedingly small if the economic process in any way approximated the equilibrium picture: Saving would be a "trickle" and by virtue of this fact alone could not give rise to any troubles. This is, in fact, the reason why "primitive" countries find it so difficult to finance the beginnings of capitalist industry themselves. It follows that, if we included savings as a major factor initiating economic change, we would be including in our premises part of what we are attempting to explain. Hence, it seems advisable to construct a model which does not contain it among the fundamental constituents. By this we may hope to get much better insight into the nature and role of saving than if, trying prematurely to be realistic, we carried it with us from the start.

To sum up, we shall designate by the term Growth changes in population and in the sum total of savings plus accumulations corrected for variation in the purchasing power of the monetary unit. That term is to emphasize not only that variation in both those variables is continuous in the mathematical sense but also that it occurs at a rate which changes but slowly and is per se incapable of producing those fluctuations in industry and trade which interest us here. This does not mean that it cannot cause any fluctuations: it obviously can. Nor do we mean, that this factor of change is irrelevant to those fluctuations which are our subject, or that it is quantitatively insignificant. Within fifty or sixty, or even nine years—which, as we shall see, are for us important periods—the cumulative change due to Growth will assert itself in many of our figures. All it means is that the effects of Growth are capable of being currently absorbed—in the sense that any disequilibrium created by every newcomer in the labor market or every dollar newly saved in the money market could under ordinary circumstances be corrected without giving rise to any visible disturbance—hence, cannot by themselves create the alternation of booms and depressions we observe. Moreover, Growth, but especially saving, owes its actual quantitative importance to another factor of change without which its modus operandi in the capitalist world cannot be understood. To be sure, there is interaction and interdependence and actual results are the product both of Growth and that other factor. But the modus operandi of the latter does account for booms and depressions and can be understood without Growth, which, therefore, we will relegate until we must call it up again in order to complete our survey.

3. By changes in the methods of supplying commodities we mean a range of events much broader than the phrase covers in its literal accepance. We include the introduction of new commodities which may even serve as the standard case. Technological change in the production of commodities already in use, the opening up of new markets or of new sources of supply, Taylorization of work, improved handling of material, the setting up of new business organizations such as department stores—in short, any "doing things differently" in the realm of economic life—all these are instances of what we shall refer to by the term Innovation. It should be noticed at once that that concept is not synonymous with "invention." Whatever the latter term may mean, it has but a distant relation to ours. Moreover, it carries misleading associations.

First, it suggests a limitation which is most unfortunate because it tends to veil the true contours of the phenomenon. It is entirely immaterial whether an innovation implies scientific novelty or not. Although most innovations can be traced to some conquest in the realm of either theoretical or practical knowledge, there are many which cannot. Innovation is possible without anything we should identify as invention and invention does not necessarily induce innovation, but produces of itself no economically revelant effect at all. The economic phenomena which we observe in the special case in which innovation and invention coincide do not differ from those we observe in cases in which preexisting knowledge is made use of. Stressing the element of invention or defining innovation by invention would, therefore, not only mean stressing an element without importance to economic analysis, but it would also narrow down the relevant phenomenon to what really is but a part of it.

Second, even where innovation consists in giving effect, by business action, to a particular invention which has either emerged autonomously or has been made specially in response to a given business situation,[1] the making of the invention and the carrying out of the corresponding innovation are two entirely different things. They often have been performed by the same person; but this is merely a chance coincidence which does not affect the validity of the distinction. Personal aptitudes—primarily intellectual in the case of the inventor, primarily volitional in the case of the businessman who turns the invention into an innovation—and the methods by which the one and the other work, belong to different spheres. The social process which produces inventions and the social process which produces innovations do not stand in any invariant relation to each other and

[1] In many important cases, invention and innovation are the result of conscious efforts to cope with a problem independently presented by an economic situation or certain features of it, such as, for example, the shortage of timber in England in the sixteenth, seventeenth, and eighteenth centuries. Sometimes *innovation* is so conditioned, whereas the corresponding *invention* occurred independently of any practical need. This is necessarily so whenever innovation makes use of an invention or a discovery due to a happy accident, but also in other cases. It might be thought that innovation can never be anything else but an effort to cope with a given economic situation. In a sense this is true. For a given innovation will satisfy them, and as a rule they can be satisfied in many different ways. Most important of all, they may remain unsatisfied for an indefinite time, which shows that they are not in themselves sufficient to produce an innovation. The rise of the motorcar industry may serve as an example. The sense in which it may be true that motorcars emerged when conditions called for them is not relevant to an economic inquiry. For any "need" for them that may have existed was certainly subconscious and not an element in the then existing system of economic values. The "need," as far as economically relevant, was created by the industry, and people could obviously have gone on without any motorcars. Therefore, it seems reasonable, on the one hand, when everybody calls for a certain innovation and everybody endeavors to effect it, to recognize this fact and, on the other hand, not to insist on seeing it when it is not there. The problem of determining how far "necessity is the mother of invention" is a difficult one. Its solution may well read differently for different purposes of analysis. We shall have to emphasize this more than once. Meanwhile, it should be pointed out that we may accept a theory of invention as presented, for example, by Mr. S. C. Gilfillan in his Sociology of Invention—the present writer, as a matter of fact, substantially does—and yet adopt another point of view for our purposes.

such relation as they display is much more complex than appears at first sight.

As soon as it is divorced from invention, innovation is readily seen to be a distinct internal factor of change. It is an *internal* factor because the turning of existing factors of production to new uses is a purely economic process and, in capitalist society, purely a matter of business behavior. It is a *distinct* internal factor because it is not implied in, nor a mere consequence of, any other. Of course, in reality, all three factors—changes in tastes, growth, and innovation—interact and mutually condition each other, and observed historic changes are the result of them all. But we can satisfy ourselves of their logical independence by visualizing societies in which internal change is merely caused by autonomous change in consumers' tastes or merely by growth or merely by innovation.

If we do this, we immediately realize that innovation is the outstanding fact in the economic history of capitalist society or in what is purely economic in that history, and also that it is largely responsible for most of what we would at first sight attribute to other factors. To illustrate this by an example: modern economic processes are to a great extent contingent upon agglomerations of population in cities and upon the facilities put at the disposal of the business community by public action. But these conditions of further innovations themselves are in most cases the results of industrial processes which come within our concept of innovation, and either directly produced or made possible by them.[1]

The changes in the economic process brought about by innovation, together with all their effects, and the response to them by the economic system, we shall designate by the term Economic Evolution. Although this term is objectionable on several counts, it comes nearer to expressing our meaning than does any other, and it has the advantage of avoiding the associations suggested by the cognate term Progress, particularly the complacency the latter seems to imply. This terminological decision is

[1] That proposition has meaning only for the purpose of economic analysis. In a wider setting, it is other social factors by which, among other things, innovation itself is determined and which make economic as well as general history. It cannot too often be repeated that every sentence of this book is to serve but a restricted purpose and moves within a restricted horizon appropriate to that purpose.

but the expression of an analytic intention, namely, the intention to make the facts of innovation the basis of our model of the process of economic change. Nothing but success in showing that the processes incident to innovation do account for the phenomena we want to understand can justify that intention. But the reader is invited to observe how very natural it is. The worst that could befall the analytic schema presented in this book would be an impression to the effect that it is ingenious or farfetched. Surely, nothing can be more plain than the proposition that innovation, as conceived by us, is at the center of practically all the phenomena, difficulties, and problems of economic life in capitalist society and that they, as well as the extreme sensitiveness of capitalism to disturbance, would be absent if productive resources flowed every year through substantially the same channels toward substantially the same goals, or were prevented from doing so only by external influences. And however difficult it may turn out to be to develop that simple idea so as to fit it for the task of coping with all the complex patterns with which it will have to be confronted, and however completely it may lose its simplicity on the way before us, it should never be forgotten that at the outset all we need to say to anyone who doubts is: Look around you!

B. The Theory of Innovation.—We will now define innovation more rigorously by means of the production function previously introduced. This function describes the way in which quantity of product varies if quantities of factors vary. If, instead of quantities of factors, we vary the form of the function, we have an innovation. But this not only limits us, at first blush at least, to the case in which the innovation consists in producing the same kind of product that had been produced before by the same kind of means of production that had been used before, but also raises more delicate questions. Therefore, we will simply define innovation as the setting up of a new production function. This covers the case of a new commodity, as well as those of a new form of organization such as a merger, of the opening up of new markets, and so on. Recalling that production in the economic sense is nothing but combining productive services, we may express the same thing by saying that innovation combines factors in a new way, or that it consists in carrying out New Combinations, although, taken literally, the latter phrases would also include what we do not now mean to include—namely, those current adaptations of the coefficients of production which are part and parcel of the most ordinary run of economic routine within given production functions.

For cases in which innovation is of the technological kind we could have defined it directly with reference to the so-called laws of physical returns. Barring indivisibility or lumpiness, the physical marginal productivity of every factor must, in the absence of innovation, montonically decrease. Innovation breaks off any such "curve" and replaces it by another which, again except for indivisibility, displays higher increments of product throughout,[1] although, of course, it also decreases monotonically. Or if we take the Ricardian law of decreasing returns and generalize it to cover industry as well, we can say that innovation interrupts its action, which again means that it replaces the law that had so far described the effects of additional doses of resources by another one. In both cases transition is made by a jump from the old to the new curve, which now applies throughout *and not only beyond that output which had been produced before by the old method.*

We can define innovation also with reference to money cost. Total costs to individual firms must, in the absence of innovation and with constant prices of factors, monotonically increase in function of their output. Whenever a given quantity of output costs less to produce than the same or a smaller quantity did cost or would have cost before, we may be sure, if prices of factors have not fallen, that there has been innovation some-

[1] This does not mean that unless there be innovation every *coefficient of production* necessarily increases in function of output, or that every coefficient of production is necessarily decreased by innovation. This bars us from measuring innovation by the behavior of these coefficients. Still less admissible is it to try to measure it by the change in one of them, for instance man-hours per unit of product or the reciprocal. The danger of such mistakes as that of comparing, say, the hours of work *on the farm* that went to produce a bushel of wheat in 1700 and 1900 and of overlooking that at the former date much more of the total work that ultimately issues into a bushel of wheat was done on the farm than at the later date, is the least of all that beset this path. The presence of other factors, and particularly of substitutable factors, makes any such measure all but meaningless. However, innovation must certainly reduce *some* coefficients, and if we are content with what amounts to almost heroic roughness, we may use product per man-hour for some purposes as an Index of Rationalization with respect to labor.

where.[1] It would be incorrect to say that in this case innovation produces falling long-run marginal cost curves or makes, in certain intervals, marginal cost negative. What should be said is that the old total or marginal cost curve is destroyed and a new one put in its place each time there is an innovation. If there are indivisibilities and the innovation becomes possible only beyond a certain quantity of output, while below it the old method remains superior and would promptly be resorted to again, should output fall sufficiently, we may indeed draw one cost curve to combine costs with the old method in one interval and costs with the new method in another interval. But this is possible only when the new method has become familiar and the whole system is adapted to it, which means that it enters the production functions—*i.e.*, the practical range of choice open to all—and is no longer an innovation.

If prices of factors are not constant but change independently of the action of the firm, the effect on its cost curves—total, average, and marginal—is exactly analogous to the effect of innovation: they break off and new ones emerge instead. It is easy to see that we cannot construct a theoretical cost curve that would in one stretch refer to, say, a given wage rate and, in another stretch, to a different one. The analogy may, hence, serve to illustrate still more clearly the impossibility of representing marginal costs in function of output as falling (whether continuously or not) and total costs as falling or rising less than they otherwise would, under the influence of successive innovations. If prices of factors change in function of the action of the firm it is no longer so, and cost curves have to take account of such changes. But, in general, prices of factors could then, unless there is lumpiness or innovation in their production or supply, change only in the same direction as the quantity of the product, so that we need not apprehend that any fall along cost curves arises from this source.

[1] It need not necessarily have occurred in the industry under observation, which may only be applying, or benefiting from, an innovation that has occurred in another. On the other hand, that criterion may be extended to apply to new commodities, if we compare the revenue that can be derived from a certain outlay in the new line with the revenue that can be derived from the same outlay in the most advantageous of the old lines. It should be observed that, unless we bar indivisibilities, the criterion is only sufficient, but need not hold for every quantity of output.

This helps to clear up some points about the theory of cost which are of considerable importance for our subject. For the sake of brevity, we shall consider total cost per unit (average cost) only and define the so-called Law of Increasing Cost (not quite correctly) with reference to it. In the long run—that is to say, when overhead may be treated as variable in function of output—average cost curves can be falling only because of the presence of lumpy factors, while all other causes that may bring about fall in average cost do not produce fall along these curves, but a downward shift of them. Hence, they can never be falling throughout, but only in intervals the length of which is determined by the nature of the lumpy factor or factors, and after which they must rise again. Now, disregarding the effects of lumpiness or smoothing them out by drawing a monotonic curve through the alternating stretches of rising and falling average costs, we should, strictly speaking, get a curve which would for a small individual firm, be parallel to the quantity axis, *i.e.*, constant unit costs. A Law of Increasing Cost comes in, however, if we admit that some factor is in absolutely inelastic supply even in the long run—the factor management for instance. For an industry or a big firm we may, in addition, get increasing total unit costs if factor prices rise against it as it increases output. This not only disposes, in the realm of fundamental principles, of the difficulties that have been raised about competitive equilibrium under conditions of decreasing cost, but also enables us to take care, by means of the concept of innovation, of a multitude of industrial patterns which seem recalcitrant to those principles.

In fact, since decreasing total unit costs are mere interruptions of the fundamental property of any given total unit cost curve either to rise or to be horizontal, increasing and decreasing costs are not coordinated alternatives. Only the former is a genuine "law"; the latter expresses but a modification of it by an accidental technical circumstance, which while it acts will indeed prevent perfectly competitive equilibrium from emerging but cannot do so indefinitely, because it must ultimately surrender. There is, hence, no Law of Decreasing Cost to parallel the Law of Increasing Cost on equal terms and there is no warrant for the monotonically descending cost curves that are sometimes drawn. At the same time, however, we recognize first, that in some cases lumpy factors may be so big—a railroad track for instance—that for a very long time ahead the whole of the useful range of total unit cost lies within the falling interval, and second, that in practically all cases there is an important falling interval, owing to fixity of overhead, on short-run total unit cost curves within which firms may be moving for years together. In cases of "building ahead of demand" and with imperfect competition, in particular in the presence of oligopolistic struggles, the latter situation will be much in evidence—firms may possibly even move within the descending interval of their marginal cost curves—and account for many instances of "overproduction" and "overcapacity."

But what dominates the picture of capitalistic life and is more than anything else responsible for our impression of a prevalence of decreasing cost, causing disequilibria, cutthroat competition and so on, is innovation, the intrusion into the system of new production functions which incessantly shift existing cost curves. Thus, having been led by other reasons to question the validity of the analysis which rests upon the concept of monotonically descending cost curves, we also see that we do not need it, for the concept of cost curves that shift under the impact of innovation gives us all we want in order to handle the mass of facts for the sake of which those descending cost curves were devised. Even the cases above alluded to, in which decreasing cost actually does not constitute an important element of a business situation—of those "cramped" situations in which everybody tries to contract while everybody could expand sometimes even at falling prime costs per unit—find their proper setting and their interpretation within this analysis, which, as pointed out before, gives to Short-time Analysis and to the Theory of Imperfect Competition what seems to the writer to be their true significance. The impression that firms moving in intervals of decreasing costs are often in the center of the vicissitudes of industrial life is not wrong. But this links up with innovation, because the firms which, rushing down along such intervals, are upsetting existing industrial structure and heading toward monopoly, are in general precisely those which have set up new production functions and which are struggling to conquer their market. If it were not for this, the space that decreasing costs fill in the economists' thought would rapidly dwindle to very modest proportions.

Before going on, it will be well to repeat the same argument in terms of the two familiar concepts due to Marshall, Internal and External Economies. As to the former, it may seem strange to say that economies of scale internal to the individual firm, if they are to explain the shape of a cost curve, necessarily reduce to effects of lumpiness. Yet it is so, not only in the case exemplified by costly machinery, but also in the cases of more rational division of labor or, more generally, better "organization" of factors which is held to occur when output expands. For if, for instance, a small tailor decides to employ a specialist in sewing on buttons because, and only because, his business expands, and if he would have taken that decision from the outset had his output been from the outset what it now is, then the only possible reason why he did not take that decision sooner is that, in his modest circumstances, labor is a lumpy factor. If internal economics are meant to designate the outstanding industrial fact we actually think of when referring to large-scale industry, they are due to innovation and cannot be expressed as a simple function of output even if they should historically be conditioned by an increase in the latter. In neither case does any difficulty arise about decreasing costs being incompatible with competitive equilibrium or about explaining the disequilibria we actually observe.

External economies are reductions in unit costs that are due to favorable circumstances incident to the growth of an industry, notably to its growth in a certain locality. They are not always easy to distinguish from internal economies and there are many intermediate cases. This, however, we will disregard. Much more important is it that "external economies must usually take their ultimate origin in the internal economics of some subsidiary industry" (R. F. Kahn, *Economic Journal* for March 1935, p. 11). If an industry grows, some firm may specialize in the production of machinery needed by that industry and no other, or somebody may set up a broker's business to provide it with raw material or start a trade journal. Cases of this type arise either from lumpiness—the journal's overhead, including, say, an owner-manager, requires a minimum of readers and advertisers in order to pay for itself—or else they constitute innovations: the journal may very well be one. Neither alternative puts external economies on a par with external diseconomies or, at all events, their most important instance, which consists in the rise of the price of factors in response to increase in the demand for them. Nor would discussion of other cases alter the result. Take the instance of the growth of a supply of workmen specially skilled in the work of an industry. Lack of it is indeed one of the major difficulties which innovation frequently meets. It is overcome as the industry develops and reaches maturity, which means that it becomes adapted in size to its environment. While this process lasts, the industrial as well as the individual cost curves are incessantly shifting and no single cost curve describing this process can have any but a historical meaning. When it is over, this source of external economies ceases to flow. In fact, it would be hard to find any instance of the phenomenon in question except in connection with new industries. Therefore, no monotonically declining cost curves can be deduced from external economies. The term is still useful in order to denote some of the effects on one industry of innovations in another, which are, of course, a most important piece of the mechanism of economic evolution in our sense. But it must not be allowed to act as a screen to hide the innovations behind it, or be represented as a factor distinct from them.

We return to our argument. In order to bring out strongly the *modus operandi* of innovation, we will now promote to the rank of assumptions a few facts of common observation which present themselves in connection with our analysis of costs.

First, major innovations and also many minor ones entail construction of New Plant (and equipment)—or the rebuilding of old plant—requiring nonnegligible time and outlay. We shall reason on the assumption that they always do. If they did not, a great part of the theoretical schema which we are going to use would have to be modified. But these modifications, while of great theoretical interest, would be practically important only if the innovations that can be carried out instantaneously and without appreciable expense were themselves important. Experience seems to teach, however, that as a matter of fact they are not, that is to say, that our assumption fails to conform to fact only in the case of innovations which are of such small importance that we can safely neglect them although we must always be prepared to meet cases which cannot be thus disposed of. Therefore, we shall impose a restriction on our concept of innovation and henceforth understand by an innovation *a change in some production function which is of the first and not of the second or a still higher order of magnitude.* A number of propositions which will be read in this book are true only of innovation in this resstricted sense.

Of course the reverse would not be true: not every new plant embodies an innovation; some are mere additions to the existing apparatus of an industry bearing either no relation to innovation or no other relation than is implied in their being built in response to an increase in demand ultimately traceable to the effects of innovations that have occurred elsewhere. The relative importance of these cases varies, of course, and is extremely difficult to estimate. In fact, we meet here one of the most serious statistical difficulties of our subject. In a system in which the process of evolution goes on strongly, practically all new plant that is being constructed beyond replacement, and much of what is being constructed by way of replacement, either embodies some innovation or is a response to situations traceable to some innovation.

Second, we shall in general argue as if every innovation—as now defined—were embodied in a New Firm founded for the purpose. There is obviously no lack of realism about this assumption.[1] The one significant exception will, together with the reason for it, be noticed under the next heading. Even the reverse proposition would be much more nearly true than it appears to be at first sight: Most new firms are founded with an idea and for a definite purpose. The life goes out of them when that idea or purpose has been fulfilled or has become obsolete or even if, without having become obsolete, it has ceased to be new. That is the fundamental reason why firms do not exist forever. Many of them are, of course, failures from the start. Like human beings, firms are constantly being born that cannot live. Others may meet what is akin, in the case of men, to death from accident or illness. Still others die a "natural" death, as men die of old age. And the "natural" cause, in the case of firms, is precisely their inability to keep up the pace in innovating which they themselves had been instrumental in setting in the time of their vigor. No firm which is merely run on established lines, however conscientious the management of its routine business may be, remains in capitalist society a source of profit, and the day comes for each when it ceases to pay interest and even depreciation. Everyone who looks around knows the

[1] It is most instructively exemplified by Professor McGregor's essay on Enterprise and the Trade Cycle, in Enterprise, Purpose and Profit, 1934. He shows very convincingly that entrepreneurial activity as reflected by the formation of new concerns is the decisive influence in starting prosperities, less convincingly, that failures initiate downward movements.

type of firm we are thinking of—living on the name, connections, quasi-rent, and reserves acquired in their youth, decorously dropping into the background, lingering in the fatally deepening dusk of respectable decay. Analytically, our assumption is a device to bring within the reach of theory an important feature of capitalist reality in general and a material element in the causation of economic flutcuations. We visualize new production functions as intruding into the system through the action of new firms founded for the purpose, while the existing or "old" firms for a time work on as before, and then react adaptively to the new state of things under the pressure of competition from downward shifting cost curves. This arrangement accurately describes the situations and struggles that we actually observe in surveying capitalist evolution, and in particular the nature of its disequilibria and fluctuations. It also describes that process of incessant rise and decay of firms and industries which is the central—though much neglected—fact about the capitalist machine.

Third, we will assume that innovations are always associated with the rise to leadership of New Men. Again, there is no lack of realism about this assumption, which but formulates a fundamental truth of the sociology of industrial society. Verifications abound and may be gleaned from any textbook on, say, the industrial revolution, although the full extent and importance of the fact will not be realized until we know more than we do at present about what may be termed the personal history of industry. The main reason for introducing this assumption into a purely economic argument not primarily concerned with the structure of society, is that it provides the rationale for the preceding assumption. In fact, it explains why new production functions do not typically grow out of old businesses—if a new man takes hold of an old firm, they may—and hence, why their insertion proceeds by competing the old ones out of existence or by enforcing the transformation of them. Since this is part of our model and will be used to explain features characteristic of the process which is the subject of this book, we must notice the case of big, particularly of "giant," concerns which often are but shells within which an ever-changing personnel may go from innovation to innovation. They are, thus, no exceptions to our third assumption, but they may be exceptions to the second, because with such concerns innovation may and, in fact frequently does, come about within one and the same firm which coordinates it with its existing apparatus, and therefore need not assert itself in the industry by way of a distinct process of competition.

In order to take care of this case, which in future may steadily gain in importance, we introduce the concept Trustified Capitalism, in distinction from Competitive Capitalism. Economic evolution or "progress" would differ substantially from the picture we are about to draw, if that form of organization prevailed throughout the economic organism. Giant concerns still have to react to each other's innovations, of course, but they do so in other and less predictable ways than firms which are drops in a competitive sea, and many details—in some points, more than details—would then have to be altered in our model. We have to recognize, in this as in other respects, that we are dealing with a process subject to institutional change and therefore must, for every historical period, see whether or not our model, however faithfully copied from the history of other periods, still fits facts. However, the sector of concerns which are "big," not only in the usual sense of the writers who figure out what percentage of the total national capital of the United States is controlled by the 20 biggest concerns, but in the sense required by the present argument, is as yet not great enough to dominate the picture in any country. Even in the world of giant firms, new ones arise and others fall into the background. Innovations still emerge primarily with the "young" ones, and the "old" ones display as a rule symptoms of what is euphemistically called conservatism. On the whole, the exception seems, therefore, to reduce to modifications to be dealt with on the merits of each practical case.

Our third assumption, then, inserts into our model of economic life a class of facts of the behavioristic type. It helps to localize the sources and effects of those downward shifts of cost curves which we saw were inadequately described by the device of monotonically descending curves, and to describe the way in which the system reacts to them. In particular, it explains why innovations are not carried into effect simultaneously and as a matter of course, either by all firms or, if they involve the use of lumpy factors, by all firms beyond a certain size, in the same manner as all firms will, other things being equal, try to employ more labor if it becomes cheaper. If this were so, all major innovations would still create disequilibria. But if action in order to carry them out were equally open to all as soon as they became technically and commercially possible, those disequilibria would not be different from those which arise currently from changes in data and are currently absorbed without very great difficulties and without "revolutions" or upheavals—which, in the political sphere also, would not occur in the way in which they actually do occur, if all people accepted new political facts with equal promptitude. Innovations which may be thought of as becoming "objectively" possible in a continuous stream, would then induce a current and continuous process of absorption, save in exceptional cases which should not display any regularity. However, the disequilibria which we observe are of a different nature. Their characteristic feature is precisely that they recur with some regularity and that they can be absorbed only by means of a distinct and painful process. This is because only some firms carry out innovations and then act along new cost curves, while the others cannot and have merely to adapt themselves, in many cases by dying. This fact, in turn, forces upon us recognition of the element formulated by our third assumption.

What we are doing amounts to this: we do not attack traditional theory, Walrasian or Marshallian, on its own gorund. In particular, we do not take offense at its fundamental assumptions about business behavior—at the picture of prompt recognition of the data of a situation and of rational action in response to them. We know, of course, that these assumptions are very far from reality but we hold that the logical schema of that theory is yet right "in principle" and that deviations from it can be adequately taken care of by introducing friction, lags, and so on, and that they are, in fact, being taken care of, with increasing success, by recent work developing from the traditional bases. We also hold, however, that this model covers less ground than is commonly supposed and that the whole economic process cannot be adequately described by it or in terms of (secondary) deviations from it. This is satisfactory only if the process to be analyzed is either stationary or "steadily growing" in the sense of our definition of the term Growth: any external disturbances may enter, of course, provided adaptation to them is passive. And this is equivalent to saying that the assumption that business behavior is ideally rational and prompt, and also that in principle it is the same with all firms, works tolerably well only within the precincts of tried experience and familiar motive. It breaks down as soon as we leave those precincts and allow the business community under study to be faced by new possibilities of business action which are as yet untried and about which the most complete command of routine teaches nothing. Those differences in the behavior of different people which within those precincts account for secondary phenomena only, become essential in the sense that they now account for the outstanding features of reality and that a picture drawn on the Walras-Marshallian lines ceases to be true—even in the qualified sense in which it is true of stationary and growing processes: it misses those features, and becomes wrong in the endeavor to account by means of its own analysis for phenomena which the assumptions of that analysis exclude. The reasonable thing for us to do, therefore, sems to be to confine the traditional analysis to the ground on which we find it useful, and to adopt other assumptions—the above three—for the purpose of describing a class of facts which lies beyond that ground. In the analysis of the process dominated by these facts traditional theory, of course, still retains its place: it will describe the responses to innovation by those firms which are not innovating themselves.

We may formulate the same point by means of the concept of Horizon. This we define as that range of choice within which a businessman moves freely and within which his decision for a course of action can be described exclusively in terms of profitability and foresight.[1] It differs widely with different types and individuals. But within a stationary or a growing process, we may

[1] It will be seen that foresight, or anticipation, and horizon are not made synonymous. A trivial example may serve to elucidate one of the differences. Tire trouble is nowadays so rare an event that any given case cannot be said to be foreseen. But, provided a motorist knows perfectly well how to manage the situation if the case arises, it is still within his horizon. Foresight is, of course, more difficult in an environment disturbed by innovation and, as soon as we have independently explained the situations, in which it becomes more difficult from this cause, we are within our rights if we in turn explain secondary features by lack of foresight, without laying ourselves open to the charge of thoughtlessly appealing to a *deus ex machina*. But such lack is not primarily linked to innovation and emphasizing it with respect to innovation would be emphasizing the wrong spot. Also, differences in foresight are undoubtedly the source of many phenomena relevant to the study of business cycles. But differences in foresight are not coterminous with differences in the ability to "walk alone" and to act on ground untried by experience.

assume that the management of each firm commands that horizon which enables it to transact its current business and to handle ordinary emergencies. Outside of such processes however, horizons of different people differ according to the criterion that the horizons of some are and the horizons of others are not confined to the range of possibilities tried out in business practice. This ability to decide in favor of untried possibilities or to choose not only between tried but also between tried and untried ones, may, however, be distributed in the population according to the Gaussian—though more plausibly a skew—law, and should not be thought of as confined to a few exceptional cases.

We neither can nor need go fully into this matter, but will be content to point to the common-sense justification of our emphasis on this difference in behavior. Everyone knows, of course, that to do something new is very much more difficult than to do something that belongs to the realm of routine, and that the two tasks differ qualitatively and not only in degree. This is due to many reasons, which we may group in three classes. First, in the case of something new being attempted, the environment resists while it looks on with—at least—benevolent neutrality at repetition of familiar acts. Resistance may consist in simple disapproval—of machine-made products—for instance—in prevention—prohibition of the use of new machinery—or aggression—smashing new machinery. Second, for the repetition of acts of routine the environment offers the prerequisites, in the case of new things it sometimes lacks, sometimes refuses, them: lenders readily lend for routine purposes; labor of the right type is available for them in the right place; customers buy freely what they understand. Third, most people feel an inhibition when the possibility of treading a new path offers itself. This may, in part, have rational foundation: it makes, in fact, a great difference whether the items entering our calculations derive from facts of daily experience or entirely from estimation. Even familiar data vary, of course, and their behavior may often be difficult to foresee, but within a familiar frame the average businessman knows how to manage them. If a new frame is to be constructed, the task changes its character. In order to see this, we need only visualize the situation of a man who would, at the present time, consider the possibility of setting up a new plant for the production of cheap aeroplanes which would pay only if all people who now drive motorcars could be induced to fly. The major elements in such an undertaking simply cannot be known. The situation is not different in the case of a new perfume. But also, irrational inhibitions enter. Neither error nor risk expresses adequately what we mean.

Whenever a new production function has been set up successfully and the trade beholds the new thing done and its major problems solved, it becomes much easier for other people to do the same thing and even to improve upon it. In fact, they are driven to copying it if they can, and some people will do so forthwith. It should be observed that it becomes easier not only to do the same thing, but also to do similar things in similar lines—either subsidiary or competitive ones—while certain innovations, such as the steam engine, directly affect a wide variety of industries. This seems to offer perfectly simple and realistic interpretations of two outstanding facts of observation: First, that innovations do not remain isolated events, and are not evenly distributed in time, but that on the contrary they tend to cluster, to come about in bunches, simply because first some, and then most, firms follow in the wake of successful innovation; second, that innovations are not at any time distributed over the whole economic system at random, but tend to concentrate in certain sectors and their surroundings. Neither observation can be new to anyone. The point we wish to make is that both follow from our premises and find their place within our analytic schema, instead of remaining outside of it in the class of deviations or modifying circumstances. The first puts into its proper light our former statement, that disturbances of equilibrium arising from innovation cannot be currently and smoothly absorbed. In fact, it is now easy to realize that those disturbances must necessarily be "big," in the sense that they will disrupt the existing system and *enforce a distinct process of adaptation.* This is independent either of the size of the innovating firm or firms or of the importance of the immediate effects their action would in itself entail. What we see at first glance may well be a multitude of reactions not easily traceable to any definite innovation behind them. But in many cases comprising historically important types, individual innovations imply, by virtue of their nature, a "big" step and a "big" change. A railroad through new country, *i.e.*, country not yet served by railroads, as soon as it gets into working order upsets all conditions of location, all cost calculations, all production functions within its radius of influence and hardly any "ways of doing things" which have been optimal before remain so afterward. The case may be put still more forcibly if we consider the railroadization and the electrification of the whole world as single processes. There is, however, some danger in overstressing such obvious instances, because this may easily lead to the familiar attitude of confining the phenomenon to this class and overlooking it in all others—hence, to missing its true dimensions.[1]

The second observation, the explanation of which follows naturally from our general schema, is no less obvious. Industrial change is never harmonious advance with all elements of the system tending to move in step. At any given time, some industries move on, others stay behind; and the discrepancies arising from this are an essential element in the situations that develop. Progress—in the industrial as well as in any other sector of social or cultural life—not only proceeds by jerks and rushes but also by one-sided rushes productive of consequences other than those which would ensue in the case of coordinated rushes. In every span of historic time it is easy to locate the ignition of the process and to associate it with certain industries and, within these industries, with certain firms, from which the disturbances then spread over the system.

The facts which our three assumptions are the means of introducing into our analytic model explain not secondary phenomena only but the essential features of the process of economic evolution in our sense of the term. We shall meet with many examples of this, as in the theory of profit to be outlined in the next section. Here we will notice one only, namely, their bearing upon our general conception of progress. Evidently, we must cease to think of it as by nature smooth and harmonious in the sense that rough passage and disharmonies present phenomena foreign to its mechanism and require special explanations by facts not embodied in its pure model. On the contrary, we must recog-

[1] As stated before, this is our fundamental reason for doubting the value of the concept of Revolutionary Inventions (opposite: Minor Inventions) if it is to suggest that they or their effects differ qualitatively from others. We shall not use the concept of Autonomous Inventions either, although this seems to carry a connotation more relevant to our argument. But the concept Induced Innovations we shall occasionally use in order to denote those additional improvements which present themselves in the process of copying the first innovators in a field and of adaptation by existing firms to their doings.

nize that evolution is lopsided, discontinuous, disharmonious by nature—that the disharmony is inherent in the very *modus operandi* of the factors of progress. Surely, this is not out of keeping with observation: the history of capitalism is studded with violent bursts and catastrophes which do not accord well with the alternative hypothesis we herewith discard, and the reader may well find that we have taken unnecessary trouble to come to the conclusion that evolution is a disturbance of existing structures and more like a series of explosions than a gentle, though incessant, transformation.

C. The Entrepreneur and His Profit.—For actions which consist in carrying out innovations we reserve the term Enterprise; the individuals who carry them out we call Entrepreneurs. This terminological decision is based on a historical fact and a theoretical proposition, namely, that carrying out innovations is the only function which is fundamental in history and essential in theory to the type usually designated by that term. The distinction between the entrepreneur and the mere head or manager of a firm who runs it on established lines or, as both functions will often coincide in one and the same person, between the entrepreneurial and the managerial function, is no more difficult than the distinction between a workman and a landowner, who may also happen to form a composite economic personality called a farmer. And surely it is but common sense to recognize that the economic function of deciding how much wool to buy for one's process of production and the function of introducing a new process of production do not stand on the same footing, either in practice or logic.

The outlines of an economic and sociological analysis of both types and both functions have been given elsewhere.[1] We will briefly note the points that are most important for our purpose.

1. It is not always easy to tell who the entrepreneur is in a given case. This is not, however, due to any lack of precision in our definition of the entrepreneurial function, but simply to the difficulty of finding out what person actually fills it. Nobody ever is an entrepreneur all the time, and nobody can ever be only an entrepreneur. This follows from the nature of the function,

[1] See the writer's Theory of Economic Development, notably Chaps. II and IV. Compare, also, the historical sketch in the writer's article Unternehmer in the Handwörterbuch der Staatswissenschaften.

which must always be combined with, and lead to, others. A man who carries out a "new combination" will unavoidably have to perform current nonentrepreneurial work in the course of doing so, and successful enterprise in our sense will normally lead to an industrial position which thenceforth involves no other functions than those of managing an old firm. Nevertheless, we have little difficulty in identifying entrepreneurship in the times of competitive capitalism. The entrepreneur will there be found among the heads of firms, mostly among the owners. Generally, he will be the founder of a firm and of an industrial family as well. In the times of giant concerns the question is often as difficult to answer as, in the case of a modern army, the question who is the leading man or who really won a given battle. The leading man may, but need not, hold or acquire the position that is officially the leading one. He may be the manager or some other salaried employee. Sometimes, he is the owner of a controlling parcel of shares without appearing on the list of responsible executives at all. Although company promoters are not as a rule entrepreneurs, a promoter may fill that function occasionally and then come near to presenting the only instance there is of a type which is entrepreneur by profession and nothing else.

2. But it should be easy to distinguish our function from those others which, though often found in combination with it, are yet not essential to it. We have already seen that the entrepreneur may, but need not, be the "inventor" of the good or process he introduces. Also, the entrepreneur may, but need not, be the person who furnishes the capital. This is a very important point. In the institutional pattern of capitalism there is machinery, the presence of which forms an essential characteristic of it, which makes it possible for people to function as entrepreneurs without having previously acquired the necessary means. It is leadership rather than ownership that matters. The failure to see this and, as a consequence, to visualize clearly entrepreneurial activity as a distinct function *sui generis,* is the common fault of both the economic and the sociological analysis of the classics and of Karl Marx. It is partly explained by the fact that previous ownership of the requisite producers' goods or of assets that may serve as collateral, or of money, makes it easier to become an entrepreneur, and the additional fact that successful entrepreneurship leads to a capitalist position for the entrepreneur and, normally,

his descendants, so that we find successful entrepreneurs very soon in possession of a plant and the other paraphernalia of a going concern. Two consequences follow, one of which is of an economic, the other of a sociological, nature.

First, risk bearing is no part of the entrepreneurial function.[1] It is the capitalist who bears the risk. The entrepreneur does so only to the extent to which, besides being an entrepreneur, he is also a capitalist, but qua entrepreneur he loses other people's money. Second, entrepreneurs as such do not form a social class. Although, in case of success, they or their descendants rise into the capitalist class, they do not from the outset belong to it or to any other definite class. As a matter of historical fact, entrepreneurs come from all classes which at the time of their emergence happen to exist. Their genealogies display most varied origins—the working class, aristocracy, the professional groups, peasants and farmers, and the artisan class, all have contributed to what is sociologically not a uniform type.

The above implies that although entrepreneurs may be or become stockholders in their firms, mere holding of stock does not, any more than would mere ownership, make an enterpreneur. The only realistic definition of stockholders is that they are creditors (capitalists) who forego part of the legal protection usually extended to creditors, in exchange for the right to participate in profits.

3. Let us visualize an entrepreneur who, in a perfect competitive society, carries out an innovation which consists in producing a commodity already in common use at a total cost per unit lower than that of any existing firm because his new method uses a smaller amount of some or all factors per unit of product. In this case, he will buy the producers' goods he needs at the prevailing prices which are adjusted to the conditions under which "old" firms work, and he will sell his product at the prevailing price adjusted to the costs of those "old" firms. It follows that his receipts will exceed his costs. The difference we shall call Entrepreneurs' Profit, or simply Profit. It is the premium

[1] Risk, nevertheless, enters into the pattern in which entrepreneurs work. But it does so indirectly and at one remove: riskiness—and every new thing is risky in a sense in which no routine action is—makes it more difficult to obtain the necessary capital and thus forms one of the obstacles entrepreneurs have to overcome and one of the instances of resistance of the environment which explain why innovations are not carried out smoothly and as a matter of course.

put upon successful innovation in capitalist society and is temporary by nature: it will vanish in the subsequent process of competition and adaptation. There is no tendency toward equilization of these temporary premia. Although we have thus deduced profit only for one particular case of innovation and only for conditions of perfect competition, the argument can readily be extended to cover all other cases and conditions. In any case, it is evident that, though temporary, profit is a net gain, *i.e.*, that is not absorbed by the value of any cost factor through a process of Imputation. For profits to emerge, however, it is essential that the "suicidal stimulus of profits" should not act instantaneously. In the preceding section we have seen the reasons why, as a rule, it does not. But cases occasionally occur, and may in the future be expected to occur more frequently, in which it does. We then get innovation without profit, or almost without it, and thus realize the possibility of what, anticipating later argument, we may term Profitless Prosperities.

In a stationary economy, even if disturbed by action of external factors, both the entrepreneurial function and the entrepreneurial profit would be absent, and so would the bulk of what is in common parlance described as profits. For, although there would be rents and quasi-rents of factors owned by firms (also in the case of a manager-proprietor, his "earnings of management" or wages, to which we may for the sake of argument add various interest items), and although there may be monopoly gains and if we admit external disturbances) also windfalls and possibly speculative gains, all these items would, in the conditions of a stationary or even of a growing economy, sum up to much smaller totals than they do in reality. Innovation is not only the most important immediate source of gains, but also indirectly produces, through the process it sets going, most of those situations from which windfall gains and losses arise and in which speculative operations acquire significant scope.

It follows that the bulk of private fortunes is, in capitalist society, directly or indirectly the result of the process of which innovation is the "prime mover." Speculative maneuvers which are responsible for some, are evidently incidents to the process of economic evolution in our sense, and so are largely the unearned increments reaped by owners of natural resources—urban land, for instance—which account for others. Saving, consistently carried on through generations, could not have been nearly so successful as it was if there had not been surpluses, due to innovation, from which to save. But the position of the typical industrial or commercial or financial family directly originates in some act of innovation. When their period of entrepreneurship is past, those families live, it is true, on quasi-rents, often supported by monopoloid situations, or, if they entirely sever their connection with business, on interest. But a new production function practically always emerges if we follow up those quasi-rents or monopoloid gains or monetary capitals to their sources. Of this we shall see many examples in our historical survey, which the writer believes to be sufficient, in spite of its fragmentary character, to establish the main points of this analysis beyond reasonable doubt.

4. Profit, in our sense, is a functional return, but it would not always be safe to locate the entrepreneurial function according to the criterion of accrual. Whether it accrues to entrepreneurs or not is a matter of institutional pattern. It does so most completely in that form of organization which is characterized by the prevalence of the family firm. It is there that it has most regularly served as the economic basis of industrial dynasties, by being reinvested or simply embodied in the ownership of a plant. In corporate industry profits accrue to the firm as such, and their distribution ceases to be automatic and becomes a matter of policy—shareholders, executives (whether entrepreneurs or not), and employees receiving in the most varied forms (bonuses, tantièmes, and so on) indeterminate shares in it or contractual equivalents for shares in it.

Struggles for a share in profits are less important for our subject than the struggles to conserve the stream of profit itself. Secrecy regarding processes, patents, judicious differentiation of products, advertising, and the like, occasionally also aggression directed against actual and would-be competitors, are instances of a familiar strategy, which in the public, as well as in the professional, mind have done much to veil the source and nature of profits in our sense, especially because that strategy may be resorted to in other cases as well. These devices are the same as those which play a role in cases of monopolistic competition, and the fact that they are met with in our case is precisely due to the other fact that an enterprise in our sense almost necessarily finds itself in an "imperfect" situation, even if the system be otherwise a perfectly competitive one. This is one of the reasons why we so persistently stress the relation between evolution and imperfection of competition. Profits might, as far as this goes, be also included in the category of monopoloid gains. This, however, would blur the specific character of our case: not every generalization is profitable to the analyst—any more than every innovation is to the innovator.

Not only is practically every enterprise threatened and put on the defensive as soon as it comes into existence, but it also threatens the existing structure of its industry or sector almost as unavoidably as it creates unemployment somewhere or other. An innovation sometimes may do so by its mere possibility and even before it is embodied in an enterprise. That structure resents the threat and perceives possibilities of defense other than adaptation by a competitive struggle which generally means death for many of its units. Situations ensue which produce the paradox that industry sometimes tries to sabotage that "progress," which it inexorably evolves by virtue of the very law of its own life. There is no contradiction in this. Our general schema, however, derives some support from the fact that it resolves that paradox so easily and shows us how and why industrial "progress" comes to the majority of firms existing at a given time as an attack from outside. Taking industry as a whole, there is always an innovating sphere warring with an "old" sphere, which sometimes tries to secure prohibition of the new ways of doing things.

5. It has been stated above that our assumption about New Firms carrying the new things into effect against resisting strata of old firms, which was to embody the characteristically different behavior in the face of new possibilities, may occasionally fail us. For the past it is obviously very realistic. Even in the present [1939] the writer is not aware of important instances which would prove it to be contrary to fact. But several minor ones he has observed. It is interesting to note that such absence of friction does not always make the path of progress smoother. In the country X, for example, all firms existing in the industry Y took at exactly the same time, about 15 years ago, to producing the article Z according to a new and much cheaper method. A deadlock ensued, very quickly remedied by an agreement which deprived that innovation of any effect beyond a surplus, unemployment, and some excess capacity. There is some reason to expect that such cases will increase in importance: on the one hand, technological research becomes increasingly mechanized

and organized; on the other hand, resistance to new ways weakens. Any technological improvement which is becoming "objectively possible," tends to be carried into effect as a matter of course. This must affect the phenomenon which is the subject of this book. It must also affect the importance of the social function, and in consequence the economic and social position, of that stratum of capitalist society which exists by entrepreneurial achievement as the knights of the Middle Ages existed by virtue of a certain technique of warfare.

Already, the volitional aptitudes that made the successful entrepreneur of old are much less necessary and have much less scope than they used to have. It is no chance coincidence that the epoch in which this decrease in importance of the entrepreneurial function first aserted itself is also the epoch in which the social and political position of the *bourgeoisie* first began to display obvious symptoms of weakness and to be attacked with success. However, it would be as great a mistake to overrate the length to which the process has as yet gone as it would be to ignore it. For our theme, it will be seen not to have proceeded far enough to matter for general contours, even in the the postwar period.

D. The Role of Money and Banking in the Process of Evolution.—This subject will be more fully discussed in the historical survey. In this section we will merely try to unravel its logical, as distinguished from its historical, roots and in so doing move on the same level of abstraction as we do throughout this chapter. Results cannot fail to look extremely unrealistic and, in this case more than in others, utterly contrary to facts. It is in no case easy to discern the element of innovation under the mass of induced, derivative, and adventitious phenomena that overlies it. But in the sphere of money and credit the layer is so thick and the surface so entirely at variance with the processes below, that the first impression of the reader may well be fatal. The proof of the analytic pudding, however, is in the eating, and the monetary part of our model is nothing but a device to get hold of those very facts to which the reader may feel inclined to point in refutation.

1. We will discard, on the understanding that they will be introduced later, consumers' borrowing, both public and private, on the one hand, and saving and accumulation, on the other.

Discarding the first, in a discussion of fundamental principle, will presumably not meet with insuperable objection. It is merely a measure of simplification and does not mean that consumers' borrowing is held to be of no importance in the cyclical process. The contrary is obvious: consumers' borrowing is one of the most conspicuous danger points in the secondary phenomena of prosperity, and consumers' debts are among the most conspicuous weak spots in recession and depression. Discarding the second is more than a measure of simplification. It implies the view that financing innovation from funds that have been saved or accumulated, presupposes previous profits, hence previous waves of evolution, and therefore has no claim to a place on the ground floor, as it were, of a model that is to display logical essentials. This follows from the argument in sec. A of this chapter, and does not imply anything about the role which financing of innovation by savings plays in any actual historical situation. In later discussions we shall assign it all the importance we conceive it to have, and also develop its *modus operandi*, although the writer thinks the importance to be smaller than, and the *modus operandi* different from, what is is commonly believed to be.

In accordance with our conception of New Men setting up New Firms, we also assume that would-be entrepreneurs do not already happen to own part or the whole of the assemblage of producers' goods which they need in order to carry out their plans, or any assets which they could exchange for what they need. There will always be such cases, although, they can become as frequent as we know them to be only when the evolutionary process is in full swing and when it has brought into existence a machinery for selling assets which we cannot assume now.[1] But they present no problem beyond those which we have dealt with in the preceding sections. Nor does a distinct problem of financing arise with the "old" firms in the stationary process from which we start. They have their plant and equipment, and their current expenditure—including repairs and replacement—can be financed from current receipts. Assuming, finally, that they are so financed, we arrive at the following three propositions, which sound strange but are tautologically true for eco-

[1] This instance illustrates well one of the source of objections to our model: we behold a fully developed industrial and financial system, and are prone to introduce the features of the building into a discussion of the scaffolding.

nomic world embodying our assumptions: Entrepreneurs borrow all the "funds" they need both for creating and for operating their plants—*i.e.*, for acquiring both their fixed and their working capital. Nobody else borrows. Those "funds" consist in means of payment created *ad hoc*. But although in themselves these propositions are nothing but pieces of analytic scaffolding, to be removed when they have served their purpose, the logical relation which they embody, between what is called "credit creation by banks" and innovation, will not be lost again. This relation, which is fundamental to the understanding of the capitalist engine, is at the bottom of all the problems of money and credit, at least as far as they are not simply problems of public finance.

2. Before going on, we will try to clarify the meaning of "credit creation" *considered as the monetary complement of innovation*, by a comparison with what would correspond to it in a socialist society. Since the central authority of the socialist state controls all existing means of production, all it has to do in case it decides to set up new production functions is simply to issue orders to those in charge of the productive functions to withdraw part of them from the employments in which they are engaged, and to apply the quantities so withdrawn to the new purposes envisaged. We may think of a kind of Gosplan as an illustration. In capitalist society the means of production required must also be withdrawn from their employments—the case of unemployed resources can easily be taken into account—and directed into the new ones but, being privately owned, they must be bought in their respective markets. The issue to the entrepreneurs of new means of payments created *ad hoc* is, since our entrepreneurs have no means of their own and since there are—so far—no savings, what corresponds in capitalist society to the order issued by the central bureau in the socialist state.

In both cases, the carrying into effect of an innovation involves, not primarily an increase in existing factors of production, but the shifting of existing factors from old to new uses.[1] There is,

[1] Even with respect to those quantities of factors which currently acrue, say, in an increasing population, and can be used for the new purposes without having previously served any old ones, it is more correct to say that they are shifted from the uses they would have served had the new purposes not been decided on, than simply to say that they go to the new uses directly. The point is of some importance, because in the traditional model it was increase in factors, rather than the shifting of factors, that was made the chief vehicle of economic progress.

however, this difference between the two methods of shifting the factors: in the case of the socialist community the new order to those in charge of the factors cancels the old one. If innovation were financed by savings, the capitalist method would be analogous, for the way in which saving and lending to entrepreneurs effects a shifting of factors through a shifting of means of payment may, indeed, be likened to the canceling of an old and the issuing of a new "order" to the owners of factors. But if innovation is financed by credit creation, the shifting of the factors is effected not by the withdrawal of funds—"canceling the old order"—from the old firms, but by the reduction of the purchasing power of existing funds which are left with the old firms while newly created funds are put at the disposal of entrepreneurs: the new "order to the factors" comes, as it were, on top of the old one, which is not thereby canceled. It will be shown later how this will affect prices and values and produce a string of important consequences which are responsible for many characertistic features of the capitalist process. This side of credit creation may also be clarified by means of the analogy with the issue of government fiat, although in all other respects the differences are much more important than the similarities.

Now, suppose that our socialist community finds it convenient to rule that the executive submit every innovation it wishes to carry out to another body, which passes upon it and may grant or withhold assent. In case it sanctions the plan, it countersigns and issues the orders to the factors to form the new combination. This is the function which in capitalist society is filled by banks which, in providing entrepreneurs with means to buy factors of production or their services, do something akin to issuing such orders. We now introduce this new kind of firms into our model. They are nothing but establishments for the manufacture of means of payment. We distinguish *member banks*, which keep the accounts of, and manufacture balances for, firms and households, and *bankers' banks*—which keep the accounts of, and manufacture balances for, member banks. For the sake of convenience we will assume that bankers' banks have no other customers but banks and that no member bank fills bankers' banks' functions, although in discussions of actual situations we must

---

But essential phenomena of the cyclical process depend on that shifting of factors.

take account of the facts that many bankers' banks also bank for firms and households and that many member banks also bank for other member banks: there are cases, the outstanding one being that of the banking system of the United States until 1914, in which central bank functions are entirely discharged by some members of the system and, perhaps, some government department, such as the United States Treasury. It is important to bear in mind that what directly matters for businesses is the amount of credit creation by member banks. Credit creation by bankers' banks stands at one remove from this and the two are not additive.

3. By confining the manufacture of credit to banks, we are roughly conforming to fact. But this restriction is not necessary. In various ways, firms may create means of payments themselves. A bill of exchange or a note is not, in itself, such a means. On the contrary, it generally requires financing and thus figures on the demand rather than the supply side of the money market. If, however, it circulates in such a way as to effect payments, it becomes an addition to the circulating medium. Historically, this has occurred repeatedly. An example is afforded by the practice which prevailed in the Lancashire cotton industry until at least the middle of the nineteenth century. Manufacturers and traders drew bills on each other which, after acceptance, were used for the settlement of debts due to other manufacturers and traders, much as bank notes would be. This should be taken into account in any estimate of the quantity of credit creation but will here be neglected throughout, because the statistical questions involved are entirely beyond us.

Government fiat might also serve the purpose of financing enterprise. There have been cases in which it did. The Brazilian government, for instance, financed coffee plantations by this method in the seventies. More frequently, however, this method was advocated without being actually resorted to. Friedrich List for instance—proving thereby how well he knew how to generalize from American experience—wished to see railroad construction (*sic!*) financed in this way. We insisted above on the differences between the issue of government fiat and credit creation by banks, not because of the difference between the creating agencies but because of the difference in the purposes usually associated with the two, which is what accounts for the difference in effects. For it must never be forgotten that the theory of credit creation as, for that matter, the theory of saving, entirely turns on the purpose for which the created—or saved—means of payment are used and on the success which attends that purpose. The quantity-theory aspect or, as we might also say, the aggregative aspect of the practice is entirely secondary. The trouble with John Law was not that he created means of payment *in vacuo*, but that he used them for purposes which failed to succeed. This will have to be emphasized again and again. We now exclude government fiat because of its historical association with consumptive expenditure, and are thus left with "credit creation by banks."

Anticipating discussion in subsequent chapters, we may at once free our theory of banking from part of its apparent unreality. Financing of enterprise has been assigned logical priority in the sense that this is the only case in which lending and the *ad hoc* creation of means of payment are essential elements of an economic process the model of which would be logically incomplete without them. But the familiar picture of banking business as it is can easily be developed from that element. The loans to entrepreneurs need not be repaid, but can be, and often are, renewed in such a way as to make the corresponding amount of means of payment permanently part of the circulating medium. In the disequilibria caused by innovation other firms will have to undertake investments which cannot be financed from current receipts, and hence become borrowers also. Whenever the evolutionary process is in full swing, the bulk of bank credit outstanding at any time finances what has become current business and has lost its original contact with innovation or with the adaptive operations induced by innovations, although the history of every loan must lead back to the one or the other.[1] If, finally, we insert consumers' borrowing on the one hand, and saving on the other, we have before us not only all the elements of which the practice of a bank actually consists, but also the explanation of the fact that current, or "regular," business has been emphasized to the point of giving rise to a theory of banking which recognizes nothing else but the financing of current commodity trade and the lending of surplus funds to the stock exchange, and to a canon of the morals of banking by which the function to which we assign logical priority is almost excluded from the things a

[1] The above proposition will be qualified later on, when account will be taken of the case of financing business losses.

banker might properly do. We shall see, however, that this does not invalidate our view and that credit creation for the purpose of innovation asserts itself and supplies the chief motive power for the variations in credit outstanding, all the same.

The latter assertion will have to justify itself in our analysis of monetary time series. But it is necessary to advert at once to its bearing on the modern controversy—it is really the modern form of a very old controversy—about the commercial *vs.* the investment theory of banking. By commercial, or classical, theory we mean the one alluded to in the preceding paragraph. Investment theory we call the theory which defines the function of the banking system, not in terms of any specific type of transaction, but in terms of the amount of deposits which results from all the possible transactions a bank can embark upon. The term *investment theory* has been chosen because investment, in the sense of the purchase of assets, bonds in particular, is the transaction which banks can most nearly effect on their own initiative and in which they are less than in any other dependent on the initiative of their customers. Now, it is extremely difficult to convey a correctly balanced impression of the relative merits of these two "theories" and of the reasons why we have to disagree with both. This difficulty is due not only to the fact that neither is a scientific theory—both aim at giving practical advice about how bankers should behave or be made to behave—but also the fact that the propositions held by, or implied in, both of them are not simply contradictory or right or wrong all along the line.

The commercial theory with older writers often has been associated with a denial of the fact of credit creation, sometimes expressed in the phrase: Bankers can lend only what has been entrusted to them by depositors. Apart from this misconception of what deposit banking means, there is no definite error in what it holds and plenty of wisdom in what it advocates. In particular, it should be clearly realized that no argument follows from our theory against banks' specializing in the current business of discounting commercial paper or against the proposition, largely though not wholly true, that this business, together with lending surplus funds on the stock exchange, will produce that amount of deposits which will equally avoid "inflationary" and "deflationary" impulses being imparted to the system. Our objection to the commercial theory rests on its failure to reach down to the sources of the process of which it describes part of the surface, and to diagnose correctly the nature of credit creation for other purposes than that of financing current commodity trade. This also obscures the relation which even "classical" credit creation for short-time purposes bears to innovation—best exemplified by loans to the stock exchange, which help to carry new issues—and leads to a narrow view about the function of finance bills and of credits in current account. Thus the theory contributes, through the phraseology which it has been instrumental in creating, to what may be described as the mimicry of credit creation, especially of credit creation for the purpose of innovation which tends to hide behind credit creation for the purposes of current trade. In this respect the investment theory is superior. But it assigns to the "regulation of the flow of funds by banks" a causal role in the economic process which does not belong to it and, by its insistence on quantity of credit outstanding, entirely loses sight of the essential element of purpose.

It is important for the functioning of the system that the banker should know, and be able to judge, what his credit is used for and that he should be an independent agent. To realize this is to understand what banking means. To have stressed it, at least by implication, is one of the chief merits of the commercial theory of banking, just as it is one of the chief demerits of the investment theory—which is a typical outsider's idea and could never, like its rival, have grown out of practical banking experience—to have overlooked it and to have made banking a mechanical function which might just as well be filled by some government department. Even if he confines himself to the most regular of commodity bills and looks with aversion on any paper that displays a suspiciously round figure, the banker must not only know what the transaction is which he is asked to finance and how it is likely to turn out, but he must also know the customer, his business, and even his private habits, and get, by frequently "talking things over with him," a clear picture of his situation. But if banks finance innovation, all this becomes immeasurably more important. It has been denied that such knowledge is possible. The reply is that all banks who at all answer to type, have it and act upon it. The giant banking concerns of England have their organs or subsidiaries which enable them to carry on that old tradition: the necessity of looking after customers and constantly feeling their pulse is one of the reasons for the division of labor between the big banks and the discount houses in the London money market. However, this is not only highly skilled work, proficiency in which cannot be acquired in any school except that of experience, but also work which requires intellectual and moral qualities not present in all people who take to the banking profession. Hence, deviations from the theoretical type must be expected to be much more frequent than in those sectors of economic reality in which we need not require more than ordinary intellectual and moral aptitudes of the "economic man." This difficulty is not peculiar to our model. It is met by anyone who tries to describe the way in which the capitalist machine is being run. Whatever our theories, we must all recognize that the leading functions are not simple matters which people can be expected to perform as effectively as they can be expected to leave an employment that offers a lower for one that offers a higher wage, or to produce beans instead of peas if it pays better; but that they are difficult to fulfill, so much so that many of those who attempt to fill them are hopelessly below the mark in a sense in which even the subaverage workman, craftsman, farmer is not. This is, of course, so with entrepreneurs. But in their case we take account of it by recognizing from the start that a majority of would-be entrepreneurs never get their projects under sail and that, of those who do, nine out of ten fail to make a success of them. In the case of bankers, however, failure to be up to what is a very high mark interferes with the working of the system as a whole. Moreover, bankers may, at some times and in some countries, fail to be up to the mark *corporatively:* that is to say, tradition and standards may be absent to such a degree that practically anyone, however lacking in aptitude and training, can drift into the banking buisness, find customers, and deal with them according to his own ideas. In such countries or times, wildcat banking develops. This in itself is sufficient to turn the history of capitalist evolution into a history of catastrophes. One of the results of our historical sketch will, in fact, be that the failure of the banking community to function in the way required by the structure of the capitalist machine accounts for most of the events which the majority of observers would call "catastrophes." Since such failure primarily shows in dealing with novel propositions—where judgment is most difficult and temptation strongest—an association has developed between financing innovation and miscarriage or misconduct which, however understandable, does not make analysis any easier.

Not less important for the functioning of the capitalist machine is it that banks should be independent agents. If they are to fulfill the function which has above been illustrated by the analogy with that socialist board which examines and passes upon the innovations envisaged by the executive, they must first be independent of the entrepreneurs whose plans they are to sanction or to refuse. This means, practically speaking, that banks and their officers must [1] not have any stake in the gains of enterprise beyond what is implied by the loan contract. This independence, most nearly realized in English banking, has always been threatened by attempts of entrepreneurs to gain control over banks and by attempts of banks or their officers to gain control over industry. But another kind of independence must be added to the list of requirements: banks must also be independent of politics. Subservience to government or to public opinion would obviously paralyze the function of that socialist board. It also paralyzes a banking system. This fact is so serious because the banker's function is essentially a critical, checking, admonitory one. Alike in this respect to economists, bankers are worth their salt only if they make themselves thoroughly unpopular with governments, politicians, and the public. This did not matter in the times of intact capitalism. In the times of decadent capitalism this piece of machinery is likely to be put out of gear by legislation. The motive, as well as the justification, for speaking in such cases of a theoretical type and a deviating reality lies in the diagnostic value of this distinction, and will be exemplified in our historical survey.

4. There are many ways in which banks may manufacture means of payment in fulfillment of their promises to lend. Only two of them interest us here—the issue of bank notes and the creation of balances, misleadingly called *deposits*. There is no difference between them, except one of technique (which is responsible for difficulties concerning the interpretation of statistics), the note being a balance embodied in a perfectly negotiable paper and the balance being a note which is transferable,

[1] "Must" here is no moral imperative, but simply indicates the fact that, unless that requirement be fulfilled, an important element of the capitalist engine is put out of operation and that certain consequences will follow from this.

not bodily but by check. Since the former has undergone, from the forties of the nineteenth century on, a change in function which has rapidly deprived it of its role as a vehicle of industrial and commercial member-bank credit, we will in general think of the latter only, except when discussing patterns in which the bank note actually filled that role.

In a formal sense, all balances are of course "created." But we confine this term to balances the creation of which increases the sum of existing means of payment. These are not necessarily "borrowed," but may also result from sales of assets to a bank. In this case the customer acquires an "owned" balance, as he does when he deposits legal-tender money or newly mined or imported monetary metal—thus acquiring balances which are owned but not created—the only cases in which the term *deposit* (in the sense of *deposition irregulare*) is appropriate. If we use the word *deposit* instead of the word *balance*, we will distinguish these cases by the term *original deposits* from *created deposits*. Although these deposits do not increase the means of payment, the newly mined or imported monetary metal itself does, and it is worth noticing that, opportunely timed, such additions to the stock of legal tender may replace credit creation that would otherwise have come about. Depositing "old" legal tender which circulated before, also increases deposits, but not the sum of existing means of payment. During the growth of deposit banking, which in America, England, and Germany was substantially completed before the World War, legal-tender money which had previously circulated outside of the banking sphere kept on streaming into banks. As long as this process played any significant role, there was a special trend in the figure of total deposits, and a number of propositions usually made about deposits require qualification for countries and periods in which that was the case. Mostly we shall consider a perfectly developed system of deposit banking in which legal tender, while moving into and out of banks, never enters into banks for the first time unless newly issued. But it should be borne in mind that by doing so on principle we would leave out of account a fact which may be very important. For instance, the answer to the question how far the fall in gold production which occurred after 1873 can have had any effect on prices, largely depends on our estimate of the immigration of legal tender into banks which coincided with it.

If payments are made out of a "borrowed" balance, the payee acquires what for him is an "owned" deposit, although for our purpose it is preferable to say that the "borrowed" balance has been simply transferred without losing that character. We may do so because, in any case, the increase in the balance of the payee is compensated by the decrease in the balance of the borrower. Where we distinguish between time and demand deposits, transfer from demand to time account, or vice versa, causes uncompensated variation in both, but there is still compensation within the sum total of all deposits. If an original deposit of "old" legal tender be made, there is compensation within the total amount of means of payment. No new "spending power" emerges. Nor does any "spending power" vanish if a customer cashes a check. But there may be compensation in still another sense. In the case which is the ideal one from the standpoint of the commercial theory of banking, balances are, say, by discounting commercial bills, created against commodities—raw materials, for instance—which have just come into existence and are about to start on their career through the system. Those balances are uncompensated ones in any of the above meanings of the term. But they may be said to be compensated in the sense that the effect on prices of the increase in the stream of money is compensated by a simultaneous increase in the stream of goods, as it also may be whenever there are underemployed resources. This proposition is not above criticism on various counts. But it still expresses a rough common-sense truth and may serve to characterize the difference between the classic case of credit creation and the cases of credit creation for the financing of innovation on the one hand, and credit creation for the financing of consumption on the other. The balances created in the latter cases are not compensated in any sense. But their effects will be more than compensated in the case if innovation when the new products are released. Their effects will never be compensated—and can be eliminated only by a distinct and painful operation—in the case of government inflation.

For the purpose of describing prewar patterns it will be convenient to reason in general on a very special case, namely, the case of perfect gold monometallism, and to treat all other cases—gold-exchange standard, bimetallism, government paper money, and so on—as deviations from it. But it should be clearly understood that this is done for convenience only, and not because any logical priority is attributed to that case: we do not, of course, mean to hold that it is essential for legal-tender money to consist of, or to be covered by, gold. On this understanding we will, in general, assume that there is, in the domain under consideration, actual circulation of gold coins and of bank notes of the central as well as of some other banks, that those coins may be lawfully melted or exported, that gold is coined for any private party without charge or loss of interest, that member banks must on demand redeem their deposits (or notes) in gold or notes of the bankers' bank, which acts as clearing house for them and must redeem its notes in gold.

The obligation to redeem balances or notes in legal tender or, in fact, in anything which exists independently of the action of banks, obviously restricts their power to create them. In the system now envisaged, in which redemption must be effected in a money that at the same time serves in the role of small cash for the current transactions of business and private life, it means for each individual bank, on the one hand, the necessity of holding a stock of till money with which to meet the ordinary and extraordinary cash requirements of customers, and on the other hand, the necessity of keeping adverse clearing-house balances within the limits set by the practice of the bankers' bank. For the banking system as a whole the limit may be defined by the necessity of keeping the unit of account at par with the unit of legal tender, *i.e.*, in our case, a certain quantity of gold. We need not go into the various attempts which have been made to figure out, for a given system, the numerical value of that limit; but the following remarks suggest themselves.

First, redeemability is a restriction on credit creation that is not implied in the other rules of "classical banking" and will, in general, exclude transactions which, but for consideration of redeemability, would be sanctioned by even the most conservative principles. It is the safety brake which gold monometallism automatically inserts into the engine. If, in such a monetary system, law or usage imposes further restrictions, they cannot have any other meaning except to strengthen that brake and to make sure that it functions. Those attempts to evaluate the limit of credit creation are usually concerned with the effects of such legal restrictions only and hardly ever posit the fundamental problem.

Second, it would be difficult to indicate, in the absence of further legal or customary rules, the numerical value of that limit. This value depends, for the individual member bank, on the kind of customers it has and on the kind of business these customers do, on the amount of internal compensation which is effected on its books—with the giant concerns of England and Germany, a very considerable part of the sum total of checks is drawn by customers in payment to other customers of the same bank—on how great a risk it is willing to run, how far it is willing to lean on the bankers' bank, and on the attitude of the latter.

Third, the limit is, particularly over time, extremely elastic. A bank does not expand its credits singlehanded. It does so when others do the same. Hence, adverse clearing-house balances are not so likely to arise as they would be if the other banks stayed behind. Customers can be educated and to a certain extent educate themselves to use less and less actual cash in their transactions. The nonbanking sphere of circulation may be conquered. Technique may lend its aid: whenever arrangements about overdrafts take the place of crediting customers' accounts with the whole amount of loans, only the amounts actually drawn will contribute to the sum total of deposits. In Germany acceptance credit, which does not directly swell demand liabilities, was very popular also for purposes other than financing international trade. The shifting of cash between banks can be regulated so as to make it support a heavier superstructure of deposits. Thus there are many devices by which reserve requirements might be almost indefinitely reduced, some of which are operative even in the case of statutory restrictions. Finally, law and usage are themselves but modes of expression—though possibly very faulty ones—of the factors which determine our limit, and change in response to change in those factors *cf.*, the successive increases of the legal maximum amount of the notes of the Banque de France. If they do not so change, they are evaded; witness the development of the American trust companies alongside of the banks which were subject to stricter regulations.

Nothing, therefore, is so likely to give a wrong impression of the operation of credit as taking a mechanistic and static view of it and neglecting the fact that our process, by virtue of its own working, widens the limits which, *ex visu* of a given point of time, seem to be rigid fetters. If that fact be called inflation, then inflation has been going on practically all the time, nowhere more than in this country, while deflationary influence originating in the monetary system—shortage of gold and the like—is a myth. This may, according to one's standpoint, be virtue or vice. It may also be good in principle and work out badly in practice, or vice versa. It may be a reason for or a reason against monetary management or, in general, planned economy. But it is a fact which we must never lose sight of, if we are to understand capitalist evolution. How it has actually worked out we shall see in our historical discussion.

To the question how great a quantity of commodities and services will be withdrawn (Real Levy) from its previous uses by a given quantity of newly created credit, there is also no general answer. We must know the whole business situation on which the creation impinges, in order to frame an expectation as to how it will act, in this respect as in others; and that business situation will not only determine the effects of any given amount of balances created but also that amount itself. Even the amount of credit creation in terms of money is exceedingly difficult to measure, still more the net amount, *i.e.*, the sum which member banks' credit creation adds to the sum which business would use in the absence of such creation. The difficulty arises not only from the interference of credit creation with saving and the fact that created balances are used for other purposes besides productive ventures, but also from the facts that what credit business actually uses, or would use, is different from the amount of facilities put at its disposal, and that in the absence of credit creation not only price levels but also sectional relations of prices would be different from what they are.

E. Interest[1] **(Money Market; Capital).**—From what has been said about entrepreneurs' profits on the one hand, and the role of money and credit on the other, we derive certain propositions on interest as an element of the economic process which we are

[1] The theory of interest presented in this section has also, like the theory of credit, been first published, in the writer's Theory of Economic Development in 1911. The many adverse criticisms it met have failed to convince him. But since he naturally wishes to minimize avoidable differences of opinion, he has endeavored throughout to formulate the propositions in this book in such a way as to make them, wherever possible, acceptable also to those who differ from him in their views as to their nature of interest. This also applies to this section, most of the propositions of which could be couched in terms of any theory of interest.

trying to describe, or of the model which we are trying to construct. Whichever of the many explanations of the phenomenon of interest we may hold, all of us will agree to the following definition, although some of us may think it very superficial: Interest is a premium on present over future means of payment, or, as we will say *a potiori*, balances. Interest is the price paid by borrowers for a social permit to acquire commodities and services without having previously fulfilled the condition which in the institutional pattern of capitalism is normally set on the issue of such a social permit, *i.e.*, without having previously contributed other commodities and services to the social stream.

For a positive premium to emerge, it is necessary that at least some people should estimate a present dollar more highly than a future dollar. This may result from many circumstances. A man may expect, for example, while being a student, to have a larger income in the future than he has now, a government may similarly count on an increase in its revenue, or it may find itself in an emergency—as may any private individual too, of course—or all of us may systematically underestimate future wants as compared with present wants of the same rank. Business will pay a positive interest if a present sum can be so used in commerce and industry as to yield a greater sum in future, zero interest if the most lucrative operation within the horizon of businessmen is expected to yield, all costs counted, no more than the sum required to carry it out, and negative interest if, as is sometimes the case, nothing they can do will cover costs. Surely there is nothing paradoxical in that.

We may go one step further without touching controversial ground. Borrowing by consumers, particularly governments, is of itself sufficient to enforce a positive rate of interset also for industry and trade, and the writer has no wish to exclude such cases or to minimize the quantitative importance of consumers' credit. But in the sphere of business, innovation is the pillar of interest, both because the profit it yields to the successful entrepreneur is the typical reason for a readiness to pay interest—for looking upon present dollars as a means of getting more dollars in the future—and because, as we have seen, borrowing is, in the situation of an entrepreneur, the typical means of getting those present dollars. The relation of this to credit creation follows from our previous argument.

All the more controversial is the proposition that entrepreneurs' profits and related gains which arise in the disequilibria caused by the impact of innovation are, *as far as the business process itself is concerned and apart from consumers' borrowing,* the only source of interest payments and the only "cause" of the fact that positive rates of interest rule in the markets of capitalist society. This means that in perfect equilibrium interest would be zero in the sense that it would not be a necessary element of the process of production and distribution, or that pure interest tends to vanish as the system approaches perfect equilibrium. Proof of this proposition is very laborious,[1] because it involves showing why all the theories which lead to a different result are logically unsatisfactory. Happily, it is not necessary to enter upon it, because we shall not have to use that proposition except in very few instances. All that the writer has to ask is that the reader assent to the modest statement of the preceding paragraph, while reserving his rights as to the nature of interest and retaining some kind of rate of interest in his picture of the state of perfect equilibrium. We may, then, confine ourselves to a few remarks and pass on. First, the thesis that the capitalist class lives on a return which, except for the financing of consumption, derives from innovation or processes directly induced by innovation, and would, hence, disappear ıf economic evolution ceased, is of some importance for what may be termed the economic sociology of capitalism. Second, although it is possible to deny that innovation is the only "cause" of interest within the realm of production and commerce, it is not possible to deny that this "cause" is sufficient to produce it in the absence of any other, or that a premium on present balances follows from our model of the evolutionary process in a way which is not open to any of those logical objections that have been raised against other theories of interest. Whoever dissents from the writer's view, would have still to admit that cause into his picture of reality, and to expect it to assert itself in the variations of the rate of interest.[2] Third, although government borrowing, changing premiums for risk bearing, currency troubles, extra-economic pressure, and varying organization of the markets for loans can-

[1] See Theory of Economic Development, Chap. V.

[1] Hence, the concession usually made to the writer's theory of interest, that entrepreneurs' "demand for capital" is normally the most important single factor in the behavior of interest, concedes much more than it is meant to concede.

not fail to distort the picture, facts are more favorable to that theory than theorists have been so far—so much so that there is, if we accept the ordinary rules of scientific procedure, no reason to use any other.

There is, however, one point which presupposes a controversial theorem and on which it is less easy to compromise in such a way as to make it possible for the reader to accept the main argument. Interest has been defined above in monetary terms, but now it is necessary to insist that interest actually is, not only on the surface but essentially, a monetary phenomenon and that we lose it if we try to pierce that surface. It is a payment for balances with which to acquire commodities and services, not for the commodities and services themselves that may be bought with those balances. It is to this fact alone that interest owes its character as a—potentially—permanent income, for profits in our sense are an essentially temporary phenomenon and do not stay permanently with any process of production and trade or any collection of producers' goods ("real capital") that may be embodied in a firm. But the lender may still secure a permanent income by shifting his money from opportunity to opportunity as each of them arises. Some of them are, no doubt, very much more durable than others and there are concerns within which innovation goes on for generations. Besides, this necessity of shifting does not apply to lenders who lend to consumers of indefinite span of life, such as governments or municipalities. But no business venture yields eternal surpluses, as any lender is bound to find out to his cost who too confidently acts upon a belief in any of those theories of which the abstinence theory is a typical example, or simply upon a naive conviction that interest is a price of some productive service in the same sense in which wages are a price of the services of labor.

The theory of interest thus hastily sketched does away with many spurious problems which, here as everywhere else, are the consequence of logical strains in an unsatisfactory analytic structure. It also allows of a much more natural interpretation than can be derived from others, of the relations interest obviously bears to other monetary magnitudes and of its peculiar sensitiveness to monetary policy; and it seems particularly appropriate in a study of industrial flutcuation if we look upon them as deviations from a state of equilibrium. Interest or, if the reader prefer, its deviation from what he believes would be its equilibrium value, then appears, because of its central position, as a kind of *coefficient of tension in the system,* which more nearly than any other single figure expresses the degree of disequilibrium present in the latter.

The premium on present, as against future, balances is settled by borrowers—mainly governments and firms—and lenders—mainly banks and their satellites—who together form what is known as the Money Market. There, every bank has a sector of its own (whence it follows that we have before us another case of imperfect competition), consisting of its stock of more or less permanent customers, while transactions that cut across these sectors make up the Open Market. Behind this and, as we have seen, at one remove from it, is the Central Market, consisting of the transactions between the bankers' banks and their banking customers, which but indirectly influence the money market proper, except for any operations that the former may undertake in the open market.

Now, interpretation of money-market events by means of that theory of interest unavoidably runs on lines which differ substantially from those of both older and more recent doctrine. The necessity of reconciling a nonmonetary theory with obvious facts of the sphere of money and credit is, in particular, responsible for the idea that there are two kinds if interest rates, a "natural" or "real" one which would also exist in a barter economy and which represents the essence of the phenomenon, a permanent net return from physical means of production, and a monetary one, which fundamentally is but the former's reflex in the monetary sphere. The two may, nevertheless, differ of course or be made to differ by monetary policy or by an expansion or contraction of bank credit, but this constitutes a disturbance from which a definite string of consequences, among them the business cycle itself, has been deduced. The roots of this idea reach very far into the past and are clearly discernible in the English monetary discussions of the fourth and fifth decades of the nineteenth century. Its role in the thought of our own time is due to the teaching of Knut Wicksell and to the work of a brilliant group of Swedish and Austrian economists. For us, however, there is no such thing as a real rate of interest, except in the same sense in which we speak of real wages: translating both the interest and the capital items of any loan transaction into real terms by means of the expected variation in an index of prices, we may derive an expected and, by performing the same operation *ex post*, an actual rate of interest in terms of "command over commodities." But nominal and real rates in this sense are only different measurements of the same thing or, if we prefer to speak of different things even in thise case, it is the monetary rate which represents the fundamental phenomenon, and the real rate which represents the derived phenomenon. Hence, the money market with all that happens in it acquires for us a much deeper significance than can be attributed to it from the standpoint just glanced at. It becomes the heart, although it never becomes the brain, of the capitalist organism.

It is not difficult to see, however, that most of the problems traditionally dealt with under the heading of interest will also present themselves to our approach, and that many relations between interest and other elements of the system will have to be formulated in a manner not so far removed from the usual one as might be expected. Of this we can convince ourselves at once. We have just denied the very existence of what has been called the natural rate of interest and do not intend to put another imaginary entity in its place. But it does not follow that all the relations must necessarily vanish from our analysis which have been asserted to hold between it and the monetary rate. For, as far as profits are the basic fact about interest and both its source and its "cause," they will, although no permanent returns [1] and although not behaving exactly as that natural rate is supposed to behave, play a similar role in our schema, and those relations between natural and monetary interest will in many, although not in all, respects be replaced by relations between profits and interest not *toto coelo* different from them. Nor should the fact

[1] Moreover, profits in our sense display no tendency toward equalization. This and the essentially temporary character of profits in our sense should be sufficient to make it quite clear that both our distinction between profit and interest and the relation between them is not identical with an old distinction between normal business profits and contractual interest. However much the writer welcomes anything that will link his teaching to older doctrine, he must point out, first, that normal profits and interest are, according to this view, still the same thing—exactly as contractual and directly earned rent of natural agents is—which he thinks erroneous, and, second, that the analytic problem which he undertook to solve by his theory of interest was precisely to show how it is possible that a theoretically permanent income flows from essentially transient sources and that it should not disappear as a net return through a process of imputation.

that interest is here defined as a monetary phenomenon and hence must have something to do with the "quantity of the circulating medium" raise exaggerated hopes or fears to the effect that the writer is going to launch out into strikingly unorthodox conclusions. For about the immediate effects of a change in the amounts of customers' balances, there cannot be much difference of opinion in any case; and anything beyond immediate effects must unavoidably bear a relation to what the balances lent or borrowed mean in terms of all or of certain classes of commodities, hence to the values, and the expected and actual changes in the values, of the general and of sectional price levels. This necessity is not less obvious in the case of zero changes—which are likely to occur in the presence of underutilized resources—as in any others. Or, to put it differently, it is never the amount of actual and potential "funds" in the market which is relevant to the rate of interest but the proportion—which is a variable, of course—of these funds to the total of balances actually in circulation. As soon as this is realized, the gulf narrows that separates our approach from others which are more familiar.

Finally, while the theory presented in this section excludes facts which are basic to others from the explanation of the nature of interest, it is not intended to exclude them—as far as they are facts—from all arguments about interest. Abstinence affords an instance. The fact that saving does—or at least may—imply a sacrifice is held to be no more sufficient or necessary to account for the existence of interest than disutility of labor is to account for the existence of wages. The writer also thinks that neither abstinence nor disutility contributes very much to our understanding of the behavior of interest or wages. But it is not held either that abstinence or disutility are nonexistent or that they are irrelevant to interest or wages. Whenever any part of funds available for lending are provided by saving, that part and its variations must in the long run bear some—though not a simple—relation to the abstinence involved; and this relation, whatever it is, can of course be expressed by a marginal condition. Another instance is consumers' time preference. Whatever its causes and whether it is a datum, it will always contribute to the determination of the rate of interest: if the latter is not to display a tendency to change, it must in strict theory equal any marginal rate of such time preference as may exist.

To this monetary theory of interest corresponds a monetary

theory of capital, which views it, on the one hand, as an accounting concept—as measuring in terms of money the resources entrusted to a firm [1]—and, on the other hand, as a monetary quantity. It is best to avoid altogether a term which has been the source of so much confusion and to replace it by what it means in every case—equipment or intermediate goods and so on—and this we shall do, except in cases in which no misunderstanding is likely to arise. But those two monetary concepts open a serviceable door by which to introduce the element of money into general theory. Only the second is, however, relevant here. Capital in this sense is not goods but balances, not a factor of production but a distinct agent which stands between the entrepreneur and the factors. It can be created by banks because balances can. Its increase and decrease are not the same as increase and decrease of commodities or any particular class of commodities. Its market is simply the money market, and there is no other capital market. No realistic meaning attaches to the statement that, in the latter, "capital" (= some kind or other of producers' goods) is being "lent in the form of money." But again as in the case of interest the introduction into our analysis of this concept of capital does not do away with the problems of what is traditionally referred to as real capital—on the contrary, they reappear though in a new garb—and results arrived at by means of a monetary theory of capital not always invalidate, but in many cases only reformulate, the proposition of "real" theories of capital. If our understanding of the processes of capitalist society hinges on realizing the fact that monetary capital is a distinct agent, it also hinges on realizing how it is related to the world of commodities.

[1] Capital in this sense includes all debts, whether owed to a bank or to other firms or to bondholders. This is in accordance with the principles of accounting, according to which capital in the usual sense figures along with all debts on the liability side of the balance sheet.

Chapter IV

THE CONTOURS OF ECONOMIC EVOLUTION

A. The Working of the Model; First Approximation.—It will be useful to assemble the analytic tools so far described and to display the resulting skeleton—a sort of chassis of our model. Experience teaches that there is danger in doing this, and another appeal to the reader is in order, to reserve judgment and to grant provisionally all simplifications, in particular, the assumption of perfect competition (with the possible exception of isolated monopoly positions) and of a state of perfect equilibrium from which to start. There is no saving, population is constant, and everything else is as we assume it to be in a state that conforms to the idea of the Theoretical Norm. We know that, in the institutional pattern of capitalist society, there will always be possibilities of New Combinations (in the absence of all others, there would be those due to the steady increase of knowledge), and always some people able and willing to carry them out; and we know the reasons why this is so. To repeat again a point which has often been misunderstood, these people are by no means looked upon as particularly rare birds. All we postulate is that that ability is distributed as unequally as others are and all we hold is that this fact has an important influence on the mechanism of economic change—a statement which is no bolder and, if anything, more realistic than any of the set of assumptions familiar to every theorist. Motivation is supplied by the prospect of profit in our sense *which does not, be it remembered, presuppose either an actual or an expected rise in prices and expenditure.* What follows implies, besides institutional and technological assumptions that are essential, others of merely expository significance. In order to make the principle stand out clearly, we wish in particular to assume, in the first instance, absence of certain elements which in reality are very important—notably, errors in diagnosis or prognosis and other mistakes.

Some people, then, conceive and work out with varying promptness plans for innovations associated with varying anticipations of profits, and set about struggling with the obstacles incident to doing a new and unfamiliar thing—obstacles which have been discussed in the preceding chapter. We look upon ability to take the lead as a part of the entrepreneurial aptitude, and this enables us, for our present purpose, to identify one man (as we could identify the tallest individual in a population) who is the first, for example, to decide on the production of a new consumers' good. The reason why he did not do so before is in disturbances which we assume to have preceded the equilibrium from which we start. Conforming to previous considerations, we suppose that he founds a new firm, constructs a new plant, and orders new equipment from existing firms. The requisite funds he borrows from a bank. On the balance acquired by so doing he draws, either in order to hand the checks to other people who furnish him with goods and services, or in order to get currency with which to pay for these supplies. Under our assumptions he withdraws, by his bids for producers' goods, the quantities of them he needs from the uses which they served before.

Then other entrepreneurs follow, after them still others in increasing number, in the path of innovation, which becomes progressively smoothed for successors by accumulating experience and vanishing obstacles. We know the reasons why this is likely to happen in the same field or in related fields: although in some respects a successful innovation will make other innovations easier to carry out in any field, it primarily faciiltates them in the lines in which it may be directly copied as a whole or in part or for which it opens up new opportunities. Consequences begin to make themselves felt all over the system in perfectly logical concatenation. They are almost too obvious to describe. First, our entrepreneurs may, under the circumstances envisaged, be relied on to spend their deposits promptly, excepting a minimum reserve. If we multiply the amount of created balances by the velocity figure that obtained in the previous equilibrium, in the truest quantity-theory style, we shall get a fair approximation to the total by which the volume of payments will be increased by this kind of expenditure alone, since nobody of all those who receive payments from entrepreneurs, has any debts to repay or any motive to increase his cash reserve beyond its previous proportion to his transactions, and since we are considering a closed domain.[1]

Second, there being no unemployed resources to start with, prices of factors of production will rise, and so will money incomes and the rate of interest (or, as the writer thinks it would be more correct to say, a positive rate of interest will emerge). Costs will rise against "old" firms as well as against entrepreneurs. But third, their receipts will also rise correspondingly to the expenditures of entrepreneurs on producers' goods, of the workmen and so on, now employed by them at higher wages, and of the recipients of all those increased payments. How individual firms or industries or sectors of the industrial organism will fare in this process depends on the shifts in demand that will occur in consequence. There will be both gains and losses. In spite of the losses in some industries, which must be expected to be a feature of the situation, all old firms taken together will, of course, show a net surplus. Of this we can satisfy ourselves if, disregarding everything except the first two steps—*i.e.*, disbursements by entrepreneurs and again the next disbursement by income receivers—we assume that labor is the only factor, wages are the only cost. Then old firms will have to pay but a part of the increase in the sum total of the incomes that has occurred, *i.e.*, the increase in the income of those workmen whom they still retain while they will, at the second turn of the wheel and before the new products reach their markets, receive the whole of it. However unrealistic, this case brings out the principle free from all complications and independent of any reactions of marginal cost in physical terms. In any case, this is

[1] Later we shall see reason for assuming that the effect will be greater than stated above, but now we do not wish to complicate matters.

the process by which the effects of the entrepreneurial activity spread over the whole system, dislocating values, disrupting the equilibrium that existed before. The term Windfall correctly expresses the character of both these gains and losses.

Fourth, under our assumptions there could, in general, be no net increase in total output. Owing to the difficulties inherent in the latter concept, this proposition may justifiably be questioned. What we mean is simply that it is impossible for all industries to increase their output under the circumstances assumed. All those who make gains will, indeed, try to do so; but if we remember, on the one hand, that in the preceding perfect equilibrium of perfect competition they all produced their optimum output, utilizing in particular their plants up to the point at which total unit cost was a minimum, and, on the other hand, that quantities of factors of production previously used by them have been withdrawn, we shall conclude that if there were only one single consumers' good, less of it would be produced now than had been produced in the preceding state of equilibrium. Instead, more producers' goods will be produced. These, together with part of the others which used to be produced for the old firms, will be taken by our entrepreneurs. If there are many consumers' goods, and if the production of some of them increases, then the production of others must decrease in such a way as to set free more productive resources than are engaged in bringing about the expansion in the former. If we include in total output the intermediate results of the current work of building up the new plants, then total output would, in the sense alluded to, be constant. If we do not include them, it would be smaller. The output of consumers' goods will fall in any case unless there is no period of gestation at all. It should be observed, however, that demand in terms of money for consumers' goods has not decreased. On the contrary, it has increased.

This is all that happens, under our present assumptions, until the first entrepreneur's plant gets into working order. Then the scene begins to change. The new comomdities—let us say, new consumers' goods—flow into the market. They are, since everything turns out according to expectation, readily taken up at exactly those prices at which the entrepreneur expected to sell them. We will also assume that from that moment onward the new firm will go on pouring out an unchanging stream of consumers' goods without any further change in its production function. A stream of receipts will hence flow into the entrepreneur's account, at a rate sufficient to repay, during the lifetime of the plant and equipment originally acquired, the total debt incurred plus interest, and to leave a profit for the entrepreneur. Let us imagine a strong case and assume what, of course, happens only in very exceptional instances, that at the end of a period not longer than the time that elapsed between the entrepreneur's first act of borrowing and the completion of his plant, things have so worked out that, the entrepreneur having currently made all necessary replacements out of receipts and having discharged all his debts to the bank, thereby annihilating all the balances newly created in his favor, is left with plant and equipment perfectly unencumbered and in perfect working order, and also with a surplus balance sufficient to serve him as "working capital." If the same applies in the case of the other entrepreneurs that followed in the wake of the first and are just now, for argument's sake, assumed to have been similar prodigies of foresight, then the following situation arises: the new firms, getting successively into working order and throwing their products into the market of consumers' goods, increase the total output of consumers' goods which had been previously reduced. In a certain sense it may be held that under our assumptions output will eventually be increased by "more" than it had fallen during the period of gestation. That is to say, if we compare the elements which constitute total output of consumers' goods at the point of time when the new firms have all begun to produce, with total output as it was in the preceding neighborhood of equilibrium, and if we cancel all items which appear in both composites, we are left with a list of plus and minus items such that, evaluated at the prices that ruled in that neighborhood, the sum of the former would necessarily be greater than the sum of the latter. If there were only one consumers' good, and if the innovation had consisted in the introduction of a novel method of producing it, the physical quantity per unit of time of the new total output would be greater than that of the old one.

These new commodities intrude into the economic world that existed before at a rate which will, for reasons given in the preceding chapter, be too great for smooth absorption. They intrude, nevertheless, gradually: the first entrepreneur's supply will not, in general, cause visible disturbance or be sufficient to alter the complexion of the business situation as a whole, although those firms may be immediately affected with the products of which the new commodities or the commodities produced by new methods are directly competitive. But, as the process gathers momentum, these effects steadily gain in importance, and disequilibrium, enforcing a process of adaptation, begins to show.

The nature of the effects on the "old" firms is easy to understand. It superimposes itself on the disequilibrium caused by the setting up of the new plant and equipment and the expenditure incident thereto. But while the effects of this were, even in those cases in which they spelled net losses, softened by the flow of that expenditure, the new disequilibrium enforces much more obviously difficult adapatations. They proceed not exclusively under the stimulus of loss. For some of the "old" firms new opportunities for expansion open up: the new methods or commodities create New Economic Space. But for others the emergence of the new methods means economic death; for still others, contraction and drifting into the background. Finally, there are firms and industries which are forced to undergo a dfficult and painful process of modernization, rationalization and reconstruction. It should be observed that these vital parts of the mechanism of economic evolution, which are readily seen to dominate many business situations and to produce results of fundamental importance, can never be revealed statistically by measuring variation in an index of production, or analyzed theoretically in terms of total output. Such an index would not produce those effects. It is disharmonious or one-sided increase and shifts *within* the aggregative quantity which matter. Aggregative analysis, here, as elsewhere, not only does not tell the whole tale but necessarily obliterates the main point of the tale.

As long, however, as new entreprises continue to emerge and to pour their stream of expenditure into the system, all those effects may be overcompensated. The "turn" *need* not come, *i.e.*, the situation described before *need* not give way to the situation we are trying to characterize now, until entrepreneurial activity slackens and eventually stops. Hence, it is essential to visualize clearly the reasons why entrepreneurial activity in fact slackens and stops at a point which can be theoretically determined. In actual life so many accidents and incidents combine to produce this result that we are never lacking plausible reasons with which to explain that stoppage in any given case. But this obscures the question of principle with which we are now concerned—whether the mechanism described would in the absence of such incidents and accidents run on forever (on a "prosperity plateau") or come to a stop from reasons inherent in it and by virtue of its own effects and of the business situations it creates.

First, since entrepreneurial activity characteristically starts off in a definite direction and does not distribute itself equally all over the industrial field—since it aims typically at production of a given commodity or a group of commodities—its possibilities are, in every instance and in any given state of the economic body, definitely limited. The results of innovation act directly on certain individual prices, and therefore set definite limits on further advance in that direction or related directions. Anxious as we are too just now to work out only the pure logic of our subject, and to avoid anything of a consequential or incidental character, however important it may be in practice, we will even retain, for the moment, the heroic assumption that not only the full increase in the new product, which will be brought about by more and more firms taking up production, and the incident fall in its price have been perfectly correctly foreseen by the first in the field, but also that those who came later also foresaw correctly what possibilities were left to them. It is easy to see that a point will be reached at which our new commodity will be produced at minimum unit cost equal to the price at which it will sell. Profits will be eliminated, the impulse of innovation will, for the time being, have spent itself.

But second, since entrepreneurial activity upsets the equilibrium of the system and since the release of the new products brings disequilibration to a head, a revision of values of all the elements of the system becomes necessary and this, for a period of time, means fluctuations and successive attempts at adaptation to changing temporary situations. This, in turn, means the impossibility of calculating costs and receipts in a satisfactory way, even if necessary margins are not altogether absent while that goes on. Hence, the difficulty of planning new things and the risk of failure are greatly increased. In order to carry out additional innovations, it is necessary to wait until things settle down as it was in the beginning to wait for an equilibrium to be established before embarking upon the innovations the effects of which we are now discussing.[1] Therefore, along with new

[1] Although we are now concentrating on the task of carpentering our logical schema, it may be well to point to the "factual" justification of

products streaming into markets, and with repayments increasing in quantitative importance, entrepreneurial activity tends to slacken, until finally it ceases entirely.

Two things call for notice. First, the outstanding conductor that spreads effects all over the system is entrepreneurs' expenditure, and this expenditure is now being reduced. This proposition is not quite symmetrical to the analogous one in the case of the situation characteristic of the period of gestation since there, the element of "crowding out the old" being absent, all effects reached the system through that one channel. But while mere stoppage of additional borrowing (remember that so far nobody borrows but entrepreneurs) would be sufficient under the circumstances to bring discomfiture to many firms and, in particular, to depress the price level,[2] yet this is not all that happens. Repayment of bank loans by entrepreneurs, annihilating balances, comes in to accentuate effects. This process we shall designate by the term Autodeflation. It occurs without any initiative on the part of banks and would occur even if nobody ever went bankrupt or restricted operations, and if no bank ever called or refused a loan. We are not concerned with the questions whether a different and less passive reaction of the monetary mechanism would either intensify or soften the phenomena under consideration, and what monetary policy "should" be followed under the

---

this. The English boom at the end of the seventeenth century did not start before 1688, the spurt in economic activity in the United States at the end of the sixties of the nineteenth century, not before the end of the Civil War. Such examples could, of course, be readily multiplied. But if the reader admit that this is not more than self-evident in the case of external disturbance, it follows that it will equally hold true for disturbance of relative values through any other—*i.e.*, internal—cause. Professor Machlup, in an address to the writer's class on business cycles, seems to have expressed the matter felicitously (though from a somewhat different standpoint) by saying that entrepreneurial risk of failure is at a minimum in equilibrium and slowly rises as prosperity develops. Entrepreneurial activity stops at a point at which that risk is a maximum. It will be seen that such an argument is not, as it at first sight seems, incompatible with our proposition that risk bearing is no part of the entrepreneurial function.

[2] No firm could however, under our present assumptions, be submerged merely by a fall in price level that would otherwise have survived. This is a truism considering we now assume absence of fixed debt-charges and of "stickiness" in any cost elements, yet worth remembering. It suffices to dispel some of the errors surrounding that subject.

circumstances. All we are interested in at the moment is that money and credit do react in a definite way, that their behavior is nothing but adaptation to an underlying economic process by which that behavior, as well as the behavior of *all* aggregative quantities, is explained, while the reverse is not true.

Second, the sum total of the phenomena we are surveying forms a connected whole which has a definite meaning and may be said to have a definite function. It constitutes the response by the system to the results of entrepreneurial activity—adaptation to the new things created, including the elimination of what is incapable of adaptation, resorption of the results of innovation into the system, reorganization of economic life so as to make it conform to the data as altered by enterprise, remodeling of the system of values, liquidation of indebtedness. Under our assumptions and with but minor qualifications, that sequence of phenomena leads up to a new neighborhood of equilibrium, in which enterprise will start again. This new neighborhood of equilibrium is characterized, as compared to the one that preceded it, by a "greater" social product of a different pattern, new production functions, equal sum total of money incomes, a minimum (strictly zero) rate of interest, zero profits, zero loans, a different system of prices and a lower level of prices, the fundamental expression of the fact that all the lasting achievements of the particular spurt of innovation have been handed to consumers in the shape of increased real incomes. Thus, as soon as the entrepreneurial impulse ceases to act which propelled it away from its previous neighborhood, the system embarks upon a struggle toward a new one, under the influence of forces which should now be perfectly clear and which are, barring occurrence of external disturbances, to land it there eventually. The process takes time and may display oscillations and relapses. But it is at the bottom of all those apparently irregular movements during which losses seem to be strewn at random over the whole of economic life, and under present assumptions cannot cease until, through however many rearrangements that are disavowed by the next day, it has accomplished the task.

It is a long way from this schema to historical fact. Innumerable layers of secondary, incidental, accidental, and "external" fact and reactions among all of them and reactions to reactions cover that skeleton of economic life, sometimes so as to hide it entirely. But the writer must have been sadly lacking in expository skill if the reader does not recognize the common sense and the realistic counterpart of this theoretical world, every element of which links up with a fact of everyday experience. We shall refer to this construction as the Pure Model or the First Approximation.

B. Looking at the Skeleton.—When we look at the skeleton, we behold the picture of a distinct process in time which displays functional relations between its constituent parts and is logically self-contained.[1] This process of economic change or evolution, moreover, goes on in units separated from each other by neighborhoods of equilibrium. Each of those units, in turn, consists of two distinct phases, during the first of which the system, under the impulse of enterpreneurial activity, draws away from an equilibrium position, and during the second of which it draws toward another equilibrium position.

Each of those two phases is characterized by a definite succession of phenomena. The reader need only recall what they are in order to make the discovery that they are precisely the phenomenon which he associates with "prosperity" and "recession": our model reproduces, by its mere working, that very sequence of events which *we observe in the course of those fluctuations in economic life which have come to be called business cycles* and which, translated into the language of diagrams, present the picture of an undulating or wavelike movement in absolute figures or rates of change. It is worth while to pause in order to comment on this fact.

First, it is by no means farfetched or paradoxical to say that "progress" unstabilizes the economic world, or that it is by virtue of its mechanism *a cyclical process*. A theory of economic fluctuations running in terms of external factors plus innovations might be considered self-evident and only another way of stating that there would be no cycles in an undisturbed stationary, or growing, flow. The reader should keep this in mind in the midst of the complications which must inevitably follow and in the face

[1] It is, in logic and discarding the influence of external factors and of growth, as selfcontained as is the stationary circuit flow. Time enters, indeed, in a different sense, but it is still theoretic time, *i.e.*, a time which serves as an axis for a logical (and not merely historical) sequence of events. The reader should, however, bear in mind what has been said in the preceding chapter about the possibility of profitless and of prosperityless cycles.

of the fact that theory as well as public opinion have steadfastly refused to take that common-sense view of the matter and persisted in tacitly assuming that "progress" is one thing (and naturally smooth) while fluctuations are another thing, differing from it, perhaps inimical to it. It is, after all, only common sense to realize that, but for the fact that economic life is in a process of incessant *internal* change, the business cycle, as we know it, would not exist. Hence, it is just as well to try to link so obviously important an element systematically to any explanation of the capitalist economy in general and of business cycles in particular. Our proof that the few fundamental facts so far included in our model suffice to produce a "wave" pervading economic life, must in any case be of diagnostic value and shed some light on such fluctuations as we observe.

Second, the fact that innovation would suffice to produce alternating prosperities and depression does not establish, of course, that these cycles are actually the ones which we historically designate as business cycles. Even if we make the reservation as to external factors, there may be other "causes." Our proposition that innovation—again, when seen in its true extent and not confined to some part or form of what we mean by it—is actually the dominant element which accounts for those historical and statistical phenomena, is so far only a working hypothesis, which will be on trial throughout this book. Moreover, our hypothesis is not yet in a shape to serve at all and it remains to be seen how much matter unconnected with its present content will have to be added to it.

But, third, starting out from an impression, drawn from economic history, that it will in fact work well, we are encouraged not only by the rough agreement of the symptoms which our model produces with the symptoms which we actually observe in the course of business cycles, but also by the ease with which certain elements, so far banished from our picture, fit into it and can be given their due without condemning us to any eclecticism. They seem, indeed, to acquire their true place and significance only with reference to it. A few examples will show this.

Most students of the business cycle have been impressed by the logic with which one cyclical situation produces the next. This was really the discovery which ushered in the scientific studies of the cyclical mechanism and has more recently been stressed by Professor Wesley Mitchell. But if we stop there, our situation is obviously unsatisfactory, for the process then lacks the motive power and looks very much a *perpetuum mobile*. That difficult vanishes and, in particular, the crucial question of what causes the turn from prosperity into recession finds a very natural answer if we accept our schema. We acquire the right to look upon recession as the reaction to prosperity in the way first clearly recognized by Juglar, without having in turn to explain prosperity by preceding recession.[1]

Again, most people will link up recessions with errors of judgment, excesses, and misconduct. This is no explanation at all; for it is not error, etc., as such but only a cluster of errors which could possibly account for widespread depressive effects. Any "theory" that rests content with this must assume that people err periodically in the way most convenient to the economist. Our model, by showing the emergence of situations in which it is understandable that mistakes of all sorts should be more frequent than usual (*i.e.*, when untried things are being put into practice and adaptation to a state of things becomes necessary, the contours of which have not yet appeared) does away with this and shows the place of the element of error in the various phases of the process, without having to introduce it as an independent, still less as a necessary, element.

Another such *deus ex machina*, closely related to error, is "anticipation." It has been pointed out in the second chapter that the introduction of this element constitutes a material improvement of our technique, but also that expectations cannot be used as part of our ultimate data in the same way as taste for tobacco can. Unless we know why people expect what they expect, any argument is completely valueless which appeals to them as *causae efficientes*. Such appeals enter into the class of pseudo-explanations. But if we understand independently how

[1] With Juglar's formula that prosperity is the *cause unique* of depression practically all "theories" agree. But the self-generating theories also claim that the causation of prosperity lies in the conditions of easy money, low stocks, cheap labor and raw materials found in depression periods, and that prosperity is merely an outgrowth of these. This line of reasoning may perhaps serve (although there is some doubt about that) in order to account for revival up to normal, but obviously cannot serve beyond that. So far, we have not dealt with any "depression" that leads below normal, and prosperity is therefore seen to be explainable without it. The subject will be taken up later on.

the situations come about in which, for example, windfall gains, rising prices, and so on produce waves of optimism, we are free to use the fact that this optimism will feed upon itself and crystallize so as to become an element of the mechanism of cyclical events and the "cause" of secondary phenomena. But there still remains the question of fact, how important, even within their rightful domain, businessmen's optimisms and pessimisms actually are. There is some danger in generalizing from familiar facts about stock exchange or land speculation—observation of which, however, also clearly teaches that its moods are not independent causes but consequential phenomena. Industry and trade are much less given to being swayed by moods. Moreover, the writer confesses that he sometimes wonders in what world those theorists live who do not doubt for a moment the efficacy of "depressed states of mind"—to be mended, as an eminent author seems to think, by "ballyhoo"—in accentuating (let alone independently causing) depressions. His experience is to the effect that the average businessman always hopes against hope, always thinks he sees recovery "around the corner," always tries to prepare for it, and that he is forced back each time by hard objective fact which as long as possible he doggedly tries to ignore. The history of the recent world crisis could almost be written in terms of ineffectual attempts to stem the tide, undertaken in a belief, fostered in this case by all the prophets, that business would be "humming" in a few months. This does not mean that businessmen are always optimistic. Far from it. What it does mean is that waves of both optimism and pessimism are not the obvious realities they seem to be to observers who judge from manias.

Other examples of how much-emphasized facts fit into our schema abound. We have, for instance, nothing to offer in defense of the so-called overproduction and underconsumption theories. But it is readily seen how our process may produce situations which, to the untrained mind, lend color to those primitive attempts at explanation. As regards the facts that underlie the various theories which attribute business cycles to overinvestment in durable producers' goods or to investment in wrong directions (malinvestment), it is easily seen, first, that variations in real investment are, as a matter of fact, intimately connected with the causation and the mechanism of cycles; second, that in the course of our process cases of both overinvestment and malinvestment will understandably occur; and, third, that in other cases an appearance of overinvestment will be created.

The analytic schema presented in this book evidently does not belong to the family of monetary theories of business cycles. It does presuppose a certain behavior of money and credit, many features of which are essential for it; but if this were enough to constitute a monetary theory of cycles, there would be no non-monetary ones, since every theory does this either explicitly or implicitly. If we wish to make that designation distinctive, we must follow Mr. Hawtrey and define a monetary theory by the criterion that it looks upon cycles as "purely monetary phenomena" in the sense that peculiarities of the sphere of money and credit account for their existence and that but for those peculiarities they would not exist at all. The writer believes those theories to be wrong and, in their practical implications, misleading. But all the facts, and in particular all the relations of monetary time series to others, on which those theories draw, find their place and interpretation in our schema. It must be realized, however, that the fundamental logic of the cyclical process of evolution is entirely independent of all those accessories which, however important they may be, make after all poor cornerstones.

Fourth, there is a point at which the picture of the working of our model presents features that seem to differ from widely accepted, though not unanimous, opinion. It does not give to prosperity and recession, relatively to each other, the welfare connotations which public opinion attaches to them. Commonly, prosperity is associated with social well-being, and recession with a falling standard of life. In our picture they are not, and there is even an implication to the contrary. This is partly due to certain facts which have not been introduced as yet, and which to some extent justify popular opinion. But we do not wish that feature of our present picture to be lost. It contains an important truth. Prosperity in our sense is, in fact, very far from being synonymous with welfare—witness, for example, the "hungry forties." And times of prolonged "depression" are very far from being synonymous with misery—witness, for example, the progress in the standard of life of the working classes, 1873-1897. Our model supplies the explanation of this, and we shall repeatedly have to insist upon it.

The socialist form of organization has the virtue of bringing out the economic nature of things much more clearly than capitalism. In a socialist community it would, for instance, be evident to everyone that what a nation gains from international trade consists of the imports and that exports are what it sacrifices in order to secure them. Similarly, it would be obvious that times of innovation are times of effort and sacrifice, of work for the future, while the harvest comes after. This is so also in a capitalist society; and that the harvest is gathered under recessive symptoms and with more anxiety than rejoicing is easily accounted for and does not alter the principle. Recession, besides being a time of harvesting the results of preceding innovation, is also a time of harvesting its indirect effects. The new methods are being copied and improved; adaptation to them or to the impact of the new commodities consists in part in "induced inventions"; some industries expand into new investment opportunities created by the achievements of entrepreneurs; others respond by rationalization of their technological and commercial processes under pressure; much dead wood disappears. There is, thus, a good deal of truth in the popular saying that "there is more brain in business" at large during recession than there is during prosperity, an observation which is, at the same time, seen not to contradict any inference that may be drawn from our model.

Fifth, there is nothing in the working of our model to point to periodicity in the cyclical process of economic evolution if that term is taken to mean a constant period. And there is no rhythm or cycle if we choose to define either of them with reference to periodicity in that sense. But both rhythm and cycles are present in a much more relevant sense. For there is a process which systematically produces alternating phases of prosperity and depression through the working of a definite mechanism set into motion by a definite "force" or "cause." All we can thus far say about the duration of the units of that process and of each of their two phases is that it will depend on the nature of the particular innovations that carry a given cycle, the actual structure of the industrial organism that responds to them, and the financial conditions and habits prevailing in the business community in each case. But that is enough and it seems entirely unjustified to deny the existence of a phenomenon because it fails to conform to certain arbitrary standards of regularity.[1] We

[1] Professor Irving Fisher, for example, argues in his paper in the *Journal of the American Statistical Association*, 1923, that plus and

take the opportunity of recalling the self-explanatory concept of Internal Irregularity—to contrast with the concept of External Irregularities due to action of external factors.

Sixth, from the standpoint of aggregative theory, it is in the nature of a paradox to say that partial disequilibria—innovation and response to innovation create in the first instance nothing else—produce what obviously is a general disequilibrium in the system as a whole. But we realize now in what sense that is so, how it comes about, and how aggregative quantities are thereby changed. Perhaps it is only common sense to recognize that, in order to produce effects on aggregates, a factor or event need not of itself be an aggregate or directly act on an aggregate. Relations between aggregates being entirely inadequate to teach us anything about the nature of the processes which shape their variations, aggregative theories of the business cycle must be inadequate, too; and it is not a valid objection against an analysis of business cycles that it deals "only" with partial situations. This applies, of course, to many "theories" such as, for example, the harvest theory: the mere fact that it locates causes in one sector of the system only, should not be recorded aaginst it, whatever its other shortcomings may be.

Seventh, our model and its working is strongly institutional in character. It presupposes the presence, not only of the general features of capitalist society, but also of several others which we hold to be actually verified but which are not logically implied in the concepts either of economic action or of capitalism. Our argument rests on historical facts which may turn out to belong to an epoch that is rapidly passing. In this sense the analysis presented has, in fact, itself been called historical. There is no objection to this. Any application must in each case wait upon the proof that the conditions assumed actually did exist, or may reasonably be expected to have existed, at the time envisaged. We assume not only private property and private initiative but a definite type of both; not only money, banks, and banking credit but also a certain attitude, moral code, business tradition, and "usage" of the banking community; above all, a spirit of the industrial *bourgeoisie* and a schema of motivation which

---

minus deviations in time series do not reveal characteristic phases and do not recur. This is true only from the standpoint of such arbitrary standards.

within the world of giant concerns—the pattern which we have called Trustified Capitalism—and within modern attitudes of the public mind is rapidly losing both its scope and its meaning. This is why in our discussion of postwar events we shall put the question whether and how far the process still persists. But the writer is quite content to shed light, such as it is, on a piece of economic history and to leave it to the reader the decision whether or not he will consider it relevant to practical problems or not. The deep-reaching question whether it is the process of capitalistic evolution itself that creates the social situations in which it dies out will only peripherically be touched upon.

C. The Secondary Wave; Second Approximation.—If innovations are being embodied in new plant and equipment, additional consumers' spending will result practically as quickly as additional producers' spending. Both together will spread from the points in the system on which they first impinge, and create that complexion of business situations which we call prosperity. Two things are then practically sure to happen. First, old firms will react to this situation and, second, many of them will "speculate" on this situation. A new factory in a village, for example, means better business for local grocers, who will accordingly place bigger orders with wholesalers, who in turn will do the same with manufacturers, and these will expand production or try to do so, and so on. But in doing this many people will act on the assumption that the rates of change they observe will continue indefinitely, and enter into transactions which will result in losses as soon as facts fail to verify that assumption. Speculation in the narrowed sense of the word will take the hint and start on its familiar course or rather, anticipating all this, stage a boom even before prosperity in business has had time to develop. New borrowing will then no longer be confined to entrepreneurs, and "deposits" will be created to finance general expansion, each loan tending to induce another loan, each rise in prices another rise. Here those transactions enter into our picture which *presuppose* an actual or expected rise in prices in order to become possible.[1] Our analysis adds nothing to this well-

[1] While, as we have seen, no such rise is, on principle, necessary to call forth innovations and while they are, in the Pure Model, profitable without it, there may and generally will be some which show profit only if rising prices are anticipated. These belong here and not to the igniting mechanism.

known piece of mechanism except the ignition of it and the means of distinguishing it from the more fundamental process which sets it in motion. This is what we will call—retaining a perhaps questionable term introduced in the writer's book of 1911—the Secondary Wave, which superimposes its effects on those of the Primary Wave.

There is no need to emphasize how great a mass of fact now enters our picture. Indeed, the phenomena of this secondary wave may be and generally are quantitatively more important than those of the primary wave. Covering as they do a much wider surface, they are also much easier to observe; in fact they are what strikes the eye first, while it may be difficult, especially if the innovations are individually small, to find the torch responsible for the conflagration. This is one reason why the element of innovation has been so much neglected by the traditional analysis of the business cycle: it hides behind, and is sometimes entirely overlaid by, the phenomena of what appears at first glance to be simply a general prosperity, which is conspicuous in many branches and strata and apparently unconnected with any activity that could in any way be called innovating, let alone "inventing." It seems only natural to think that for this general prosperity some equally general—*e.g.*, monetary—explanation should be found and that both it and the reaction to it should be looked upon as meaningless and functionless disturbances of economic life and of the march of progress.

The cyclical clusters of errors, excesses of optimism and pessimism and the like are not necessarily inherent in the primary process—which process would produce ups and downs and, be it particularly remembered, also losses without any errors—although they can be adequately motivated by it. But now they acquire additional importance. Part of the phenomena of the secondary wave consists, in fact, of nothing else. Among the logically nonessential, but practically most important facts we now mean to inseert, one, mentioned above, may deserve a further remark. We will discuss it in terms of Professor Irving Fisher's Debt-Inflation Theory not of cycles—the existence of which he denies—but of Great Depressions. Of all the "starters" of debt "the most common appears to be *new opportunities to invest at a big prospective profit* [Professor Fisher's italics] as compared with ordinary profits and interest, such as through new inventions, new industries, development of new resources, opening of new lands or new markets" (*op. cit.*, p. 348). This is so. But if the borrowers are entrepreneurs and everything is as it was assumed to be in our Pure Model, no dire consequences need follow from this. As far as that goes, we have only to add a qualification about entrepreneurial miscalculations. Whenever loans are used in ways which will decrease costs per unit of product, the same may apply to the borrowing of nonentrepreneurs, even of old firms which borrow in order to carry out adaptations that prove sufficiently successful. Professor Fisher, therefore, rightly emphasizes *over*indebtedness induced, primarily, by easy money. But he does not define overindebtedness. Nor is it easy to do so. The only way which the writer can think of is precisely by reference to "productivity." And the processes of the secondary wave, in fact, supply us with plenty of instances of unproductive loans. Once a prosperity has got under sail, households will borrow for purposes of consumption, in the expectation that actual incomes will permanently be what they are or that they will still increase; business will borrow merely to expand on old lines, on the expectation that this demand will persist or still increase; farms will be bought at prices at which they could pay only if the prices of agricultural products kept their level or increased. In these cases there is no increase in productivity at all, and it is this fact and this fact alone which is responsible for a fall in prices sometimes spelling disaster, even without speculation in the narrower sense of the word, which however never fails to add to the structure of debt. "Evidently debt and deflation go far toward a great mass of phenomena in a very simple logical way" (p. 342).

The reader will see how easy it is to jump from this to misleading conclusions. The only conclusion that really follows is that the credit machine is so designed as to serve the improvement of the productive apparatus and to punish any other use. However, this turn of phrase must not be interpreted to mean that that design cannot be altered. Of course it can and also the existing machine can be made to work in any one of many different ways. Professor Fisher's suggestions about "reflation" by open-market operations do not now concern us. But it should be pointed out that distinction between debts according to purpose, however difficult to carry out, is always relevant to diagnosis and may be relevant to preventive policy.

The break in secondary prosperity is similarly induced by the turn of the underlying process. The latter supplies the only adequate explanation of the former, which in fact constitutes the great crux of those theories of the cycle that attempt to deal with it by itself.[1] Any prosperity, however ideally confined to essential or primary processes, induces a period of liquidation which, besides eliminating firms that have become obsolete beyond the possibility of adaptation, also involves a painful process of readjustment of prices, quantities, and values as the contours of the new equilibrium system emerge. But when we take account of the phenomena which constitute the secondary wave, we realize at once that there is much more to liquidate and to adjust. In the atmosphere of secondary prosperity there will also develop reckless, fraudulent, or otherwise unsuccessful enterprise, which cannot stand the tests administered by recession. The speculative position is likely to contain many untenable elements which the slightest impairment of the values of collateral will bring down. A considerable part of current and investment operations will show loss as soon as prices fall, as they will by virtue of the primary process. Part of the debt structure will crumble.

All this does not necessarily amount to panic or crisis—neither word is a technical term—but it easily induces panics or crises. If they occur, still another situation is created, than would otherwise prevail, and additional adjustments become necessary. But even if they do not, we readily see the two effects which define the Vicious Spiral. On the one hand, any fall in values which enforces liquidation, induces quite mechanically another fall in values. "Prices fall because they have fallen" (Marshall). Measures of defense, efforts made by firms or households to repay loans, or by banks to call them in order to improve liquidity, drive debtors in the well-known way toward the very rocks which those measures were taken to avoid. Freezing of credits, shrinkage of deposits, and all the rest follow in due course. On the other hand, not only we, the observers, but also the dramatis personae realize how much there is to liquidate, or even go into hysterics about it. Then pessimistic expectation may for a time

[1] That is the case with most theories. Hence the embarrassment voiced by the question: Why should there be a break at all—what is it that puts an end to prosperity? This is but the natural consequence of the fact that what we call the phenomena of the secondary wave is all their authors see.

acquire a causal role. But again it is necessary to warn against overrating its importance. The simplest appeal to experience should be sufficient to justify this warning. No great crisis has ever come about that was not fully explainable by the objective facts of the situation. Expectation not so conditioned never has produced more than short-lived spurts or breaks. And this is true not only for general business situations but for any particular market. No corner ever succeeded unless the course of events gave independent support. No amount of optimistic expectation could have kept up the price of copper in the twenties; no amount of pessimistic expectation could have kept it down if sources of supply as important as those which were added, had suddenly been exhausted.

Now that class of facts, whenever it is of sufficient quantitative significance, has an important bearing upon our schema. As long as we took no acocunt of it, we had only two phases—Prosperity and Recession—in every unit of the cyclical process, but now we shall understand that under pressure of the breakdown of the secondary wave and of the bearish anticipation which will be induced by it, our process will generally, although not necessarily, outrun (as a rule, also miss) the neighborhood of equilibrium toward which it was heading and enter upon a new phase, absent in our first approximation which will be characterized by Abnormal Liquidation, that is to say, by a downward revision of values and a shrinkage of operations that reduce them, often quite erratically, below their equilibrium amounts. While in recession a mechanism is at work to draw the system toward equilibrium, new disequilibrium develops now: the system again draws away from a neighborhood of equilibrium as it did during prosperity, but under the influence of a different impulse. For this phase we shall reserve the term Depression. But when depression has run its course, the system starts to feel its way back to a new neighborhood of equilibrium. This constitutes our fourth phase. We will call it Recovery or Revival. Expansion up to equilibrium amounts then sets in and yields temporary surplus gains or eliminates the losses incident to operation at the trough amounts. But even apart from imperfections, this new neighborhood will not be the same at that which would have been reached without abnormal liquidation. For, first, abnormal liquidation destroys many things which could and would have survived without it (in particular, it often liquidates and weeds out firms which do not command adequate financial support, however sound their business may be, and it leaves unliquidated concerns which do command such support, although they may never be able to pay their way), and hence produces a pattern more or less different from that which the normal process would have evolved. Second, depression and the return of the system from the depressive excursion take time. They may take several years. During that time data change and what would have been a neighborhood of equilibrium when depression started is no longer one when all is over. We will refer to prosperity and revival as the positive phases of a cycle, to recession and depression as the negative phases.

It is left to the reader to work out the picture of depression and revival. We confine ourselves to the following comments:

1. While recession and—if depression occurs—revival are necessary parts of the cyclical process of economic evolution, depression itself is not. From the business situations which necessarily obtain in recession, depression may easily develop, but in all its essential aspects the cyclical process would be logically complete without it. Whether it occurs or not is a question of fact and depends on accidental circumstances, such as the mentality and temper of the business community and the public, the prevalence of get-rich-quick morals, the way—conscientious or otherwise—in which credit is handled in prosperity, the ability of the public to form an opinion about the merits of propositions, the degree to which it is given to belief in phrases about prosperity plateaus and the wonders of monetary management and so on. Moreover, no *theoretical* expectation can be formed about the occurrence and severity of depressions. We may, in an given situation, try to appraise the extent of existing maladjustments, of the presence of fraudulent schemes, "unsound credit," and so on; but beyond such indications it is impossible to go. In a very difficult situation, aggravated, for instance, by serious external events, the business community may keep its nerves, while it may become frightened on much smaller provocation. A scare or panic may occur almost anywhere in the course of a cycle, although, of course, it is much more likely to occur at certain junctures than at others. Such a panic may mean very little and yet violently send down values and even certain physical quantities. A lesson follows from this for the analysis of time series: We must not trust our graphs implicitly. Both

peaks and troughs may easily mislead and it is hardly an exaggeration to say that, as far as information about fundamental processes goes, they are precisely the most unreliable items in an array.[1]

2. Next, what may be termed the Problem of the Recovery Point now emerges in its proper setting. The much-debated questions whether or not the system stops of itself when once it has entered upon a negative phase, and whether it then starts of itself on a positive one, only arise in the case of four-phase cycles. For we know why the process of liquidation or absorption which constitutes recession in a two-phase cycle will, barring minor oscillations, die out when it has done its work. We also know why, as long as the capitalist mechanism and capitalist motivation are intact, entrepreneurial activity will then resume without any external stimulus. So far, our analysis leads us to agree with those authors who believe in the existence of "recuperative forces," and merely gives more precise meaning to this otherwise not very helpful phrase. But this is no longer so in the case of a four-phase cycle. Depression, as we have seen, has not simply a definite amount of work to do. On the contrary, it has a way of feeding upon itself and of setting into motion a mechanism which, considered in isolation, could in fact run on indefinitely under its own steam. We have indicated above what that "vicious spiral" consists in. Various models have been constructed in order to display it. But proving from the properties of such a mechanism, the elements of which have been taken out of their setting in the economic organism, that the process will go on intensifying itself, does not amount to proving that its real counterpart will actually do so; else, we could equally well argue that, once we have a cough that irritates our throat and thus induces further coughing, we must go on coughing forever. The problem is to analyze a complex sequence of short-time situations in which the facts described by such theories of the spiral form only one of many components.

[1] To all this, however, there is a qualification the importance of which will become clear later on. What has just been said is true only so long as we keep to the hypothesis, presently to be discarded, that the cyclical process of evolution consists in a succession of units of one single type of wave. As soon as we drop it, a result more hopeful for diagnosis, and perhaps even for prognosis, presents itself. However, the fact still remains that only historical investigation can indicate whether in a given case depression has actually occurred or not.

We will first distinguish between the course of events in industrial and commercial business, on the one hand, and the course of events in the stock exchange and other speculative markets, on the other hand. The latter is quite likely to conform to the spiral pattern. Traditional doctrine relies on three factors of recovery from a slump. First, bears will cover and thus provide a parachute. So they will from time to time, and this would rally the market if there were no objective reason for relapse. If there is, because distress selling goes on and prospects are black, each bear attack will be followed by a stronger one. Moreover, older doctrine seems in general to have exaggerated the regulative and smoothing effects of speculation, as we shall see later on. Second, "insiders" will quietly buy. This, in fact, is almost always done to some extent but in general not quantitatively sufficient to turn the tide. Third, the average investor's attitude will change because of the increasing inducement to invest which falling quotations seem to offer. This seems to the writer to be most unrealistic. The average investor in such cases thinks that Doom is at hand and the higher the returns the less he buys. The argument entirely overlooks the shift that occurs in the investor's demand curve and assumes that its position is invariant to cyclical phases. It is changing business prospects, that is to say, a fact external to these markets, which pulls them out of depression.

As for industry and trade, the first step is to show that recovery will necessarily set in if the depressive process stops (in practice it is sufficient that it slackens perceptibly). This is easy. If there is a depression phase, then the trough is, as we have seen, no longer what it was in the two-phase cycle, namely a state of equilibrium. And this proposition is in itself sufficient to prove the point without any resort to optimistic expectations which, however, will soon emerge to help. For saying that firms will not act in the way which will lead to recovery and eventually to a neighborhood of equilibrium, would be synonymous with saying that they will deliberately forego gains and incur losses which it is in their individual power to make or to avoid, and scrap plant and equipment which could be profitably used. It is sometimes objected that cramped lower-level equilibria may arise from which people will not of themselves move. This may be so in individual cases, particularly in imperfectly competitive situations. But the probability that this state of things should prevail all over the system, in all industries and with all concerns—for that would be necessary to justify the inference—is indistinguishable from zero. Therefore, our problem reduces to the question whether the depressive process does stop of itself short of, theoretically, universal starvation.

To this question, however, there is no general answer. It can indeed be proved that the pressure from the spiral produces reactions in the system which tend to stop it. On the one hand, there will be what we may term diffusion or dilution of effects. The spiral process sets in by a number of unfavorable individual events, such as bankruptcies, breaks in individual markets, shutdowns. These induce similar events, but it is readily seen that each of them taken by itself loses momentum as its effects spread. The failure of a concern may cause the failures of other concerns, but part of its liabilities will be to firms which can stand the loss and which therefore act as buffers. Each addition to unemployment will cause further and further unemployment but, *taken individually*, at a decreasing rate. Individual contractions of output breed contraction all around, but the impact of each of them slackens and stops after having gone a certain way. No doubt we invariably observe a rapid deterioration of the business situation once the system has embarked upon a cumulative downward process. But this deterioration is not simply due to the fact that the spiral feeds upon itself but primarily to the other fact that it is fed from outside, *i.e.*, from breakdowns and contractions which occur independently of it. It will thus be seen that increase in total effects observed is perfectly compatible with the proposition that each individual effect tends to peter out, and that a case for believing that the spiral itself will peter out may be made on these lines.

On the other hand, there is what we may term depression business. This may be instanced by the case of the stoppage of a firm which induces unemployment that in turn causes the failure of a grocer whose customers the unemployed workmen were. This grocer's market is not completely annihilated, however, and if he disappears there will be some space for other grocers to expand into. To put the matter generally, the spiral process is a movement away from equilibrium, as we see from the increasing dispersion in prices and from the increasing deviation from equilibrium relations between physical quantities. This spells not only actual and potential losses but also actual and potential gains. Hence it will, however great total net losses may be, not only induce contractions but also expansions, although these may for the time being not show statistically. It has often been held that it is the ensuing cheapness of cost factors, labor, money, raw materials, which eventually breaks the spiral. This formulation does not seem felicitous because it leaves out of account the downward shift of demand curves which might preclude production even if, say, steel and copper were to be had for nothing. But what can be said is that since demand and cost curves do not shift uniformly, opportunities arise for transactions which would not be possible otherwise and which will do somethings to counteract the ravages of the spiral. It is no doubt true that pessimistic expectations will prevent many transactions from materializing which are profitable on paper. But it is perfectly gratuitous 'to postulate that this is the general case. Whatever the businessman's state of mind, he will take current business that offers itself. This is in fact one of the main differences in the functioning of an industrial and of a speculative market.

But though it may thus be shown that a restorative tendency will develop to work against the spiral, there is nothing to prove that it will prevail against it. As long as we keep our argument perfectly general, we must recognize the possibility of a system so conditioned and of a spiral so violent that that tendency may fight a losing battle at any given moment and that, theoretically, the system may never conquer the breathing space in which it could recover of itself. This seems in fact to be the element of truth in the popular opinion that there must be help from outside of the business organism, from government action or some favorable chance event, if there is to be recovery at all or, at any rate, recovery without a preceding period of complete disorganization and of indefinite length.

This result calls for a few additional remarks.

First, the above analysis does not make spirals identical with depressions. We might make them identical with what we shall sometimes call Deep Depressions. But the depression phases in our sense generally outlast any spiral processes which may occur in their course and are particularly likely to occur at their beginning. In general revival is from a trough in which the situation is no longer dominated by a cumulative downward process. Nevertheless, the problem of the spiral is relevant to the problem of the recovery point because, as we have seen, revival will ensue when the depressive process stops and because the presence of a spiral affords the only reason for doubting that it does stop of itself.

Second, the inconclusiveness of our result is due to our wish to face squarely a problem of general theory. A much stronger case for believing that, in the absence of exceptionally unfavorable external factors, the system will recover "of itself" under almost any practically conceivable circumstances, can be made by relying on restrictive assumptions amply verified by common sense and historical fact. One of these has frequently been expressed by means of the observation that total income fluctuates less than total output, the item wages plus salaries less than total income, expenditure on consumers' goods less than wages plus salaries. This is broadly correct and partly accounted for by our theory of dilution of effects. But partly it also rests on the presence of incomes which are insensitive to depression and of social strata little affected by it, *i.e.*, on facts which are no part of the logic of the capitalist engine. It still remains true that the question whether or not a given recovery was "natural" must in every historical instance be answered anew.

Third, it has been repeatedly emphasized that depression, unlike recession, is a pathological process to which no organic functions can be attributed. This proposition is indeed not quite true. In our schematic exposition, each phase is credited with what we conceive to be its most characteristic features and this never does justice to real life. On the one hand, much that could live according to the criterion afforded by the theory of equilibrium, may perish in an otherwise normal recession. On the other hand, much that according to the same criterion cannot live (and many maladjustments and rigidities) will not be eliminated by recession. Hence much work of reorganization and adaptation is also done in depression. But substantially our proposition holds. It follows that proof, even if it were more satisfactory than it is, that depression will find a "natural" end, does not in itself constitute an argument for letting things take their course or trusting to "the restorative forces of nature." The case for government action in depression remains, independently of humanitarian considerations, incomparably stronger than it is in recession.

3. It follows that division of the units of the cyclical process of evolution into two or four phases is not a matter of descriptive convenience. Each phase is a distinct composite phenom-

enon, not only distinguishable by a characteristic set of features, but also explainable in terms of the different "forces" which dominate it and produce those features. As we know, these "forces" consist in such concretely observable phenomena as innovation (entrepreneurs' expenditure), response of the system to the impact of the products of new plant (and autodeflation), the impetus of abnormal liquidation (and of depressive anticipation arising out of it) meeting with equilibrium (return to what now are normal quantities and values). The second and fourth phases, recession and revival, differ in the nature of the deviations they liquidate or absorb and in the signs of the latter. They are alike in the nature of the mechanism at work which in both cases consists of equilibrium relations between the elements of the economic system asserting themselves. The first and third phases, prosperity and depression, differ in the nature of the impulse that propels the system and of the deviations which develop. They are alike in that in each case the system draws away from equilibrium and into disequilibrium. In a two-phase cyclical movement a line through normals would form (erratic movements excepted) a boundary of all the items plotted on a chart, no points of our material lying above or none below it (according to the series plotted—price series would run above, unemployment series below the boundary line). The line or curve through normals in a four-phase cyclical movement, on the other hand, must cut through the graphs of series.

Since every cycle is a historical individual and not merely an arbitrary unit created by the observer, we are not at liberty to count cycles from any phase we please. The phenomenon becomes understandable only if we start with the neighborhood of equilibrium preceding prosperity and end up with the neighborhood following revival. The count from trough to trough or from peak to peak is, therefore, not only open to the objection already mentioned—that both troughs and peaks may prove very unreliable beacons—but it is never theoretically correct. It may be convenient at times, but it is likely to induce faulty analysis in several ways, one of which is of particular importance for us.

Revival is the last and not the first phase of a cycle. If we count from troughs we cut off this phase from the cycle to which it belongs and add it on to a cycle to which it does not belong. Counting in this way, we lose the fundamental distinction between revival and prosperity. Although most authors recognize at least a distinction of degree and some also one of kind, they do not recognize the difference in the propelling factor. They see indices move up from the trough and eventually on to prosperity levels (which are mostly only quantitatively defined), and they conclude naturally enough that the same factors account for the whole rise. Hence, they search the processes of *revival* for "causes" of the entire rise and find nothing more than gradual elimination of the abnormalities then existing—low stocks, unused plant, unemployed labor, idle credit facilities—and in particular, they find nothing that looks like innovation. Therefore, they arrive at the result that innovation has nothing to do with initiating *prosperity*, even if they glance at this possibility, which most of them do not. Such analysis easily misses the pivotal point and drifts into *perpetuum-mobile* explanations, particularly of the monetary sort.[1]

4. Along with the phenomena of the secondary wave, we will introduce a few other facts, to complete our Second Approximation.

First, we must drop the assumption, made for convenience of exposition, that our wave is the first of its kind and that it not only starts from a neighborhood of equilibrium—through all qualifications we must hold on to this—but that it is entirely unaffected by the results of previous evolution. That is, we must take account of the fact that each neighborhood contains undigested elements of previous prosperities and depressions, innovations not yet completely worked out, results of faulty or other-

[1] Here we should notice a question which the writer has often been asked. If we admit the possibility that, under the influence of depressive factors "crystallizing" and gathering momentum, the system outruns a neighborhood of equilibrium on its downward path, why should it be less likely that the upward tendency in the recovery phase also crystallize and gather momentum so that the neighborhood be similarly outrun on the upward path? We believe this to be less likely, owing to the absence of a phenomenon similar to the breakdown of the secondary wave. No corresponding impulse toward optimistic excess exists in recovery. But even if that were not so and speculation developed merely on the strength of favorable rates of change so as to lift the system above equilibrium, relapse to it (perhaps somewhat below it with reaction to follow) would, in the absence of stimulus from innovation (or, of course, external factors), quickly follow. In other words, return to equilibrium may indeed be attended by fluctuations around equilibrium but they will soon subside. That type of fluctuation we shall discuss later on.

wise imperfect adaptations, and so on. There is nothing in this to invalidate our model. On the contrary, these facts are but a consequence of the process described by it. But they greatly increase the difficulties of analysis and complicate the patterns of the business situations we have to deal with.

One point calls for special notice. Producers, becoming familiar with the recurrent shifts of demand in the course of the cyclical phases, learn to provide for the peak demand of prosperity. Industries more subject than others to such fluctuations (for example, industries producing industrial equipment or materials for it), which we shall call Cyclical Industries, are particularly likely to do this. They will set up productive capacity which is intended to be fully used [1] only in times of prosperity. This tendency, which practically always presupposes imperfect competition, will be strengthened by the fact that even replacement demand is strongly cyclical, sometimes quite irrationally so. Railroads, for instance, could be expected to know that depression do not last forever, yet they often order new rails or new rolling stock late in revival or even in prosperity. A number of obviously important consequences follow. Output will much more readily expand in prosperity than we should expect from the Pure Model and costs and prices will rise less than they otherwise would. Also, a peculiar kind of unemployment, akin to seasonal unemployment, may ensue; for in many cases the men who are dismissed when prosperity demand ceases will be neither able nor willing to get other employment during what they know is but a temporary interruption, to which they are accustomed, but will simply "hang around." This is an important point to remember in any short-time theory of unemployment.

Second, we must insert growth. Saving, in particular, we cannot longer disregard, because sources and motives are supplied by our process strong enough to make it quantitatively significant. In fact, it would be possible, once the cyclical process is started, to construct a model the financial wheels of which would entirely consist of saving, and which would function differently. This we

[1] That case must be distinguished from building capacity "ahead of demand." But inasmuch as doing this rests on an expectation which, in turn, rests on familiarity with the results of evolution (much more so than of growth), this case should also be mentioned here. This is another reason why so many industries are, even in prosperity, to the "left of the optimum point."

shall not do, since even a small amount of credit creation suffices to produce the phenomena we have been describing. But we must insert it in what we conceive to be its actual role. It will be convenient to defer this until we come to the discussion of the behavior of monetary time series. For the moment, it is enough to invite the reader to form his own opinion of how the financing of innovation by saving, instead of by credit creation, will affect the contours of our waves, particularly in price levels.

On the other hand, third, we must recall that credit creation spreads from its "logical" source, financing of innovation, throughout the system. It intrudes by way of credit's being created for any kind of expansion that cannot be financed by existing funds and by way of entrepreneurs' not repaying what they borrow within the cycle and very often never repaying all of it or reborrowing regularly part of their working capital. On the surface, therefore, credit creation tends to lose its relation to innovation and becomes an instrument for financing business in general, and its amount will display variations not explainable by the Pure Model. For example, it may increase in recovery, when ordinary business resumes its proportions. It will also decrease less than the first approximation indicates—or not at all—in recession, because outlay for the purpose of adaptation of old firms and the expansion of some of them into the new economic space created by recent innovation will be financed by bank credit.

Fourth, the effect of innovation in opening up new investment opportunities to industries which have not themselves reformed their method of production cannot be sufficiently emphasized. It is not confined to the opening up of possibilities best instanced by the building of American transcontinental railroads. New economic space is created also by the mere fact that additional production may call forth other production to pay for it: if there are in the closed domain only two industries producing equilibrium amounts, and if one of them introduces an innovation enabling it, for example, to produce a greater number of units with the same quantity of resources, the other industry may expand its production in response. That is what happens extensively in recession and then again in revival, depression—if sufficiently "panicky"—frequently, though not necessarily, interrupting the process.

From these cases it is necessary to distingush another which may produce similar results. Some industries are so sensitive to the rate of interest as to shape their course primarily with reference to it. In prewar Germany, for instance, apartment-house building could have been represented with satisfactory approximation as a function of the mortgage rate alone. And something of the kind is suggested by the fact that residential building in the United States precedes the Harvard barometer's curve *B* by a few months—which makes it in the short run roughly inverse to the money curve *C*.[1] This is somewhat more significant than it looks because, apart from the influence of interest, we should, if anything, expect a lag. It would not, however, be safe to trust this relation too much.

Fifth, we will repeat not only that the entrepreneurial impulse impinges upon an imperfectly competitive world but also that entrepreneurs and their satellites almost always find themselves in imperfectly competitive short-time situations even in an otherwise perfectly competitive world. In fact, evolution in our sense is the most powerful influence in creating such imperfections all around. Hence we now drop the assumption of perfect competition altogether, as well as the assumption, made at the threshold of this chapter, that there is perfect equilibrium at the start. We can assume, instead, that both competition and equilibrium are, independently of the effects of our process, imperfect from the start, or even that the system is inactive in the sense defined in the second chapter. We know what consequences this will entail: propositions and proofs will be less stringent, zones of indeterminateness will emerge, sequences of events will be less prompt, and buffers will be inserted between the parts of our mechanism so that its gears will be slower to mesh. There will be more room for individual strategy, moves and countermoves which may impede, although they may also facilitate, the system's struggle toward equilibrium. This will certainly produce many freakish patterns and the economist's engine for the production of paradoxa will be worked up to capacity. But this is all. An important point to bear in mind is the possibility, or even the likelihood, of situations in which industries may, even in equilibrium, move within intervals of decreasing average costs. In fact, theoretical expectation is, in all phases save pros-

[1] [Curve B, representing business activity, showed bank debits of 241 cities outside N.Y.C. Curve C, representing money, showed rates on short-time money.—Ed.]

perity, for this rather than for the opposite alternative, and it may well apply also to the beginning of the prosperity phase.

Since it has, with many economists, become a fashion to make the presence of unemployed resources—labor, in particular—a datum of the problem of cycles, to base their theories on it and to object to other theories on the ground that they neglect it and fail precisely because they neglect it, we will state once more where we stand concerning this matter. Imperfections of both competition and equilibrium, as well as external disturbances, may account for the presence of unemployed resources independently of the cyclical process of evolution. We have not introduced this fact into our pure model in order to relieve the latter of unessential and secondary elements; but it can now be inserted without difficulty and be taken account of in any given case which presents them. Besides, since our process itself produces both imperfections of competition and disequilibria which account for underemployment that may outlast the cyclical unit which produced it, we include, by recognizing that every cycle is heir to preceding cycles, also what this source may contribute to the total unemployment with which any given unit starts. This would have been circular reasoning in the Pure Model, but as far as any part of total underemployment is due to imperfection of competition, *full employment ceases to be a property of equilibrium states and instead indicates—paradoxical though this may sound—disequilibrium of a certain type*. This is important because it supplies the answer to the argument of those economists who look for equilibrium in the cyclical peaks. In any case, the presence of unemployment at the beginning of prosperity need not, for those who wish to stress it, be an obstacle to accepting our analysis. Difference of opinion, however, amounting in important cases to difference of diagnosis, arises only if it be held that unemployment of resources is (barring rigidities) compatible with perfect equilibrium in a perfectly competitive situation.

D. Many Simultaneous Cycles; Third Approximation.—So far we have implied that,barring the effects of external disturbance, there is in our material a single sequence of cycles, each of which is of the same type as all its predecessors and successors. Every individual cycle has been thought of as crippled or drawn out in duration, accentuated or reduced in amplitude by its historic setting (wars, crops, and so on), and as internally irregular besides; nevertheless, each was on a par with the others. But there is nothing in our theoretical schema to warrant this. There is no reason why the cyclical process of evolution should give rise to just one wavelike movement. On the contrary, there are many reasons to expect that it will set into motion an indefinite number of wavelike fluctuations which will roll on simultaneously and interfere with one another in the process. Nor does the impression we derive from any graph of economic time series lend support to a single-cycle hypothesis. On the contrary, the reader need only inspect any of the charts in this book in order to satisfy himself that it is much more natural to assume the presence of many fluctuations, of different span and intensity, which seem to be superimposed on each other. In accepting that inference from theory and in recognizing this fact, we fall in with the general tendency in the study of business cycles.

Spectacular booms and spectacular breakdowns were what first attracted the attention of both economists and businessmen. The problem thus presented itself at the outset as the problem of "crises." These were primarily looked upon as individual catastrophes, interrupting an even flow or an expansion that did not by its own mechanism produce them. Most of the arguments which even today we are in the habit of listing as "theories of the cycle" were developed then, *i.e.*, in the last quarter of the eighteenth century and in, roughly, the first half of the nineteenth century—particularly, all the monetary theories and the various theories of overproduction, underconsumption, and so on. The great advance beyond this view of the subject came about as the result of the efforts of many authors, but is primarily associated with the name of Clement Juglar, who was the first to have a clear perception of how theory, statistics, and history ought to cooperate in our field. His great merit is that he pushed the crisis into the background and that he discovered below it another, much more fundamental, phenomenon, the mechanism of alternating prosperities and liquidations, the latter of which, as pointed out in another place, he interpreted to be a reaction of the economic system to the events of the former. Henceforth, although it took decades for this new view to prevail, the *wave* ousted the *crisis* from the role of protagonist of the play. But it was the exploration and interpretation of *the* wave to which students bent their energy then. For Juglar and his followers took it for granted that what they had discovered was a single wavelike movement and were not conscious of the fact that by assuming this they were really introducing a new, bold, and very unrealistic hypothesis.

But this hypothesis worked fairly well at first. Juglar's findings from his banking figures, interest rates, and prices, supported as they were by marriage rates and other evidence, fitted in satisfactorily enough with the dates of the big crises which had been recognized before him. Difficulties arose, indeed, with increasing accuracy of observation, and the workers in the field, deprived of the guidance of the spectacular symptoms of crises, and faced with a much gentler sweep, began to waver about duration and phases. But they still kept to the hypothesis of a single wave, although one would think that recognition of the presence of several waves would have been the natural remedy for part of the irregularities which now crowded upon them. This attitude of mind, asserting itself in a reluctance to drop a familiar instrument of analysis and in a disposition to deny the reality or existence of other wavelike movements which began to be offered for consideration, is highly interesting and could be paralleled by many instances from other sciences. It is by no means extinct even now. Presumably, it would be more correct to say that the majority of students has not yet succeeded in leaving those moorings. For others, however, the problem has again changed its complexion. It is no longer the problem of *the* wave. It is the problem of identifying and, if possible, isolating the many waves and of studying their interference one with each another. The present writer who, when starting work on the business cycle nearly 30 years ago, also accepted the single-cycle hypothesis as a matter of course, considers the development to be a very important progress, but it is one of those progresses which at first create as many difficulties as they solve. And he would not be surprised if in the future economists would imitate astronomers in thinking it a matter of self-respect to have private periodicities of their own.

We will notice only those contribution to this line of advance which are directly relevant to our own work. They refer to a wavelike movement very much longer and to another wavelike movement very much shorter than the one described by Juglar. Summing up earlier work of his, Professor A. Spiethoff showed in his monograph on cycles (Krisen in Handwörterbuch der

Staatswissenschaften, 4th ed., 1923) that there are epochs in which prosperities, and other epochs in which depressions, are relatively more marked, and these epochs he considered as bigger units without, however, combining them into cycles containing an upgrade and a downgrade and also without going beyond a statement to the effect that they were probably due to other causes than what he was prepared to call *cycles*. Applying his criterion of iron consumption he found that for England the period from 1822 to 1842 constitutes such a span of (prevalence of) depression (*Stockungsspanne*) and that for Germany the years 1843 to 1873 and 1895 to 1913 make up spans of (prevalence of) prosperity (*Aufschwungsspanne*), while from 1874 to 1894 we have a span of depression. It was N. D. Kondratieff, however, who brought the phenomenon fully before the scientific community and who systematically analyzed all the material available to him on the assumption of the presence of a Long Wave, characteristic of the capitalist process. He dates the first long wave covered by his material from the end of the eighties or the beginning of the nineties of the eighteenth century to 1844–1851; the second, from 1844–1851 to 1890–1896; and the third, from 1890–1896 onward. Other students also presented evidence of the presence of movements of average period longer than that usually attributed to the Juglar cycle. We will mention Professor S. S. Kuznets (Secular Movements in Production and Prices, 1930) and Dr. C. A. R. Wardwell (An investigation of Economic Data for Major Cycles, 1927), who found average periods of roughly 25 and 15 years, respectively.

In 1923 Professor W. L. Crum published the result of a periodogram analysis of monthly commercial paper rates in New York from 1866 to 1922, clearly showing the presence of a period of roughly 40 months in the series analyzed. The importance of the contribution consists in the fact that it established, at least for one series and without any further comment, the existence of a cycle which can be observed in practically all time series and is really the most visible and most regular of all. Simultaneously, Mr. Joseph Kitchin, by a less rigorous but more pliable method, showed that cycle also in bank clearings and wholesale prices, as well as in interest rates, for both Great Britain and the United States, during the period 1890 to 1922, moreover contrasted it with the Juglar cycle and a longer swing which can be roughly identified with Spiethoff's spans and which he linked up with gold production. "The 40-month-cycle," although at first none too favorably received, has since acquired citizenship which, as we shall see, cannot reasonably be questioned. Professor Mitchell's authority may, it seems, be appealed to for qualified support, based upon analysis of five American systematic series (among them, two of clearings and one of deposits) for 1878–1923, which gives a mean duration (of cycles in general) of 42.05 months with a standard deviation of 12.37 months, while the median is 40 months. The high value of the standard deviation must not astonish us. Nothing more regular can be expected in material such as ours is.

Assertion or denial of the coexistence of several cyclical movements may, of course, mean many different things, and discussion stands to gain from a clear distinction among them in each case. An author who submits findings about what he holds to be a distinct cyclical movement, may simply claim to have established a statistical fact. He may, however, claim less or more. On the one hand, he may merely hold that assuming the existence of several cycles will prove to be a useful descriptive device. On the other hand, he may hold that his cycles correspond, each of them, to different economic processes and link up with different causes. There is such a variety of possible standpoints between and around these two, that there is hardly any sense in straight asertion or straight denial of anybody's cycles. We return to our argument, in order to make our own standpoint as clear as possible.

First, if innovations are at the root of cyclical fluctuations, these cannot be expected to form a single wavelike movement, because the periods of gestation and of absorption of effects by the economic system will not, in general, be equal for all the innovations that are undertaken at any time. There will be innovations of relatively long span, and along with them others will be undertaken which run their course, on the back of the wave created by the former, in shorter periods. This at once suggests both multiplicity of fluctuations and the kind of interference between them which we are to expect. When a wave of long span is in its prosperity phase, it will be easier for smaller waves—which, as a rule, will correspond to less important innovations—to rise, and as long as the "underlying" prosperity lasts there will be a cushion ready for them while, say, in the depression phase of the underlying wave it may be impossible for them to rise visibly at all, although they might still assert themselves by softening that depression through their prosperities and intensifying it through their depressions. The impression some of us have that seasonal fluctuations are particularly strong in times of prolonged depression may be due to that. Variations in expenditure within each class of cycle will accentuate or compensate the effects of variations in expenditure occurring in the course of all other contemporaneous cycles, and no variation will be what it would be in the absence of the others. These cycles will displace each other's peaks and troughs and between them produce contour lines that are completely understandable without due recognition of the phases of the others into which the phase of any given cycle happens to fall. Behavior of time series that seems to disavow expectation can often be explained in this way.

Second, a statistical and historical picture of a movement displaying more than one cycle may result from the fact that successive cyclical units are not so independent of each other as we assumed in constructing our model. When some innovation has been successfully carried into effect, the next wave is much more likely to start in the same or a neighboring field than anywhere else. Major innovations hardly ever emerge in their final form or cover in one throw the whole field that will ultimately be their own. The railroadization, the electrification, the motorization of the world are instances. One railroad or a few lines may be all, and more than all, that can be successfully built in a given environment at a given time. Reaction and absorption may have to follow before a new wave of railroad construction becomes possible. The motorcar would never have acquired its present importance and become so potent a reformer of life if it had remained what it was thirty years ago and if it had failed to shape the environmental conditions—roads, among them—for its own further development. In such cases, innovation is carried out in steps each of which constitutes a cycle. But these cycles may display a family likeness and a relation to one another which tends to weld them into a higher unit that will stand out as a historical individual. The case is entirely different from the previous one. There we had a multiplicity of cycles each of which was an independent entity. Here we have a sequence of cycles of one type only, and the cycle of higher order is but a product or composite of these and has no existence of its own.

Third, a sequence of cycles, whether independent of one

another or not, may be the result of processes which have also effects other than those which show in the cycles themselves. Railroadization may again serve as an example. Expenditure on, and the opening of, a new line has some immediate effects on business in general, on competing means of transport, and on the relative position of centers of production. It requires more time to bring into use the opportunities of production newly created by the railroad and to annihilate others. And it takes still longer for population to shift, new cities to develop, other cities to decay, and, generally, the new face of the country to take shape that is adapted to the environment as altered by the railroadization. Another example is the process known as the Industrial Revolution. It consisted of a cluster of cycles of various span that were superimposed on each other. But these together wrought a fundamental change in the economic and social structure of society which in itself also had some obviously cyclical characteristics. It came about in phases in which prices, interest rates, employment, incomes, credit, and output behaved much as they did in the fluctuations universally recognized as cycles. And we should be losing an obvious opportunity of pushing our analysis deeper into the material of economic history if we refused to take account of this. Again, this kind of cycle or this aspect of what it has become usual to call the Long Wave, is completely different from either the first or the second case. It differs from the latter in that it is a real phenomenon and not merely the statistical effect of a sequence of real phenomena having more in common with one another than with similar phenomena outside the sequence. It differs from the former in that it cannot be linked to a particular type of innovations as against other types carried out during the same epoch, but is the result of all industrial and commercial processes of that epoch.

We conclude, as stated in the first paragraph of this section, that there is a theoretically indefinite number of fluctuations present in our material at any time, the word *present* meaning that there are real factors at work to produce them and *not merely that the material may be decomposed into them by formal methods.* Their duration varies greatly—for we know that some of them are associated with effects of processes which run their course in a year or two, others with effects which are secular by nature—but might in a limiting case vary continuously. As a matter of fact, we shall not expect this, but rather that periods will display finite differences clustering aorund certain averages. Some of these periods will be so close together as to be undistinguishable. Others will be wide apart.

Nothing in this implies a hypothesis. All it has to do with hypotheses is that it implies the refusal to accept one, *viz.*, the single-cycle hypothesis. Nor are we going to make another hypothesis to take the place of the latter. But we are going to make a *decision*. For our purpose, as for many others, it would be highly inconvenient to leave matters at the above result and to attempt to work with an indefinite number of cycles or classes of cycles. Nor is there any necessity of doing so. It stands to reason that as we draw away from the single-cycle hypothesis we shall reap the bulk of the harvest to be hoped for at the first steps and that then these returns will be rapidly decreasing. Hence, we decide now to content ourselves, for the rough purposes of this volume, with three classes of cycles, to which we shall refer simply as Kondratieffs, Juglars and Kitchins, because the average spans by which we choose to identify the individuals belonging to each of our three classes approximately correspond to the spans of the cycles "discovered" by those three investigators, respectively. Since this arrangement plays a considerable role in the exposition that is to follow and since any misunderstandings about it might easily impair the contribution to the study of business cycles which this book may be hoped to make, it is desirable to comment upon it.

1. By saying that in adopting a three-cycle schema we are not making any hypothesis which is to replace the single-cycle hypothesis, but only a decision, we have waived any claims for that schema beyond those we are about to state. There are no particular virtues in the choice made of just three classes of cycles. Five would perhaps be better, although, after some experimenting, the writer came to the conclusion that the improvement in the picture would not warrant the increase in cumbersomeness. In particular, it cannot be emphasized too strongly that the three-cycle schema does not follow from our model—although multiplicity of cycles does—and that approval of it or objection to it does not add or detract from the value or otherwise of our fundamental idea, which would work equally well or ill with many other schemata of this kind. If we discuss the behavior of time series in terms of Kondratieffs, Juglars, and Kitchins, this will be done simply because the writer has found it useful in his own

work and in marshaling his facts. So far, then, the three-cycle schema may be looked upon as a convenient descriptive device, and readers who so wish need never look upon it in any other light. As far as this goes, it follows that we are estopped from calling the single-cycle schema wrong: the only reproach we can cast upon it is that it is inconvenient.

2. But one motive of the decision made was to have as many classes or orders of cycles as are necessary in order to assure us that all of the three reasons for the multiplicity of cycles have the opportunity of coming into play, and not more.[1] Another was to have the families of long, medium, and short cycles represented. And, finally, it was thought reasonable to require that each of the cycles to be chosen should have definite historical and statistical meaning. This requirement accounts for the fact that our cycles are precisely those "discovered" by the authors by the name of whom we designate them, for whatever exception may be taken to their material and methods and however much room there may be for difference of opinion about the details of their findings, certain broad facts, often observed without any intention to discover any cycles, stand out to bear witness to the historical and statistical meaning of those three orders of cycles.

Historically, the first Kondratieff covered by our material means the industrial revolution, including the protracted process of its absorption. We date it from the eighties of the eighteenth century to 1842. The second stretches over what has been called the age of steam and steel. It runs its course between 1842 and 1897. And the third, the Kondratieff of electricity, chemistry, and motors, we date from 1898 on. These datings do not lack historical justification. Yet they are not only tentative, but also by nature merely approximate. A considerable zone of doubt surrounds most of them, as will be seen more clearly later on. Each Juglar not only has its "big" crisis—we do not attach much importance to this—but also can be associated with definite

[1] Three turned out to be the minimum number satisfying that requirement; but this does not mean that we specifically associate each of our cycles with one of those reasons. Inasmuch as the second and third reasons refer to effects which must take a comparatively long time to assert themselves, the Kondratieff will bear a particular relation to them. Otherwise, it is merely a chance coincidence that, having seen three reasons for the multiplicity of cycles, we also chose to confine that multiplicity to three orders or classes.

innovatory processes in industry and trade. Average duration is between nine and ten years. Historical association of that kind is most doubtful in the case of the Kitchins, partly because the writer has not been able to accomplish the heavy task of investigating each of them but had to be content with a survey of a few intervals. Results were not conclusive, and it is even necessary to leave open the possibility that Kitchins are merely fluctuations of the adaptive type (sec. E).[1] Whether or not the statistical evidence supports the historical to the extent necessary to make our schema a useful tool of analysis, will be for the reader to judge. All classes or orders of cycles show differently in different series and countries: in some series, such as pig-iron consumption and unemployment, Juglars show best; in others—the majority of the series is among them—the Kitchins. The latter stand out better, on the whole, in America than in England, Juglars better in Germany than in England.[2] All this also defines the sense

[1] [Later in life, Schumpeter entirely abandoned the idea that Kitchins could be explained by his theory.—Ed.]

[2] Very little will be said, as opportunities arise, about those differences. This makes it all the more important to emphasize here that they may in future prove to be very helpful clues to a wide variety of problems. Differences in the behavior of the same (or closely related) series in different countries may tell us a great deal about the economic structure of these countries, the peculiarities of their economic engines, and their economic relations to each other. Differences in the degree to which different cycles show in different series are full of potential information about the details of the cyclical mechanism and the character of the different cycles. It should be added that, while the fact that a given class of cycle is absent or very weakly marked in any single series is, for that reason, always very interesting, it must never be recorded against the "reality" of that class of cycle. For instance, Mr. B. Greenstein, in his periodogram study, which ranks very high on the list of contribution of this type (Periodogram Analysis with Special Application to Business Failures in the United States 1867-1932—data, relative number of failures from Dun's Review—*Econometrica* for April 1935) finds a cycle of a typical duration of 9.4 years, which the present writer (but the reader knows by now how easily satisfied he is) considers extremely satisfactory and, in fact, wishes to list as one of the major statistical testimonials for the Juglar cycle. There are also minor peaks but nothing whatever to indicate anything like the Kitchin cycle. This, however, is precisely what we should expect. Fluctuations the depression phases of which are as short and gentle as those of the Kitchins are not likely to drive any abnormal number of firms into bankruptcy or, more generally, failure, while the stronger swings, due to more deepreaching industrial change, of the Juglars naturally will. In this respect

in which we claim "real existence" for our three orders of cycles.

3. From the reasons given for expecting the simultaneous presence of cycles of different order, it follows that for us the problem that arises as soon as we recognize the presence of more than one cyclical movement, is a problem of interference only and not —with the proviso just made as regards the Kitchin cycle—a problem of different causation. They are all to be explained in terms of the process of economic evolution as described by our model. Innovations, their immediate and ulterior effects and the response to them by the system, are the common "cause" of them all, although different types of innovations and different kinds of effects may play different roles in each. With this qualification and also another which will suggest itself in the next section (presence of fluctuations of different types), it is the same phenomenon and the same mechanism we observe in all of them. In particular, we have in all cases the same reasons for expecting two or four phases. Difference in duration alone suffices to alter many details in the pictures presented by cycles of different orders and in many cases expectations will have to be formulated separately for cycles of different span. But, in principle, our general propositions apply to all of them.

For the analysis of given patterns of reality this conception of the process of evolution producing a multiplicity of simultaneous waves is of considerable importance, although it does not, of course, touch upon any of those phenomena which are produced by external factors, because it allows us to see the economic process in the light of a single simple principle. Therefore, it seems to be worth while to use it as a schema of interpretation and to fit it for this service by investing it with some additional properties suggested by what we know about the mechanism of cycles and by analytical convenience. Representation of what, in reality, is indefinite multiplicity by three orders of cycles was the fundamental step. We now go on to postulate that each Kondratieff should contain an integral number of Juglars and each Juglar an integral number of Kitchins. The warrant for this is in the nature of the circumstances which give rise to multiplicity. If waves of innovations of shorter span play around a wave of a

---

the case is similar to those of unemployment percentage or pig-iron consumption mentioned above: variations of these cannot be great in the course of Kitchins.

similar character but of longer span, the sequence of the phases of the latter will so determine the conditions under which the former rise and break as to make a higher unit out of them, even if the innovations which create them are entirely independent of the innovations which carry the longer wave. There will be a relation between the phases of each of the two movements which will tend to keep the shorter ones within the longer span. The analogous proposition for the second and third causes of multiplicity is obvious. The fact that the units of a cyclical movement of a certain order cannot be considered as independent —any more than the individual items in any time sequence—accounts for many difficulties encountered in analysis by means of formal statistical methods.

The units which fall within a unit of the next higher order will display certain relations to one another which separate them from others, and the units of a cyclical movement of a certain order which happen to fall in the corresponding phases of successive units of a cyclical movement of next higher order will also have some characteristics in common which, in some respects, make a distinct universe of them. Moreover it follows that the sweep of each longer wave supplies neighborhoods of equilibrium for the wave of the next lower order. Since shorter waves must in most cases rise from a situation which is not a neighborhood of equilibrium but disturbed by the effects of the longer waves in progress at this time, we must now modify our previous proposition that the process of innovation starts from such neighborhoods only, as well as our concept of neighborhood of equilibrium itself. From the standpoint of the transactions which carry a fluctuation of short span, the sweep of the longer waves constitutes the long-time conditions of doing business, although full equilibrium could, even theoretically, exist only in the points in which all cycles pass their normals. This accords well with the attitude toward economic fluctuations of the business community. What the businessman sees, feels about, and takes account of are the relatively short waves. In our three-cycle schema they would be the Kitchins. Waves much longer than these he does not recognize as such, but only as good or bad times, new eras, and so on. He, therefore, acts as a rule on the conditions of a phase of longer cycles as if these conditions were permanent. This is obviously so in the case of the Kondratieff. The Juglar is an intermediate case. For every time series the sweep of any cycle is the trend of the cycles of next lower order. No hypothesis about the precise form of the relation between cycles of different order is implied in this. In particular, their effects are not simply additive, altough it may suffice for our rough purposes to assume that they are logarithmically additive. Even so, it is clear that the coincidence at any time of corresponding phases of all three cycles will always produce phenomena of unusual intensity, especially if the phases that coincide are those of prosperity or depression. The three deepest and longest "depressions" within the epoch covered by our matrial —1825–1830, 1873–1878, and 1929–1934—all display that characteristic.

As the reader sees, there is some rational justification for the two additional properties of the cyclical movement which we have now introduced. But there is no rational justification that the writer can see for assuming that the integral number of Kitchins in a Juglar or of Juglars in a Kondratieff should always be the same. Yet from the study of our time series we derive a rough impression that this is so. Barring very few cases in which difficulties arise, it is possible to count off, historically as well as statistically, six Juglars to a Kondratieff and three Kitchins to a Juglar—not as an average but in every individual case. We shall make use of this fact in our exposition, but the writer is very anxious to make it quite clear, not only that no major result depends on this, but also that no part of his theoretical schema is tied up with it. There is nothing in it to warrant expectation of any such regularity. On the contrary, the logical expectation from the fundamental idea would be irregularity; for why innovations which differ so much in period of gestation and in the time it takes to absorb them into the system should always produce cycles of respectively somewhat less than 60 years, somewhat less than 10 years, and somewhat less than 40 months, is indeed difficult to see. We state the fact of what seems to us considerable regularity,[1] deviations from which are in every case easily ac-

[1] Of course, it is largely a matter of opinion—or of tests, the validity of which is a matter of opinion—how far we should recognize that fact at all. Having made it abundantly clear that cycles are an irregular phenomenon playing in an environment disturbed by additional irregularities, the writer would feel safe against any misunderstanding of the meaning of his schema if such misunderstandings had not frequently arisen. From standards which are clearly inapplicable to material such as ours, it is, of course, easy to argue that no regularity has been proved

counted for by external disturbances, because we believe it to be a fact but not on account of any theoretical preconception in its favor. If the reader accepts that fact, he ought to record it, not for, but against the analytical schema presented. If he refuses to accept it, such disagreement will not entail any consquences beyond complicating description. It should be added, however, that our observation is in rough accord with many well-known estimates of the duration of cycles and looks as strange as it does only because we combine estimates not usually presented together.

E. Other Fluctuations.—Obviously, the waves of which we have been trying to describe the mechanism and the causes are not the only economic fluctuations. The reader need only think of seasonal fluctuations in order to satisfy himself of this. Statistical and theoretical analysis reveals the presence in our material of very many other wavelike movements. Except for the purposes of the theory of static equilibrium, the economic process ought really to be thought of as an infinitely complex composite of many synchronous waves of different nature, quite apart from the class which interests us here. One of the most important tasks of the theory of the future lies in this direction.

The business cycles with which we are concerned are really

---

either by the present or any other writer and that, in particular, our three cycles are not adequately established by the evidence to be presented later. Therefore, it may not be superfluous to insist once more on the sense in which we are going to speak of, say, the Kitchin. We mean that there are fluctuations, shorter than those of the Juglar group, but which we nevertheless believe to be of similar nature and which we think to be tolerably represented by a typical duration somewhat exceeding three years. We do not mean that they are exactly 40 months—mostly, they are shorter. Nor do we believe that that "somewhat exceeding three years" represents a mean or mode that meets any formal dispersion test. The writer thinks that any such test would not have had much sense. That is why he left the duration so little determinate. He remembers that the most valued assistant he ever had once threw up his hands in holy horror when he expressed himself satisfied, in a certain case, with a "periodicity" of 48 months as showing the presence of the "40-month cycle." He frankly admits that this sounds absurd, but what he meant was not so at all. *Traces* of fluctuations substantially longer than 1 and substantially shorter than 9 years was all he felt justified in looking for. And these he always found, though often only in rates of change.

not at all what one thinks of when using the terms Wave Fluctuation. They are the result of a process which, indeed, produces upward and downward movements in our graphs, but these movements are not analogous to the oscillation of an elastic string or membrane—which, once set into motion, would, but for friction, go on indefinitely—because they are due to the intermittent action of the "force" of innovation, by which the action of the equilibrium "force" is each time brought into play. But there are other economic fluctuations which answer more nearly to the physical analogy.

1. Before discussing a few of these, however, it is necessary to point out again that our cycles are not even alone in their own class. Very many external factors will act so as to produce a sequence of phenomena which will look in many respects similar to a unit of the cyclical process. If they occur often enough, the graphs of the time series of a world in which they are the only ones to act on an otherwise stationary process may easily present the picture of a wavelike movement, even if there were no oscillation around it. War finance affords an instance. While war demand is being financed by inflationary methods, we shall observe many of the phenomena which we associate with the prosperity phases of our cycles. When the war demand ceases and budgets are balanced again, we shall have before us most of the surface phenomena of recession and depression—with secondary waves superimposed—after which a period will follow which should display many of the characteristics of a cyclical recovery. The shifts occurring during the process in the industrial organism, first from peace to war production and then again from war to peace production, will present further analogies. Causes and effects are all different, of course, but there will be "waves" nevertheless. In fact, many authors reason on the cyclical process in a way which would be much more appropriate in the case of such war waves than it is in the case of the former. And no inconsiderable part of what to us seems faulty analysis may be due to the analogy with the *modus operandi* of external disturbance. There would, hence, be some point in working out systematically both similarities and differences, particularly with reference to the behavior of the monetary mechanisms, but we cannot stay to do this.

Another external factor which may be responsible for wavelike behavior is variation in gold production as far as due to chance or "autonomous" discovery. Since the theories which use it as a basis for the explanation of shorter cycles seem no longer to have adherents, the only question is whether the long wave can be explained by them. Such contributions to an answer as the present writer has to offer will be found in various places, especially in the historical chapters. Here, risking repetition, we will merely state first, that we are not faced with an alternative explanation, acceptance of which would imply abandonment of the explanation presented in this book and vice versa. This is obvious as regards variations in gold production that may be thought of as induced by our process, but also true of autonomous discoveries. They simply alter some of the conditions of entrepreneurial activity: it would be nothing short of absurd to say that Californian and Australian gold discoveries *called forth* railroad construction, or South African gold discoveries the "electrification" of the economic world, both of which had begun before, or that these events would have been impossible without them. Second, gold discoveries act on the system through interest rates and prices, and on interest rates wholly, on prices mainly, through the banking mechanism. Effects can, hence, never be read off directly from gold production—or variations in gold in monetary use, which is also a function of other variables than gold production—but embody the reaction of banks and their customers. But, third, prices and values will, in the long run, be different from what they would be if gold production were substantially different from what it is, provided gold plays any major role in monetary systems, although not in general to the extent one would expect on quantity-theory grounds. Many details of the picture of events will be traceable to its behavior. And since "levels" and "trends" of prices and values will also be influenced, we may in fact speak of a wave *sui generis*, due to the influence of gold, on which the waves of our process are (though not additively) superimposed.

Still more instructive is the "harvest cycle," because it is commonly spoken of as a cycle and because it has by some authors been made the basis of a theory of the (medium-length) general business cycle (W. St. Jevons and H. L. Moore). Just how harvests affect the general business situation, is less simple than we might think. In itself, the mere fact of autonomous variation of crops is more relevant to welfare than to prosperity or depression. What matters for the latter is only the influence on values and incomes which such an event will exert. There will be no great effect at all if the abnormal harvest sells for the same amount of money as a normal one would, though there will be some disturbance unless every individual household and firm spends the same amount on agrarian products which it spent before. If it sells for more or less, there will be a shift in incomes and expenditures, but in an isolated country prosperity or depression does not necessarily follow. For the prosperity or depression of the agrarian sector which does follow is compensated by conditions of opposite complexion in other sectors.

If that conclusion seems to run counter to all experience and if, in particular, everybody in this country used to expect better business from a good harvest, this is primarily due to the fact that, in most cases and especially if it coincided with poor harvests in Europe, it meant increase in value of exports, which directly acted on the system as a whole. But while chance variations in crops will exert an influence on general business situations, even apart from their effects on values of exports, this influence mainly rests on the reaction of the credit structure—meaning thereby reaction of both borrowers and lenders—and is neither so dependable nor so strong as is commonly believed. It may mitigate or accentuate depressions or prosperities and thus often help to turn the tide. But any claim that it explains the cyclical character of the economic process is disposed of by the proof that this process would display cycles of its own, even if no external fator ever acted upon it. The natural thing to do, therefore, is to recognize the recurrent fluctuations caused by fortuitious variations of crops as a special type of cycles (Special Cycles) which will superimpose themselves—again, not additively—on the cycles which are the object of this study. There is no theoretical presumption as to the relative importance of these special cycles. It varies obviously historically and geographically. At some times and in some countries they may dominate observed fluctuations. Russia to about 1900 affords an instance, though not a simple one.

It is, of course, a question of fact whether this is the only instance of a Special Cycle. If we answer in the affirmative, that only means that we do not know of any others. We have seen in the instance of building that what strongly looks like a very special movement can yet be brought within the schema of cyclical events and understood as a consequence of conditions which, in turn, can be traced to our process. The writer has not met with any case other than crops as influenced by weather in which that was impossible unless, indeed, we choose to include wars and autonomous gold discoveries.

2. We now pass on to consider fluctuations which more nearly fit the model of elastic (acoustic) waves. We have just had another instance—the mechanism of innovation being the outstanding one—of the fact that an all-pervading cycle may arise in the system from a particular or sectional cause, such as the chance variation of output in the agrarian sector. In order to produce wavelike movements, an impulse or "force" or factor need not itself act intermittently or in a wavelike fashion. One case of this sort we can visualize by means of the analogy with a vessel into'which water flows at a perfectly steady rate, but which is so constructed that it releases the water by a valve each time a certain weight has been accumulated. Saving might afford an economic instance, although we do not believe it would act in this way independently of our process which opens and shuts the valve. For an illustration of another case we will fall back on the analogy with the elastic string which, in response to a single pull, continues ever after to oscillate—in the absence of friction. This case primarily interests us here. Both cases, however, arise obviously from the properties of the system on which our "something" acts and are largely independent of the nature of the latter. Economic waves of this kind constitute a distinct class. Professor Tinbergen even goes so far as to regard them as the only type of "endogenous" waves and as the main object of exact business-cycle anaylsis. The reasons why that type of wave plays but a subordinate role in this book, are clear from the design of our model. But in studying our material we must always look out for them and we now define their relation to our cycles. We shall refer to them as Waves of Adaptation or Oscillations.

Setting aside the nice question whether an economic system can, without any particular "force" impinging upon it, work in a wavelike fashion merely by virtue of its structure, we will next notice the possibility suggested by Professor E. Slutsky, that a great number of small random shocks so acts upon a process as to give it an undulatory character (Slutsky effect). The model devised in order to display the phenomenon was this: Series consisting of purely random items, such as the last digits of the numbers drawn in Russian lotteries, were turned into series consisting of correlated items by the operation of moving summation of the nth *order,* so that in the latter "each of two adjacent items has one particular cause of its own and $n - 1$ causes in common with the other." And a strongly cyclical movement revealed itself at once, which, in the case of an unweighted 10-year moving summation, imitated the graph of Dr. Dorothy S. Thomas' quarterly index of British Business (trend eliminated) exceedingly well.

We cannot here enter into the economic, statistical and epistemological questions raised by this most interesting result. Common sense tells us that cumulation of the effects of small disturbances will often be met with in economic life, although, owing to the presence of shock absorbers in the system, this fact should not be relied on without previous exploration of the economics of each case. The possibility of undulatory movements solely due to this fact may be granted at once. But the manner in which Professor Slutsky posits the problem of application to the economic process suggests, first, that he thinks of it as a possible explanation of the business cycles of reality and, second, that he attaches some weight to the covariation of his series with that index of cycles. It is, hence, not superfluous to remark, concerning the first point, that a model of the economic process for which such explanation could be defended would have to be entirely unrealistic, and, concerning the latter point, that the elimination of trend by least squares or a method using similar assumptions will, of course, go far toward making deviations conform to the Slutsky model. Even if there is no trend to eliminate, any series undulating with sufficient regularity will be amenable to approximate reproduction from any random series, provided the period be suitably chosen. Let us assume, for argument's sake, that all our series moved in regular sines. Then the proof that these sines may be produced by cumulation of random causes, however interesting in itself, is not only no proof, but even no reason to suspect, that they are so produced. Else all sinelike processes would have to be. But that proof did two things for us: first, it removed the argument that, since our series display obvious regularities, therefore their behavior cannot result from the impact of random causes; second, it opened an avenue to an important part of the economic mechaism, which has since been explored by R. Frisch in a powerful piece of work.[1]

Cumulation of effects is as obvious a reality in many economic processes as are acceleration, self-reinforcement, multiplication. All these phenomena belong to the oldest stock in trade of the usual type of historical reporting on booms and crises—in some cases they are the whole of it. The reason why their role in the mechanism of cycles has not throughout our exposition been emphasized more strongly is simply that it seemed to be sufficiently taken care of in various ways, particularly by such concepts as the Secondary Wave and the Vicious Spiral, which must be understood to include them and to give them their proper setting and motivation.

These phenomena can, of course, be also produced by the impact of external factors, chance occurrences among them, and will, hence, reproduce part of the cyclial mehanism whenever such factors impinge on the system. There seems, however, some danger of accepting them as such for an adequate explanation of the historical cycles. It has been remarked in the first chapter that an external-factor theory of business fluctuations would by no means be obviously absurd. These external factors would then work through cumulations, accelerations, and so on, and there would be no need for them to be important in order to create important ups and downs. It is, in particular, possible to argue that if some such event has once set into motion a self-reinforcing process of prosperity, this will go on of itself—each increase in demand for, say, consumers' goods increasing the demand for equipment goods, production of which increases again consumer's purchasing power, and so on—and thereby create increasingly precarious situations, so that the longer it lasts the smaller the influence will be which is required to bring about a crash when an equally self-reinforcing depressive process will set in. The inadequacy of such explanations does not rest with the fact that in the popular and semipopular literature on individual crises, in which they primarily occur, cumulation, acceleration, and so on are little more than words loosely connected with sur-

[1] R. Frisch, Propagation and Impulse Problems, Economic Essays in Honour of G. Cassel, Sec. 5: Erratic shocks as a source of energy in maintaining oscillations. Although he quotes both Wicksell's and Slutsky's work as a starting point, his argument is really quite a different one. Witness his concept of Changing Harmonics.

face observations lacking in precision. It is, no doubt, possible to put up a better showing. Against this we urge, first, that in order to establish such a theory *as a fundamental explanation* satisfactory in logic, it would be necessary to show that, by means of the elements comprised under the heading self-reinforcement, a small disturbance could create a cycle from a strictly stationary process in which all the steadying forces and mechanisms of the system are perfectly intact and the burning cigarette falls upon moist grass. Failure successfully to meet this test, throws the theory back upon big disturbances, such as wars or serious social unrest or sudden changes in monetary or commercial policy, about which there cannot be any difference of opinion. Refusal to meet this test, on the ground that actual states are never stationary, amounts to evading the point at issue.[1] Second, we urge again, as we did when discussing the Vicious Spiral, that historically there never was a case in which any wave would have had to be explained like this. The proposition itself that small disturbances may induce larger one is not entirely invalidated by these considerations.

3. The simplest case of Waves of Adaptation or Oscillation may be illustrated by any individual price which happens to be out of equilibrium. Even if no further disturbance occurs, we do not observe that it at once assumes its equilibrium value or that it makes straight for that value and stops there. As a rule, it will miss it or outrun it and turn back again. Most of our series will behave like this. Sometimes there are technical reasons for it. On the stock exchange, for instance, bulls and bears will from time to time consolidate their positions and cover before they go on. But this is not necessary. The graphs of our weekly, or

[1] In one case, such a refusal would have to be accepted, although this would but open the door on a long discussion of principle. The refusal can be based on the denial of the existence of any equilibrium tendency or equilibrating mechanism or conservative forces in the system, the equations of which would then have no stationary solution at all. This would imply a picture of economic reality altogether different from the one we have been trying to draw throughout. Since both, however, are nothing but analytic schemata, choice between them, as far as not due to extrascientific preference, would have to turn on results. In a system that always reacts, and reacts to reaction, exclusively by acceleration until it meets catastrophe or, at the low point, an upward pull, explanation of fluctuations would indeed be easy. It would, in fact, be superfluous.

even monthly, series reveal oscillations of this nature by the sawtooth-like contour of their larger movements. We might call them Hesitations. If the change to which a series responds in this way has not originated in it, but in another series we speak of Vibrations.

Hesitations and vibrations are part and parcel of the cyclical mechanism, although in this book, which cannot adequately deal with anything except principles and the broadest of contours of facts, they will not show up as they should. But again, they are not confined to specifically cyclical disturbances. Any disturbance, whatever its nature, will produce them. The surface similarly between our cycles and other fluctuations will be intensified thereby and all the oscillations they start will interfere with each other. The same is true of those waves of adaptation which may result from the introduction of lags, or lags and time derivatives, or of the influence of past and (expected) future values of our variables. Cases in which, say, the quantity of a commodity —as, for instance, in the cases which give rise to the spider-web problem—adapts itself with a lag or in which lags or velocities of adaptation differ in different parts of the system, thus creating intermediate situations which may be reacted to in such a manner that wave-like movements will ensue, have been met in Chap. II. Their occurrence is perfectly easy to understand on obvious common-sense considerations. Their exact theory, a most important and hopeful contribution to the general theory of prices, is, with the exception of a few instances, beyond the scope of this book. However much light it sheds on details of the mechanism both of the cyclical process and of other disturbances, it has to be coupled with other propositions in order to make of it a theory of the cyclical process. Unless this be done, that apparatus is compatible with any explanation and renders the same kind of service to each.

4. A few other matters may conveniently be disposed of here. *Replacement of industrial equipment* has been linked sporadically with business cycles ever since Marx's time, some authors coming near to making it the central element of causation. Into our analysis replacement enters in two ways. First, cyclical situations are not a matter of indifference for the decision to replace. Replacement becomes necessary, either because of wear and tear or because of obsolescence. Obsolete or obsolescent machinery is not typically replaced in properities. We find, rather, that the

intense competition of the recession and depression periods will, with a qualification for the prostration and paralysis of deep depression, in general force firms to install the newest available types. The reverse, however, holds true, if we may trust the incomplete information we have, for the replacement of machinery that is wearing out. There is no doubt, for instance, that the American and the English cotton-textile industries renew their equipment when business is brisk, although there is some doubt as to the interpretation of this fact. The life of a building or a machine is, of course, not a purely technological, but an economic, variable. Barring obsolescence, it is rationally determined by the point of time from which the unit of product can be produced more cheaply by installing a new machine than by keeping the old one, and therefore a function of many quantities, actual and expected, rate of interest included. These quantities fluctuate cyclically and, particularly if the technolgical superiority of a new machine varies with the degree of utilization and if the price of the machine is inflexible, replacement may often figure out more advantageously in prosperity than in recession. But such considerations are hardly relevant, since in any case the lifetime of the average machine is very much longer than any but the longest cycles. Most of the common textile machinery remains fully efficient for from 30 to 40 years—mules that have been well treated, even longer than that. Such statistics as we have do not, in fact, encourage a belief that either those or other rational considerations play a dominant role in the decision to replace, and in old-established industries with a (substantially) stationary technique, a considerable percentage of the machinery in use at any time is of greater age than experts' standards seem to justify. That fact is beyond doubt, perhaps as the simple consequence of the other fact that, when prices fall, people are quite naively and a-rationally discouraged and so have to make up for deferred replacement when things look better again. This is not an important item in the list of secondary phenomena, but, of course, it presupposes the existence of acyclical movement. Not even the theory of the "lower turning point" can safely be based upon it; for the situation is in practice never such that it would at a given time become necessary, under penalty of breakdown, to replace. It is, as we have seen before, only when recovery has set in for other reasons that this demand for equipment goods revives.

Second, there will be genuine replacement waves if the age distribution of an industry's equipment clusters around certain values. This will have to be explained in each individual case and cannot be appealed to *in abstracto* as an independent cause of fluctuations. But as a rule such reasons are not difficult to find. External factors will often supply them. If, for instance, the equipment of a district has been destroyed by an earthquake, and replaced in, say, the subsequent two or three years, we can, at the expense of assuming that the lifetimes of all elements are actually replaced thereafter, derive what will look like an ideally regular wave rolling on forever. But it is clear how unreasonable such assumptions would be. Bulges of decreasing amplitude will, however, in most cases persist, and influence the behavior of our time series, for a while. Now our model supplies us with an "endogenous" instance: when innovators have ridden to success in some branch of industry and the new combination is spreading, we shall readily understand that new machinery will be installed in this and in complementary branches, often also in others, owing to the impulse imparted to business in general, at a velocity which will in fact produce the required (skew-bell-shaped) age distribution. This is part of our mechanism and contingent upon its working. But it is no new or independent cause of fluctuations, least of all of permanent ones: the effect will, as regards specialized machinery, tend to vanish from diffusion (different firms replacing at different times, some not replacing at all) though successive innovations in different fields will tend to keep it alive in the higher stages of nonspecialized semifinished metal products.

Wavelike bulges in the output of equipment and construction industries, for use in the explanation of ups and downs, have been derived in many other ways, one of which should be noticed. In its crudest form the argument may be put like this: let us assume, to bring out the essential point, that an industry uses one million units of a certain strictly homogeneous type of machinery which we will baptize *hobby horse* and which lives exactly 10 years, not more nor less. These hobby horses have been evenly installed—at a constant rate of 100,000 hobby horses a year—the industry using, and also the industry furnishing, the hobby horses has reached perfect equilibrium—100,000 hobby horses being produced and sold for replacement each year. This schema would not be substantially affected if we assumed further expansion at a constant rate known to all firms. But instead we assume now that "something" permanently but suddenly raises the demand for the product by 10 per cent. If hobby horses have been previously utilized to optimum point, 10 per cent more of them will be demanded now. Producers will, therefore, sell 200,000 hobby horses, say, next year; but after that demand will again drop to the 100,000 necessary for replacement until the new ones will themselves have to be replaced, when another bulge will show. Those producers are supposed to have doubled their capacity, and the firms in the higher stages above the hobby-horse producers, to have expanded correspondingly—this is the intensification or multiplication of effects—and the consequences are obvious.

Nobody, of course, has ever presented this argument in so grotesque a form, but reasoning not far removed from it keeps on turning up. It is, therefore, worth while to stay in order to realize the absurdity of it. "Something" is not an admissible cause. If it be made more concrete, it will be seen that such sudden jerks are not likely to occur except in consequence of innovation, and if the increase be *not* sudden many of the consequences will fail to follow for this reason alone. But even if demand for the product increase suddenly, it does not follow that the producing firms will promptly demand proportionally more hobby horses. In practice, there will be the buffer of excess capacity. Even if perfect equilibrium of perfect competition should have prevailed, they will not all act equally promptly and in the same way—some, for instance, overworking their hobby horses or using them beyond their ususal lifetime for the rigid lifetime is, of course, a most unrealistic assumption). Granting, however, that they all order 1 per cent more hobby horses, this will not necessarily induce the manufacturers of the latter to increase plant capacity all at once to the full amount. They may equally well raise their prices or add to their unfilled orders. Owing to the presence of buffers at every step of the process and also to normal foresight, the impact, instead of gathering force at every step, will tend to spend itself. If it does not, this is no verification of the argument but merely a proof that there is another process at work. The neglect of all equilibrating influences amounts in this, as it does in all similar cases, to theoretical fault.

But what should be stressed more than this is the lack of

realism displayed by the argument under discussion. No attempt at technical improvement—for instance, insertion of a considerable lag between the effect of the new expenditure for investment goods on the prices of consumers' goods and the effect of the consequent increase in the supply of investment goods—can do away with the fact that a picture of business behavior is being drawn, not from reality, but from the needs of the theorist. Moreover, there is no reason to believe that any such bulges would be sufficiently synchronized to matter. But again it must be observed that this criticism applies only if that argument is to stand by itself as a major contribution to the explanation of cycles. It is not denied that hobby-horse manufacturers, or some of them, may thus foolishly behave and that they are most likely to do so in the atmosphere of prosperity which, however, would then have to be independently explained.

Chapter V

TIME SERIES AND THEIR NORMAL

A. Introduction.—In this chapter we will assemble into one connected argument what for our purpose it seems necessary to say on questions of principle concerning statistical method. This is indeed but little.[1] No exposition of technique can be attempted here and the reader unfamiliar with usual procedure should turn to some treatise on the subject. The problem of the elimination of seasoned variations remains excluded. Our discussion thus reduces to analysis of time series which reflect economic growth and the cyclical process of evolution as distorted by the influence of external factors.

In order to put into relief the nature of time series and of the statistical problem they present, we will distinguish three types of variables, which we shall call *theoretical, random* or *stochastic,* and *historical variables.* If we have before us a system, *i.e.,* a set of quantities between which certain relations are known to exist, we may investigate these relations by allowing those quantities to vary "virtually." As a result we get theoretical "laws" with which to operate. Time, if it enters at all, has no reference to any particular date and serves only as one of the coordinates. The

[1] [Even so, I have cut this chapter heavily.—Ed.]

theoretical law, once established, is raised above the sphere of the actual findings from which it was gleaned, by the decision to rely on it until further notice. Of course, every law in this sense is relative to the general properties of the system. A variable thus related by a "law" to one or more or all variables within the general conditions of a system, we call a *theoretical variable.* Any quantity occurring in a proposition of classical mechanics will illustrate this. An economic instance of such a variable is the quantity of a commodity that is effectively demanded within a Walrasian world.

The logical counterpart of a theoretical is a stochastic variable. It is not defined by a functional relation, known or supposed to be known, to another variable. On the contrary, the absence of any such relation is its outstanding characteristic. We do not "Understand" its variations in the sense in which we "understand" the variations of a theoretical variable; they are mere experimental or observational facts. Instead, we note the relative frequency of the occurrence of different values of a quantity in the course of experiments or observations carried out under conditions under which a theoretical variable would display a constant value. We may think of those experiments as consisting of sets of drawings from an urn known to contain black and white balls in unchanging proportions, and base upon them certain measurements and (whatever the logic of this may be) mathematical expectations, everything in fact that centers around the unfortunate term Probability or the less objectionable one, Limiting value of Relative Frequency. It is the prerequisite of all reasoning about random variables that their values, actual and possible, should constitute a *universe* in the technical sense, and that we are on safe ground only when moving within the walls of this severely restrictive condition.

As soon as we step out of the world of thoretical schemata and try to link to actual fact any of the theoretical relations that hold within them, we get hybrid variables which are neither theoretical nor random but borrow characteristics from both categories. If, in particular, we wish to derive a form of some theoretical function more concrete than that which theory supplies —say, of a Marshallian demand function—we face all the difficulties of distinguishing between both classes of characteristics and the danger of being entirely misled by our inability to do so. Disregarding this, however, we may illustrate the difference between theoretic and stochastic variables and their simultaneous presence in the actual material as follows: suppose we know that a given set of price-quantity data represents a Marshallian demand curve which is ideally invariant in the interval of time covered by those data. Then, to every quantity within the interval corresponds one single "true" price which is a theoretical variable. Now, let the observations of the prices be subject to small random errors. We shall get either several price quotations for each quantity or else single quotations which deviate to an unknown extent from their "true" value. Each quotation, taken by itself, is therefore a stochastic variable and may be looked upon as an observation in the technical sense. If there are several prices to one quantity, they are all observations of the same thing, form (a sample of) a universe, and may be said to represent fragments of a frequency distribution. But obviously the whole set of prices cannot be so interpreted. In the graph of all of them the theoretical variation asserts itself. However, since in our case we know that the theoretical law is invariant we may be able to find it from the material by purely statistical methods;[1] but it is that knowledge and not the statistical logic per se that enables us to do so.

A historic variable is, in one sense, precisely that kind of hybrid. But it differs from the case just discussed by the fact that its theoretical law is in a process of change. We assume for simplicity's sake that the frequency distribution about each "true" point remains invariant. Let us start with an economy in perfect Walrasian equilibrium and fasten upon the price of any commodity the quality of which is to remain strictly the same. This price is, as everything else, at Theoretical Normal (now in the sense defined in the second chapter) and any variations we observe in quotations would (unless we allow small variations in quantity, which we do not just now) be due only to errors of observation or small chance events which can be treated as if they were errors of observation. Hence, it would reveal nothing except a frequency distribution. Let the system embark upon

[1] Success will in this case depend on the "law of the movement" being sufficiently obvious for us to be able to hit it by the formula we choose. [The case reduces] to the schema of shots being fired at a target moving according to an unknown law. If the demand curve shifts, then the analogy would be with shots fired at a target moving according to an unknown law that changes in an unknown way.

a prosperity excursion under entrepreneurial impulse. Both price and quantity of our commodity will change now, but the new values they assume cannot be directly used for the derivation of its (Marshallian) demand curve, because they do not lie either on the original or any other single demand curve, but successively on different ones—which it is usual, though not quite correct, to express by saying that the demand curve shifts. The old Theoretical Normal has been destroyed without being replaced by another. We may, indeed, imagine that every price-quantity pair lies on a temporary demand curve, and interpret its values as the result of two components: a movement of, and a movement along, a demand curve. But, in general, we cannot distinguish between the two without further information or hypotheses.

This situation lasts throughout the cycle and until a new equilibrium is reached. Then we shall have again a Theoretical Normal as before, but a different one: price and quantity of our commodity will then be adapted to the conditions of a new Walrasian world in which new equilibrium values result from, and may vary along new demand, supply, cost functions, and so on. This property of belonging at different times to different systems, or of representing different Theoretical Normals, is the outstanding fact about historic variables which determines their nature. Among other things, it is that fact and that fact alone which brings in the axis of *historic* time and makes the actual dates of those variables or their actual location on that axis essential to their very meaning. Without it, dates would be irrelevant, and arraying items according to their dates would be nothing but a very inconvenient and unenlightening mode of presentation. Hence we may, for our purpose, define a historic variable as a variable, the Stochastic Normal of which changes owing to a change of its Theoretical Norm.[1] A sequence of values of such a variable we call a *time sequence* or, slightly incorrectly, *series*. We may now also adopt the usual definition,

[1] The writer, having been told that the above is liable to be misunderstood, wishes to add an explanation, though he does not himself see the necessity of it. We assume that nothing disturbs the economic process except cyclical evolution in our sense. We observe a variable in two successive states of ideal Walrasian equilibrium, *A* and *B*. Its value is constant at equilibrium amount in *A* and in *B*, though differing as between *A* and *B*. In both cases we are supposed to be able to make many observations which are subject to errors of measurement and form

which would not, taken by itself, convey our meaning: a sequence of values of a variable arrayed according to consecutive dates of occurrence.

Now, the only thing that is universally true about time series is that they do not fulfill probability requirements. We have to add that, since the evolutionary process reflected in every time series goes on in distinct cyclical units, the individual items within each unit are not independent of each other. Neither, strictly speaking, are the cycles themselves independent; but we may overlook this in a first approximation and make them our observational units. This, however, reduces the number of our observations to a dangerous degree. The fact is that only for what we have called the Kitchins our material covers a number of units at all sufficient for statistical treatment and the value even of this is much impaired by the possibility of systematic change during all that time. For most series, available Juglars are few. For no series are they "many" in the technical sense: from 12 to 14 are all we have, in the most favorable cases, for prewar times. And of Kondratieffs we have, up to 1914, a little more than 2¼. If, finally, we recall the external and internal irregularities to which our process is subject, we have before us the nature of the statistical task involved in Time-series Analysis.

That heading commonly denotes two problems. First, the problem of splitting up any individual time series into the components present in it. As a matter of common sense, we look upon it as a composite which we naturally would like to decompose by formal methods, *i.e.*, methods which involve as little theory as possible, because one of our main objects in doing so is precisely to confront results with theoretical propositions. Second, the problem of "correlation" of different time series with each other. Again as a matter of common sense, we look

---

in both the same frequency distribution, say a symmetrical one. This distribution, of course, could change, but is for simplicity's sake assumed not to do so. By the Statistical Normal which does change we, of course, do not mean the function descriptive of the distribution but the values of the variable which in A and in *B* would turn out to be the "true" ones in the sense of the theory of errors of observation. Under our assumptions, these coincide with the values that are theoretically normal ones, and the reason why they are different as between *A* and *B* is that the theoretical or equilibrium value of the variable in *A* has been changed into the equlibrium value of the same variable in *B* by the process of the evolution.

upon each series as one element of what we feel to be a process, which it is no less natural to try to explore by putting our time series in such a shape that they will display the relations between variations of economic quantities peculiar to that process. It is again very understandable that we should wish these relations to be derived by formal methods so as to make them as independent as possible of theories. But as we have seen before from other standpoints, so we see now from the standpoint of statistical theory that neither problem is amenable to solution by formal methods or, indeed, has any sense if stated in terms of formal methods.

It is important for the reader to grasp clearly what that means and what it does not mean. Of course it is a well-known proposition that any material can be split into components—say of the sine-cosine type—in an infinite number of ways and that even if the constants of the function that is to represent it are subject to restrictions sufficient to make the problem determinate, such as are implied in the Fourier analysis, no amount of closeness of fit proves in itself that the individual components have any meaning in the sense that distinct phenomena correspond to them. Therefore, there is, in a formal sense and in the absence of further information, no logical meaning to the question what components are "present" in any given material, and even periodicity that seems to stand out visually, as well as obvious absence of periodicity, may prove very misleading. Not only is it, for example, possible to approximate, to any desired degree, a straight line by a Fourier series, but a straight line may really be the resultant of two sine movements of equal period and amplitude and opposite phase. But our analysis leads us much beyond these and similarly familiar arguments. By formal methods we understand here methods deriving from, and making use of, probability schemata: and our point is that these schemata become, in strict logic, inapplicable under the conditions which give rise to time series as defined, and that application of methods based upon them may hence give spurious results. We must introduce further information or postulates in order to make them work at all. But even then they may work faultily. Hence, they cannot be relied on to discover and isolate any components and for this reason alone, even if there were no others, would also fail to solve the second problem of time-series analysis.

We do not however go so far as to say that they must work

faultily and can never turn out results that are at least justifiable in the first approximation. To clear the ground in order to make room for judicious use of them, at least in some classes of cases, is on the contrary one of the objects of the above analysis, as it was one of the objects of many of the arrangements decided on in the fourth chapter. We have, for instance, so chosen our three cycles as to make them significantly differ in period. This will open the door to several methods that would otherwise be excluded. Moreover, we have stressed that virtue of the three-cycle schema which consists in making it less absurd than it otherwise would be to assure approximate equality of periods for each class of cycles. This does not amount to justification, to be sure, and even if it did, would not suffice to render application of either Fourier or Schuster analysis plain sailing, but it certainly makes matters easier for both.[1] We have also pointed out, that each of our "higher" cycles may be plausibly assumed to span an integral number of the next lower ones. As the Fourier analysis consists of a fundamental term and its harmonics, this removes one of the difficulties its application encounters. In a sense, the mere fact that our analysis of the business cycle shows essential sameness of the process all along, both in nature and symptoms, goes some way toward discouraging that extreme scepticism which, at first sight, might seem to follow from the above considerations: to us, therefore, it does not seem correct to say that statisticians have, in their time-series analyses, been completely stepping on clouds.

[1] Be it repeated again: there is no connection between our theory of the cyclical process of evolution and that assumption. However, if it were too wide from the facts, the Fourier method would become impossible, and so would the periodogram method. Hence, it is not superfluous to emphasize that the argument, "it is one of the very characteristics of business cycles that their length varies greatly even over short periods" (comment by Dr. Tintner on above passage), is not as convincing as it seems, as soon as we give up the single-cycle hypothesis. In this connection arises the question whether suitable reforms in both the practice and the theory of those methods might not improve their value. One example may suffice. We sometimes observe that while the ordinates of the periodogram nowhere reach heights significant within the meaning of the usual tests, there is a tendency for relatively high ones to cluster together. The writer speaks with diffidence on a matter which belongs to the realm of the specialist in statistical method. But it seems to him, that these clusters are not without significance and should be taken notice of, independently of mere height.

The fundamental indictment, however, remains. We may express it in a nutshell by saying that statistical methods are not general in the sense in which our logic is and that, outside of the range of probability schemata, they must grow out of the theory of the patterns to which they are to apply. From knowledge about the phenomena to be handled, which is of course basically empirical but at the same time a priori with reference to each individual task in hand, we must try to form an idea about the properties of statistical contours and to devise statistical procedure appropriate to expressing those properties. This requirement we call the Principle of Economic Meaning. The whole of the argument of this book may be looked upon as an attempt to provide material with which to satisfy it.

B. Trend.—The strong impression which all but compels us to distinguish trends and cycles may be embodied in quite noncommittal definitions. We may say that a series displays a *trend* if it is possible to divide the whole time interval covered by it into subintervals such that the mean values of the time integrals over these subintervals are monotonically increasing or decreasing in function of time, or that they display recurrence of the same figures once only. By the term *cycle* we designate the fact, that a given series corrected for seasonal displays recurrence of values either in its items or in its first or higher time derivatives more than once. Inasmuch as these fluctuations do not occur independently in individual series but display either instantaneous or lagged association with fluctuations in others, we may define the concept of cycle so as to cover this additional fact. Series which do not display such cycles we call Clean Trend Series; series which do not display a trend in the sense defined, Clean Cyclical Series. As these purely formal definitions do not involve any restriction as to the length of the interval to be studied, there are, of course, instances of both. For those intervals, however, which we consider in this book there are no instances of clean trend series, and only two major ones of clean cyclical series: unemployment percentage and interest rate.

C. A Single Cyclical Movement.—We return to the principle of economic meaning and our definition of time series. In order to facilitate exposition, we will in this section assume not only that seasonal variation and growth (in our sense) are absent or have been successfully eliminated, but also that the process of economic evolution embodied in our model works in such a way as to produce one cyclical movement only. Of course, these assumptions already constitute "additional knowledge." We know, further, the nature of the process that any time series fulfilling those requirements would reflect. Each item of such a series indicates, in a way appropriate to the nature of the element represented by the series, a stage in that process which, as we know, sometimes propels the system away from, and at other times draws the system toward, a neighborhood of equilibrium. It follows, even without formal proof, that there must exist on the graph discrete points or, slightly more realistically, discrete intervals in which the series passes through neighborhoods of equilibrium or comes, at all events, as near to such neighborhoods as it will go and as its inactivity, rigidity, or sloppiness allows. This is a fact of fundamental importance for us. It supplies the link between what we have called the Theoretical Normal and its statistical shadow, the Statistical Normal. This term, as we shall henceforth use it, has nothing to do with frequency distributions. Its meaning is analogous to what the business services mean when they say that business is above or below normal. In fact, what we are trying to do is merely to offer a more precise definition and a somewhat different interpretation of this very idea, so familiar to business practice.

To locate the points on our graphs which correspond to points of equilibrium, or the intervals on our graphs which correspond to neighborhoods of equilibrium, therefore, is from our standpoint the first and foremost task of time-series analysis. For the state of the economic system in those neighborhoods sums up and presents, however roughly, the net result of the preceding spurts of evolution as shaped and absorbed by the response of the system. They mark the path of economic evolution as steppingstones mark the path across a brook. They are the most relevant items of a series most pregnant with information and most important as reference points for the rest. A line or curve through those points, or a band or narrow zone through those neighborhoods, supplies a trend that really has economic significance. We shall use the term primarily in this sense. We know from the analysis in the second and fourth chapters that this trend does not describe a phenomenon distinct from the cycle. On the contrary, since evolution is essentially a process which moves in cycles, the trend is nothing but the result of the cyclical process or a property of it. In order to express this, we will call our trend the trend of results or Result Trend. Moreover, we also know that it carries realistic meaning only in discrete points or intervals. If we connect them by straight lines or fit a smooth curve to them, it must be borne in mind that the stretches between the neighborhoods are nothing but a visual help and devoid of realistic meaning. No facts correspond to them. Real is only the cycle itself.

Just as statement of the problem was possible only from the economics of the case, so methods for its solution canot be derived from anything else: they are but a translation into statistical tools of such information as we may be able to command. Historical information about each individual case is the only means by which to reduce to bearable proportions the influence of external factors, and study and discussion of each situation which seems to have some claim to being called a neighborhood of equilibrium and unavoidably rough estimates will be the surest way to reliable results, at least for some time to come. It is this method on which the writer has chiefly relied and it is in order to illustrate principles rather than for the sake of the use we make in our work on time series that we now attack the question of the purely statistical procedure.

In the case of two-phase cycles solution would be easy. First, we should have to estabilsh the fact that a given cycle displays two phases only, and to make sure that the points between cycles are really normal and not freakish—for there could obviously be cases in which some or all symptoms outrun equilibrium, but rebound so quickly that there is practically no depression and consequently no recovery. Second, having satisfied ourselves on those points, all we have to do is to mark the highest or the lowest points, as the case may be, according to the nature of each series. A smooth curve connecting those points will then give the trends which in this case do not go through the material but trace lines bordering on it in certain places and deviating from it in others. Of course, external factors must be expected to produce at least dents—but, as a rule, fluctuations also—which will upset the cyclical schema unless historically diagnosed. That they deflect the whole series for good must be recognized. What we get is, hence, never a trend produced by the cyclical process alone, but by the cyclical process as distorted by external factors.

In the case of a four-phase cycle the problem and the principle of its solution are the same, but practical difficulties arise. The price level, for instance, would in strict theory rise both in prosperity and recovery and fall both in recession and depression. But even if in fact it always behaved like this, the neighborhood of equilibrium might still lie anywhere between the peaks and troughs and there is obviously no prima-facie warrant for assuming that it should lie, for example, midway. Hence, our only hope of identifying neighborhoods from time series themselves reduces to the possibility that their graphs display some characteristic behavior in or around those neighborhoods. This might, of course, consist simply in their assuming a particular numerical value, which, however, is obviously out of the question. But equilibrium positions might also be betrayed by more general properties of the graph. Consideration of this opening imposes on us, it is true, a big toll at the outset. For unless we rest content with a visual impression, we will first have to perform a smoothing operation in order to get rid of oscillations, vibrations, hesitations, and also of some of the effects of some of the external factors. As soon, however, as this toll is paid, we reap all the advantages incident to being able to deal with differential properties of the smooth courve only, *i.e.*, with rates of change at every point.

D. Many Simultaneous Waves. The above analysis only served to lead up to the really relevant case of a complex cyclical movement. We will, for the sake of simplicity, let it consist of our Kondratieffs, Juglars, and Kitchins only, and disregard all the other types of fluctuations noticed in sec. E of the preceding chapter. Since we have nothing to add to what was previously said about effects of external disturbances and the possibility of eliminating them, it will also be convenient to assume their absence as well as absence of Seasonals and Growth. Although, of course, we do not, as a matter of principle, postulate either internal regularity or sine form, there is some use in presenting (Chart I) the graph of the sum of three sine curves the amplitudes of which are proportional to their duration and (Chart II) the graph of the first differences of the composite curve. There is, however, no trend: the cyclical movements represented are, in our terminology, "clean." Barring this, we may look upon the charts as an illustration of all the boldest assumptions which it is possible, and to some extent permissible, to make in order to simplify description and to construct an ideal schema with which to compare observations. In particular, all cycles have four phases of equal length, amplitudes of plus and minus excursions are equal and constant, periods are also constant, and each of the two higher cycles consists of an integral and constant number of units of the next lower movement. For the stranger to statistical technique the fact alone that extreme regularity of but three components may result in so very irregular-looking a composite should be instructive.

Many methods which would be available for the analysis of such a composite and are not, in strict logic, applicable to the economic time series we meet with in practice, may yet produce results which historical analysis permits us to accept as approximations. This fact again suggests that our material satisfies certain conditions of regularity, in particular those required by the Fourier and the Schuster analysis, more nearly than we should expect on theoretical grounds. It also gives additional importance, for our field, to an elegant method due to Dr. N. S. Georgescu, although it consists in fitting sine curves according to a probability test—the most probable values of the unknown periods of a known number of sinelike fluctuations being found under the assumption that "errors" are distributed according to the Gaussian law.[1] And the same fact also lends some support to quite primitive methods of proceeding by inspection—simply counting off what we see—or by means of average periods that hardly ever get very seriously out of step with observations except in cases which we may reasonably explain on the score of external disturbance. The success which Mr. Kitchin (Cycles and Trends in Economic Factors, quoted above) undoubtedly achieved simply by counting off his short cycles, observing that two or three of them seem to form higher units and that there is a sort of ground swell below both, illustrates the point very well.

[1] See Académie des Sciences, séance du 7 juillet, 1930, Sur un problème de calcul des probabilités avec application à la recherche des périodes inconnues d'un phénomène cyclique. Note de M. N.S. Georgescu, présenté par M. Émile Borel, which gives the fundamental idea.

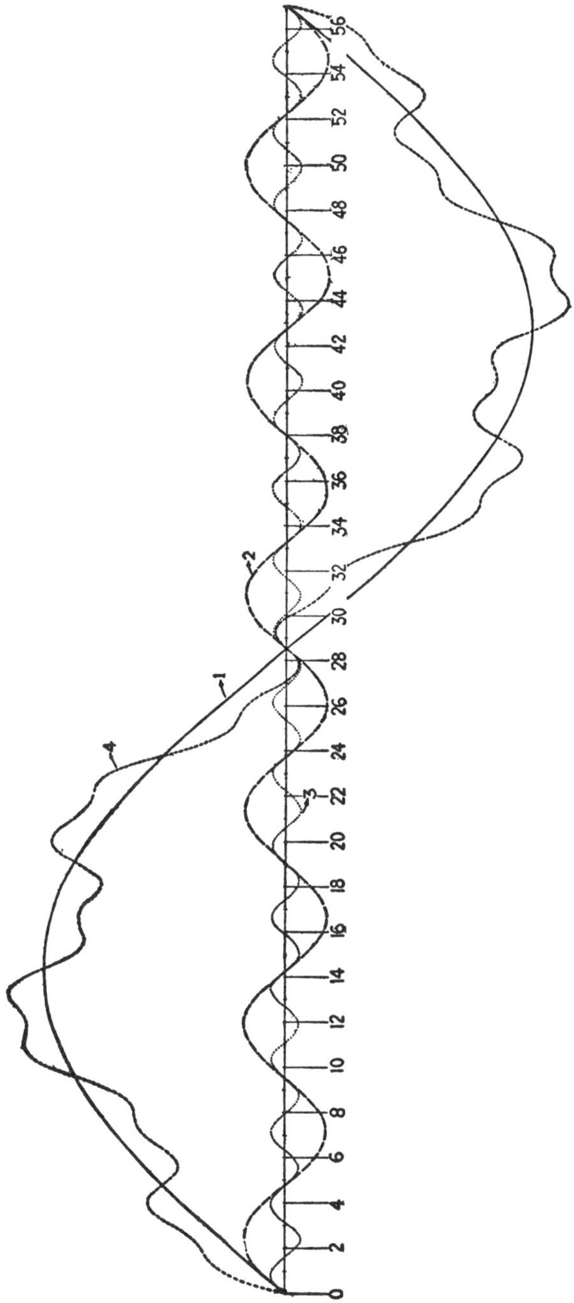

CHART I.—Curve 1, long cycle; curve 2, intermediate cycle; curve 3, short cycle; sum of 1–3.

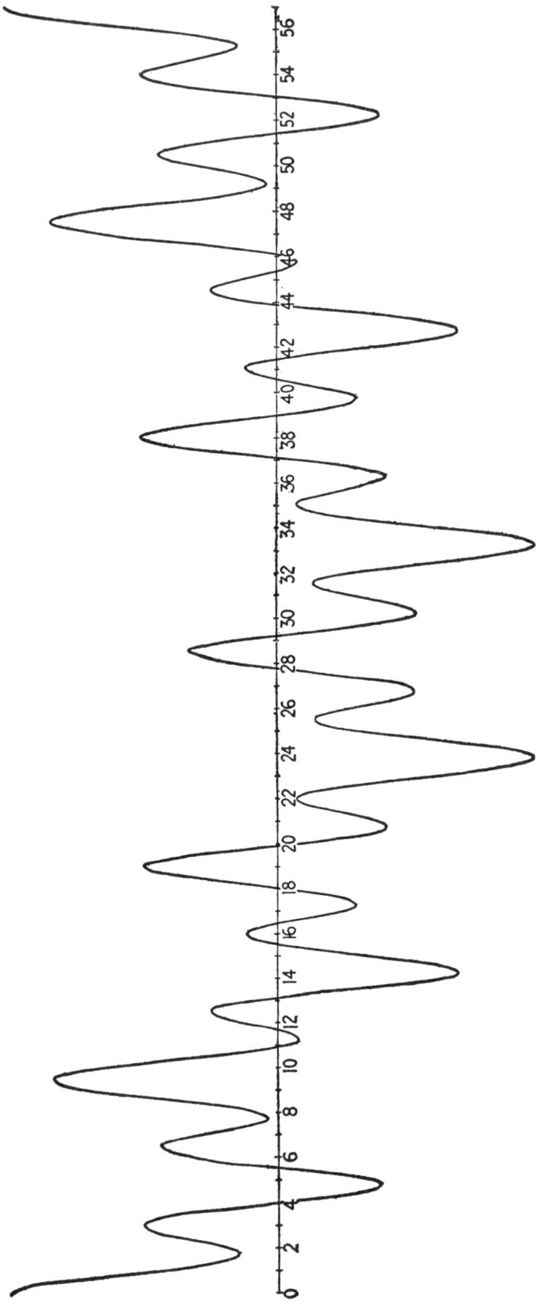
0
2
4
6
8
10
12
14
16
18
20
22
24
26
28
30
32
34
36
38
40
42
44
46
48
50
52
54
56

CHART II.

Chapter VI

HISTORICAL OUTLINES.
I. INTRODUCTION; 1786-1842

A. The Fundamental Importance of the Historical Approach to the Problems of the Cyclical Process of Evolution.—The importance of such an approach has been emphasized from the outset. Since what we are trying to understand is economic change in historic time, there is little exaggeration in saying that the ultimate goal is simply a reasoned history, not of crises only, nor of cycles or waves, but of the economic process in all its aspects and bearings to which theory merely supplies some tools and schemata, and statistics merely part of the material. Only detailed historic knowledge can definitively answer most of the questions of individual causation and mechanism; without it the study of time series must remain inconclusive, and theoretical analysis empty. Contemporaneous facts or even historic facts covering the last quarter or half of a century are perfectly inadequate. For no phenomenon of an essentially historic nature can be expected to reveal itself unless it is studied over a long interval. An intensive study of the process in the last quarter of the seventeenth and in the eighteenth century is hence a most urgent task, for a quantitaive and carefully dated account of a period of 250 years may be called the minimum of existence of the student of business cycles.

Of course, this is being increasingly realized. Histories of "crises" and detailed descriptions of individual crises have been written from the beginning of the nineteenth century. That literature is richer than appears at first sight because it includes all the descriptions of particular aspects, as well as those written from particular standpoints—notably, most of the attempts to analyze the working of the monetary mechanism and of speculation, with both of which the phenomenon of crises has been linked up from the first. But that is not what we mean. Since the development generated by the economic system is "cyclical" by nature, the task to be accomplished grows far beyond mere description of spectacular breakdowns, on the one hand, and of the behavior of aggregative quantities, on the other, into the formidable one of describing in detail the industrial processes behind them. Historians of crises primarily talk about stock exchange events, banking, price level, failures, unemployment, total production, and so on—all of which are readily recognized as surface phenomena or as compounds which sum up underlying processes in such a way as to hide their real features. Hence, the value of that kind of historical work is not only impaired by the fact that much of it is not up to minimum requirements of scholarship, but also by the still more important fact that, except incidentally, it did not touch upon the essential things at all. The same objection applies to more recent attempts, very meritorious in themselves, to follow up changing business situations year by year so as to supply us with business annals.

What we really need we are more likely to find in general economic histories: they bring us much nearer to the process which produces the waves we observe in our time series. But much more important are the innumerable monographs on individual industries. Although not aiming at our range of problems and withholding, almost tantalizingly sometimes, the information and the exact dating required for our purpose, they indicate how an industry arises, how it is absorbed into the economic organism, how it affects that organism and how it is reacted upon, and what its cyclical behavior is. In fact, they largely agree in what they consider relevant or interesting, and a general schema could readily be sketched which would fit the large majority of them and could easily be improved upon. Coordination and systemization of this kind of work would be extremely useful and is perhaps not too much to hope for. Furthermore, we have an increasing number of monographs on individual concerns and entrepreneurs, jubilee volumes, biographies, and so on which, whatever their shortcomings, are a storehouse of relevant material. The growing interest in the genealogy of nonaristocratic families opens up further possibilities. Additional raw material for the annals of the future is, of course, in the archives of banks and concerns, trade associations, public departments that have to do with industrial questions, and also in the information to be derived from the daily and weekly press and from trade journals. The history of technology, of trade routes, of individual towns and industrial districts gives in some instances even now what we want.

Compared with this vast program, the following comments or sketches, though the result of more labor than a first impression would indicate, are of course pitifully inadequate. What can be presented are mere illustrations and indications which it is hoped will go some way toward filling the bloodless theoretical schemata and statistical countour lines with live fact and toward making our meaning clearer and more vivid. But even the urgent task of locating cycles historically has been not more than broached. Moreover, no satisfactory history of capitalism can be written without taking account of Dutch and Italian "origins" and of the later developments in France. Yet it has not only proved impossible to present Dutch, Italian, and French material, but the writer has also been unable to work it up for himself beyond the most common general treatises and the most outstanding monographs. Finally, American, English, and German economic history has been more intensively analyzed only from about 1780 on, and even in this restricted field there are many lacunae, not only in the following exposition, but also in the knowledge of its author. Details, although the core of the matter is precisely in the details, can come in only by way of example and in order to teach application of our theoretical schema.

B. Questions of Principle.—A few questions of principle must be disposed of first.

1. Excluding as we do noncapitalist change, we have to define that word which good economists always try to avoid: capitalism is that form of private property economy in which innovations are carried out by means of borrowed money, which in general,

though not by logical necessity, implies credit creation. A society, the economic life of which is characterized by private property and controlled by private initiative, is according to this definition not necessarily capitalist, even if there are, for instance, privately owned factories, salaried workers, and free exchange of goods and services, either in kind or through the medium of money. The entrepreneurial function itself is not confined to capitalist society, since such economic leadership as it implies would be present, though in other forms, even in a primitive tribe or in a socialist community.

If by this definition we merely meant to exercise our logical right of terminological freedom, no more would have to be said about it. With some authors, prominent among whom is Boehm-Bawerk, defining capital, capitalist production, and capitalism does, in fact, not mean more than this. With others—Marx or Sombart may be quoted as instances—the definitions which they give or which can be gleaned from their texts, imply a statement of fact, namely, that the defining characteristic gives the essence of a definite historical phenomena. But also definitions of the latter type may legitimately differ according to point of view and purpose, and such differences need not imply difference of opinion as to the nature of the phenomenon. Our definition belongs to this class. It undoubtedly appears strange at a first reading, but a little reflection will satisfy the reader that most of the features which are commonly associated with the concept of capitalism would be absent from the economic and from the cultural process of a society without credit creation. Our characteristic is not, however, intended to imply causal connotation. It should also be observed that, like most other definitions of capitalism, ours is institutional. But of course the institutions which, with very rare exceptions, we treat as data throughout, are themselves the results of and elements in the process we wish to study. The only thing that could be controversial about this is our proposition that the economic process of capitalist society is identical with the sequence of events that gives rise to the business cycle.

Therefore, we shall date capitalism as far back as the element of credit creation. And this, in turn, at least as far back as negotiable credit instruments, the presence of which gives the practical, if not the logical, certainty of the presence of credit creation—in the same sense as the discovery of arms in some prehistoric deposit gives the practical certainty of the presence of the practice of fighting. But we must go further than this to the non-negotiable instrument which precedes the imperfectly negotiable one, and to the possibility of transferring, by however clumsy a method, deposits lodged with banks. This, of course, has not in itself anything to do with credit creation; but such information as we have strongly suggests that the practice of credit creation is as old as deposit banking. For Southern Europe this would carry us to the close of the twelfth and the beginning of the thirteenth century.

2. Finally, a point properly pertaining to the realm of general methodology must be touched upon in order to eliminate an apparent contradiction between our way of looking at economic or social change and the principle of historic continuity which tends to assert itself in historical analysis *pari passu* with increasing material and improving methods of research. Our theory of the mechanism of change stresses discontinuity. It takes the view that evolution proceeds by successive revolutions, or that there are in the process jerks or jumps which account for many of its features. As soon, however, as we survey the history of society or of any particular sector of social life, we become aware of a fact which seems, at first sight, to be incompatible with that view: every change seems to consist in the accumulation of many small influences and events and comes about precisely by steps so small as to make any exact dating and any sharp distinction of epochs almost meaningless. Evolution of productive technique may serve as an example. What we designate as a big invention hardly ever springs out of the current of events as Athene did from the head of Zeus, and practically every exception we might think of vanishes on closer investigation. Cooperation of many minds and many small experiences acting on a given objective situation and coordinated by it slowly evolve what appears as really new only if we leave out intermediate steps and compare types distant in time or space. The decisive step in bringing about a new thing or ultimate practical success is, in most cases, only the last straw and often relatively insignificant in itself. Needless to say, this holds true also of the process of change in social institutions and so on. What is technically called a revolution never can be understood from itself, *i.e.*, without refernce to the developments that led up to it; it sums up rather than initiates. Now, it is important to note that there is no contradiction whatever between our theory and a theory of history which

bases itself on these facts. What difference there is, is a difference of purpose and method only. This becomes evident if we reflect that any given industrial development, for instance the electrification of the household, may involve many discontinuities incident to the setting up of new production functions when looked at from the standpoint of individual firms and yet appear, when looked at from other standpoints, as a continuous process proceeding steadily from roots centuries back. By one of the many roughnesses forced upon us by the nature of the task which this volume is to fulfill, we may characterize this as a difference between microscopic and macroscopic points of view: there is as little contradiction between them as there is between calling the contour of a forest discontinuous for some and smooth for other purposes.

C. The Long Wave from 1787 to 1842.—Those years cover what according to our tentative schema we call a Long Cycle or Kondratieff. We have seen reasons to believe that this long wave was not the first of its kind. It is, however, the first to admit of reasonably clear statistical description. Owing both to inadequate information and to the presence of serious political disturbance (mainly the troubles associated with the American Revolution and its aftermath),[1] dating is very uncertain at the beginning.

[1] As soon as we admit the validity, for certain limited purposes, of an analysis which looks upon economic evolution as a distinct process having a logic of its own but going on in a disturbed environment, it obviously must be expected that cyclical phases which are due according to that logic or mechanism will often fail to show, owing to the opposing influence of such external disturbance. No argument against cyclical schemata follows from this and, in the particular case of this country, there would be no point in objecting that we are allowing our Kondratieff to "rise," in flagrant violation of our schema, at a time which is known to have been one of depression (1783-1790). To begin with, the fact is not beyond question. Moreover, the objection rests upon what we know to be incorrect, an identification of depression and suffering. Suffering there certainly was, witness the rebellion of 1786, but this is not conclusive evidence about what the cyclical phase was. Finally, there was the obvious and independent factor of physical impoverishment owing to the war of independence and to the equally important effects of the inflation incident to it. The bankruptcy of 1780, the issue of the "bills of a new tenor," and the final liquidation of the "continental paper currency" were the landmarks on a route that went through all the vicissitudes of unbridled inflation. This, by virtue of a vicious circle which ought to be, but is not, common

Nor is the end beyond doubt. Our choice rests on a combination of statistical and industrial fact, mainly about the cotton textile and iron trades, which further study may easily disavow. But few students will deny the reality of the process, usually referred to as the industrial revolution, which we identify with that Kondratieff.

1. It is necessary, however, to guard against possible misunderstanding by making quite clear in what sense we accept the term industrial revolution and its implications. The writer agrees with modern economic historians who frown upon it. It is not only outmoded, but also misleading, if it is intended to convey either the idea that what it designates was a unique event or series of events that created a new economic and social order, or the idea that, unconnected with previous developments, it suddenly burst upon the world in the last two or three decades of the eighteenth century.

Tugan-Baranowsky's dictum that "if one wishes to refer the industrial revolution to a definite historical epoch it can be located more justifiably in the second quarter of the nineteenth than in the end of the eighteenth century" accords with our view. As we know, it is in recession, depression, and revival that the achievements initiated in the prosperity phase mature and fully unfold themselves, thus bringing about a general reorganization of industry and commerce, the full exploitation of the opportunities newly created, and the elimination of obsolete and inadaptable elements, which is exactly what happened and what accounts for what everyone admits to have been a prolonged, though often interrupted, "depression"—from the Napoleonic Wars into the forties.

Exactly as the innovations which "carried" the industrial upswing of the eighties and nineties of the eighteenth century in many cases emerged much earlier—in a preparatory state that in some cases amounted to real, though quantitatively unimportant, success—so the twenties and thirties of the nineteenth century already display the first successes of the innovations which were to "carry" the next Kondratieff. The next big thing in particular, railroadization of the world, then asserted itself even to the point of playing a significant role in the last Juglar of the Kondratieff

knowledge among economists, called for ever new inflation in cure of situations created by antecedent inflation.

now under discussion. We observe the same phenomenon on the downgrade and in the revival of the second Kondratieff when, notably in the eighties, electrification, the most important innovation of the third, developed beyond the experimental state. Why this should be is so readily understandable that we might be tempted to consider it, by way of generalizing from our few observations, as a normal feature of the evolutionary process, and to insert it into our model. This has not been done because the intention was to keep the latter as simple as possible, in order to qualify it for the task of conveying essentials; but there would have been no difficulty in making the insertion. Wherever we fiind the phenomenon, it constitutes an additional link between successive cycles—there is no reason to confine it to Kondratieffs. What matters here is that the reader should realize that it does not invalidate our schema.

2. In addition to blurring contours at the beginning of this period, external factors exerted paramount influence until, roughly, 1820. The rest of the period was much less disturbed: the influence of events was small, or only local or of but minor moment. The effects of the friction between the United States and England (1826–1830), of the Texan war with Mexico, of the American monetary and tariff policy, though important, were never dominant in the sense of seriously interfering with the interpretation of cyclical situations. But the world wars of 1793 to 1815 obviously were. Nothing illustrates better than does the figure of Napoleon what we mean by an external factor. However, that factor was so important as to raise the question of principle whether we are within our rights if we continue to speak of a distinct process of economic evolution *sui generis* going on that was merely disturbed and distorted by political events.

In order to form an opinion about this it is necessary to note first that the process of industrial innovation obviously began before February 1793, when England declared war upon France. Moreover, we can follow it up and conclude from our knowledge of its mechanism that it would have produced a peak of prosperity, and afterward recession, without those political events. That what we claim to be cyclical fluctuations were in a number of instances associated with political events is as true as that there were several other fluctuations which are directly traceable to the latter. But we must guard against an optical delusion which often arises from interpretation of the behavior of time series in terms of spectacular events. Where these coincide with, or immediately precede, a business situation that seems to accord with them, this is uncritically accepted as proof of a causal relation. But where a political event fails to produce a corresponding effect on business, the fact is likely to be overlooked: England's international situation in 1806, for instance, was anything but comfortable, yet the year was one of prosperity.

Second, we will classify effects roughly into wastage, dislocation, and inflation. Physical destruction and real cost of armaments—in the case of Germany, also of plunder and exactions both in money and in kind—were of course considerable, but only locally and temporarily went to the point of destroying or paralyzing business processes.

In the case of the United States the influence of the European events was complicated and in some respects counteracted by the war, and by conditions verging on war, with England. Even so, American shipping, shipbuilding, and its subsidiaries reaped considerable windfall gains from abnormally high freight rates and a profitable transit trade. This, of course, helped financing and conditioned enterprise in other directions. Subsequent embargoes, non-intercourse acts, and the war put an end to much of this and account for depressive phenomena which would not have been present to the same degree without that temporary stimulus and its removal. But America, as far as it was not a farming nation, would then have been primarily a seafaring and trading nation an any case, and her farming interest would have felt the impulse of England's industrial development—which made her a wheat-importing country in the eighties—even without the obstacles that impeded exports from the continent of Europe.

Conversely, first the war of independence and then the war of 1812 to 1814 together with its antecedents, affected industry much as prohibitive tariffs would have done and encouraged investment that was bound to become unremunerative as soon as those conditions were removed. The year 1815 brought a regular postwar spurt and 1816 a no less regular postwar slump, such as we always observe in such cases. Time series and industrial history, of course, reflect both. They would do so whatever the underlying cyclical phase might have been. But again, this is no reason to deny the reality of the cyclical component on principle or to assume a priori, as soon as we realize the presence of noncyclical components, that they were the only ones to act. In our particular case depth as well as duration (to 1821) of the ensuing depressive conditions could hardly be understood without reference to the location of those years in the Kondratieff.

3. Although the result of much more complex social, economic, and fiscal motivations, the American tariffs of 1789 and 1816 may, from our standpoint, be looked upon as attempts to prolong the conditions that prevailed during the preceding wars and to preserve the industrial war structures. Whatever their effects in other respects and on other interests, this purpose was actually served by them as was the cognate purpose of keeping alive structures that owed their existence to inflation and, barring further inflation, could not have survived without protection. As it was, tariffs certainly softened downgrades and accentuated upgrades. Removal, even if gradual, might even have produced depressive situations, sudden removal panics, that could not otherwise be explained. Fear—perhaps, exaggerated fear—of immediate consequences paralyzed the badly organized and badly led interests which were injured by that policy; and the vicious circle of protection making itself necessary and creating situations that call for more protection, is at the bottom of American protectionism to this day.

But this does not mean that changes in tariff policy dominate the cyclical movement, although they powerfully determine what the industrial structure will be. It does not mean this, as a matter of fact, in the American case (even beyond our period). And it does not mean this, as a matter of analytical principle. In the former respect, we will note that the tariff of 1789 did not more than protect a number of weak industrial striplings. Of the acts from 1816, when protection got really under sail, to the "tariff of abominations" (1828) none turned any tide. We will now formulate more generally: imposition and removal of tariffs changes the conditions both for enterprise and for current business. As regards enterprise, protection will stimulate it in some directions and bridle it in others, so that a distorted industrial organism will be the consequence. Net effects there may be, although there need not, but positive ones will always be more visible than the (largely conjectural) negative ones. In no case is it correct to list this influence among alternatives to the influence of the entrepreneurial factor, through which alone it acts as does any other change in data. This in part explains the ineffectiveness of protection in creating booms: all it can possibly do is to add one favoring circumstance, while it is perfectly consonant with this that the removal of protection may produce a slump by upsetting calculations.

In its role as a condition of entrepreneurial activity, imposition of tariffs will thus act similarly to cheap money policy: it creates margins which would not otherwise exist and therefore calls forth enterprise and secondary expansion that may become a source of troubles. However, protection acts not only on enterprise, but also on current business or what we call the world of old firms. As far as it does this, it may directly change the complexion of the economic situation as a whole. Here it has what may be termed a mechanical or automatic effect, although this effect is never one way only.

4. The question remains to what extent the external factors Inflation and Deflation shaped events and whether they provide an alternative explanation of the economic history of the time that could stand by itself, thereby proving the futility of looking for any cycles of autonomous causation, particularly for the Kondratieff. The answer is comparatively simple if by inflation we mean merely the financing of public expenditure by legal tender or credit instruments created *ad hoc,* and if by its effects we mean merely the impact of the amount thus created times a suitable coefficient of velocity. But such situations are invariably complicated by an expansion of business credit which superimposes itself on the direct effects and is very difficult to distinguish from expansion of business credit that during the same time would have occurred in the ordinary course of prosperity phases. For America we have also at various junctures to take account of inflationary impulses, given quite independently of any fiscal vicissitudes and often without any change in the quantity and character of legal tender, by soft and cheap money policies and "reckless banking," which in America was fostered by the inflationist temper of the public mind. This Gordian knot interpretation has got to face, however convenient it may be to slur over these difficulties by aggregative propositions. We shall class with external factors, not only inflationary financing of government expenditure, but also inflationary impulses of the last-mentioned type, provided they proceed from the political world—which mainly, though not exclusively, means legislation—while "reckless banking" will be classed with speculative manias, swindle,

and the like, by which we wish to express, on the one hand, that it does not belong to those features without which our model would not be logically complete and, on the other hand, that it does belong to those features which understandably present themselves under certain environmental circumstances and in certain stages in the career of capitalism.

It is only with regard to "reckless banking" that the question of inflation arises at all for the United States. Broadly speaking, sound money policy prevailed during the whole of this period, and the Constitution—which at the time was understood to have deprived both state legislatures and Congress of the power of issuing not only "bills of credit" but legal-tende:r fiat—reflects acknowledgment of the lesson taught by the war inflation. It ratified the temporary defeat of inflationism and substantially settled monetary matters until the Civil War.

5. In the United States the production of agricultural raw materials in general followed rather than preceded the development of the industries that use them. This is especially true of wool, which, in spite of many efforts by manufacturers, of protection, of the impulses given by the English war and by the growing demand for mutton, and of the introduction of the Merino breed (1801), developed slowly until, just beyond our period, it temporarily became an article of export. Cotton continued to be imported and also to be an article of transit trade—net exports began in 1794—until a growing industry almost impelled its production on a larger scale. The great investment in cotton planting in the South began in the recession of that Kondratieff: a typical example of an induced development or of what we have called expansion into new economic space created by previous innovation. Lumbering was, of course, basic to the general growth of the country from the start, but not very interesting cyclically, since so much of it was done for local purposes. The great development was in wheat growing. Stimulated by abundance of cheap credit due to what has above been referred to as "reckless banking," and by foreign demand, it experienced a boom 1790–1795, which together with the development of milling incident to it was one of the most important elements of that Kondratieff prosperity. Since that boom was primarily. though by no means wholly—a matter of ability to export, the setback and America's share in the ensuing agrarian depression must be interpreted in terms of foreign conditions, falling prices, and protection in Eng-

land in particular, the effects of which were, for the country taken as a whole, alleviated by the favorably developing cotton situation.

But another phenomenon calls for attention which plays a role in all agrarian depressions in this country. That is a type of innovation which from the start has been peculiar to it and has remained so into the twenties of this century: innovation which creates the conditions for bringing new regions into cultivation. Grain production shifted its center from the New England States to Virginia and Maryland already in colonial times, and in our period began to shift it again to the Ohio and the Great Lakes. Each process of this kind spells increase of production and, at the same time, prosperity in the new and depression in the old regions—the latter well illustrating that important piece of the cyclical mechanism, the competition between the new and the old production functions. It should be noted in passing that this also illustrates the difficulty of talking about the "long-period depressions in the world's agriculture" as homogeneous phenomena.

6. In the United States, agricultural and commercial enterprise (the latter also including shipping) was the chief determinant of business situations throughout our period. Also, we must bear in mind that evolution in our sense in America—and this holds true to this day or in any case to the end of the second Kondratieff—was supported by a rate of growth in our sense which had no parallel in either England or Germany. Simple expansion along obvious lines, exploitation of opportunities which, once created, lay at hand ready and inexhaustible for a mightly host of followers, and immigration of men and capital in response to those opportunities supplied a much greater part of the propelling forces here than anywhere else. Entrepreneurial activity was generally faced with favorable changes in its data. Foreign evolution and growth, on the whole, worked in the same direction. The extension of the wheat and cotton areas, notably after 1830, was possible without destroying the conditions for further extension. These facts are too obvious to require proof or illustration, nor is it necessary to insist on the consequent dependence of American on English business situations. We will notice, however, that these conditions, as soon as the troubles of the eighties of the eighteenth century were over, produced two features that were

prominent in the boom of the nineties as well as in many of those that were to follow—land companies and the speculation in land.

A great part of industrial production was carried on in the farmer's home or by workshop crafts throughout our period, as it had been in colonial times, or it worked under conditions which practically exempted it from the repercussions described in our model: a sawmill sawing on toll, located in an agrarian neighborhood, may pay or not, may work or not, but it has nothing to "compete down," nor will its processes react on other industrial organisms—the agrarian milieu acts as a shock absorber. How considerable, nevertheless, industrial enterprise must already have been before the Revolution is proved by the fact that embargoes and actual war with the mother country caused so little serious embarrassment, and that, in particular, domestic furnaces and forges were quite up to the requirements of cannon casting and of the other kinds of demand incident to the military operations. Massachusetts and Connecticut and the neighborhoods of Philadelphia and New York were by that time industrialized to a considerable extent; there had been occasional exports of manufactured products as early as the middle of the seventeenth century, and industrial towns (Wilmington, Lancaster) had sprung up while water-power developments were of quantitative importance at least several decades before our period. Flour milling, even before the innovations associated with the name of Oliver Evans, was technologically ahead of the rest of the world. The construction of glass works by the Virginia Company and then by "Baron" Stiegel can serve as typical illustrations of our process. There were some considerable iron works. Textile interests had risen to political influence. Shipbuilding, like other industries, was fostered by bounties.

The British colonial enterprises, such as the Virginia and the Plymouth companies, had from the first included industrial development in their programs. And the War of Independence, of course, gave a great impulse to most of this. But up to its end the violent fluctuations and the spectacular crises must primarily be described in terms of external factors—such as wars, sudden changes in the political data, English conditions, and so on, which acted on the industries through commerce—rather than in terms of the industrial mechanisms itself. Since external factors obviously dominate the picture and are naturally stressed by both contemporaneous and historical reports, an attempt to answer the question whether there were also genuinely cyclical fluctuations would involve an extremely difficult piece of analysis which the writer has been unable to undertake. But the colonial issues of paper money and the other inflationist policies of the colonies cannot simply be put in the same class with European government inflations. In part at least, they stood instead of cyclical expansions of bank credit and, directly (by loans and subsidies) and indirectly, financed innovations for the financing of which there were no other means. Some of the breakdowns which studded that expansion are, hence, more akin to ordinary crises, and the processes within which they occurred are possibly more akin to cycles in our sense than we could ever realize if we saw in those colonial issues nothing but ordinary inflation. The use made of that tool was often so improvident and unsystematic that the usual comments on them may be amply justified all the same, but they do not cover the whole of the case. Contemporaneous observers, as well as some historians, such as Chalmers and Weeden, may have put the cart before the horse, and presumably implied a lot of wrong theory, but they were hardly wrong as to the facts when they associated some industrial developments, in shipbuilding and ironmaking in particular, with the paper money, although most of them failed to associate also ensuing depression with it.

Taking account of the previously mentioned disturbances of the eighties of the eighteenth century, by saying either that they interfered with the rising tide of enterprise so as to blot out the symptoms generally associated with prosperity, or that they delayed the rise of the tide until about 1786, we see the setting in of the process that, fostered by land grants, loans and subsidies, and other facilities extended by manufacturers and would-be manufacturers by states and municipalities, was eventually to transform American industries in much the same way as the corresponding process did in England. Advance was spread over a wide variety of industries and was in full swing by the time Alexander Hamilton submitted his famous report. The main feature, in industry in the strict sense, was the introduction of power machinery which began to turn the workshop of the craft type into the factory. As an example we will mention the development of the cotton and woolen mills in New England and Pennsylvania—the Beverly Cotton Manufactory was chartered in 1789—which in the nineties culminated in the "cotton mania," the most striking single phenomenon of what might be be termed the positive phase of the American industrial revolution. This was, of course, intimately connected with water-power developments. The great Hamiltonian project for the exploitation of the falls of the Passaic, which after initial vicissitudes. eventually created the industrial center of Paterson, may serve as an example. These water-power developments, together with improved means of communication—turnpikes and canals, partly constructed by public enterprise—and shipbuilding, made the backbone of the strictly industrial component of what we interpret as Kondratieff prosperity. *Technological* innovation, let alone "invention," was not in prominence. The only one of first-rate importance was the Whitney cotton gin, though there were many minor ones, particularly in the field of agricultural implements. Even the introduction of English innovations was at first but slow. Though, for example, jennies, Arkwright frames, and mules all came in about 1790, they made very little headway before the turn of the century.

Whoever looks at quantities only and neglects the distinction between initiation and development of results, will be inclined, in this case as in that of England, to date the "revolution" from the first, the second, or even the third decade of the nineteenth century. That time was, however, clearly one of derivative development of the type which we associate with Kondratieff downgrades and revivals. The nature of technological innovation, in particular, accords with this. Water-power development went on along the lines previously chalked out, met its great successes, in spite of the primitive and wasteful pitch-back wheel, especially —after Paterson—in Lowell, Lawrence, Manchester, Holyoke, Philadelphia, and Fall River, and remained the main source of industrial power to the end of our period. This, together with what it induced, was the great industrial feature in the Juglars after 1820. Steam came in but slowly, both because of the abundance of water power, and because cheap freight rates were, for the greater part of the country, a prerequisite of its extended use. Within our period it had quantitative significance only in the neighborhood of cheap coal, the introduction of the iron boiler notwithstanding.

The rise of industry in the Middle West, another feature of this Kondratieff downgrade, is, however, bound up with it, and its use spread from there to the South and even into the heart of the water-power regions and to cotton textiles (Eagle Cotton Mills, 1831). After about 1810, O. Evans' high-pressure engines began to compete with the imported (low-pressure) Watt engines. But the production of engines for industrial purposes in Cleveland and Pittsburgh was, as far as the writer knows, small even at the end of the period, although it was of more importance for steamboat use. Since smelting, the other great source of industrial demand for fuel, met with a plentiful supply of charcoal, which did not begin to give out until the first decade of the nineteenth century, coal, though discovered in colonial times and even, in small quantities, imported from England before 1800, was of little importance until the thirties. Then imports rose, and the technological difficulties were overcome which had stood in the way of large-scale use of domestic coal. F. W. Geissenhainer's invention, if this is the word, the introduction of the hot blast, already successful in England, and coking, all contributed to the prosperity of the last Juglar, although the great development came after 1842.

The iron industry in general and rolling in particular had, as we should expect, expanded in the upswing of the nineties, but they outgrew the small-scale type and old methods in the downswing. The puddling process came in 1817, rolling mills became bigger (Pittsburgh) and began to crowd out forge hammers. But the production of cast steel in Cincinnati and the output of the crucible-steel works in Jersey and Pittsburgh, although dating from the upswing preceding 1837, did not attain quantitative importance within the period. We have here a typical instance of an industry drawn along by foreign innovation and increasing home demand, expanding in response to the general march of things. Downgrade and revival developments in the textiles, particularly in cotton, were of a different character because this industry, which expanded still more vigorously "into new economic space" during the first 40 years of the nineteenth century, had created that space itself and did not merely respond to the growth of the environment. In Massachusetts alone about 90 companies for making cotton and woolen goods were incorporated between 1807 and 1818 (V. Clark, Vol. I, p. 266) a fact which yet indicates the rate of expansion, greatly surpassed, of course, after 1820. A number of domestic improvements of the technological type attended this downgrade process. The most important was F. C. Lowell's loom (1814), which almost immediately induced a great increase in weaving by power, the application to woolens succeeding in the course of the twenties. It was preceded by the invention of "pickers" and "willows" (according to Mr. Clark, 1807) and was followed by the Goulding condenser, which revolutionized the woolen industry in the thirties (Kondratieff revival), and a considerable list of minor new devices. What we know of quantities of product and prices behaved accordingly.

In transportation the great thing was the construction of canals. Within the last three decades of our period, cost of transportation between the East and the Middle West fell spectacularly in consequence, both per ton-mile and because of the saving in time and distance. Philadelphia became the center of a system of waterways. The canal between the Hudson and Lake Champlain was opened in 1823; the most important of all, the Erie canal, in 1825. The truly revolutionary effect of this on physical production, prices, and location—an ideal instance by which to illustrate the nature and *modus operandi* of innovation, in particular the way in which innovation produces prosperity and depression—is luckily so obvious and its quantitative importance so palpable that we need not stay to prove it.[1] While canal traffic reached its peak about the end of the Kondratieff (1840), railroads—there were about 1,500 miles in operation by 1837 and about 4,000 by 1842—cannot have been a major factor in the upswing of the last Juglar, except locally and by the contribution of railroad projects to the speculative situation of 1837, when they featured along with banks and land companies.

Demand for rails began before 1830, but the steam locomotive, tracks, and roadbeds did not get into a serviceable shape until, roughly, 1835. Comparative slowness of beginnings is accounted for also by the fact that the entrepreneurial task of breaking down the resistance of the environment proved astonishingly difficult. Impediments, such as constraint to pay tolls to canal companies in cases of competition, local jealousies obstructing necessary connections, and so on, were not overcome until much later. Public enterprise in the field began in 1836 and 1837

[1] The developments in the West, largely induced by that innovation, are but inadequately characterized by the fact that between 1820 and 1840, the population of Ohio increased from 581,295 to 1,519,497; that of Illinois, from 55,162 to 476,182.

(Illinois, Michigan, Indiana). As elsewhere, the first railroads were local and sponsored by businessmen in important towns on the coast or other navigable water, with a view to opening up the hinterland. The Mohawk and Hudson was an Albany enterprise to cut Troy out of the transshipment trade between the Erie Canal and the Hudson. The Baltimore and Ohio was Baltimore's bid for interior trade, the Charleston and Hamburg was an effort on the part of Charleston to divert the trade which went down the river from Hamburg to Savannah. The "competing-down element" is thus obvious from the outset, and even absolute losses—as distinguished from the relative losses equal to the net result of general development and this competition—must have been felt almost immediately, not only by canal and highway companies, but in general by business in towns that lagged behind. Freight rates fell quickly to—on a rough average—three cents per ton-mile which, however, was still about double the charge on canals, though only one-fifth of the cost of transportation on a turnpike.

7. In the United States profits and the *ad hoc* creation of means of payment were obviously the main domestic sources of the "funds" which financed industrial and other enterprises. After 1780 sound money principles prevailed as far as Federal policy was concerned. Repayment of the national debt, substantially accomplished between 1832 and 1835, was in keeping with this, yet there are several qualifications to be made, two of which are relevant to our subject. At no time, first, did the Federal government really support the two Banks of the United States in such attempts as they made to acquire the position of central banks and to exert a restraining influence on loose or even semicriminal practice; in the autumn of 1833 it even weakened the position of the second bank and materially helped to urge on private banking by withdrawing its deposits from the former and distributing them among the state banks—a measure that was partly counteracted, only when it had taken full effect, by the Specie Circular (1836), stopping sales of public land on credit and insisting on payment in specie, which, under the circumstances, amounted to an official declaration to the effect that the state banks were not to be trusted. And at no time, secondly, was the Federal government able to restrain the states from fostering methods of banking obviously at variance with the principles of monetary policy it professed. In the country at large,

though with notable exceptions, the inflationist mentality that had developed in colonial times continued unabated, and each depression brought its attack on the monetary system with the utmost regularity. Politics in some states was entirely swayed by it. For instance, Kentucky founded (1820) the Bank of the Commonwealth of Kentucky, in order to issue paper money to the amount of two millions to be lent on mortgages. Pennsylvania in 1840 authorized the banks of the state to issue three millions in notes redeemable in state bonds.

The first bank of issue, the Bank of North America, was established in 1782. During the first four years of its existence, it confined itself to discounting for not more than 45 days. Others followed in quick succession. According to Gouge there were 21 of them by 1795 and—in spite of the crash of 1809—119 by 1812. In 1829 there were 329, by 1837 the number had increased to 788, a peak of 901 was reached in 1840. They lent on promissory notes secured by collateral or endorsement, often on mortgage, keeping very scanty reserves and not caring too much about such details as the paying in of capital or redemption, in spite of the facts that there was no central bank to fall back upon and that supporting relations between banks developed but slowly after 1820. The passionate inflationism of the public mind protected them, although we also read of complaints about the "deluge of paper money." In some communities the attempt to present notes for payment involved the danger of seizure of the notes or arrest or even danger to life and limb. Although it is the notes about which we read the picturesque stories, checking deposits were also very freely created. The rule of lending short and acquiring quick assets broke down from the first—although there were banks and bankers who kept to it throughout; deviating practice went to very different lengths in different parts of the country—and was soon challenged on principle by the copious writings of valiant pamphleteers. The notes of many banks depreciated seriously between 1814 and 1817, suspensions of specie payments (1814 and 1837, in particular), and failures were of frequent occurrence. We hear of industrial concerns applying for power to form banks in order to finance themselves by note issues and some Midwestern states gave railroad companies such powers for this very purpose.

This detail is significant. It provides a clue to the interpretation both of that practice and of the inflationist mentality of that time which made such practice possible in communities that were in other respects supernormally strict about moral standards. Neither of them can be disposed of by an expression of moral disapproval. Nor does it help us to criticize them from the standpoint of the classical theory of banking. Whatever our opinion might be if we placed ourselves on other possible standpoints, however strongly we may feel it our duty to condemn both the misconduct involved and the public opinion that not only condoned but fostered it, the fact still remains that we have before us the clearest historical instance by which to illustrate the function of credit creation. It was the financing of innovation by credit creation—the only method available, as we have seen in the course of our theoretical argument, in the absence of sufficient results of previous evolution—which is at the bottom of that "reckless banking." This undoubtedly sheds a different light upon it. Those banks filled their function sometimes dishonestly and even criminally, but they filled a function which can be distinguished from their dishonesty or criminality. Sound money men of all times, hence, threw and still throw away the baby with the bath by condemning the principles of that practice, however understandable their clamor for policing and controlling the practice itself may have been. The people felt this. So did some of the advocates of inflation, though they were unable to formulate their case correctly.

That this is so, we can also see from the long-run behavior of the level of domestic prices. It is not as we would expect it to be if there really had been "paper inflation" *sans phrase*. On the contrary, it is distinctly as we would expect it to be from the normal working of our model—namely up in the Kondratieff prosperity, and down afterward. Increase of output eventually overtook the effects of bank expansion each time and exerted its downward pull on the price level exactly as it should according to the *modus operandi* of our mechanism of innovation. There is no such difference between the behavior of the American and the British price indices as we would assuredly find if our diagnosis were seriously at fault.

This does not cover the case, however. In 1812 and 1813, then again from 1834 to 1836, we find spectacular rises which are contrary to expectation. The first is accounted for by the English war. The second is due to what, even from our standpoint obviously was excess, *i.e.*, more than the usual Juglar expansion.

Jacksonian policies—the hostility to central banking or, in fact, any control of credit creation—may be held responsible for its violence, as well as for the violence of the subsequent fall. The case provides interesting material for study with reference to contemporaneous problems. Moreover, we do not, of course, deny the presence, during practically the whole of the period, of "reckless banking." There can be no doubt, not only that unsound and fraudulent schemes were readily financed in many instances, but also that credit was freely extended for other purposes than innovation, most of which would only pay at rising or at least, constant prices. The Secondary Wave loomed large in every Juglar and many secondary maladjustments were the consequence, requiring additional processes of liquidation and accentuating those violent crashes which would have been much milder without them, although the vicissitudes incident to economic development, within a young country of such possibilities, could not have been avoided entirely by even the most conservative behavior of banks.

8. Finally, we will try to locate the Juglars. The Kitchins are, as has been pointed out before, in any case beyond the reach of the historical information at the writer's command and can, therefore, be established from time series only, although some support can be and has been derived from annals of the general business situation. But as regards the first Kondratieff, at all events until about 1820, that information is not even quite adequate for the Juglars. The reader should recall, moreover, what has been said in the fourth chapter about the meaning of our dating and the unavoidable roughness of it. It is for him to judge how far what follows suffices to make a common-sense case.

As regards dating, we meet, of course, the difficulty, already encountered, about the beginning of the Kondratieff. The wave of cotton and water power, of wheat growing, and of a few minor innovations is obvious. In the early nineties it was certainly running strongly. But how far back we are to go and how we are to appraise the relative importance of the various unfavorable external factors that acted on the industrial process—such as Shay's Rebellion—the writer feels unable to say. Nor do our difficulties stop there. We are able to follow, from 1788 to 1789, the rising tide until the last quarter of 1796. Till then there were only the financial troubles of 1792, which did not amount to much. Prosperous conditions continued to prevail in the South after 1796, but in New England preponderatingly unfavorable situations followed until a rally in 1804. This makes a picture of one big two-phase cycle with smaller fluctuations of an erratic character in its second half. But all it really shows is that aggregative contour lines and the complexion of general business situations are unsafe guides to the deeper things in the economic process. The reason for that impression is not far to seek. The American general business situation was at the time largely a function of European war demand. Farmers, merchants, and shipowners were dependent on it. In 1797 and 1798 trading was imperilled by privateering and the country was on the verge of a war with France. This passed and trade recovered, but the peace of Amiens meant nothing less than a catastrophe, sending down prices, inducing failures and idle tonnage. All this impinged on the rest of the organism through a highly precarious banking situation.

The same factors acted the other way again in 1805 and 1806, but the Jeffersonian embargo (December 1807 to March 1809) exerted, of course, a strongly depressive effect. February 1811 brought the Nonintercourse Act to life again, then came the war with England and the damage it did to trade and shipping, and the stimulus it gave to domestic manufactures, followed by the reverse state of affairs (enhanced by European crop failures) in and after 1815, until the crisis which broke out in the last quarter of 1818 liquidated, for America, the abnormalities of the Napoleonic time. But, once more, that an organism lives in a stormy environment which tosses it and alternately benefits and injures it does not prove that it has no life of its own. How strong that life was, shows on occasion, for instance in 1793, which was a year of prosperous business, although trading and shipping interests were affected considerably by the events in England, or in the prosperous conditions that prevailed in the South while the trading and financial centers suffered. In the situations of 1795, 1807, and 1814, however much colored they were by the influence of foreign situations, the specifically American component may yet be recognized and linked to industrial processes and, as their complement, banking developments. Since, however, the question could in any case only be whether or not there were traces of the endogenous rhythm of economic life, we need not insist. The tentative dating is: 1787-1794, 1795-1804, 1805-1813, 1814-1822. There is no doubt about the period which, in case we accept this, would have to be called the fifth Juglar: 1823-1831. Nor is there any doubt about the reality of that unit in the evolutionary process which ran its course in the thirties and early forties: 1832–1842, as the writer thinks. But it displays many irregularities.

Chapter VII

HISTORICAL OUTLINES. II. 1843-1913

A. The Period 1843-1897.—This period covers the second of our Long Waves. There is some difference of opinion among those students of the business cycle who use that concept at all, as to whether the forties are to be included with the first or the second, while some historians date the beginnings of what they feel to have been another economic revolution, from earlier developments. The important thing is that nobody doubts the reality of that revolution which in nature and importance is perfectly comparable to the one that occurred in the last two decades of the eighteenth century, and that nobody could fail to associate it with what we call the railroadization of the world, which obviously was its outstanding feature. The latter statement particularly applies to this country, the Western and Middle Western parts of which were, economically speaking, created by the railroad. Nor need we stay to show more fully than we did in the course of unfolding our theoretical schema, how railroad construction produces both prosperities and recessions—with the latter, situations which easily slide off into depressions—and, in particular, simultaneous cycles of different span. For railroadization is our standard example by which to illustrate the working of our model. The comparatively long periods of gestation, both of the individual line—each is an innovation within our meaning of the term—and of the sectional or national system—which, as such, constitute innovations of a higher order—the quantitative importance of the expenditure involved, the consequent dislocation of all the data of economic life, the new investment opportunities and the new possibilities that are created for further innovation, and the (cyclical) disturbances in turn caused by these, combine to make the essential features of our evolutionary process more obvious in this than they are in any other case. More easily than in any other can the usual objections to our anaylsis be silenced by a simple refêrence to obvious facts.

1. While railroad developments in the forties are our chief reason for dating the beginning of the second Kondratieff as we do, it is not, of course, implied that railroads were of no cyclical importance after 1897, which would, for this country at least, be as untrue as it would be to assert that the cyclical role of cotton textiles ceased in 1842. Innovations which "carry" a Kondratieff, continue to contribute to the next, just as we have already seen that they develop—as did, for instance, railroads themselves or at least one of the "great things" of the third Kondratieff, electricity—from beginnings in the downgrade and revival of the preceding one. Yet there is little difference of opinion about dating the end of the second Kondratieff. What difference there is turns on months or, at most, a year. This comparative agreement is, of course, due to the strong testimony of aggregative and systematic series and to the unmistakable complexion of business, which at that time emerged from what has come down to posterity as the Great Depression. But it can also be justified from the nature of the business processes behind those series.

The properties of the social pattern as revealed, for example, by the foreign, social, and financial policies of the great nations, also lend support to the view that 1897 may be taken to mark the end of an era and the beginning of another. Although the whole process we are analyzing in this book is essentially the process of capitalist evolution—economic evolution as conditioning, and being conditioned by, the institutional pattern of bourgeois society—yet the second Kondratieff has a special claim to the epitheton *bourgeois*. By this we mean that the interests and attitudes of the industrial and commercial classes controlled policies and all manifestations of culture in a sense in which this cannot be asserted for any preceding or any subsequent period.

2. The rule of the *beourgeoisie* and of bourgeois rationalism extended, as could easily be shown, to the religions, the arts, the sciences, the style of life, to everything social in fact, with the single exception of the Catholic Church, which hence became an object of aversion and of temporarily successful attack. All that matters for our purpose, however, is the fact that the bourgeois world behaved politically in such a way as to minimize external disturbance of our process. What institutional change of the kind relevant to our subject there was, grew much more clearly out of the immediate economic situations than such changes did at any other time.

As for the United States, the free trade that really mattered was the free trade within the country. Compared with this—and the economic history of the Middle West and West is no doubt the greatest historical example of free-trade achievement—the regulation of foreign commerce, very important during the first Kondratieff, steadily declined in economic, although only temporarily in political, importance. In spite, however, of that fact and of the influence of the South, protection was retained throughout. Fiscal considerations had their part in determining the increases of 1842 and the reductions of 1857, but the long-lived Walker Act of 1846, which may be taken to represent what to Americans seems to be moderate protection, still kept all the more significant items at 25 or 30 per cent ad valorem. After the Civil War, duties on wool and woolens again moved into the center of the political game about the tariff (1867). The law of 1872 and the general revision of 1883 brought small reductions, but the McKinley tariff of 1890 gratified manufacturers (worsted manufacturers, in particular), while giving to the farmers a full measure of protection to wool, the only thing protectionists had to offer to them. The Wilson Act abolished the tariff on wool and reduced the duties on woolens on the average from 91 to 49 per cent, only to provoke the violent reaction embodied in the Dingley tariff, which, unfortunately for the standing of free trade in the public eye, happened to come at the threshold of the third Kondratieff, as the reductions of 1872 and 1883 had come at the threshold of crises.[1] As far as the writer is able to see, this policy may have alleviated temporary difficulties for some industries—while changes such as that brought about by the Wilson Act certainly created *some* disturbance—but on the whole it hardly influenced the march of things substantially. It never was a major factor in cyclical turning points and still less turned depressions into prosperities or vice versa. Its provable influence on trends is confined to a small number of industries, and there is something curiously unreal about the place it held in party politics and in the thought and talk of a large sector of the community.

In the sphere of banking, the outstanding institutional change was the creation of the National Banking System. Two developments which almost amounted to institutional changes should be noticed, however. One was the rise of the New York banking center to something like the position of a central bank. The other was the gradual reform of banking practice, in some states —for instance in Louisiana (1842)—enforced by law, in others, like Massachusetts, by the banking community itself. In New York the safety fund and bond security systems were improved; in South Carolina and some Middle Western states serious banking also prevailed, although "bogus" and "mushroom" banks, the notes of which were dealt in at discounts up to 90 per cent, were still frequent in the West and the South. The National Banking Act did much, directly and indirectly, to improve matters further and, until the setback caused by the early practices of trust companies, progress in that direction was all but unbroken.

It is neither possible nor necessary to discuss the details of the fiscal policy of our period, but it is necessary to advert to its spirit. In the United States, the tariff as a rule took care of Federal expenditure and even yielded surpluses so large as to be almost embarrassing, except during the Civil War and some years after it. In England the income tax reappeared for good, but throughout the period behaved with the restraint of a new-

[1] These are good instances by which to illustrate the dangers of arguing by coincidences, in particular in explaining business situations by external factors. They are so valuable because it is plain that those measures cannot be held to have produced the cyclical phases that happened to follow upon them. This should make us careful in other cases also.

comer not quite certain of his right to a place. In Germany the same holds true for the various state income taxes which were introduced or reformed and among which Miquel's Prussian income and property tax (1891) was the supreme achievement. The writer has been told, though he has not been able to verify it, that Miquel believed an income tax which in the highest brackets asymptotically approaches 5 per cent to be dangerously high. The practice of German municipalities of levying an additional percentage for their own purposes, which was soon to make even that income tax a serious burden, did not develop within our period. All this, of course, implies acceptance of the bourgeois schema of things economic. No group that had any political significance doubted anyone's right to his private income or inheritance. Income was earned primarily for private purposes and the state and other public bodies were to take away as little as they could. Taxes were a necesary evil, to be confined to amounts and to be laid on in ways that would as little as possible interfere with the disposal of returns as it would have been in their absence. Retrenchment or, at all events, economy was meritorious in the management of public affairs; saving or accumulation, in the management of private affairs. Supported and controlled by the approval of the political powers, the bourgeois worked and saved—within a firm framework including a safe and sound monetary system—for an indefinite family future, and invariably took as long a view as he could afford to take.

3. The bourgeois Kondratieff spans a long list of wars, foreign entanglements, revolutions.[1] Space forbids explanation of why they seem to the writer to have been, even in a deeper sense than that which is implied in the narrow purposes of this book, factors external to that social pattern. We will confine ourselves to discussing the importance of a few instances, or types of instances, for the working of the mechanism of economic evolution. There is, first, the group of what, from our standpoint at least, we may designate as minor ones, such as the various frictions that arose between this country and England. Some of these the business community rightly refused to take cognizance

[1] The behavior of gold—the California and Australian discoveries certainly were external factors since, primarily at least, they were due to chance—will be more conveniently considered at other turns of our way.

of; others caused small ripples. Even disturbances involving military operations come within this category, such as the war between the United States and Mexico which, through the payments of the latter to the former, exerted some influence, though only on short-run money-market situations, for some time after its close. The detailed study of time series has, of course, to take account of this type of disturbance, but it is safe to say that no major effects are overlooked by neglecting them here. Minor also, for this country—if we except effects on immigration—was the repercussion from the continental revolutions of 1848, the troubles in Russian Poland, and even from most other European events, however momentous they were in themselves. This country was not, to be sure, a world sufficient unto itself; but the nature of those events was such as not to interfere materially either with agricultural exports or with capital imports.

4. By far the greatest and most interesting "external disturbance" of the period was the American Civil War. Barring the physical injuries to the productive apparatus of the country, which (again illustrating the difference between misery and depression, or welfare and prosperity) had very little cyclical importance[1] (what cyclical importance they had was in the prosperity direction, for reconstruction supplied the basis for a postwar boom), its effects bear a striking resemblance to the effects on this country of the first World War of this century. We have an understandable financial and commercial earthquake at the beginning, and stringency and stagnation lasting almost to the end of the first year of hostilities. Then, helped by a good crop, a typical war boom developed in response to government demand supported by the issue of the greenbacks. The conflicting forces of the postwar boom and of postwar liquidation impinged on a rising cyclical (Juglar) tide which in this case it is very easy to distinguish from the effects of the external factor, because it was so clearly based on a development that had nothing to do with the war—railroad construction. Most of the effects and after-effects of the war were drowned in the rise and break

[1] Physical destruction of plant and stock was quickly repaired—J. Stuart Mill commented on this—as it always will be so long as the capitalist engine is intact. What matters economically in such cases is impairment of the capitalist motive power and mechanism, rather than physical loss. And that motive power and mechanism had in this case not suffered at all.

of that wave, and although some of the fluctuations in the last sixties have to be attributed to them, neither the cyclical rhythms nor trend results were affected enough to become unrecognizable. Even the difficulties in 1866 and 1867 were not due to postwar adjustments alone. But the question still remains what importance we are to attach to the monetary element during the seventeen years of the greenback standard.

It is a matter of definition whether we can speak of deflation at all. In our sense there was none, for there was neither net contraction of the volume of the circulating media nor any pressure on the money market, such we might expect would attend a policy of raising exchanges to gold parity. A sector of public opinion was in favor of both, and Secretary Hugh McCulloch's report of December 1865 actually envisaged both. Looking upon greenbacks and compound-interest notes in the most orthodox light, he proposed to fund them by means of bond issues and in fact set about retiring them out of surplus revenue. This policy at first met with an astonishing amount of approval, both from the President and from Congress. But it was presently curbed by the act of April 12, 1866. Retirement actually affected was quite small and more than compensated by the expanding circulation of the national banks' notes. The Secretary was probably right when, several years later, he stated that but for the Treasury's monthly statements nobody would have known that there was any retirement at all. What eventually happened was what his successor and Congress professed to aim at—the economic organism was allowed to grow into its monetary coat.

Pressure on the money market was also avoided through various favorable circumstances. No great efforts, such as might have crippled business success, were needed to restore the Federal budget to order. On the contrary, it was possible to begin reducing the Federal debt from its 1865 peak of 2,675 million dollars. The situation of banks was further eased by the emigration of American bonds to Europe, which set in almost immediately, and by other foreign credits which became available to American business; but it was strong from the beginning. In 1866 national banks held legal-tender reserves to the amount of 211 millons against deposits of 539 millions. This is but one symptom of a fact that is most important for the diagnosis of the inflation as it stood at the end of the war. It had not taken full effect, *i.e.*, it had never gone beyond that stage in which part of the swelled receipts are being used for increasing cash and paying off debts —it had never become "wild." Part of the rise in prices in 1864 was not the mechanical effect of the quantity of greenbacks but was due to the impediments to production and trade and to speculative anticipation, and the whole of the fall to the end of 1865 (a fall of, roughly, 22 per cent of the level of September 1864) was simply the reversal of this, an adjustment to the actual amount of fiat, not the consequence of any stringency or pull at the monetary rein.

On the whole, industry emerged from the period of hostilities in a liquid state, though not so much so as it did in 1918. Banks, being still more liquid, soon began to expand credit in the rising wave of prosperity. Loans and discounts of national banks increased from 500 to 900 millions from 1866 to the end of 1872, while loans of the New York City clearing house banks moved around a fairly even level till the end of 1869. This is not contradiction. Moreover, the monetary element obviously did not depress output which, on the contrary, made new records throughout the period to the Resumption Act—except in 1871, 1874, and 1876—and increased by 50 per cent per capita, in spite of the huge wave of postwar immigration. It did not prevent increase of money wage rates to 1872, nor decrease in rates of interest, nor even lax habits of lending and speculative excesses. As far as it has anything to do with Black Friday and the crisis of 1873, it was not through stringency but through its opposite. The inference seems to be unavoidable that stabilization of the dollar at the peak of the gold premium or, in fact, any devaluation, would have enforced continuance of inflation, still more excesses, and a still more severe crisis. This is not to deny that the fall in greenback prices—rapid to 1871—spelled hardship for large sectors of the community, the agricultural sector in particular—wheat fell to nearly half the 1866 price by 1870, cotton to less than half within a year—nor that, although the monetary factor evidently accounts for only a minor part of this devaluation and continuing inflation would have brought temporary relief to those sectors. Finally, the importance for our understanding the nature of the cyclical process of evolution, of this case of prosperities accompanied by prices that were not only falling (1866–1880, at an average rate of about 4 per cent per year) but also expected to fall, cannot be too strongly pressed upon the reader's attention.

5. After 1878 progress toward full ratification of the gold standard, which eventually came in 1900 (Gold Standard Act of March 14), need not have been difficult. If, nevertheless, it proved to be so, this was not due to any hitches in the working of the monetary or the economic system, but to the temporary success of the silver interests. This "external factor" from 1876 to 1896 repeatedly threatened to block the road and adversely influenced business situations mainly in two ways. First, both American and European business opinion, seeing some and anticipating further success of silver politicians, tried to prepare for possibilities and responded in a way which should be highly instructive for any mind at all open to factual evidence about the economic importance of safe and stable currency conditions. Second, the mechanical effect, as distinguished from the effect on anticipations, of the silver actually bought was to jeopardize the gold position of the country, which but for this would have been very favorable throughout. For instance, from 1891 to 1893 there was an export of gold to the amount of $155,000,000 for which neither the unsatisfactory crops and prices of 1892 and 1893 nor any other element in the situation will fully account. The Treasury, then the only guardian of the national gold reserve, had, for both reasons, to face a task that at some junctures (1884 was the first) looked hopeless.

The currency factor was a major source of weakness during the vicissitudes of 1893 and was primarily responsible for what proved a specifically American catastrophe, not otherwise fully motivated, in 1896. But while silver thus undoubtedly influenced cyclical situations, it did not do so in the manner we should expect from a perusal of the Bland (1878) and Sherman (1890) acts. The provisions of the former were in themselves quite sufficient to impart an "inflationary" impulse to the system. Yet the price level continued to decline from 1866 on, as mentioned above, even more than in England. The explanation lies in the policy of the Treasury. The passing of that bill really meant a drawn battle: the sound money front had had to give way, but it stuck to the guns of the gold standard. In moving, as it were, on the resultant of these two component forces, the Treasury, while obeying the letter of the law, buying silver in the amount required and doing something toward putting it into circulation, at the same time did its best to prevent it from taking effect. The issue of small greenbacks, for instance, was discontinued in 1885.

Some gold in the New York associated banks was, at the same time, replaced by silver. Besides, silver was allowed to accumulate in the Treasury's vaults and thereby was "sterilized." This policy meant sailing close to the wind, but it succeeded because of several favorable circumstances.

As has already been pointed out, barring the effects of the silver experiment, the gold position of the country was favorable, in some years that might have been critical exceptionally so. Moreover, the fall in interest rates induced an increase in United States bond prices, which backed the notes of national banks. The value of the right to issue notes being decreased thereby, the amount of national bank notes outstanding shrank by about 200 millions during the eighties—a process which was, of course, quickened by the Treasury's policy of debt redemption. Finally, the surpluses which made that policy possible also facilitated accumulation of idle silver. Whatever may be thought of the spending of 300 million dollars or so on the purpose set by the Bland act, effects on prices and on the rhythm and the trends of the cyclical process must have been small, if not altogether absent. The same, or almost the same, is true of the Sherman Act, which much more obviously suggests a compromise between the necessity of satisfying the silver interests and the wish to keep the gold standard. It is particularly significant that the monthly amount of silver to be bought (4,500,000) ounces) was to be paid for in "treasury notes" which were legal tender in every respect but redeemable *in gold* or silver, as the secretary might see fit. Tactics veil intentions. But facts seem to warrant the interpretation that the leaders of the gold party, faced with an attack which was irresistible because some of them needed the support of the silver party in order to gratify their own protectionist desires, decided to *reculer por mieux sauter* on the strength of two observations and a hope. The observations from recent experience were, first, that the Treasury could stand a lot of strain and, second, that silver could be turned into redeemable fiat—which is the way that in fact, though not in law, it had been worked under the Bland Act—and thus prevented, for a time at least, from swamping the monetary system. The hope, according to this interpretation, was that tactical and economic situations would sooner or later arise in which the dragon might be killed. They had not long to wait. Eighteen hundred ninety-three came and brought repeal.

B. The Agricultural Situations of the Period.—In a first approximation, the story of the way in which civilized humanity got and fought cheap bread is, for our period, the story of American railroads and American machinery (toward the end of the period, dry farming must be added). We will at once notice some points which in part account for peculiarities in the *modus operandi* of these two innovations. First, the policy of land settlement entered upon after the Civil War greatly helped to propel the process and stands in a relation of interaction with railroad building. It increased and it directed toward the land a stream of immigrants which, but for it, would have flowed in more slowly. This qualifies the sweeping statement just made: neither immigration nor land policy comes entirely within our schema, but neither of them is independent of the process it describes. Second, those two innovations did not arise in the agricultural sphere. Transportation service was wholly, agricultural machinery mainly, the product of industrial initiative. This entailed an important consequence, particularly obvious in the case of transportation. Typically, a railroad opened a region, built elevators, prepared many things for the would-be farmer, sometimes even furnished instructions about products and methods. Any handy couple could go out to the Middle West or the Far West and know exactly what to do and how to do it. Therefore, the agricultural effects of each railroad asserted themselves with a rapidity which would have been altogether impossible in the case of a genuinely agrarian innovation, and this tended to shorten periods of agrarian prosperity in our sense.[1]

For America, however, the consequences were, third, mitigated—during by far the greater part of the period even reversed—by the fact that wheat and cotton production faced a world-demand schedule that, in real terms, shifted upward all the time. If that production had been monopolized instead of being perfectly competitive, it might still have been during that Kondratieff the best long-run policy to extend acreage and to produce simply as much as possible. For the time being, and before competing

[1] The case was not one of innovation without profits (compare the third chapter) or of cycles without prosperity phase (compare the fourth chapter). But both profits and prosperities in our sense showed rather in the railroad and in the industrial than in the farming business. What farmers earned (in good times) was of the nature of exceptionally high wages.

sources of supply were opened (Argentina in particular), progress in shipping and fall in ocean freight rates worked in the same direction. But, fourth, those consequences were intensified by the fact that in agriculture the "old firms" in our sense are not eliminated so quickly as in industry but go on producing much longer. This is the phenomenon which, if there were not objections to using a term which is associated with so much faulty reasoning, we should call agrarian overproduction. Although the old, on which those innovations would, if our process had been allowed free sway, have passed sentence of economic death, was mainly located in Europe, some effects of this type show also in the Northeast of this country. But dairying, vegetable growing, and so on then, before the time of modern refrigeration and canning, afforded much more compensation than they do today, and New England farming was able to contract by the comparatively painless method of the farmers, without ceasing to be farmers, moving to the West at the expense of abandoning investment.

In order to bring out a very simple but also very important point, we will, for the argument of this paragraph, assume that there are not any chance variations in crops or any effects on yield per acre of innovations which are assumed to act on costs and acreage only—so that the latter remains constant from year to year. Then we can say that for American agriculture, taken as a whole, variations in earnings and variations in prices of products were indeed very different things and that, in particular, falling prices were perfectly compatible with rising earnings—to some extent even the conditions for increase in earnings from sales to Europe. But it is also true that for considerable sectors, and for many individual cases in all sectors, money earnings were, under our assumptions, simply proportional to prices. These sectors and individuals were bound to suffer from any fall of prices below the level to which their locations and methods were adapted. Such a fall must occur by the working of our process and is, in fact, an essential part of the mechanism which spreads the fruits of progress and redistributes productive resources in accordance with the requirements of the new situation. It would have occurred even if there had been no other innovations: agrarian developments alone would have been sufficient to depress the general price *level*, but all other innovations worked in the same direction.

Now, because of the favorable shift in European as well as American demand, and because of those other innovations, agrarian prices did not substantially decline, during our period, relatively to other prices. Even those farmers whose earnings were proportional to prices of products suffered only to the extent to which the prices of what they bought were retail prices which did not fall as much as the wholesale prices they got, and to the extent to which protection prevented nonagrarian prices from reacting as they would have done without it. It was debts, particularly debts incurred for the acquisition of the holding, which gave to the fall in the price level its sinister connotation. This would have been so in the absence of any speculation in farm land and even if nobody had ever bought a farm in erroneous anticipation of rising product prices. But both these factors added dark hues to the picture. This seems to do justice, and at the same time to assign limits, to the view which links agrarian prosperity and distress simply with prices. According to *Technical Bulletin* 288, U. S. Department of Agriculture (D. L. Wickens), 27.8 per cent of all farms operated by owners were mortgaged in 1890, to 35.5 per cent of their value—figures which, while showing the seriousness of the situation, also show that at least three-quarters of all farms (for among the mortgaged ones there must have been some that carried the burden without distress) cannot have been vitally affected. There were other debts besides the mortgages, of course, for which the writer has not been able to make any reliable estimate; but these were mostly short-term bank debts and all, in all normal cases, amenable to current adjustment.

This analysis supplies the theory of what is generally known as the argricultural depression of the last quarter of the nineteenth century, which bears, mainly because it occurred in about the same segment of the Kondratieff, so unmistakable a family likeness to the agricultural depression of the post-Napoleonic period. For America, it should be dated 1882 to 1890, for in 1891 the acreage harvested again starts expanding, and 1877 to 1881 were years of either good harvests or good prices or both, the bumper year, 1879 (rich crop plus high prices owing to failures in Europe) and 1881, the year of maximum price of wheat (119.2 cents per bushel, December farm price) being among them. The reader will observe that the monetary factor has not so far been assigned any independent (causal) role, our analysis having been exclusively in terms of the process described by our model. It is, indeed, believed that this explanation accounts for the essentials of the case. But by itself it is, nevertheless, inadequate for the period 1848–1869.

Californian and Australian gold was, of course, a factor in the expansion and in the behavior of prices during that time. The rise in prices to 1866 and the incident speculation in farm land induced an agrarian postwar crisis which, however, lasted three years only. But after that our process is subject to much less disturbance and is much more nearly adequate to explain the course of things. From 1866 to 1880, the acreage harvested increased from 15.4 to over 38 millions. This is quite enough to bear out the view taken.[1] The long-run tendency of prices accords perfectly though short time peaks and troughs occur irregularly in response to variations in American and European harvests. Prices of farm products in general rose fairly steadily from 1843 to 1857

[1] Exception to the above analysis will be taken, not only by those economists who make agrarian prosperities and depressions (these terms do not now carry the technical meaning assigned to them in this book) wholly a matter of the behavior of money, but also by some who do not. The latter may hold that by our neglect of the decrease in gold production in the seventies and eighties, we make ourselves guilty of a one-sidedness similar to that of the purely monetary explanations. This is not so. The gold factor is not neglected but, though only implicitly, fully taken account of. It is not mentioned explicitly, except for the fifties and sixties, because it was only then that it played an autonomous role. Nor do we deny that the monetary factor could have behaved, or have been made to behave, in such a way as to avoid that fall in price level. Any effective inflation would have done that and brought relief to debtors, agrarian and other. What is objected to, in any diagnosis of the agrarian depression which makes gold production the central fact about it, is that not only does it look merely at the agrarian problem, failing to see it as an element of the process of economic evolution, but also that it looks even at the agrarian problem only from the standpoint of a single surface fact. And what is objected to in the motivation of any policy based on that diagnosis, is that it not only looks at the agrarian problem exclusively from the standpoint of the interest of the agricultural producer, but even neglects all the real problems of that producer. To avoid misunderstandings, the writer wishes to say what may be gleaned also from other remarks in this book—that he is not out of sympathy with measures in support of a healthy class of bona fide farmers, and does not think it ought to be allowed to perish. But there are ways of helping them without interfering with the efficiency of the capitalist machine and without producing consequences other than those that such a policy is intended to serve.

—a rise which almost exactly covers the prosperity phase of the second Kondratieff—and then fell, as again they should have done according to our schema, to a level in 1861 (75, on a 1910–1914 basis), somewhat above the level they again reached at the time when the effects of the Civil War disturbance were substantially digested (1878: 72). They continued their downward course, as we should expect, to 1896 (56). The minimum in December farm price of wheat (48.9 cents) occurs in 1894 (cotton was near its minimum in the same year) and in 10 years, during the period from the Civil War to 1897, it was below 75 cents. Of these, nine years were between 1884 and 1897, the fall after 1891 being again asociated with increase of acreage.

C. **Railroadization.** 1. While for this country railroadization was obviously the "big thing" or "backbone" of the bourgeois Kondratieff, it really got under way, if we judge by mileage added, in 1849, *i.e.*, about six years later than in England. The, roughly, 1720 miles added in 1840, 1841, and 1842 failed to produce any of the symptoms of prosperity and were, moreover, the leavings of the boom of the thirties rather than the first installment of new developments. The New England railroad boom which contributed so much to Boston's prominence at that time began in 1847, but meant little until 1849. By not dating accordingly—but the reader is welcome to do so; it does not make any difference to the analytic schema presented—we are acting on the theory that the irregular twin peak in the thirties upset the course of events which would otherwise have been more like that in England or Germany and that we are but "reconstructing the temple in ruins" if we date as we do. The ruins in question or, without metaphor, the indications that guide us, are the time series: receipts from land sales began to increase in 1842, deposits and stock prices soared in 1843, when also prices started to rise. Liquidation of the excesses associated with wildcat banking stunted the beginnings of the prosperity phase of the new Kondratieff, and this accounts for the mildness of the setback at the end of 1847. Several good crops, English free trade, and the Californian boom helped to shorten the ensuing depression, which covers not quite a year (1848) and to accentuate revival, which also made up for what the stunted prosperity had failed to bring about.

Transition to the prosperity of what, then, has to be counted as the second Juglar was effected in an atmosphere of boom, unusual expansion of credit and speculation, particularly in land and railroad stock, to all of which Californian gold (since 1850) and the favorable development of foreign trade lent their aid. The warrant for speaking of a new Juglar, although the curve of new (less abandoned) mileage displays nothing but a dip in the year from which we date it (1852), is in the shift of building activity from New England to the Central Atlantic and the Middle Western states, which clearly meant a distinct new step within the Kondratieff process: this statement should be compared with the discussion on possible relations between longer and shorter cycles in the fourth chapter. The reason why we do not attach more weight to the setback which occurred as early as autumn 1853 and lasted through 1854 and almost to the end of 1855 is that it seems to have been entirely due to speculative excesses—in part, no doubt, fostered by the new gold—and to their repercussion on railroad construction. Therefore, we date prosperity plus recession of that Juglar from the beginning of 1852 to the second half of 1856. Finally, the reason why we do not attribute to gold anything beyond excesses and reaction to excesses (and such disturbances as the failure of the rates of interest to rise promptly and "tight" situations *consequent* upon this) is that the railroad construction was clearly under sail before the Californian gold began to act, and that, looking at the data of the situation, we do not see any justification for holding that that process would, barring those excesses, not have run its course or produced its effects without it. Part of the rise in price level we do attribute to it.

The quantitative adequacy of expenditure on railroad construction is beyond doubt: the trackage operated reached about 30,000 miles by 1860, and the capital debt of railroads alone then was about 900 million dollars; for actual cost of construction, there is no reliable estimate, but it certainly exceeded that sum, of which about three-quarters were spent in that decade. Beyond doubt, too, is the truly revolutionary effect of the mileage opened. Freight rates fell drastically and by 1854 averaged between two and three cents per ton-mile. The entrepreneurial function consisted, in this case, not so much in visualizing possibilities—everyone saw them and speculated on them—or in the solution of technological problems—the locomotive functioned sufficiently well by that time and was thenceforth improved almost automatically by a series of typically "induced" inventions, and no major problems impeded the building of the lines—as in the leadership of groups, in successfully dealing with politicians and local interests, in the solution of problems of management and of development in the regions the roads opened up. It was "getting things done" and nothing else, a variety of pure entrepreneurship stripped of all accessories. But this entrepreneurship was often split between several individuals and is not always easy to atribute to any single one.

2. As regards financing, we must distinguish the task of creating the conditions of profitableness of the enterprise from the task of providing the money for construction. That the first should have been a distinct task is due to the fact that the Middle Western and Western projects could not be expected to pay for themselves within a period such as most investors care to envisage. Many of them meant building ahead of demand in the boldest acceptance of the phrase and everyone understood them to mean that. Operating deficits for a period which it was impossible to estimate with any accuracy were part of the data of the problem. In a sense, any construction under such circumstances implies "overdoing it." But this concept is hardly applicable to a situation in which, without producing some of the effects of overdoing, the thing could not have been done at all. Under different environmental conditions and with a political structure different from what it was, those circumstances might have constituted a strong case for railroadization's being planned and executed by the national government, as it was in Russia by the imperial bureaucracy. State enterprise was, in fact, prominent in the early stages of American railroad development; but by that time it had failed.

Since many projects that were obviously socially productive (in Professor Pigou's sense) were not at that time paying propositions, additional sources of revenue, or contributions to the costs, had to be found. Where it proved possible to secure subsidies or loans amounting to subsidies, this at the same time helped to solve the problem of financing construction. But the solution presently hit upon in the case of the Illinois Central Railroad, the donation of land by Congress (1850; the immediate grantees were the states of Illinois, Mississippi, and Alabama) did not. Previous profits or domestic savings being inadequate, railroad construction was, therefore, mainly financed by credit creation.

From the standpoint of the United States, foreign buying of American railroad bonds amounted to this—even if the bonds were paid for out of, say, English savings—as did European credits extended in anticipation of bond issues or simply as overdrafts. Foreign investing was at times heavy. According to the estimate given in Sumner's History of the American Currency, English investments in this country (not only in railroads) amounted to about 400 million dollars before 1857. Overdrafts (though mainly for what purported to be "regular" commercial credit) were granted, in many cases, with almost unbelievable freedom and carelessness. Domestic credit creation was even more freely resorted to. We do not know its amount, but we can, in most cases, trace it in one or more of the following forms: direct lending by banks to companies against their notes or on bonds to be sold later to the public; financing the subscriptions of the promoting groups or of the public (in which case we must also take account of the fact that a customer may borrow for other purposes because by subscribing he binds means which would otherwise serve these); and financing speculation—there is a significant coincidence between the increase of railroad stock prices and of deposits in 1852. The fact that credit, created *ad hoc* by both the preexisting banks and the many new ones that emerged, to a large extent financed railroad and other innovation, has often been emphasized and never been contested. We may illustrate, however, by one instance, the case of the Illinois Central Railroad.

The burst of speculation which occurred in the Middle West in the twenties and thirties and led up to the peak in land sales in the middle of the latter decade, had really no other basis than everybody's conviction of the imminence of great developments. What these developments were to be and which part of the region would lead in them was in this case entirely indefinite, no particular locality holding any particular advantages. Preferential positions had to be created largely by political action, and an anarchic struggle ensued between local communities, each controlled by its own group of speculators—railroad and canal projects, which for the moment were mostly bubbles, being the chief bones of contention. Moves and countermoves in this struggle constituted state politics and dominated the state legislature of Illinois, which under the circumstances was the only possible source of powers and means. Plans of a central railroad, which came to nothing, emerged in 1818 and 1835. The Internal Improvement Bill, passed in 1837, provided a little over 10 millions for the carrying out of various railroad and waterways projects, one of which may be looked upon as a second attempt to do what eventually was done by the Illinois Central Roailroad Company. This time a beginning was made, but it soon ended in collapse and discredit. Another attempt to make headway was made in 1843, when a charter was granted for the Great Western Railroad Company, which after failure was renewed in 1849. Soon after this, however, the campaign in Washington, first for a right of preemption of land, and after that for a straight land grant, met with success and the Illinois Central Railroad Company was chartered and organized in 1851.

There is no need for any comment on the nature of the proceedings which thus inaugurated the colonization of a great part of the country, or for explanation of what the entrepreneurial function so far consisted in. The financial group which eventually found themselves in control of the enterprise (the same which had bought the Michigan Central in 1846) were well connected and by no means lacking in seriousness. Their methods and attitudes were fully up to the standard of their time in such matters. The charter, which among other things provided that 7 per cent of the gross income was to go to the state, cannot be said to have failed to take account of public interest. But the fact had to be faced that there simply were no means available at all commensurate with building costs, which were budgeted at 16-1/2 millions. On the stock, which at first the group had thought of keeping to themselves, they looked very much in the light of what in French finance is termed *parts de fondateurs* or, to use an American expression, of velvet. They were businessmen who had their means and more than their means engaged in other ventures, and their behavior but too well illustrates our theory of the logical primacy of created credit in the financing of innovation. They did, however, pay in an assessment of 20 per cent on the first million of stock, and both the directors and their business connections took 2 millions of bonds, to be paid for by installments. They thus proved that they meant business, but it is not unfair to suspect that the money they actually paid was borrowed from banks. This was the war chest with which they embarked upon surveying. They also induced the Michigan Central, which they controlled, to enter into an agreement to carry, in consideration of certain concessions, another 2 millions of bonds of the Illinois Central. The fundamental idea, however, was from the beginning to sell, or borrow upon, mortgage bonds secured on the land grant and the right of way plus improvements. This method then was a recognized one and for a time became still more so—in other cases existing contracts of a nonexisting enterprise were used as security—and it was far from being disapproved of, so long as it did not coincide with fraudulent representations. They offered these bonds in England and, in spite of the refusal of the Rothschilds and the Barings, succeeded in forming a syndicate. The means so provided ran out by 1855, when the promoters had to take additional bonds. Further calls on the stockholders and borowing on short-term notes became necessary before the work was completed in 1856. Embarrassments were not ended thereby, and in 1857 catastrophe was—even apart from damaging revelations—perilously near, but the company, under the able management of an extraordinary man, stood its ground and, with sales of land developing steadily, consolidated its position. The effect of the line on the development—or, rather, the economic creation—of its territory and the whole country needs no emphasis.

3. Our analysis contains all the elements necessary for a diagnosis of the crisis of 1857. It will be convenient, however, to add a few minor points and to round off the picture, in order to show once more how what we consider the fundamental mechanism of fluctuations combines with accidents and incidents not inherent to its logic. To begin with, the crisis was an international one, commercial and financial relations between our countries (and others) being strong enough to synchronize events remarkably and to play a large role in shaping the surface. But it is nonetheless a fact that fundamental explanation could run for each country in terms of its own development. Second, the crisis coincides with, or rather lags behind, the upper turning point of that Kondratieff. All statistical indications combine to support this finding, which is all the more remarkable because gold production could have been expected to interfere with their behavior. It actually did to some extent, but not enough to alter the fundamental contour. This happened later, when the Civil War and other external factors make it possible to speak for Europe of a "rising trend" in prices up to 1873. But in the United States wholesale prices recovered only moderately in

1859 from the sharp fall in the preceding year and then continued to fall until the first quarter of 1861. Although gold thus failed to keep up the price level, it had, as stated before, undoubtedly a share in bringing about the preceding rise. This influence was exerted partly through the expenditure of gold miners and partly through the additional facilities for credit creation it provided. But through the whole of the upswing we observe recurrent situations of stringency, which is exactly what we should expect. The case shows very well how easy money, due to the action of external factors, will on a rising tide of business always produce stringency and, hence, is the most ineffective of means to prevent recessions.

Third, the increase in gold production and what, without explaining again, we term *reckless banking* actually do account for many surface phenomena. In particular these factors account for the sharp and short panic that followed upon the failure of the Ohio Life and Trust Company on Aug. 25, 1857, after which 150 banks failed up to Oct. 17: there was a spectacular run on Oct. 13. It is only natural that public attention concentrated on this, and that many writers at that time and later simply formulated the popular theory that the whole catastrophe was due to the shortsightedness of banks which called in loans in a panicky way. Although neither this contraction nor the preceding "recklessness" provide fundamental explanations, both played a very real role in the "abnormal liquidation" that ensued, and our theory neither requires nor justifies any attempt to discount their importance. Difference of opinion arises only if it be held that either the credit expansion or the credit contraction was the essence of the matter, and that without either of the two everything would have been well. But we may go some way with those more careful analysts of that situation who pointed to a number of auxiliary factors which intensified the boom and the removal of which intensified the depression. One of these factors—the speculation in land—went to lengths entirely out of proportion with what would have been a normal incident of the contemporaneous development and must hence be classed as a separate factor requiring in turn special sociological explanation. Stock exchange speculation played a smaller role. Railroad stocks reached their peak toward the end of 1852 and then fell sharply to the end of 1854 in the course of what in September of that year amounted to a financial panic and entailed a considerable number of failures. The air being thus cleared, no speculative crash occurred afterward and the abrupt fall in the crisis of 1857 gave way to partial recovery within the year. Another factor was of course the import of capital, of which the unfavorable balance in commodity trade between 1850 and 1857 was a symptom. This certainly contributed to making the situation more sensitive than it otherwise would have been. The very good wheat and cotton crops of 1855, which were sold at favorable prices, also gave an impetus to all sorts of activities which then added to the difficulties of liquidation. Of other causes contributing to the slump there is a long list.

Fourth and finally, however, there cannot be any doubt in this case of the reality of the fundamental explanation from our schema. Railroad construction was the main but not the only factor that carried that wave of evolution. Taken together, the innovation of the period and the adaptations they enforced explain primarily the turn of the Kondratieff. Again, as in earlier cases, it is not claimed that they explain the crisis also, except in the sense that they make it understandable that speculative furors broke out and that error and misconduct accumulated: they thus furnish a reason why the situation became so sensitive as to be easily turned into a crisis by unfavorable events or by troubles arising out of those weak spots. The actual picture of the crisis could never be understood from innovations alone. Many things in that upswing—railroad construction in particular—were done under the influence of artificial stimuli, by which we mean that a number of them would not have been undertaken at all or would not have been undertaken just then and on such a scale without encouragement from the political and the financial sphere. No critique is implied by this. On the contrary we have said before that the term *overdoing* must be applied with caution. But this accounts of course for some of the difficulties of the ensuing situation and also for the presence of a Hayek effect: in a very obvious sense the period of production was lengthened beyond what the economic organism could stand for the moment.

4. At the time of the crisis the Juglar turned into depression. There were many failures in 1858, prices fell sharply, and construction decreased further—exports and imports nearly balanced for the *fiscal* year. In spite of easy money, good crops in the South (five successive supernormal cotton crops, in 1859

also coupled with high prices), and all-around activity, the general atmosphere, as recorded by the press of that time, was anything but cheerful until into 1860; but revival asserted itself, below this surface, from the beginning of 1859. The fact that this revival differed so much from its predecessor (1850, 1851) we attribute primarily to the underlying Kondratieff which had by then completed its prosperity, and entered upon its recession. This recession underlay the shorter ups and downs of those years and shaded off into the Civil War, the approach of which intensified, although it did not altogether create, the troubles of 1860.[1] The war dominated the third Juglar (1861–1869; diag-

[1] In 1859 imports again approached the 1857 level—for the second half of the fiscal year they were even considerably higher—and there was a vigorous expansion of bank loans, with specie in banks declining, that led to stringency in the fall. Moreover, new banks were founded and capital of banks was increased in the West (which until 1860 suffered from bad crops and low prices of breadstuffs). These Western banks, mostly modeled after the New York Free Banking System, but with much less sound and stable securities to back their issues and with arrangements about redemption amounting to evasion, rapidly became a source of weakness of the situation, although the banks in the South, particularly in Louisiana, and, to a lesser extent, those of New York and New England were still in a strong position. The Western record crop of 1860 and other favorable circumstances might have availed to prevent trouble, but for the political situation. Its seriousness was first realized in the South, the banks of New Orleans beginning to restrict and to look askance at Northern paper in August. This affected New York banks, while in the West many banks got into trouble through the decline in the bonds of Southern states that formed a great part of the basis of their note issue. There was a premonitory panic in the New York Stock Exchange in October, in spite of easy money. After the presidential election on Nov. 6 panic and disorganization spread through all sectors of the country's economic system, of no greater industrial significance, however, than the panic of 1914. The one point calling for notice is the novel method which was resorted to in order to handle the situation and which constitutes a more important step in the development of banking than many a reform act. The 50 New York banks which formed the Clearing House Association decided on corporative action, in order to extend credit instead of restricting it, by means of practically pooling their cash reserves and creating clearing-house certificates against deposit of adequate security including receivables, to be accepted in settlement of claims between themselves. Only one bank held aloof. Success was complete and almost immediate. Boston followed with similar results; in other parts of the country banks had to suspend. Both the device and its success are highly instructive. The latter, never again quite repeated, although this bit of central bank policy thenceforth became

nosis of 1861 is doubtful owing to political events) and of course interfered both with the behavior of our series and the processes behind them, displacing peaks and deferring steps in industrial development, thus crowding them into the years immediately preceding 1872.

New trackage (minus abandonments) in 1869 began its unprecedented increase, which reached a peak in 1871. The success of the first transcontinental route, which had been pushed as a war measure to link California to the North, led the way and indicated what was to be the particular feature of this boom. We have again the same pattern of entrepreneurial activity and financing: promoters securing options of right of way, having the company chartered and endowed with land grants, selling the options to it and taking securities in payment, finally placing the bonds—the stock being commonly treated as a bonus—in order to provide the means for construction, and buying equipment on installments through equipment trust certificates. In case of success, issue of further securities would then become possible to consolidate the situation. Failing this, there was reconstruction. In almost every major instance, promoters might have plagiarized the Duke of Wellington's (alleged) saying at Waterloo, "Blücher or the night." The Blücher in our case was primarily English (and other European) capital, which took the responsibility for a great part of the 2 billions which are said to have been expended on American railroads from 1867 to 1873. A very efficient machinery for pressing European capital into the service had by that time replaced the individual efforts of early times.

Two things are perfectly clear. First, that development which quantitativly outstripped the one of the forties and fifties as it was outstripped by the development in the eighties (the all-time peak in miles added comes in 1887) was a typical downgrade development within the meaning of our model. It was a Juglar prosperity superimposed on a Kondratieff recession,[1] a new step

part of the household remedies in such situations, was precisely due to the fact that there was not much wrong with either the industrial or the banking situation and that disturbance by an external factor was all that had to be faced.

[1] [Presumably a slip. Below Schumpeter dates the beginning of Kondratieff *depression* in 1870, the same date he gives for the beginning of the Juglar prosperity.—Ed.]

in what no longer was fundamentally new, but a process of carrying out what had previously been inititated. Railroad construction was now swimming with the stream in a sense in which it had not been before. What was to be done, how it had to be done, was chalked out, and all the characteristics of induced or completing development were present. This left plenty of problems for the individual case, but they were comparatively easy to solve, further eased by the growth of the environment, and of the type which is characteristic of "exploiting investment opportunity" and "pushing into new economic space." Moreover, the general features of the period support this interpretation. There was a great building boom. The well-being of all classes in the years 1869 to 1873 of which we read (and which we are able to verify as far as our information goes)—the fact in particular that wages rose and wholesale prices fell while the former had risen less than wholesale prices in the early fifties—is obviously due to the expansion of production which our schema leads us to expect in every Kondratieff recession.[1] But it is not less clear, in the second place, that that method of financing which so well illustrates our theory, was handled with such carelessness as to make it an additional cause of the situation of 1873. It not only induced but really also presupposed abnormal speculative activity and could not without it have gone to anything like the length it did.

The phenomena of the Secondary Wave were developed to an unusual degree thereby, and errors and cases of misconduct became possible which our model does not account for per se. The Gold Corner, Black Friday, bank failures, campaigns between stock exchange operators, and other purely financial incidents were symptoms of this, and it becomes understandable that even as regards the railroad business these things were more obviously in evidence than the underlying process and that it seemed as if construction had been brought to a stop and the success of existing lines had been jeopardized by them rather than by any "logic of evolution." But even so, nobody can deny that railroad construction had temporarily exhausted possibilities—a formulation which is more correct than the more common phrase of things having been overdone—and it should be easy to see that this, together with the dislocating consequences immediate and ulte-

[1] [The same mistake pointed out in the previous footnote.—Ed.]

rior, for the economic system, of new construction was what created the situation in which the Secondary Wave broke, and with it untenable credit situations and speculative bubbles all over the field of industry and commerce.

Although the abnormal liquidation which has come down to posterity as the crisis of 1873 clearly first broke out abroad (in Vienna), and the American scaffolding received its first decisive shock on the wire of foreign credit, our diagnosis seems to stand. It is not astonishing that the impact was primarily on the new, instead of on those elements that progress had made obsolete. For, as was pointed out in our theoretical chapter, this will always happen if the new things stand on a slender and the old things on a safe financial basis. Thus, the role played in the drama by the Northern Pacific failure does not any more contradict expectation from our model than does the fact that, in general, danger signals first became visible in the railroad field. Railroad stocks reached their peak in 1869, *i.e.*, in the revival of the preceding Juglar, were no more than steady in the boom of 1871, and declined in 1872 while industrial stocks rose. Tightness of money, smallness of bank reserves, a premonitory panic on the stock exchange in October 1871, all link up with railroad finance, as do the slackening in increase of exports and the sharp rise of imports that occurred in 1872. Once the panic had broken out in the fall of 1873—up till then general business kept up well—the typical sequence of events followed. Speculation in land and stocks collapsed, prices fell, exports increased, imports decreased, firms of all types failed in large numbers, the stock exchange had to be closed, banks suspended payment, unemployment became serious almost immediately. We shall not repeat what has been said in the discussion of the crisis of 1857. The fact is significant, however, that, as far as mechanisms go, there would have to be repetition.

But this time the breakdown was much more serious and a prolonged depression followed. It is hazardous to rely on statistical evidence for an appraisal of relative severities of crises, because equal reactions of identical symptoms may mean very different things at different times, and presence or absence of others may be accidental or due to difference in the handling of the situations. As far as mere figures go, however, some aspects, at any rate, of the depression were quite as dark in 1873 to 1877 as they were in 1929 to 1933. Data about unemployment, for instance, are, it is true, entirely untrustworthy and incomparable. But if we could believe in the figure, mentioned by some authors, of 3 millions of "tramps" (in the winter of 1873 to 1874) then this, considering the smaller quantitative importance of the industrial sector and the absence at that time of any tendency to exaggeration, would indicate that relative unemployment was actually worse than it was during the recent world crisis. Prices fell less sharply than they did in and after 1930. But this is because their downward movement from the Civil War peak had not, except in 1872, been previously checked. The decline was more gentle then because it was more even, but it was not smaller if we consider, as we must, ultimate results and not only what happened in the crisis proper. The political complement also was similar, granger movement, agitation for inflation, strikes and riots being, if we take account of differences in social and political structure and attitude, more than fair counterparts of corresponding phenomena in the recent instance, although in the bourgeois Kondratieff they were handled in a different way.

5. According to contemporaneous report, 1874 to (the first half of) 1878 were years of almost unrelieved gloom. But adjustment and the elimination of untenable positions went on steadily, and the path was cleared for recovery. The process is well reflected in the figures of railroad construction. It touched low point as early as 1875 and suffered another setback in 1877, but there was significant increase in 1876, both in new trackage and in locomotives built, in the midst of a renewed outbreak of failures and a great fall of railroad stock prices. Thus the tide began to turn before either people's "depressed state of mind" had changed for the better or surface mechanisms had ceased to work in the downward direction, also before the revival on the stock exchange (1877). It was the improvement in the *objective elements of the situation* which turned both the psychic states (expectations) and the mechanisms (cumulation of depressive effects and that sort of thing), and not vice versa. Nor was it external circumstances which stopped the downward course. Crops were good in 1878, but prices of wheat and cotton were low and improvement in any case set in before good crops became a certainty. *The system recovered of its own and this in the face of steadily declining general prices.* We date the fourth Juglar 1870–1879.

Now the eighth decade of the nineteenth century lies, according to our schema, entirely within the depression phase of the second Kondriatieff, which turned from recession into depression about 1870.[1] A whole Juglar as well as the prosperity and recession of another which began with 1880, therefore, completed their course on what statisticians would call a downward trend. And this is our explanation of the severity of the crisis, the depth of the subsequent depression—which is, in all respects, as strikingly similar to the one of 1826 to 1830 and the one of 1929 to 1933 as were the prosperities that preceded them—and the fact that gloom and difficulties persisted far into recovery. All three cases were characterized by the fact that the shorter wave had to subside to what was a falling level while, in other cases that did not lead to such breakdown or prolonged depression, it had only to subside to a rising level.

In the case under discussion, nobody can doubt the reality of the particular process that constituted the Juglar in the course of which the crisis occurred. Nor is it farfetched to say that the larger process—mainly associated with railroad construction—within which the events of 1870 to 1873 constitute a step, had so revolutionized the economic system that liquidation, absorption, adaptation—all of what these terms mean can be clearly observed—was an unusually long and painful affair. If objection to the three-cycle schema be insuperable, we do not insist on it. The facts remain, whatever the merits or demerits of the schema by which we present them. But what it is necessary to insist on is, first, that in the other two cases which are in an analogous position on the two other Kondratieffs and stand in approximately the same time relation to preceding industrial revolutions, we also find similarly severe and prolonged depressions and, second, that we do not find such depressions in any other case.

As soon as paralysis due to the shock was over, expansion of physical production resumed *within the Kondratieff depression,*

[1] This turn occurred, therefore, before the last boom which preceded the great crisis. Without unduly stressing the regularities which form the basis of our schema, we should recall that this is perfectly in accordance with it, since it makes the beginning of a Kondratieff depression coincide with a Juglar prosperity. The reasons why an "about" should be inserted are, on the one hand, that the gentle sweep of the Kondratieff displays broad heights and depth and not any peaks or troughs, so that precise location is always difficult, and, on the other hand, that aftereffects of the Civil War must be taken into account.

as we should expect. Railroad construction, going on to be the carrier of the cyclical movement, soared from 1878, to a peak in new trackage in 1882 and (from the fall to 1885) to the all-time peak of 1887 (nearly 13,000 miles). This almost gives, if the lag is taken into account, the history of the cyclical fluctuations of that period. But this does not mean now, as it did before, that the relation of railroad construction and general business was primarily one of cause and effect. On the contrary, the more an innovation becomes established, the more it loses the character of an innovation and the more it begins to follow impulses, instead of giving them. Besides, Kondratieff downgrades and revivals precisely display a wide variety of induced or completing innovations which develop and carry to their limit possibilities opened up before, of which railroad building was but the most important. Accordingly, railroad construction, increasingly settling into a predetermined framework and exploiting preexisting investment opportunities, became during the period under discussion much more (though not yet entirely) a function of railroad business and, hence, of the rest of the business organism than it had been before, and the relation became substantially one of mutual dependence. However, the railroad industry had not sown its wild oats as yet, either as regards boldness of advance or as regards financial methods.

Traffic and earnings had revived by 1878 (1877 marks the low point in the latter), which we consider as the last year of the recovery phase of the fourth Juglar. Then they strongly increased, with general business, to 1881, when the flow of new capital into railroads reached the peak corresponding to the peak in miles added that occurred one year later. Investment continued, though at a decreasing rate, until 1883, when it experienced a check, with the Juglar turning into its recession (1882), followed by a depression in the ordinary course. But although the above shows that we make as full allowance for the influence of business on railroads as we do for the influence of railroad construction on business, railroads still set the pace. It would not be correct, in particular, to emphasize the part played by the crops of 1878, 1879, and 1880 to the point of making them the main factor in railroad construction. They constituted a favoring circumstance. But farm products after all made up less than 20 per cent of total tonnage hauled, and average range of variation was roughly 5 per cent.

We may date Juglar depression from the end of 1883. It lasted through 1884 and 1885 and is marked by a crisis in the former year, panic on the stock exchange, strain in the money market necessitating issue of clearinghouse certicates, failures of banks and stock exchange firms, unemployment, and so on. According to the schema the Kondratieff would have been due to embark upon revival in that year, and this accounts for the further fact that neither severity nor duration of that depression were at all comparable to the severity and duration of the events of 1873 to 1877. One point calls for attention, however. In expounding the working of our model we have laid stress on the fall in the price of new products, which is a major piece of the mechanism that conveys the results of progress to the masses. We also saw that this fall, though as a matter of general theory it should primarily affect competing industries as well as old firms in the same industry, will also react on the innovating industry itself, especially if it stands financially on slippery ground and if further steps in the path of evolution begin to compete with the creations of earlier steps.

The history of railroads affords a good illustration for this. Freight rates began of course to fall at a very early stage, but they still averaged about 2½ cents in 1868. Then they fell sharply, though at a decreasing rate, to 1874, when they averaged 1.8 cents, and still more sharply during that depression. They increased slightly in 1878, but reached the one-cent level in 1885. Now this process was perfectly normal, but it upset many a financial structure in the railroad business. And because of the imperfections of competition in this industry, it did its work by way of spectacular struggles between controlling groups, which exercised the public mind and set everybody talking about freight wars, cutthroat competition, discrimination, and the evils of unregulated enterprise, to the exclusion of what the thing really meant. As a matter of fact, it paved the way to consolidation, efficient administration, and sound finance, thus ushering in the last step of America's railroadization.

It took another Juglar, however, to accomplish this (1889 to 1897), the last one to be dominated by the railroad industry, although the days of new companies had passed. Some of its features have been and will be discussed in their various places, when also certain difficulties of dating and interpretation will be mentioned. For the moment it is sufficient to note that the crisis of 1893 has in a sense more claim to be called a crisis of railroads than has any other. While the preceding crises of that Kondratieff were railroad prices primarily in the sense that railroadization played the leading role in the process of economic evolution which produced the situations that developed into crises, and railroads were but secondarily affected, the case of 1893 was primarily a crisis of the roads themselves—roughly one-quarter of which (measured by capital) went into the receiver's hands. Earnings fell off in 1894, when for the second time in the history of American railroads there was an absolute decrease in traffic, and construction displayed the lowest figure since 1851. Duration of that depression—abnormal for a Juglar in a Kondratieff revival—and irregularity of ensuing fluctuations, though also conditioned by external factors, are substantially accounted for by the effects of that house cleaning in what had then become an "old," and after the World War was to become a declining, industry. A final boom in construction and new organization was still to follow and to contribute to the prosperity of the next Kondratieff—as the leading innovations of every Kondratieff seem to do—which carried mileage to about 250,000 by 1910. After that year, net construction rapidly decreased to zero and below.

D. Some Features of the Development of Manufactures.— For the United States, a history of the cyclical process could, in the period of the second Kondratieff, be written almost exclusively in terms of railroad development. Inserting immigration of capital and men—about 14 millions immigrated, from the end of the Civil War to 1900—harvests, and the Civil War, we would get practically all the fluctuations and trends there are. By 1897, "net capital" of the railroads stood at $9,168,072,000 (a little over $50,000 per mile in operation). Everything else turned on the roads and was either created or conditioned by them, and large-scale financing found its main object in them. But we must not exaggerate. The railroads did not teach Americans capitalist methods and attitudes. These, as well as large-scale industrial enterprise, existed before. Nor were the industrial processes of the period mere adaptations to, or exploitations of, the conditions created by the roads. Scarcity of labor and wealth of natural resources presented problems and conditioned achievements of their own. These—efficient labor saving machinery, in particular—became characteristic of American innovation, which no longer internationally lagged but increasingly began to lead during that Kondratieff.

In that environment which contained no large, antiquated structures it is not easy to find decaying industries. Whaling, which steadily declined (with one short interruption) after the sixties, is, however, one. It affords a good example of the mechanism that draws resources toward new goals. Shipping in general reflects, apart from coastal, river, and lake shipping, the same tendency. During the first two Juglars, in the days of the clippers and also during the fifties, the American merchant marine had almost defied competition in the Atlantic trade. But it lost much of its ground during and after the Civil War, in spite of many attempts and in spite of subsidies. This was not due to any shortcomings in shipbuilding, which was more progressive than the English and repeatedly competed successfully even as to price. America simply turned away from the sea. We will merely note that in the construction of the wooden sailing vessel America was supreme, and that this was a feature of the prosperities of the forties and fifties. The iron steamer, also the iron sailing ship, was being successfully built in the prosperity of the fourth Juglar (John Roach and Son, Cramp and Sons), and shipbuilding was conspicuous by precedence in the processes that started the fifth—in fact it was active already in 1877. In the fifth and sixth, the all-steel ship established itself and the triple-expansion engine put in its appearance. Colliers, tankers, greatly improved coastal and river steamers, after 1890 battleships, also continued to give employment, and in 1891 one of the greatest yards of the world started launching (Newport News Shipyard and Drydock Co.).

Coal mining, though perhaps to a greater degree the object of active enterprise than it was in England, was more pushed along than pushing. Developments of new districts, availing themselves either of existing or *ad hoc* created new transport facilities, constitute in the American case definite innovations and contribute to definite prosperities. For anthracite this was true before our period—an outstanding instance being the Lehigh Coal and Navigation Company—bituminous coal first featured in the forties, during which steam began to push out water power—a process more characteristic of that Juglar than railroads were. Coking did not play any role and was done in very primitive ways until the prosperity that preceded 1873. Then it developed in the Connellsville field, producing mainly for the Pittsburgh district. Production spread and went on growing during the depression and made a big stride in the prosperity of the penultimate Juglar. The census of 1890 enumerates 13 districts. But to the end of that Kondratieff (and beyond) the wasteful beehive even prevailed.

The use of petroleum for other purposes than lighting is, like electricity, a "carrying" innovation of the next Kondratieff, and was in the incubating stage during the second. "In 1878 a vaporizing device for burning a residuum of petroleum and coal tar in conjunction with superheated steam was tested at the Brooklyn Navy Yard. Nearly nine years later, an oil-burning locomotive . . . was reported to represent the first practical application of this fuel to land transportation. The following year oil was used at the plant of the North Chicago Rolling Mill Company."[1] All sorts of applications were experimented with and by-products gained rapidly in importance (gasoline, lubricants); but none of them was a major feature of entrepreneurial activity during that period.

Petroleum for lighting purposes was one of the great innovations—a New Commodity in our sense—of the second Kondratieff, and all the features of an innovation of this type stand out very well. It had been used occasionally before, but wells were first drilled in 1859 (drilling and pipe lines were the two great innovations of the period). In the very limited field it entered, it first competed out kerosene (made from shale and coal) as well as other illuminants (for example, whale oil). Later it had to meet gas and electricity, which eventually competed it out in turn. Quantities, prices, profits behaved in the process as we should expect. The first wave of this innovation starts in—and helped starting, of course—the prosperity of the third Juglar. As a result, there were 194 refineries by 1865, mostly in Ohio (the biggest enterprise being that of Rockefeller, Andrews, and Flagler), Pennsylvania and New York. The expansion thus induced went on in the Juglar downgrade and revival, powerfully propelled by the discoveries in California, the price of refined and still more of crude petroleum falling accordingly. Pipe lines and tank cars also emerged at that time and consumers' resistance

[1] V. S. Clark, History of Manufactures in the United States, vol. II, p. 517.

was speedily overcome. The regular situation of the Juglar downgrade led to the organization of the Continental Improvement Company (1868), which developed into the South Improvement Company (1872). The fifth Juglar then brought the completion of the organizational innovation that was to set the outstanding example for other industries,[1] the Standard Oil. It remained a "trust" for a decade only, and independent refineries continued to exist. But the ideas of the centralized management of an industry, of running it as a unit according to a plan, and of acquiring control of some of its conditioning factors—railroads, in particular—persisted.

Gas was also a major element in the entrepreneurial activity that carried the second Kondratieff—though it had a much more important previous history than had petroleum—and similarly completed its career substantially within the period. In England gas is reported to have been first used for lighting a house as early as 1792. Boulton and Watts' installation at Soho (1804) made it widely known. London began using it in 1807, and most of the larger cities followed suit in 1816–1819. In this country Baltimore adopted it first, in 1816, New York in 1823, Boston in 1828; and there were many other installations previous to the crisis of 1837. But it was in the forties that the first great wave set in. The process lasted into the seventies—the westward expansion of the country continuing to supply new objects, though in the East it was substantially completed by the end of the first Juglar, when coal gas also began to supplant gas from rosin and whale oil. Municipal initiative and regulation, naturally much concerned with this commodity, accounts for the deviations of investment from the cyclical schema. Prices were still high for the private household, partly because of the discrimination in favor of the public consumer (the city rate in Baltimore was, for instance in 1848 $1 per 1,000 cubic feet, as compared with $4 for private consumers). The great difficulty which hampered enterprise at the beginning, the lack of an adequate meter, was

[1] In 1884 it was followed, though on a much lower level of efficiency, in the cottonseed oil industry (American Cotton Oil Trust), which never really conquered. In 1887 the Southern Cotton Oil Company was founded, a many-plant concern which was to play a great role in the industry. The cotton-oil case is particularly interesting because of the complications and changes in the competitive position of the product. Cyclically, it was important throughout the last three Juglars. Its innovating stage was in the late sixties and early seventies.

definitely overcome in 1843. Until 1872, gas was distilled from coal—a process that was to regain importance when markets had been found for the by-products—but in that year water gas was patented. This innovation, although introduced in Philadelphia the year after, entered upon its career in the eighties. Carburetted water gas was successful in warding off the attack threatening from kerosene, and the Welsbach mantle (preceded by the Bunsen burner, 1855, and the Lungren mantle, 1881), in deferring defeat by electricity for about a decade. In the fifth Juglar, also, gas began to invade other uses besides lighting. There was a considerable development of gas motors, gas stoves appeared in 1879, circulating-tank water heaters in 1883 (the improved Ruud heater came in 1897).

Another competitor arose, however—natural gas, which had been used for lighting before our period (Fredonia, New York, 1821) and had conquered considerable ground in this capacity. It had sometimes a price advantage over manufactured gas and always other advantages which made it preferable for industrial use. This began in the boiling of salt brine in West Virginia (1841), but the first important case was its use in Pennsylvania iron works in 1873. The first pipe line of any length was opened in 1875. The big wave of this innovation was an important element of the penultimate Juglar and culminated in a boom in 1886. Its importance from our standpoint consists in the fact that it shifted industrial location, newly creating several centers, and powerfully affected the coal situation in Pennsylvania, Ohio, Indiana, and Kansas. But production of the wells of that district then rapidly declined. We will add here that the great increase in the use of natural gas about 1908 accounts for the break in the curve of sales of manufactured gas that occurred at that time.

Technologically, iron-ore mining was a simple affair. It was the object of entrepreneurial activity in two ways. First, there was the task of exploring and developing a district before mining operations could be started. Northern Minnesota (1884) may serve as an example. Transport questions and new commercial combinations attended the development of the Lake Superior districts: the Marquette range in the second Juglar, the Menominee mines in the fourth, the Gogebic mines in the fifth (1885) —the Mesabi mines belong to the next period. Second, there were organizational innovations in the eighties and early nineties, some horizontal combinations, which for the greater part failed

—the Lake Superior Consolidated iron mines, 1893, however, was also a horizontal combination, although it owned its ships and linked up with the railroad interests of its shareholders—and the vertical ones which arose from the intrusion of the steel concerns. The competing-down process was, to a great extent, geographical. We have seen that this was so in many other cases and that it explains certain features of American cycles and certain local result trends: it is essential to notice that this rise and decline of industrial centers is part of our cyclical mechanism. The case in hand presents one of the most familiar instances. Migration of the iron industry from New England, New York, New Jersey, and Pennsylvania (which as late as 1880 produced nearly half of the 4 million tons of iron then put out) to the Central Western states and to the South was in part conditioned by ore and coal developments. Output of the Lake Superior district increased roughly from 1 to 9 million tons between 1870 and 1890. Together with the ores of Alabama and Tennessee, the Champlain ores and imports, it brought price down to roughly one-third during that time.

This rapid shift of the centers of iron production was one of the reasons why from the time of the Civil War there was, even in prosperity, so large a percentage of idle furnaces, which is thus seen to have nothing to do with any inherent tendency to overproduction or overcapacity. The furnaces in the districts that were being competed down simply did not disappear at once. But there was also rapid technological obsolescence during the last three Juglars: up to 1850, when the drop bottom came in to facilitate the handling of the cupola furnace, there had been hardly any change since colonal times. Charcoal furnaces had to go, though they did so slowly. Coke and bituminous coal furnaces adopted the same improvements that were being introduced in Europe—the introduction of the fuel-saving regenerative stove was one of the most important of them—and grew in size and efficiency. This is the reason for the failure of attempts made after 1873 to limit output by agreement: the up-to-date firms were perfectly able to produce at a price which fell, with fluctuations, from 1872 to 1897. The great stride in absolute quantities was a feature of the penultimate Juglar. It becomes still more impressive if we consider that by then the iron-saving effect of the use of steel had already asserted itself.

In spite of the fact that the fundamental principle of the Bessemer process was independently discovered in this country (W. Kelly, 1851), introduction of this process was one of the achievements of the prosperity which preceded 1873. Only eight firms had adopted it by 1875, though a few other Bessemer plants—running into the depression with their period of gestation—were then being built. Other novelties came at the same time, but the open-hearth process was not among them. It was still an innovation in the last Juglar, when the Homestead works took it up (1888). The same applies to the Thomas-Gilchrist process, although the license for America had been bought in 1881 by the Bessemer Steel Company.[1] Alloys (chrome and nickel steel) put in an appearance in the seventies and eighties, but more effectively in the last Juglar, in which also the Harvey armor-plate process was developed in works built for the purpose. Steel casting was then greatly improved. Scrap was coming widely into use as a raw material of the steel industry.

Organizational innovation may be instanced by the two outstanding cases. The first Bessemer plant in Pittsburgh was the Edgar Thomson Steel Company, in the foundation of which the iron-manufacturing firm of Carnegie Brothers took a leading interest. This was the first of a series of conquests (Homestead, Union Mills, Duquesne) which in 1891 culminated in the foundation of Carnegie Steel. An equally comprehensive structure of the vertical-combination type had by then been erected in the Illinois Steel (1889 or 1891, since it grew to full size in the later year). The Colorado Fuel and Steel dates from the same epoch. Consumption of iron and steel reached a cyclical maximum in 1890. Then a decline set in which eventually issued into the crisis of 1893, in which 32 failures occurred to the end of June, among them the failures of concerns so considerable as the Philadelphia and Reading Coal and Iron and the Pennsylvania Steel. In itself, this does not show more about the nature of

[1] The picture of the cyclical rhythm of innovation could, of course, be much improved if space allowed going adequately into the history of iron and steel production. For instance, puddling was, till the end of the seventies, competing with the Bessemer process. During the fourth Juglar, its position was strengthened by two inventions which deserve notice. The Ellershausen process and Dank's puddling mill (John Fitz, 1857) spread during the sixties, its superiority over the English two-high mill mainly resting on American labor conditions. There were half a dozen other improvements in rolling about the same time.

that crisis than do the railroad failures; but taken together with what has been said before, it seems to justify the diagnosis that that crisis was the "abnormal liquidation" of positions which had become inadaptable in the course of an evolution that primarily centered in iron and steel.

Tools, mechanical objects of use, and machinery are among the things which it is very difficult to quantify and the importance of which would not be adequately rendered by quantity even if we could quantify them. The importance for the cyclical process and for the resulting trends of that bold originality which characterizes American achievement in this field and to which European industry owes so much, is obvious but hard to follow up in detail, because it covers a wide surface and because it consisted much more in devices to make things work economically and efficiently, than in spectacular "invention." Export statistics reveal, by the sixties, how very wide that surface was and how far it extended beyond what had become American specialties, such as sewing machines and agricultural implements. Locomotives and "unspecified machines and other iron and steel products," taken together, were more important than either. A few instances must suffice. Though "quantity" came in the downgrade, foundations were laid and leading innovations introduced in the upgrade of that Kondratieff.

Cyrus McCormick's invention is usually dated 1834, but he himself tells us that his reaper got into really workable shape by 1845. Innovation—the "carrying into effect"—was an element of the second Juglar. Induced improvement and diffusion contributed to all the other Juglars up to the organizational innovation which occurred in the last (foundation of the American Harvester, 1890). Other steps in the mechanization of agriculture could readily be inserted. Still more than in other cases, the fact of—and the reason for—progress going on in cyclical jerks is evident.

The sewing machine (invention by E. Howe in 1846), produced in its practical form by the Singer concern in 1850, also was one of the innovations of the second Juglar, and had already become an international success in the third. Except for its application to bootmaking, its effects on the system were different from those of the majority, and similar to those of a minority, of innovations. Since it can be used by the individual worker, it did not in itself induce the regular competing-down process, though it wrought a revolution in efficiency. Specialized forms of it, facilitating increased division of labor, did, however. We may proceed to notice some of the industries of metal consumers' goods in which innovation consisted in successful standardization, specialization, and mass production—locks (New Haven), clocks and watches (also Connecticut, and Waltham, the dollar watch competing successfully all over the world), and small arms (for example, Colt) were all in their innovating stages either in the first or in the second Juglar and became established in the next one. The pioneer concern in the field of watches, the American Watch Company, struggled with the problems of mechanical watchmaking in the fifties—1857 found it insolvent—but was highly successful in the sixties, when the host began to follow (New York Watch, National Watch, in the next Juglar: Illinois Watch, Rockford Watch, to mention a few). Typewriters reached the manufacturing stage about 1873. No notice was taken of them in the census of 1880, but there were thirty factories in 1890.

Woodworking and metalworking machinery (circular saw, revolving-disk cutting machine), Blanshard's copying lathe, Sellers' planing and blot-screwing machines, the milling machine and the turning tool, wood screws, precision gauges, nuts and bolts, the dry-clay brickmaking machine, Blake's machine for stone breaking, the continuous-feeding printing press, the typesetting machine (working indifferently in the sixties), great improvement in boiler making, the Corliss engine, later the Porter-Allen engine for electric dynamos—all that this medley stands for had, with few exceptions, its initial struggles and successes in the Juglars of the Kondratieff upswing and its diffusion in the Kondratieff downswing and revival, as we should expect. Quantitative importance in the cyclical mechanism is certain, and in the cases, frequent in New England, in which this type of industry formed the core of industrial agglomerations, even obvious. Large concerns emerged (Axe and Edge Tool, 1889; National Saw, 1893). The principle was the same in all cases. It consisted, even, in applying labor- and power-saving devices to the production of labor- and power-saving devices themselves. Everything was subordinated to cheapness. Where wood was cheaper, it was used. Painting was preferred to polishing. Englishmen called these machines flimsy. But standardized mass production was the result. Very few branches remained unaffected.

We will choose the boot and shoe industry as an example for the revolutions which machinery wrought in consumers' goods industries during the second Kondratieff. No machines were used in the American shoe industry before our period, though in some towns a fairly advanced division of labor had turned to good account the ample sources of the raw material and the developed practice of tanning. Wooden pegs for fastening soles were used, however, from 1880, and in 1820, a peg-cutting machine was introduced. The rolling machine for hardening sole leather, 90 times as fast as hammering by hand, came in 1845, and the Howe sewing machine as such meant a step in the mechanization of the industry, since cloth uppers were much used for women's shoes as late as the eighties. Its adaptation to upper leather sewing (1851) is said to have quadrupled the output per man. The same year brought the machine that pegged around a sole in one minute. A number of other innovations were introduced in the course of subsequent Juglars, in fact about 4,000 patents were taken out between 1850 and the end of our period. The most important was the McKay sewing machine (1858; practical success in 1860), which is still used on two-thirds of the total output of shoes, and on nearly all women's shoes. This innovation then induced the "avalanche" in the Kondratieff downgrade—a truly typical case in this as in another respect, for the nature of entrepreneur's profits is well brought out by the practice, then established, not to sell shoe machinery but to lease it.

By 1895 there were 4,000 McKay machines in use, turning out about 120 millions of pairs. They had been improved in 1867 and are said to have reduced costs of sewing on soles from 75 to 3 cents a pair. The Goodyear welt-sewing machine (invented in 1862), which became practical in 1877, was 54 times as fast as welt sewing by awl and needle. But its success was a matter of the last Juglar, and within our period it did not get beyond 25 millions of pairs (1895). The Cable screw bottoming machine for heavy shoes (1869), the heel-building machine (1870; by 1889 there were 200 establishments in this country producing heels only), the standard screw bottoming machine (1875), which is still used, substantially complete the story for our period. We will, however, add that the success of the lasting machine, the feature in shoemaking of the first Juglar of the third Kondratieff (in general use by 1900, though patented in 1882) increased output per workman twelve times at least. The net fall in monetary labor cost which that list of innovations brought about from 1850 to 1900, was from $408 per hundred pairs to $35. There was no further reduction after 1900. Horsepower installed increased from about 3,000 in 1869 to about 50,000 in 1899. But the number of wage earners employed increased steadily until 1923.

The cyclical behavior and the resulting trends in the major textile industries is not, as in England, completely described by the schema of an established industry that expands with the environment, innovating moderately in the process. But some of its traits are present[1] in the cases of cotton and wool, the former of which was, of course, also propelled by the development in the production of its raw material. Worsted, though experimented with in the thirties by the Lowell Company, was practically a new industry. Not much success attended its beginning in the first Juglar, but it got into its stride as one of the major innovations of the second. Combing was then done by hand. The combing machine, although invented, was not yet a success. After the Civil War the Lister comb came in, and even in the eighties this machine was largely imported. Expansion of the worsted industry was a feature of the last three Juglars of that Kondratieff.

As regards cotton, the impulse of innovation came—apart from migration to the South, which first became important in the eighties—from machinery. In this respect the case would be analogous to that of the shoe industry, were it not for the fact that textile men had a much larger share in the evolution of their machinery than had the shoe manufacturers. They displayed much more initiative in ordering it and they took a hand in producing it, although the production of textile-mill machinery as

[1] The reader will, it is hoped, excuse the pedantry and observe again: It is always possible and perfectly sound analysis to explain the expansion of an industry by an appeal to Growth in our sense, in this case also to such external factors as immigration of men and capital. It is also permissible, in dealing with any single industry, to include within the phrase, expansion of environment, innovation outside of that industry, although this phrase then does not any longer connote a single distinct process. But it is not permissible to take expansion of environment in the latter sense as a full explanation of the development of any individual industry as far as this development implies changes in production functions elsewhere.

a distinct industry dates from the beginning of the century. In Worcester, Paterson, Lawrence, Fall River, and Philadelphia this specialty, and all the specialties within this specialty, had risen to considerable importance in the downgrade and revival of the preceding Kondratieff. This simply continued on an increasing scale in the forties and afterward. Technological development in the cotton industry itself lies between the two great specifically American innovations, the introduction of ring spinning (invented in 1828 or 1831), which spread in the period, and the Northrop battery loom (successful in 1894) which properly belongs to the third Kondratieff. The eighties were the time when Fall River flourished, although it lost its iron industry. Many interesting incidents, for example struggles between different methods of production, should, if space permitted, be noticed in that process of expansion. But it went on almost uninterruptedly and there was no vision about it of possibilities differing in kind from what, at every step, actually was. In this sense the great things had by then been done. There is, hence, much less reason for us to stay with the case than there would be for the purpose of general economic history. Investment does, as a matter of fact, cluster in prosperities and contributes to them, but they are in this period, from the standpoint of this industry, independently given "conjunctures" with which it swims but which it does not initiate by its own operations.

In the downswing and revival of the Kondratieff came the great expansion of output, and in the depressions, particularly those of the middle seventies and the middle eighties, there were losses, failures, shutdowns, complaints about overproduction. These spells of bad business with very different severity, not only on different districts—the astonishingly great difference in wages, taxes, costs of power and raw materials might account for that—but also on different firms. In 1883 for instance, when "overproduction" began to show itself, some firms were losing and restricting, others paying high dividends and working overtime (the young worsted industry was booming). From this we may infer that in spite of the standardization of mills—which also was one of the major novelties of the period—there was a good deal of difference in the production functions (including commercial combinations) of individual firms, which was due to inconspicuous innovations of the type that a Kondratieff downgrade is apt to induce. In consequence, costs probably differed widely and a competing-down process was running strongly. If this be true, it would follow that there was nothing in the general outcry about overproduction—those crying out, simply, who were not able to keep the pace and whose concerns were being made obsolete—although the surface presented a picture almost ideally conforming to the conceptions of the theory of overproduction.

The woolen industry suffered from the price of its raw material, and although consumption of wool nearly doubled from 1870 to 1890, there were few major new developments. The Goulding condenser (1826) had come before; the Crompton mule was applied to the production of cashmeres and woolens from the beginning of our period; in 1841 a new loom for carpet weaving was invented (E. Bigelow), which, improved and developed in various directions, practically started an important carpet industry that, after its innovating stages in the fifties, expanded throughout the period; an invention for card cleaning was made in 1853; the seventies saw the transition from the spinning jack to the mule. Shoddy, cotton mixtures, progress in dyeing, and, of course, the great innovation of ready-made clothing (victorious in the fourth Juglar)—all lent their help. The industry felt crises, particularly some of them, such as the one of 1857, very acutely—more acutely than the writer is able to explain. Behavior in the Kondratieff downgrade and revival as compared with the behavior in the Kondratieff prosperity is according to expectation.

In the last three Juglars, but particularly in the last one, production of fertilizers (phosphates) made considerable strides. The dogged survival of the use of charcoal in the production of iron led to the distilling of the timber and to the production of acetates as a by-product—an innovation of the penultimate Juglar, as was the production of soda by the Solvay process. Manufacture of sulphuric acid on a large scale begins with the third. The stories of the American sugar refining industry, which, for the time being, culminated (1887) in a combination that controlled 90 per cent of the production, and of the American Tobacco Company (1890), highly interesting though they are cannot be dealt with here. Nor can developments in the industries of glass (tank furnaces were an innovation of the last Juglar), cement (Portland cement—innovating stage in the fifth and sixth Juglar), paper (new uses: paper collars, paper carwheels;

new processes: mechanical and sulphite pulp, successful in the eighties), and rubber (rubber boots, rubber reclaiming; substantial consolidation in U.S. Rubber Company and Mechanical Rubber Company, both 1892).

But we cannot pass over the beginnings of the electrical industry. Both names and investments are too big for that. Since, however, the former are so familiar, we can confine ourselves to noticing, in passing, the type of entrepreneur to which they belong and of which they are among the best instances. Since the first Morse patent was taken out in 1840 and telegraph lines extended as far as Pittsburgh in 1847, the commercial history of electricity actually dates from the beginning of that Kondratieff. Telephones began their career in 1877, when A. G. Bell floated a company for the exploitation of his patent, adopting the policy, similar to that of the McKay shoe machinery concern, of leasing the instruments. Percentage increase of telephones connected was very rapid in the prosperity of the penultimate Juglar, then slackened in 1895. In 1897 over 500,000 were installed (as compared with 20,200,000 in 1930). An electrical equipment industry—motors, electric wiring, and so on; not exclusively telegraph and telephone appliances—produced values of 2.7 millions in 1879 and 92.4 in 1899 (not including machinery and supplies made in establishments belonging to other industries). In the latter year, kilowatt-hours produced were a little over 3 billions; in 1960, 96 billions.

Electric current for light and power dates really from 1892, when Edison's hydroelectric station in Appleton, Wis., his thermoelectric station in New York, and the one in Chicago went into operation. By then, the Edison Electric Light Company (1878) and the American Electrical Company (later, the Thomson-Houston Company; E. Thomson in 1886 patented electric welding) were already in existence; and electric light, according to the principle of C. S. Brush, had been installed in a few cotton mills and in San Francisco. The arc lamp and Edison's incandescent lamp then competed with each other. In 1886 W. Stanley constructed the first station using alternating current. Problems of transmission were being solved. In manufacture, electric power was coming into use, especially in cotton mills, from 1882. This established all the fundaments of the technique, bore down resistance, and prepared the great development that was to follow and to turn revival into a Kondratieff prosperity.

But quantitatively it did not signify. Only traction did. After a number of more or less experimental ventures, an electric tram service was installed at Richmond in 1887; then this innovation spread rapidly. In Massachusetts, for instance, 1,400 miles of overhead trolley street railways were constructed from 1890 to 1897.[1]

Not only the technological but also the financial and organizational bases were laid during the last two Juglars. The Edison Electric Light and the Edison General Electric (1889) were successful and had a number of subsidiaries, some of them abroad. Then there were the Westinghouse and the Thomson-Houston concerns. When the latter coalesced with the Edison General Electrical (General Electric, 1892, capital 50 million dollars), which by that time, at Schenectady and elsewhere, employed over 6,000 hands, a concern emerged that controlled practically all the more important patents, supplied 1,277 stations and 435 traction companies operating nearly 5,000 miles—in itself a powerful engine of economic revolution.

Since we sketched the course of the Juglars when describing railroad developments, and since we have so framed the above comments on American industrial history as to make it easy for the reader to insert innovations in their proper places, we need not now add a detailed survey but only a bald calendar. With the qualification mentioned, we take 1843 as the first year of the first Juglar, its prosperity lasting until the middle of 1845, its recession until the end of 1847, its depression covering 1848, and its revival, 1849, 1850, and 1851. The prosperity and recession phases of the second (1852 to 1860) ran from the beginning of 1852 to the middle of 1856 (irregularities making it difficult to distinguish between them); depression lasted to the end of 1858; and 1859 and 1860 make up the recovery phase. The rise of the third Juglar is blurred by, and uncertain because of, political events, and so is its course. We simply count it from 1861 to 1869, on the strength of the aspects of the period 1867 to

[1] Trams in general were substantially an achievement of the second Kondratieff—the bus was one of the downgrade of the first Kondratieff. In Philadelphia, for instance, the oldest companies received their charters in 1857 and there was an outburst of promotions after 1858. Horses and mules were used until 1885, then the underground cable. From 1893 on, trams were electrified. In financing, holding companies began to play a role during the fourth Juglar.

1869, which seems to conform to our idea of a revival as modified by those external factors. The prosperity phase of the fourth Juglar (1870 to the middle of 1879) covers 1870, 1871, and the first half of 1872; the recession phase, the second half of 1872 and 1873; the next three years form the depression; and 1877, 1878, and the first half of 1879, the recovery phase, the beginning of which was still under the clouds of the preceding storm. The fifth Juglar covers the period from the middle of 1879 to the end of 1888. It prosperity lasted to the middle of 1881; recession, from the middle of 1881 to the end of 1883; depression covered 1884 and the greater part of 1885 and was followed by more than three years of recovery. The sixth Juglar (1889 to 1897) illustrates our proposition about the irregularity of panics or crises. The course of things in the last quarter of 1890 and the first half of 1891 interrupted and distorted what, nevertheless, we consider as the prosperity phase of that Juglar. The rest of 1891, 1892, and the first half of 1893 make up the recession; the second half of 1893, 1894, and the first half of 1895, depression. Revival then set in—and symptoms shaded off, by the end of 1897, into a new prosperity—but 1896 interrupted its course, though in a way which can be satisfactorily accounted for.

E. The First Sixteen Years of the Third Kondratieff (1893-1913).—The sixteen years preceding the first World War cover a little more than the prosperity phase of the Kondratieff, the whole of its first and about half of its second Juglar. An application of our schema which involves, as it must in this case, speaking of a Long Wave that is still incomplete, will no doubt seem hazardous, to say the least. The future course of events may entirely fail to justify the hypothesis that this implies. But evidence tending to justify it will presently be submitted, and we shall also have the opportunity to test it by confronting the expectations that follow from it with postwar facts. For the moment, it is sufficient to agree that a significant "break in trends" occurred about 1897—few people will deny that; there is even not much doubt to cloud the exact date—and to state our thesis that what caused it was once more an economic revolution, analogous in every respect to the "industrial revolution" of textbook fame and to the other revolution, which was wrought by railroads, steel, and steam. By speaking of still another economic revolution we are not departing from prevalent opinion—hardly even by making it the basis of our analysis of the cycles which occurred during the period—for the New Industrial Revolution has become a very common phrase by now. Again we observe the tendency, noticed in the case of the first Kondratieff, to apply that phrase to the downgrade—which in this case, since the war dominated all things while it lasted, practically means the postwar period—rather than to the span which is the subject of this section. To do this right and wrong in the same sense in which it was right and wrong in the other case, and not only does not contradict our view, but in one vital point actually lends support to it: for the reason why more of "revolution" is found in the downgrade than they do in prosperity, exactly as they should according to our model.

In the same sense in which it is possible to associate the second Kondratieff with railroads, and with the same qualifications, the third can be associated with electricity. In order to see this statement in its true light, it is necessary to observe, first, that it refers to ignition only and does not imply that all economic changes of our period are due to electricity—growth and the phenomena of the Secondary Wave would in any case have to be added; second, that quantitatively very important developments were either simple continuations, or continuations induced by the impact of the new things, of the innovations that carried the second Kondratieff; third, that electricity was not the only new thing and that several others of first importance were as independent of it as the new shoe machinery was of railroads; finally, that electricity, though an innovation in our sense—the same sense in which railroads were innovations in the second Kondratieff in spite of the railroad boom of the thirties—yet has had a previous industrial history going back to the forties, while its history as an invention goes back to Volta at least. It seems idle to ask whether the importance of electricity was greater or smaller than that of steam. It has certainly created new industries and commodities, new attitudes, new forms of social action and reaction. It has upset previous industrial locations by practically eliminating the element of power from the list of determining factors. It has changed the relative economic positions of nations, and the conditions of foreign trade. Only a small fraction of this, however, asserted itself in the sixteen years under discussion, although all the fundamental conquests and extensive investments were then made, and all the bases were laid. Not before 1908 did installations of power, even in this country, spell the victory of electricity. Immediate cost advantage was at first small, in many cases negative—as it was, for example, in the case of the all-steel ship—and reciprocating and similar steam engines kept often more than their own, a most interesting case, in its complexity, of reaction to innovation. Even in lighting, electricity was expensive, and the difficulty arising from the necessity of supplying current for disproportionately great peak loads, hence at a low percentage of average utilization, was overcome but slowly.

1. For want of a more adequate label, we will speak of the Neomercantilist Kondratieff. Few will deny that the social atmosphere characteristically changed about the late nineties, though not everyone who recognizes that change will be ready to grant the claims we make for the "symbolic" year 1897, and most people will also agree with the proposition that those changes were of two kinds—the one represented by such symptoms as the recrudescence of protection and the increase in expenditure on armaments, the other by such symptoms as the new spirit in fiscal and social legislation, the rising tide of political radicalism and socialism, the growth and changing attitudes of trade unionism, and so on. In America (Dingley tariff, 1897) protectionism meant little more than another victory of a tendency that had been present from the first; in England, no more than a slow change of public opinion on the subject of free trade. In Germany the social insurance item rose to 1.1 billion marks in 1913, while in America there was little of this beyond social legislation in some states (Wisconsin) and a general hostility to "big business," satisfied for the time being with prosecutions under the Sherman Act and regulation of utilities. Whatever we may think of the importance of immediate economic effects, looking back today, it is impossible to mistake the significance of these symptoms of a changing attitude toward capitalism.

The deepest problem of the economic sociology of our epoch is whether those tendencies grew out of the very logic of capitalist evolution, or were distortions of it traceable to extra-capitalist influences. Those tendencies, whatever their nature, sourccs, and relation to each other, hardly asserted themselves strongly enough in prewar America to have to be listed among the main factors that shaped American economic history. The

Cuban war—and what Europeans loved to call American Imperialism, in general—conditioned not unimportant innovations, but it is here assumed to have had no great influence in distorting any cycles.

2. American agriculture has to be listed among the industries which added important developments on the lines chalked out by the innovations of the second Kondratieff. Since some of the problems of the agricultural depression of the third will have to be taken up in the chapters on the postwar period, we will here merely recall the agricultural conquest of the Far West, completed by the end of the century, improvement of agricultural machinery (big threshers and combines for instance), increased use of gas engines—light tractors came into use in the first decade of the century; 3,000 were sold in 1914—the beginning use of electric power—total horsepower employed rose by 32 per cent from 1899 to 1909—and rapidly increasing consumption of fertilizers (from under 2 million tons at the beginning of the period to over 7 millions in 1914). All of this increased wheat acreage by about one-third as between the average of the last decade of the second and the average of the first decade of the third Kondratieff, and also yield per acre. Cotton increased its acreage still more and similarly displayed increase in yield per acre.

3. The last installment of railroad construction, a typical instance of completing development on established bases and in part merely the reflex of the sharp rise in net earnings which set in during 1897 and continued until 1911 (with peaks in 1904, 1907, and 1910), contributed substantially to the prosperity phase in this country. About 70,000 miles were added and "net capital" increased from a little over 9 billions in 1897 to 15-1/3 billions in 1913. There is thus reason to speak of another railroad boom—secondary phenomena though it was, in spite of its quantitative importance—and to remind the reader of the meaning of this way of fitting things together. Ignition and quantitative importance do not necessarily go together. Quantitatively or statistically, the processes of every cycle are always contributed to by the completion and the working of the inheritance of preceding evolution, even as they hand over their own contribution to the next cycles.

The "induced" or "completing" character of railroad achievement during that time shows not only in construction—in the commercial nature of the new trackage and the fact that it was largely built in response to existing demand within an existing framework—but also, and still better, in other elements. The great clearing of the ground that the crisis of 1893 and its aftermath had effected, brought control over many roads into new hands. New types of men took hold of them, very different from the type of earlier railroad entrepreneurs. Some of them were not entrepreneurs at all, but simply efficient administrators. According to Mr. H. Jerome's index "product' per man-hour in steam railroad operation rose from 104 (base, 1890) to 138.9 during the period 1895 to 1910. The new administrations improved tracks and roadbeds, raised horsepower installed (between 1899 and 1909) from roughly 21 millions to roughly 45 millions, accepted improvements in safety devices, began to accept automatic train control and mechanical stokers, new types of locomotives and cars, and thus evolved the railroad service that since has come to be looked upon as a matter of course, though many of these things—the electric and the oil-burning locomotive, in particular—did not spread until the postwar downgrade.

As far as the new men were not administrators, they were organizers and financiers. In both these respects, 1893 had indeed left many problems. The situation may even be said to have set a definite task to which the financial groups that had carried out the liquidation and reconstruction, and the executives they had put into power or accepted, now applied themselves. This task was one of consolidation in a very comprehensive sense of this word and it implied consolidation in the particular sense of combination, amalgamation, and merger. What the public and the political world saw and felt about was, on the one hand, the creation of new economic positions invested by the imagination of the man in the street with a power that was both immense and sinister and, on the other hand, the spectacle of financial maneuvers and of the struggles between financial groups that offered as much food for the prevalent propensity to gamble as for moral indignation. Since it is these aspects which still dominate the economic historiography also of the industrial "merger boom," it is necesary to point out that for us the latter means something which the public mind either did not realize at all or entirely failed to link up with those financial operations: new production functions, reorganization of large sectors of the system, increase of productive efficiency all round.

Mergers must, therefore, be listed among the innovations that carried that prosperity.

4. Of course, consolidation was not a new phenomenon. Railroad systems, in particular, had been built up before, and industrial combination had begun in the sixties and been a feature of the late eighties. New, however, were the scale, some of the methods, and, to a certain extent, the meaning. In all cases, whatever the legal garb, those mergers meant new units of control, new principles of management, new possibilities of industrial research, and, at least eventually, new types of plant and equipment—also, new locations—intended to achieve, often built to exceed, the absolute optimum of known, if untried, technology. The productive capacity that was thus created and could not have been created without them ranks high on the list of the factors that explain the torrent of products that broke forth in the postwar part of the downgrade. It is hence not correct to call those combinations monopolies simply, without adding that they were monopolies of a special kind, very different in theory and practice from the genuine case. What such combinations, provided they go far enough, might mean for the mechanism of the business cycle has been pointed out, under the heading of trustified capitalism, in the third chapter. As a matter of fact, however, the course of events in the period under discussion and its statistical picture hardly bear out the expectation that the cyclical movement would be substantially altered by their policies. This statement requires the following qualifications, which do not, however, invalidate it: individual prices were frequently deflected (those of steel rails, for instance) from the course they would otherwise have taken, though this did not amount to more than what combinations had done at all times; the combinations frequently included firms which otherwise would presently have been competed out of existence, and thus may be said to have provided a method for the elimination of the obsolescent elements of the system that obviated the death struggle by anticipating its results. Once formed, the giants in some cases threatened the life of outsiders—both new and old—also in other ways than by their technological commercial superiority.[1]

[1] That superiority has often been denied. It is, of course, true that mere size is not necessarily an advantage and may well be a disadvantage. Judgment must turn on the merits of each case. But statistical evidence to the effect that smaller concerns often do better than the

Difficulties arise in some cases in settling who the entrepreneur was. In the two outstanding instances in the railroad field, all the criteria were present in the two leading men (Harriman and Hill). One of them was as much an organizer and reformer of administrative routine as he was a stock exchange leader. But this combination of aptitudes only serves to show how rare, with this kind of innovation, must be the cases in which one man can be said to have been "the" entrepreneur. The industrial function which amalgamations fulfilled was in most cases entirely divorced from the task of bringing them about. Yet that traveling salesman who turned into a promoter of combinations was no mere financial peddler, though he probably understood little and cared less about anything except a profitable deal in industrial properties. In some cases, bankers played a leading role, although one must be careful not to overrate the initiating importance of an agent whom negotiations place in the limelight. The Mercantile Marine, which, among the transactions of first importance, came nearest to being a bankers' venture, was no success. The steel combine was almost exclusively determined by the dominating position of the Carnegie concern and practically dictated by its head. The average banker's contribution was a subordinate one and consisted mainly in forgetting what banks exist for in capitalist society.

The movement started in 1898, immediately after recovery from the troubles of 1896. The year 1899 saw it in full swing, especially in iron and steel. The big events came in the first years of the century; then 1907 called a temporary halt. The policy of the Union Pacific may serve as an example from the railroad field, which will at the same time contribute to the understanding of the crisis of 1907. Obviously it was no mere attempt to secure a monopoly position as such—which, as must have been clear to anyone, could never have been exploited in the sense of the classical theory of monopoly price—or simply financial piracy, but an attempt to build a system so circum-

---

giants should not be uncritically accepted. The smaller concerns may *now* often be in the position of the new, and the giants in the position of the old firms in our model. It is held above that the big concerns (there may be exceptions, of course) implied technological and organizational improvement when they were founded. It is not held that they retained their advantages until the present day. Our theory would in fact lead us to expect the contrary.

stanced as to realize maximum economy, and to make it yield surpluses *through this increase in efficiency.* The way was found barred at the very beginning: the most important link in that system, the Chicago, Burlington, and Quincy, had been conquered by the Northern Pacific and the Great Northern. By this transaction the "collateral trust bond" came into prominence. The buyers of the stock of the Chicago, Burlington, and Quincy handed it to the Northern Pacific and the Great Northern at a price almost 50 per cent above what it had sold for before the buying began, and this price was paid in bonds that were issued by these two companies and then gradually sold to the public.

When the Union Pacific interests saw the road blocked, they tried to unseat the blockaders by acquiring a controlling parcel of the Northern Pacific itself. What strikes the observer is not this move as such, but the absolute disregard of costs and consequences that characterized its execution. The Union Pacific troops were set to storm the concrete trenches of the Morgan position, perfectly impervious to frontal attack. Europeans helped, against their will, by selling short when the attacked stock soared, and by lending, though English banks tried to discourage this whenever the purpose was detected or suspected. The Northern Pacific Corner of 1901 ended in a draw from which an understanding emerged (Northern Securities Company, to be presently prosecuted under the Sherman Act), but the harm done to the financial structure and to the international position of American currency and credit accounts for a sequence of events that lasted through 1903 ("rich men's panic") and was serious enough to affect somewhat, though not to the extent one might have expected, the industrial processes below that surface. We note two things. First, innovation in the formative stages of trustified capitalism will regularly produce such events owing to the fact that large-scale financial operations of a type entirely lacking in the mechanism of innovation in competitive capitalism are in this case necessary for the entrepreneur to get his hand on the wheel. It would always do that even in later stages, if there were not the alternative method of the rise of new men to leading positions within the giant concerns, once these are formed. Second, the maneuvres and excesses of those as of earlier times, and hence the crisis that ensued, are not simply accounted for by the fact that in one way or another they served, or were induced by, the purposes of large-scale innovation. Crises, be it repeated, are historic individuals, into the making of which enter many peculiarities of individuals and environments, besides external factors. Our model explains the underlying process and even, in most cases, approximately the location in time of the turning points, and the *modus operandi* of the features peculiar to each situation. But these remain distinct facts and exert distinct consequences, all the same. In the case in hand, a less speculative-minded public, a banking system of firmer tradition, entrepreneurs less bent on immediate financial success and less free from inhibitions would of course have made a great difference to the behavior of our time series and would have eased the difficulty we have in dating Juglars in that period.

Another aspect is best displayed by the next step in the Union Pacific's financial career. After the dissolution of the Northern Securities Company, it had no interest in holding the parcel of Northern Pacific and Great Northern stocks which had come to it in the liquidation, and it began to sell out, acquiring, up to the middle of 1906, about 56 millions in cash and on call. This sum was obviously assembled by way of preparing a new campaign in the fields, this time, of the New York Central, the Santa Fe, and the Baltimore and Ohio. In this campaign, what we may term *seriousness of purpose* is, at last from the standpoint of the Union Pacific itself, very much less obvious than is the deliberate fostering in 1906 of a speculative craze that had already set in. We note first, the spending of the Union Pacific's funds for this campaign and the straining of its credit to the extent of 75 millions borrowed on notes; second, the fact that banks offered less than no resistance to this borrowing and not much resistance to speculators' borrowing in general; third, that, European capital being drawn to this country by high rates and prospects of speculative gain, an additional relation between the American and the European short-money markets, normally inoperative at that time, was set up which was bound to act as an ideal conductor of repercussions. The importance of such things is clear and so is the consequence that for us follows for the diagnosis of 1907.

5. Industrial mergers displayed similar phenomena and call for but little additional comment. The theory of their financial construction may, in case innovation consists simply in the cheapening of the costs per unit of a product already in use,

formulated like this. Entrepreneurs' profits may be expressed as the difference between the present value of a set of factors of production, evaluated with regard to the net returns they are expected to yield if used within a given new production function, and the present value of the same set, evaluated on the basis of the net returns they are expected to yield within their old one. In the limiting case of perfect competition and perfect absence of friction they can be bought at prices corresponding to the latter while, until competition steps in to reestablish normal relations of values—in acordance with the theory of imputation— the products of the new combination that is being envisaged would also sell at their old prices, hence, at more than cost. Suppose that the factors required for a new combination consist of the plants of a number of independent going concerns and that these concerns can be acquired at prices corresponding to the conditions prevailing in the preceding neighborhood of equilibrium. Then we get estimated entrepreneurial profits by deducting these values from those higher ones which the plants are expected to realize within the new combination. If we further assume that in payment of the former, bonds (or preferred shares, or bonds with common shares thrown in as a bonus, to supply the motive for selling out) are issued to vendors and that profit expectations are embodied in common shares, we have the rationale of a method which in itself but expresses the economic logic of the situation. Its peculiarity so far consists only in the facility it affords for cashing unrealized profits which may never be actually earned and which, even if they eventually are, exert, by being cashed in advance, an influence on the monetary part of the mechanism entirely different from that which profits exert in the ordinary case. In particular they must be financed, unless that common stock is held indefinitely by the founding group and its associates. This may for instance be done by the savings of the public or by credit created in order to enable the public to buy.

Attention is called especially to the effects that, thus applied, saving will have on producing excesses in consumption as far as those non-existent but realized profits are spent on consumers' goods. As far as they are not, these savings probably fulfill their normal social function of improving the productive apparatus, although, *even if everything had always been done with ideal correctness,* the private interest of those savers who bought common stock would, in many cases, have been better served by a game of poker. Apart from such sales to the public of the securities created, mergers as such—as distinguished from their industrial programs—did not require any funds. This is one reason why it is idle to speculate about where the "huge sums" came from that figured in those capital transactions. Already for 1899, for instance, stocks and bonds alone of new industrial combinations that were "absorbed by investors" are said to have amounted to nearly 3.6 billion dollars, three-quarters of which was common stock. This does not mean, of course, that existing funds, let alone savings, were actually spent on those stocks and bonds to anything like that amount. Some vendors kept their bonds, and some "entrepreneurs" their stock. Nor was there new investment if, instead of keeping them, they sold in order to buy other securities with the proceeds, for this was equivalent to an exchange of securities. And even as far as they simply sold for "money, *i.e.*, against existing or *ad hoc* created deposits, that money was, of course, not bound or absorbed by the transaction. Any sums thus withdrawn from their channels were speedily returned to them again. As far as that goes, it was not the supply of "capital" that was exhausted in 1907, but the supply of folly.

That interpretative schema is, of course, entirely independent from actual financial practice. The vast scope for irresponsibility and misconduct which is inherent in that method and immeasurably increased by the fact that the evolution of an environment's system of moral ideas and legal safeguards tends to lag behind its economic evolution, is mainly relevant for the explanation of the details of particular situations which so easily veil the fundamental facts under a surface of "shortage of credit," "lack of confidence," "hoarding," or "shortage of reserves." Combinations of all types emerged all over the industrial field but we will confine ourselves, for the purpose of illustration, to one instance only—one which presents the essential features with unusual clearness—the United States Steel Corporation (1901). The financial construction—the form was simply that of a holding company—was practically determined by the Carnegie Company which in the Juglar recession of 1900 was tactically in a still more advantageous position than it had been before and not only impregnable to attack, but also perfectly ready to attack, itself—such an attack was actually expected and, in fact, announced in the shape of an extensive program of new construction. In order to apply our schema to the case, we must recognize that the chief vendor combined the role which it assigns to vendors, with the function of the entrepreneur who creates the future possibilities so that securities transferred to him would represent both the value of his plant as it was, irrespective of and previous to the new combination and the additional value of capitalized expected profits. To a minor degree this applied also to other vendors who, in fact, were less favorably treated. So far, deviation from our schema can only have resulted from the possibility that fixed interest bonds of the new corporation formed, within the "payments" to vendors, a larger part than they should have according to the relation between preexisting and expected values. This is all we would have to say, had the vendors kept their common stock. But it was clear from the outset that this was precisely what they—or most of them—did not wish to do. In order to gratify them, a syndicate was formed and a market was created by methods of high-pressure salesmanhsip that included "matching orders" and the like. This seems to have been more than "cashing unrealized profits."

The further career of the United States Steel Corporation is, owing to its central position in the typically cyclical industry and to the accuracy of the information it puts at the disposal of the public, a subject of commanding interest. Only one remark is necessary here, however. The 301 millions of bonds were, of course, a heavy burden, but the 1,018 millions of capital stock were no burden at all. If our diagnosis of the economic nature of this stock (or a great part of it) be true, absence or smallness of dividends would not be a sign of bad financial health; and their gradual dwindling and final disappearance is what would have to be expected from the standpoint of our theory. As a matter of fact, so far they have not dwindled to zero. But we also observe that the concerns' real earning power over time—*i.e.*, earning power independent of short-time fluctuations and of the effects of the rise in the *level* of prices and of such events as the World War—was kept only by incessant "ploughing back" of surpluses and by a sequence of innovations, mostly minor ones. The case is thus seen not to contradict, but on the contrary to illustrate, our thesis that no structure of real capital is ever the source of permanent net returns, although this proposition is, in strict theory, true in the case of perfect competition only.

6. We return to what, in the sense defined in the introduction

to this section, is the backbone of the purely industrial process of this Kondratieff. The stage having been set before, both technologically and economically, the electric developments that we observe in the later nineties, spreading their effects over the industrial field, would in themselves have been sufficient to produce what we call a Kondratieff prosperity and to impress a dominant contour line on the successive business situations of that time, although independent innovations in some sectors, completing developments in other sectors, growth, external factors are just as important for the analysis of actual long-run results and more important for the analysis of short-run situations. To save space, we will neglect the progress of the telegraph, the telephone (numbers of telephones installed in 1897, 515,200; in 1914, just over 10 millions) and of electric lighting (arc lamp, incandescent lamp, metallic filaments), the two last of which practically exhaust what advance there was during the prosperity phase toward the electrification of the household, which became so important a downgrade development. The essential thing was the production of electric power: 3,150 million kilowatt-hours in 1899 and 19,652 million kilowatt-hours in 1914, no year showing decrease and only 1908 the same figure as the preceding year.

Soon after the turn of the century long-distance transmission, the triphase current, the spread of the steam turbine, improvement of hydroelectric motors, construction of hydroelectric and thermoelectric plants of ever-increasing capacities, and the victory of the big power stations over the plants of individual industrial consumers became the leading features of the period, which also persisted, on the much larger scale characteristic of Kondratieff recessions and depressions, in the postwar epoch. As mentioned before, hydroelectric enterprise had started on a large scale in 1895, when the plant at Niagara Falls went into operation. It supplied industrial power from the first and in 1900 embarked upon a still more ambitious program. In New England (Holyoke Water Power Company), on the Mississippi (Keokuk), in Montana (Great Falls), on the St. Mary's River (Consolidated Lake Superior Company), on the Pacific Coast, in the South (many local companies; Southern Power Company, 1906, the first onc of importance beyond its neighborhood; Alabama Power Company; the plant of the Aluminum Company in Tennessee; then an interesting development of transmission lines that led to a cooperation between several systems in the Southern Appalachian region, buying current from each other and helping each other in cases of breakdown and so on), the foundations were laid, during the first two Juglars of the third Kondratieff of the electric system of the country, as the foundations of its railroad system had been laid during the first three Juglars of the second Kondratieff.

Only in exceptional cases did large-scale electrical enterprise proceed from the industrial consumer, the outstanding instance being the Aluminum Company's venture. New industrial enterprise proceeded from electrical enterprise also only exceptionally, the outstanding case being that of the Consolidated Lake Superior Company, which set out to create a whole industrial district by taking up pulp and suphide production, copper refining, and steelmaking. Comment that would well illustrate some properties of our model is invited by the plan and its execution. The former was perfectly sound and the latter perfectly competent from a technological standpoint. The water power, the ores, the timber, were all there and their role within a comprehensive scheme was easy to visualize. But this is not enough. One essential peculiarity of the working of the capitalist system is that it imposes sequences and rules of timing. Its effectiveness largely rests on this and on the promptness with which it punishes infringement of those sequences and rules. For success in capitalist society it is not sufficient to be right *in abstracto*; one must be right at given dates.

The general rule was that industries expanded on the new supply of power. Cotton textile and paper mills, the metallurgical and the chemical industries installed electricity. Some iron-works, however, used their furnace gas for thermoelectric purposes. A most important development ensued in steel. This movement was well under way before the first Juglar had run its course, but assumed much larger dimensions later on as the price of current fell. The superiority of new over old plant was considerably increased because in many cases—that of cotton mills, for instance—different types of factory buildings were necessary in order to take full advantage of the installation of electric power. Electrical equipment was produced by the General Electric and the Westinghouse concerns and also by many other firms, some dating from the eighties (as, for instance, the Electric Storage Battery Company). Some of the most important ones were highly specialized (Electric Boat Company, National Carbon Company). Electric dynamos gained ground fairly rapidly; the water turbine less so. Both the General Electric and the Westinghouse exported successfully and also started enterprise abroad (British Westinghouse in 1899). But total added value under the census heading of Electrical Machinery and Apparatus was only about 180 millions in 1914. A great feature of the first Juglar were electric trams, of which about 25,000 miles were built up to 1907. The competition of the motorcar and the motorbus then stepped in to dim prospects. Though maximum trackage was not reached until 1917, they were no longer of cyclical importance after that year; but until 1907 they were in the foreground of speculative interest and railroads were so concerned about the danger to their local traffic that one great system impaired its financial position in the attempt to buy up lines in its territory. The equipment of the London Underground Railway was supplied by American firms (1897). Finally, it should not be forgotten that in 1914 there were still above 40 firms fighting the losing fight of the electric automobile.

The writer frankly despairs of his ability to give, within the space at his command, anything like an adequate picture, both of the ramifications of the transforming influence of electricity and of the other innovations which—independently of it or induced by it—grouped themselves around it and, together with it, set a pace to output of producers' goods that, in spite of "responsive" extension of capacities, repeatedly resulted in steel and even coal "famines" or conditions approaching serious shortage.[1] These conditions were particularly remarkable in the case

[1] This strain on a productive apparatus, that at the same time was being expanded at an unprecedented rate reflects, of course, the fever induced by the proceedings in the sphere of finance and speculation and was, in this sense, a harbinger of future difficulties. But it does not seem correct to argue that the mere fact of full (or more than what should be called full, that is, optimal) employment of resources would suffice to bring about the upper turning point. Increase of physical output is not necessary to prosperity. For its symptoms to persist, it is sufficient that people *try* to increase output. In fact, if it cannot for the time being be increased, this would only accentuate those symptoms, and any rise in cost would always be at least compensated for by an increase of prices of products, until new products emerge. That such periods of superheated atmosphere put also a strain on the moral and social framework of society and are productive of serious problems is perfectly true, but that is another matter.

of coal, because hydroelectricity itself and many other innovations were obviously so fuel-saving that something like technological unemployment of coal (which did come about in the downgrade) could reasonably have been expected: consumption of coal in the Edison Chicago works, for instance, was 6.9 pounds per kilowatt-hour in 1900, and 2.87 pounds in 1913. We must confine ourselves to a few desultory remarks.

7. First, steam engineering reacted to electricity in two ways, by the improvement of competing engines—of the compound (reciprocating) engine and of high-pressure boilers (superheating) and by offering the completing steam engine turbine (turbogenerator). On both lines it would be possible to array, in descending order of importance, a vast amount of new industrial activity. The reader recalls that the entrepreneurial role and the change in production functions that defines our concept of innovation, are both capable of many gradations. They include Edison and Carnegie achievements, but also achievements that may be exemplified by a man who first carries out the idea of letting cars on the drive-yourself system. And those who follow the pioneers are still entrepreneurs, though to a degree that continuously decreases to zero. The doings of all of them must be visualized if a correct idea is to be formed about the nature, role, and quantitative importance of innovation. Nonelectric engineering enterprise in the epoch of electricity fills densely the whole scale, but crowds particularly in the middle range. All types of toolmaking were, for instance, in a process of transformation in which firms producing specialties rose and fell quickly. Of large-scale enterprise in this field and of this kind, the two plants of the American Bridge Company (1902) may be mentioned, but the whole huge development in steel shapes, though mostly under the control of the steel concerns (the Bethlehem, for example, bought H. Grey's patents of the steel section, which was so great an improvement in the rolling of big beams for structural purposes), really belongs here. Railroad locomotives and rolling stock, bicycles, agricultural machinery, ships, all had their minor innovations directly induced or indirectly conditioned (via creation of new demand) by the "carrying" ones. We proceed, however, to the second great innovation of this Kondratieff.

The automobile industry affords a good example of a purely entrepreneurial achievement turning to new uses not only existing resources but also existing technology, *viz.*, the Lenoir-Otto internal combustion engine, the principle of interchangeable parts, the possibilities offered by steel developments and modern machine tools. Among modern industries it also was, in its beginnings, almost in a class by itself with respect to financial methods. Its own productive process consisted in assembling intermediate goods which it was possible to buy on credit (on 60 to 90 days' open account, for instance), so that the resulting product, sold for cash, could directly pay for itself. Later on, the retailer, or institutions that financed him, came in to bridge the gap by remitting not only in advance of his sale to the consumer, but also of delivery to him. Thus, the manufacturer need not borrow at all from banks and may still induce expansion of deposits to an extent amounting to inflation. No better instance could be found to show how credit creation for the purpose of innovation can hide. This industry, though not a starter yet one of the most important carriers of this Kondratieff, revealed its full meaning for the economic process and for civilization—it has altered the style of life and the outlook on life probably more than any prophet ever did—in the downgrade span after the war, exactly as cotton textiles asserted themselves fully in the downgrade of their Kondratieff. In the prosperity it did not get so far.

The problems of assembling were solved in Germany and France. G. Daimler and K. Benz produced vehicles in the eighties; Elwood Haynes, C. and F. Duryea, R. E. Olds, by 1893; A. Winton, in 1894. Half a dozen small companies, with a quantitative importance practically equal to zero, were founded in the next six years by these men (Duryea Motor Wagon Company, Winton Motor Company, 1897): Registration in this country totaled 8,624 in 1899, and in 1900 the Olds Motor Works of Detroit started what to them seemed mass production, reaching the figure of 4,000 in 1903. Ford, somewhat hampered in the nineties by a struggle with the Selden patent, reached incorporation stage in 1903 ($100,000 capital, $28,000 paid up). Mortality among pioneers was as high as in such a case we would naturally expect. With the (temporarily) successful ones, profits paid for expansion. Along with the gasoline car came the gasoline mower. The first bus routes and stage lines were established about 1905. Between 1902 and 1907, 322 companies started operations. In the latter year, 8,423 cars were sold for about 5-1/2 million dollars, of which 1 million was profit. The year 1908 closes the first stage.

In that year innovation turned against itself. The great new thing appeared in the shape of the light and cheap four-cylinder Ford car for the masses, which drove from the field many of what by then were old firms in our sense. That the increased mortality—the modal firm founded in 1902 lasted until 1910, and the modal firm founded in 1908, also—was mainly among firms under four years of age, does not contradict this statement, because in a period of such rapid change a great many new foundations will start on a plan that has already become obsolete, although the failure of others was no doubt due to unsuccessful innovations of their own. General Motors, founded in 1908 (Durant), provided the first occasion for bankers to enter the field (1910), which until then had been entirely outside their sphere of influence and substantially remained so to the war. Ratio of net profit to net worth, though declining, remained on a level about twice as high as in the postwar period and equal to six or seven times the "normal rate of interest."[1] Prices, also

[1] That suffices to give an idea, although both the meaning of normal rate of interest in this connection and comparison with it of net worth are not free from doubt as to significance. It should be observed that these high, in one case at least spectacular, profits—they were profits in the full sense of our definition of the concept and a very good instance by which to illustrate it—were earned, despite the fact that the period of gestation of the automobile plant of the time was quite short, so that there hardly was a span during which spending on plant could have exerted influence undisturbed by the impact of additional products, while in all other respects entry into the industry was perfectly unimpeded. The case thus serves to show that neither prolonged gestation nor bars to entry are so essential for the emergence of profit as might be thought—although in many cases both do play a role. It also serves to show what it is that prevents competition from stepping in promptly and effectively and how realistic the fundamental distinction is between the behavior of the mere economic man and the entrepreneur. Enticement for entry was not wanting. Nor was there any friction to hold back would-be competitors or any lack of promptness among them. There was nothing but the difficulty of doing a new thing and making a success of it. Competitors crowded along and, in an industry requiring but little capital, not only hovered around, but actually entered the field. Only, most of them failed to produce a car that would sell at a price covering cost, there being absolutely no other reason for this than the one embodied in our theory of entrepreneurial activity. Coincidence of high mortality and high profits ideally expresses this situation.

declining, moved on a level still further above that of the twenties, which loose statement applies even if no account be taken of the difference in quality, which defies comparison, and of the change in the price level. Product per man-hour, whatever it may mean in such a case, rose (logarithmically) more sharply between 1909 and 1914 than ever before or after. Designs became more stable, parts more standardized, after 1912—the year that closes the heroic age of the industry. In 1914, 338 firms produced a total of 573,114 cars, to which Ford contributed almost one-half. The importance of the industry and of its demand for the products of other industries was, therefore, perfectly adequate to "ignite" the second Juglar, although, even in 1914, value added was only 210.6 millions. Subsidiaries developed quickly. In 1914, 971 firms existed producing bodies and parts, and motors infused new life into the rubber industry.

Also in this country, there had been a considerable amount of enterprise in the field of rubber clothing fabrics in the thirties of the nineteenth century, but it ended in failure and disappeared in the crisis of 1837 to 1839. Vulcanization accounts for a new start that was a minor feature of the first Juglar of the second Kondratieff (from 1842, on). The next event, following upon a long period of quiet and rather passive expansion, was the merger that combined 10 concerns into the United States Rubber Company (incorporated in 1892), which conquered more and more ground in the Kondratieff prosperity under discussion (later on it also acquired plantations of its own). This industry felt the impulse of the new demand from the motorcar innovation soon after 1908, when production of tires, tubes and other accessories began to count in production programs.[1]

The oil industry also became almost a subsidiary to the gasoline engine. In 1899, only 12.8 per cent of crude oil on stills went to the production of gasoline, kerosene still absorbing 57.7 per cent; but in our period the former and the use of oil for fueling purposes in general aproached their postwar importance. From the standpoint of the industry, this was but a favorable external fact, without which decay would have been unavoid-

[1] The third new industry, rayon, met during the period under discussion with so little success in this country—the companies that were founded from 1897 to 1911 were unqualified failures and the American Viscose, founded in 1911, was a foreign-owned enterprise—that we need not mention it at all.

able, and the considerable development during the period—value added in petroleum refining increased from about 21 to about 71 millions between 1899 and 1914, and output of crude petroleum from about 60 million to nearly 250 million barrels between 1897 and 1913—was primarily a case of "being drawn along" or of passive adaptation. The rise which occurred in prices bears witness to that.[1] Pipe lines, tank ships, tank cars were no longer novelties. There was progress in the methods of prospecting, in drilling to greater depths—the rotary drill came after the war—and in rational treatment of oil fields by gas and water pressure. Refining was still done in "skimming" and in complete straight-run plants, and gasoline yield from crude was still only 18.6 per cent in 1914—the cracking process was to increase it and hydrogenation to raise it to 100 per cent in postwar times. Profits were high all the time and partly financed new investment, particularly within the Standard Oil concern. Its dissolution by judicial decree in 1911 did not, within our period, affect the division of labor between the constituent companies, although it did so later.[2]

Among old industries, glass production was thoroughly revolutionized by innovations that were almost entirely independent of anything that happened elsewhere. Up to 1898, slow introduction of tank furnaces had been practically the only change that had come to the bottle-glass blower's old trade for decades, and this had left his function untouched. In 1898 came the semiautomatic machine, which, though it eliminated blowers, still required skilled labor; and in 1905, the completely auto-

[1] As regards prices of crude oil, this was in spite of the fact that production was highly competitive—in fact, various circumstances, natural and legal, combined to make it almost perfectly so and to force everybody to produce what he could. The Standard Oil concern never controlled more than 33.5 per cent of output (1898), and mostly much less (in 1907, for instance, 11 per cent). Its position rested entirely on the pipe lines and on refineries. That is why pipe-line companies were subjected to the obligations of common carriers in 1906.

[2] As mentioned in the preceding section, production of natural gas started in the middle nineties on the increase that was to carry consumption, mainly for industrial purposes, to 1,918 billions of cubic feet. In 1900 it was 509 billions. A number of innovations in the industry make it necessary to include it in the list of those that contributed to the third Kondratieff, particularly to its second and to postwar Juglars.

matic (Owens) machine. A later development started in 1917 ("feed and flow" machine). Almost simultaneously the window-glass production was mechanized (cylinder machine, J. H. Lubbers, 1903, introduced about 1905). Again a later development, the steel process (Colburn, Fourcault), should be mentioned here. A minor innovation was migration (from Pittsburgh to Indiana and Ohio), mainly motivated by the desire to use natural gas. While value added (in the group of stone, clay, and glass products) increased between 1899 and 1914 by 204 per cent, employment fell strongly and *permanently*. For instance, employment in the bottle (and jar) industry was, after a spectacular increase of physical output, even in 1925 only three-quarters of what it had been in 1899. In other respects the case was normal. We find quite as much increase in physical output and quite as much fall in price as we have a right to expect.

This is interesting, because the industry was by no means untouched by the merger movement or by the tendency toward giant concerns irrespective of mergers. The American Window Glass Company, which controlled nearly three-fourths of the capacity, was incorporated in 1899. The first thing it did, however, was reduce prices drastically. No doubt this move was not only interpreted by observers, but even motivated by the executive, as an attack on actual and potential competitors, intended to cut throats and to establish a monopoly. But the point is that even if such monopoly position had been attained, *i.e.*, if the result had really been to leave but a single seller in the industry, that seller could never have behaved according to the theoretical schema of monopoly without losing that position. The implications of this resolve the paradox of modern industry, which, while struggling for monopoloid control, yet surpasses all historical records in efficiency as measured by physical output, as well as the other paradox that, monopolistic tendencies notwithstanding, our schema fits statistical fact not less well in the period of "big business" than it did in more competitive times. Other branches of the glass industry also display instances of the tendency toward the big concern (Pittsburgh Plate Glass, 1895; National Glass (tableware), 1899).

We pass by paper. There was little change in production functions—though much expansion of output—except what is implied in the use of hydroelectric power and in some interesting amalgamations (such as the International Paper Company in

1898 or the American Writing Paper Company in 1899). We also pass by printing. Hoe's revolving-cylinder press had won out by the sixties; it was developed later on; color printing and typography came in the eighties and nineties, as did the Mergenthaler linotype and the Lanston monotype and automatic type casting, but the advance beyond that belongs to the downgrade of the third Kondratieff. Finally, we pass by the developments in the chemical industry: progress in the production of heavy chemicals, use of electricity, mergers.

We must, however, make a remark on cement, developments in which induced enthusiasts to speak of a cement age. As a matter of fact, the increase in output is as striking as the fall in price that accompanied it, in spite of the protective duty, the absence of perfect competition, the violent booms during which it occurred, and the fact that owing to the contemporaneous innovations in building (steel-concrete) the demand curve for its product shifted upward still more than it would have done under the mere influence of general conditions of prosperity. The rise of the industry dates, as was mentioned in the preceding section, from the fifth and sixth Juglars of the second Kondratieff and development simply continued during the period under review. The first stride had been made in the middle eighties, when the price of Portland cement started on its downward course in response to a fall in costs and output began to increase. About 2.7 million barrels were produced and the factory price was $1.61 in 1897. Output was over 88 millions, and price was $0.93 in 1914—still lower, in fact, if improvement of quality is taken into account. Absence of distress in the industry suggests that money costs per unit must have fallen, and fallen fairly generally for the large majority of firms, to something like the German level. An innovation of the last Juglar of the preceding Kondratieff, the rotary kiln—which conquered, and increased in size, as soon as it became more economical through the use of powdered coal—and more powerful grinding machinery must be responsible. Competition by natural and slag cement may have had something to do with the promptness with which the benefit was handed over to the consumer. Many new firms—but no giants—emerged, and we can repeatedly follow up progress from higher prices, which threatened the manufacturers' margins, to lower prices a few years later, which did not.

How remarkable that is and how closely it was associated with the conditions characteristic of a new and innovating industry we can see from a comparison with the cotton industry. This also expanded, cotton consumption roughly doubling in the period. Nor was innovation absent. The Northrop-Draper loom came into its own in this period and the Crompton (1905) and Knowles (1910) looms were then new. Ring spindles were improved with considerable success as to the reduction of cost and, as mentioned before, electricity lent its aid. Yet the price of print cloth rose from 1900 to and above the level of the second half of the eighties: the character of the old established industry that is drawn along by the environment asserted itself. There were some amalgamations—New England Cotton Yarn Company; American Thread Company; also an attempt to form a cartel: Fall River Printcloth pool, 1898 to 1901. The feature in woolen textiles was the large worsted mill—the carded-wool industry declined even absolutely—but, partly because of the high price of the raw material, there were no developments that need detain us. Silk made considerable headway, largely by innovations which, in part at least, overcame the difficulties incident to the American labor situation; but this was only continuation of what had been achieved before.

Of course, all the industrial processes of the time reflect themselves in the development of iron and steel. But they were to a much lesser degree initiated by it than the processes of, say, the eighties. We have already noticed the relation of give and take between electricity and steel and the role of the latter in the merger movement and we will but add a few outstanding facts. In mining, the old iron-ore districts declined and the Lake Superior ores dominated the market. The innovation was the development of the Mesabi range after the technological and transportation problems incident to the quality and the location of that ore had been successfully overcome. Also the period saw the rise and decay of the tendency toward complete vertical integration—although integration to the extent of combining mining, railroads, docks, and fleets proved successful and may be considered responsible for part of the great increase in productive efficiency that occurred—and several attempts at reorganization of the trade. The really decisive fall in the prices of ores occurred, however, before our period. Prices of pig iron rose very considerably and the inference that there was no great reform in its production function is borne out by the history of the industry, which, as far as direct use of iron is concerned (wrought iron), naturally declined. Output of pig iron rose in the Kondratieff upswing, but not much more, even in the high tide of prosperity, than it did in the eighties. This is due, of course, to the fact that the same quantity went so much further than before.

All the significant progress was in steel. The open-hearth process, the use of scrap, basic steel, and alloys are the main headings. The first three can hardly be called novelties. Moreover, in the case of the open-hearth process, it was largely consumers' demand, particularly from producers and users of structural material, that gave it the victory over the Bessemer process. New plants—the Gary plant, for instance—hence adopted it as a matter of course, although, for many individual producers, it still involved innovation to dismantle their Bessemer plant and to throw in their fortunes with the (basic) open-hearth process. It should be observed in passing that the open-hearth process, working with scrap, gave a new stimulus to the smaller concern, because the economies of large-scale production were much less than in the Bessemer plant. Alloys, which were to gain great importance, were practically new. They had scored their first successes in the eighties, especially for forgings (crankshafts for the Boston Elevated, for instance, or the moving parts of the pumps of the Calumet and Hecla mines).

The important development, however, with which the Bethlehem steel was particularly associated, came in our period. High-speed cutting steel for the machine shop and various other specialties, for motorcars, railroads, oil drills, and so on, were beginning to play a role. Still, however important these developments and however great their quantitative contribution to the Kondratieff, it was, nevertheless, one more case of the great things having been done. The quantity of crude steel consumed increased fully as much as we should expect it to do in a Kondratieff prosperity, but the behavior of prices clearly does not place steel production in the van of innovation. In the case of specialties this behavior may enter into the class of prices of branded articles and also veil an actual fall per efficiency unit. In other cases, for example the standard one of the price of rails, which stood at 28 from 1902 to 1915, it may be due to another type of monopoloid situations, although rails had displayed a tentency to rise before 1901. In other cases there was competition enough to enforce a fall if conditions of production had warranted it. Yet none ensued, except such as would occur in the course of Juglar situations.

Copper mining illustrates very well some of the ways of innovation. Its American history begins in Michigan (Keweenaw peninsula, 1854). Output increased rapidly—there was plenty of demand in the fifties from the brass and copper works in Connecticut (kitchen utensils; brass and copper tubing; both not important innovations), from producers of oil lamps and burners, shipbuilders, and so on. By the sixties, a considerable industry had developed, which profited greatly from the war, and the products of which began to compete with iron—as iron, a century before, had almost crowded out copper in Europe. Professor Taussig is presumably right in his opinion that it owed but little to the special bill of 1869, which gave it additional protection. The Calumet and Hecla mines got into their stride in that year and figured in the subsequent boom. The annual average price of copper in 1872 almost reached the annual average of 1864, and then fell, with sharply marked Juglar fluctuations, to 1894. This fall, which was greater than that of the price level, was as much due to innovations of the downgrade type (power drills, high-power explosives, all sorts of mechanizations) that reduced costs so as to enforce a policy of "nursing demand" in order to extend old and create new uses, as it was to new competition from the Arizona and Montana mines that were discovered in the seventies. Output of the Montana mines (Butte, vein ores—expensive to win but of high copper content—the basis of the position of the Anaconda concern) outstripped that of the Michigan mines in 1887. These new sources of supply were one of the by-products of railroad developments, both in the sense that the railroads induced their discovery and in the sense that they made exploitation possible, since there was no fuel for smelting and refining in their neighborhood.

The great increase in output during our period, at the very beginning of which there was a copper boom culminated in 1899 and was followed by another from 1904 to 1906, was induced, however, by the developments of the electric industry and, later on, of the motorcar industry. Already in the eighties the innovation of hard drawing of copper wire had established that contact which then became the dominant factor in the demand for copper. At the same time electricity had contributed the new method of refining which in the course of the nineties reduced costs to about half. New discoveries (porphyry ores) in Utah, Nevada, New Mexico, Alaska (1900 to 1911), the great expansion in Arizona which began in the middle nineties, and various improvements in mining methods complete the list of innovations. Interpretation in the light of our model is obvious; the competitive struggles with iron (for example, early telegraph wires were made of iron) and aluminum are particularly interesting. The foundation in 1899, and the success from 1899 to 1901 and again from 1905 to 1907 of a holding concern primarily aiming at control of prices with a view to creating short-run monopoly situations (Amalgamated Copper) deserves notice precisely because it affords one of those rare instances to which the ordinary theory of monopoly approximately applies. It also illustrates the conditions, the limitations, and the essentially temporary character of all such cases and the difference between them and the ordinary industrial combines.

The only other subject we can afford to touch is aluminum. Both its commercially successful methods of production are branches of electrical metallurgy (the brothers Cowles; Héroult-Hull). Their invention in the eighties led to quick expansion in the last Juglar of the second Kondratieff, and prices fell to one dollar per pound by about 1890. The two firms in control of the industry (The Pittsburgh Reduction, later American Aluminum Company and the Cowles Electric Smelting Company, Cleveland) afford as instructive a case study as the single seller of later date does under similar conditions. Prices continued to fall and in the middle nineties had reached the level at which mass production for structural purposes became possible. The use for railroads, motorcars, and electrical appliances, in the food industries, in chemistry, and so on, begins in our period.

8. As usual, we cannot hope to explain every individual spurt and breakdown by the factors which enter into our model. All the latter can do for us, is to describe the industrial processes that underlie such spurts and breakdowns and create conditions that favor their occurrence. Enough facts have been presented to justify the statement that those 16 years were a period of rapid industrial evolution, tapering off at the end, displaying all those characteristics that we imply when speaking of a Kondratieff prosperity, and centering in the electrical innovation with all that was induced by it. This Kondratieff prosperity naturally divides up—within the developments associated with electricity,

which went on with hardly any break—into two periods each characterized by industrial processes of its own, the first primarily by mergers, the second primarly by the automobile industry, though both were also influenced by other items, among them some that were merely "completing." The processes of the second period are discernible by 1907, but do not dominate the economic situation before 1909, though the processes of the first period had clearly come to a provisional stop before. We have before us a complete and an incomplete Juglar, the end of the latter being submerged in the effects of the war.

But, worse than usual, the picture of general business situations during several years completely fails to bear out the expectations which, on the evidence from industrial history, we should form as to their complexion, so much so as to make the dating of cyclical phases uncertain. The nature of the difficulty is well brought out by the behavior of time series. On the one hand, prices, output, pig-iron consumption, clearings, and so on reflect very well the general features of a Kondratieff prosperity and also the division into two sub-periods. If we eliminate trends, the Kondratieff effect is lost, but that division stands out quite strongly: two sequences of well-marked Kitchins are separated by an abrupt trough in 1907-1908. On the other hand, this trough is irregular from the standpoint of our schema, as well as from the standpoint of industrial history. For 1907 we should have expected the situation which we do not find before the second half of 1909. Hence our schema does not explain that crisis—not, at all events, for the precise date at which it occurred and at which either continued revival or prosperity ought to have commanded the scene.

The writer wished to put the case thus strongly in order to enable his readers to record it against the three-cycle schema. He does not do so himself, however, because those irregularities seem to him adequately accounted for by a factor which in the preceding historical report has repeatedly been stressed, *viz.*, the course of events in the financial sphere, which in the period under discussion acquired an abnormal importance. We have seen that one class of the innovations that carried that Kondratieff prosperity and in particular its first Juglar—mergers—tended more than others to induce disturbances of a purely financial nature. We have also seen that the banking system failed to function according to design. The practices of the trust companies in fact revived, in a modernized form, the wildcat banking of the thirties of the nineteenth century. But recklessness in the handling of the most difficult part of a bank's business—that part which has to do with the financing of innovation and of speculative transactions incident to innovation—was not confined to them. Even the national banks maneuvered themselves into positions of strain, almost from the start, and were repeatedly unable to respond to current requirements, because they had lent on new securities that syndicates were unable to place. Both at the time and later, responsibility for this state of things was attributed to the absence of a central institution and to the legal framework within which the banking system had to work, reserve requirements in particular. This, however, was putting the cart before the horse. It is true that adequate machinery did not exist for the handling of a crisis after the event. But this has nothing to do with the way in which the conditions of strain arose. On the contrary, the *strain restrained* what otherwise would have gone on entirely unbridled. If any lesson can be drawn at all from the experience of those days, it is exactly opposite to the one that recommended itself both to the banking community and to the public mind. Blaming the brake for the results of reckless driving is, however, part of the political psychology of cycles.

This factor did more than disturb the surface. It is understandable that, in an atmosphere in which everyone lived on, and worked with, what as yet were future possibilities, the industrial process also should be profoundly affected. Remembering this, we shall now venture upon an interpretation of events year by year.

Eighteen ninety-eight makes a very normal first year of a Kondratieff prosperity. But a significant reaction to a pace, particularly in the financial sphere, which was clearly abnormal and very strongly displayed the features that we subsume under the heading Secondary Wave, occurred as early as February 1899, and liquidation, not quite confined to the financial sphere, lasted to the end of May (death of Flower, May 12). Another setback came in December—call money at 186 per cent on the eighteenth of that month actually had a sobering effect for a year, although caused by English troubles; it threw much light on the situation—but industry did not slacken until the middle of 1900. This completes the prosperity of the first Juglar, the recession of which should, according to our schema, display much the same symptoms, because of the location of that Juglar in the Kondratieff. So it does through 1902, witness the "steel famine." The wheat harvests of 1901 and 1902 were favorable external factors. But the way was studded with financial vicissitudes of which that outbreak of speculative frenzy centering in the Northern Pacific corner and the reaction thereto were the most important. However, while upsetting the international money market and the normal functioning of the domestiic banking system, they did not blot out the industrial rhythm. What can be interpreted as a regular Juglar depression, mitigated by the underlying Kondratieff swell, set in at the begining of 1903 and lasted till nearly the end of 1904, the so-called "rich men's panic" being its complement in the financial sphere. Recovery followed, and under the circumstances there is no reason to wonder at its violence, which may be held to account for a short reaction. The latter or the recovery from it would then complete that Juglar's third Kitchin. This carries us to about the middle of 1906.

Then followed indeed a strong upswing in the second half of 1906, sustained though on a stationary level until the autumn 1907; but it does not link up with any new processes in industry and suddenly gave way to what looks like deep depression for the rest of the year, followed by an only less sudden recovery in 1908. The year 1909 displays all the features of a regular prosperity milder in character than that of the first Juglar, which we should expect from its location in the Kondratieff, although we should not have expected, and must trace to aftereffects of preceding irregularities, the early relapse in 1910 and 1911. 1912 was a year of good business and is true to form, and in 1913 and 1914 the system was sliding into what bears interpretation as a regular Juglar depression. Although not wholly, irregularity is, therefore, mainly confined to 1907 and 1980, *i.e.*, to the crisis of 1907 and its aftermath. This crisis is an intermezzo, which falls outside of our schema. Once we accept that explanation of it which is offered here, it becomes as understandable that the setting in of the industrial processes that carried the second Juglar should have been deferred by it, as the same effect would have been understandable if, instead of the crisis, a natural catastrophe or a social disturbance of sufficient magnitude had occurred. For the crisis would, not less than events of the latter type, interfere with entrepreneurial activity by destroying the neighborhhod of equilibrium from which alone it starts. Also, it would follow that we should not accept at face value what looks like an overgrown Kitchin—extending, if we count from trough to trough, from 1904 to 1908—but rather allow the dent in 1906 to split it so that the first Juglar ends in (the middle of) that year.

We will not go into the details of the crisis of 1907 or into the technique by which that crisis was handled. But, since our diagnosis attributes its violence and its location in time entirely to the doings in the financial sector, both defense and explanation seem to be called for. As to the first, a survey of events since 1898, the elements of which have been presented above, clearly yields supporting evidence. In particular, it should be observed that the manner in which the financial engine was from the start handled by the groups and individuals at or near the steering wheel, while perfectly adequate to produce breakdowns, at the same time produced, for those groups and individuals, results which offered ample enticement to repeat abuses on an ever-enlarging scale. That a major breakdown, when it eventually occurred, did not remain confined to the stock exchange and to the banks, but also paralyzed the economic process, is not surprising. But the short duration of this "depression," as well as the fact that it was not nearly so deep as we might infer from indices that heavily weight the output in the most affected sectors, and as we might expect from the violence of the financial catastrophe, lend support to our view that it was not a depression in our sense at all. Nor can it be urged, as an argument against the above analysis, that the crisis was international. For Germany and a few other countries, such as Egypt, a very similar state of things can be shown to have existed and to have produced largely autonomously, similar results, synchonization of which is easily accounted for by existing financial relations. As regards the rest of the world, which was much less affected, these relations—and infection by the speculative excesses in America—are sufficient to account for such crises as occurred. In fact, foreign capital played a considerable role in the American stock exchange and money market at the critical time.

If, then, this diagnosis seem acceptable, it follows that, barring those surface phenomena that characterize any crisis, there is no analogy between 1907 and either 1873 or 1929. This is indeed obvious from the character and duration of the depressions that ensued in the two latter cases. There is more similarity between 1907 and 1857. We should not attach much importance to such details as that each of these cases centered around a conspicuous failure (in 1907 that of the Knickerbocker Trust on Oct. 22). But it is more relevant that both occurred in the first half of the Kondratieff. The reader should observe how many of the actual facts of both cases are covered by this formula, and how well the similarities between them and the differences between these two and other cases are expressed by it. The analogy should not, howver, be pressed too far. The location of both crises in their Kondratieffs is not exactly the same. That in 1857 occurred at a later stage and hence it can, to a much greater extent, be explained by the underlying phase of the evolutionary process. But the ever-forgotten lesson about what causes such spectacular breakdowns of the capitalist engine and how they could be prevented or mitigated is the same in both, and in fact all, cases.

Explanation is due because our diagnosis explains the occurrence of the crisis of 1907 by a disturbance of the normal working of the cyclical process of evolution, which was not attributable to an external factor but to the systematic abuse of the financial apparatus. Speaking of a disturbance of the capitalist process by a factor that arises out of that process itself obviously raises a methodological question. Any economic or social system has its logic and the standards inherent to that logic. Effects due to action conforming to this logic and those standards are one thing, effects of deviations from them another thing. In matters of human behavior, both conforming and deviating action must be separately taken into account, for both are equally real. This should also explain why we can speak of abuse as distinguished from use of institutions without thereby committing ourselves to a moral—or any other—value judgment. The former term is intended merely to indicate the fact that the behavior deviates from standards which follow from the structure of an economic system. The only question that matters is whether or not that distinction is supported by the facts and in turn serves to elucidate them. If this be answered in the affirmative, "faulty" handling of institutions may induce breakdowns exactly as an external factor, and disturbance of this nature can autonomously arise in the financial as in any other sphere of economic activity.

Chapter VIII

1919-1929

A. Postwar Events and Postwar Problems.—The formidable task of interpreting, economically and sociologically, our own time cannot be attacked in this book. Whatever of this the reader may find in the following pages, is incidental to an argument the very restricted purpose of which should be borne in mind throughout. That purpose is to answer the question how far the cyclical process of capitalist evolution, as analyzed for the 130 years that preceded the World War,* can be proved to have persisted in the postwar period, and to see how our model works under the conditions and with the richer material of that period. The contribution toward an understanding of the postwar-world which an investigation of this kind can be expected to make may prove worse than valueless, if its character, methodological background, and analytic intention are allowed to drop out of sight. Wherever it seemed possible, an attempt has been made to save space and to rely on the fact that current economic events are, and have been since the war, very much more efficiently reported than before, and on the hope that general contour lines are, therefore, familiar to the reader.

* Author refers to World War I, throughout, as World War.

We exclude the years 1914 to 1918 on the ground that those years were dominateed by "external factors" to an extent that makes their figures valueless for our purpose. That is, indeed, not quite true. The rhythm of economic life clearly persisted in the United States, and some aspects of war events are not without relevance for the study of business cycles. In particular, war expenditure affords as good experimental evidence as we can ever hope to get about the nature and consequences of a boom which has nothing to do with innovation and is brought about by expanding credit and stimulating consumption alone. The fact that expenditure was not directed into channels which would commend themselves to advocates of such a policy is entirely irrelevant, for all that matters is that depressions were actually impending or in progress in 1914 and that public expenditure turned them into prosperity first and created untenable situations afterward. But although the case almost ideally complements and illustrates part of the argument of this book, we will follow the practice of the majority of students and eliminate those violent "irregularities" by leaving out the figures of those years.

External factors in our sense continued to play a supernormally important rôle throughout the postwar period. That our second component of economic change, the cyclical process of evolution, was still present and asserted itself in the same manner as before is not so obvious. Owing to the historic character of our subject —or the fact that it is "institutionally conditioned"—this question would arise in any case, even if there had been no war: whenever we wish to apply our analysis to an additional span of time, we must always ask whether our process still persists. The method of deriving an answer is to locate the postwar period in our cyclical schema, to formulate the expectations which follow from that, and to see how far they agree with observed fact. According to that schema the postwar time up to the world crisis covers parts of the recession and depression phases of our third Kondratieff which underlie two incomplete Juglars. If fluctuations behave as they did before the war, those Juglars would be the third and fourth of that Kondratieff. The third would complete the recession, the fourth would entirely lie on (but not complete) the depression phase of the latter. We ought to be able, finally, to discern the Kitchin wave superimposed on those two. *The time series picture of all this must then link up with the historical facts of the industrial process behind it.* Expectations are perfectly definite and will be formulated as our picture unfolds.

B. Comments on Postwar Patterns.–Now we will drop, if only for a few paragraphs, the practice, imposed upon us by the nature of our task, of treating the institutional framework of society, the attitudes of individuals and groups, and the policies resulting from a given social pattern as data of our economic process, and changes in these data as external factors. We will glance at the social process as a whole and in so doing adopt the convenient, though possibly inadequate, hypothesis of Marxism, according to which social, cultural, political situations and the spirit in which and the measures by which they are met, derive from the working of that capitalist machine. Our cyclical schema lends itself to this view, not only because of the length of its longest wave, which brings long-run social changes within the reach of business-cycle analysis, but also because it stresses that kind of economic change that is particularly likely to break up existing patterns and to create new ones, thereby breaking up old and creating new positions of power, civilizations, valuations, beliefs, and policies which from this standpoint are, therefore, no longer "external." The standard illustration is afforded by those innovations which drove the artisan's shop into modest reservations and, together with the artisan's shop, also the artisan's world. Gathering up the threads that lie all over our edifice we might thus try to understand the social configuration of the postwar period from the economic process we have analyzed.

But we should find the task more difficult than the analogous one in the cases of the first and second Kondratieffs. There the social process and its cultural and political complements were not difficult to interpret in the sense of the working hypothesis which for the moment we have adopted. All that was not covered by it we could comfortably stow away as atavisms. This is not so in the case of the Neomercantilist Kondratieff. If the reader refers to Chap. VII, Sec. E, he will find that we had to recognize, besides phenomena that indicated consistent development of previous tendencies, the presence of other phenomena that did not seem to fit into the same current but rather to fight against it: they looked like a revolt against the rational or rationalistic civilization of that epoch. Of course, it is easy to label them, too, as atavisms. This sounds convincing in some cases, for instance, in the case of the German legislation for the protection of the artisan class. Here we see a dying stratum trying to defend its crumbling basis by political means. It is not so convincing in others, and any open mind must admit the possibility that a movement of such breadth and depth may have been more than an atavism or the last card of a decaying class. The fact that the writer had no better name to offer for it than *Neomercantilism* sufficiently shows that so far he has not succeeded in interpreting it to his own satisfaction. For that term, at best, gets hold of one of many aspects and is as inadequate as Nationalism or Anti-rationalism would be. Now that tendency or attitude did not perish. On the contrary, it developed during the postwar period and in developing revealed itself more fully in the Corporative or Totalitarian or Fascist State and also became ideologically articulate. However much the war—and the circumstances of the "Have-not nations"—may have had to do with concrete forms, mechanisms, timings, and surface events, that departure from the road that leads from capitalism to orthodox socialism is not "due" to it, and the general drift of this page might have been the same had it never occurred. The answer to the question how this development may be expected to affect our cyclical process depends on the kind of planning that a fascist government undertakes: given sufficient power and insight in a central authority, innovation may of course be planned for in such a way as to minimize disturbance.

1. If this component of postwar history can be traced to prewar sources, everything can. For the only other component—the "socialist" one—is perfectly *en règle* from the standpoint of our working hypothesis and may readily be described in terms of the rationalizing, leveling, mechanizing, and democratizing effects of capitalist evolution. This is too obvious to detain us, and only a few points of particular relevance to our subject need elaboration.

First, the rise of the labor interest to a position of political power and sometimes of responsibility, which is but the most conspicuous of the symptoms of a profound change in social structures, is clearly a product of capitalism in our sense of the term, which created a political world and political attitudes fundamentally incompatible with itself even where, as in the United States, the labor interest was (within our period) not politically dominant. The habit of the old-fashioned liberal—in the European sense of the word—of blaming "politics" for almost everything he considers less than satisfactory in the capitalist world is, as far as this goes, in fact open to the objection that in blaming "politics" he is blaming a product and an essential element of the system he approves. Taking the social system of capitalism as a whole, it is meaningless to say that it—or any element of it, *e.g.*, the gold standard—is checkmated by "politics." What ought to be said—on this level of analysis—is that it checkmates itself.

Second, it is worth mentioning that capitalism, also by its own working, evolves a phenomenon the importance of which was not foreseen by Marx: the clerical class. The growth of the laboring stratum proper, relatively to the increase of gainfully occupied persons, ceased in the first decade of this century, but the relative growth of the salaried employee (roughly equal to "white collar") then became spectacular—for obvious reasons of capitalist technique. The interests of this class—the "logic of its situation"—and its attitudes differing considerably from the interests and attitudes of "workmen," we have here a factor to the power of which much of the politics and policies of postwar times may be traced, particularly in Germany. This New Middle Class, as it has been called, forms in some countries and comes near to forming in others, together with farmers (peasants) and small businessmen (mainly retailers), a majority of the population, which, though split into widely differing sections, yet feels and acts uniformly in many cases; and that in fundamental attitude it is as hostile to the interests of the bigger and big bourgeoisie as is the working class in the narrower sense of the term, though also hostile to the interests of the latter. It is in the light of these facts and not in the light of the simple but entirely unrealistic contrast between property owners and proletarians that postwar patterns must be understood.

Third, capitalist evolution not only upsets social structures
titude it is as hostile to the interests of the bigger and big bour-
which protected the capitalist interests, by progressively eliminating precapitalist strata from politics and public administration and by creating new positions of political power, but also undermines the attitudes, motivations, and beliefs of the capitalist stratum itself. Even if an industrial family happens to own a given concern, wholly or nearly so, and if its members actually manage it, they do not under modern conditions

look upon it in the way industrial families used to do in the past. Their attitude is more distant, less personal, more rationalized. But the leading men of the giant concerns as a rule fill a specialized function in a spirit which resembles that of the employee properly so called, and tend to distinguish between their success and that of the concern, let alone that of the shareholders. Moreover, the loosening of the family tie—a typical feature of the culture of capitalism—removes or weakens what, no doubt, was the center of the motivation of the businessman of old. Finally, the top group—say, 40,000 men and their families in this country and just about as many in Germany—absorbs, subconsciously and by no infinite number of channels, views, habits, valuations cultural worlds—that are not its own. "Capitalists" cease to believe in the standards and moral schemata of their own class. They adopt, or connive at, many things which their predecessors would have considered not only injurious to their interests but dishonorable: in surveying modern economic fact, one cannot but be struck by the discovery of how much of the typical behavior of the bourgeoisie of the nineteenth century was extra-economically conditioned. All this, of course, links up, in a way that hardly requires explanation, with the decrease in the importance of the entrepreneurial function noticed in Chap. III and Chap. IV.

Fourth, both the rise to power of strata untinged by bourgeois attitudes and the fact that these attitudes lose their hold on the bourgeois stratum itself, which to an increasing extent allows itself to be educated by its new masters and the intellectual exponents of these masters combine to produce the anti-saving attitude of our epoch so clearly voiced in its popular, as well as scientific, literature on economic theory and policy. Saving with a view to providing revenue for an indefinite family future was part not only of the economic but also of the moral scheme of life of the typical bourgeois. The attempt to prove that such thrift is harmful to the interest of the masses always has been a major element in anti-capitalist arguments, which without it would be open to a dangerously obvious reply. Attempts to prove that it is also harmful to the capitalist interest itself have never been wanting. But in our time the lesson is being learned and beginning to motivate public policy. Whatever its merits or demerits, its success must be understood as part of a general short-run attitude of modern man toward economic problems and situations, which follows from the changes in social structure.

All this spells a profound change in the environment within which the capitalist engine works.

2. But recognizing thus fully the relation which exists between capitalist evolution and its social and sociopsychological complement, no more debars us from recognizing the existence of distinguishable spheres of social activity between which in a given case given effects may be apportioned, than recognition of universal interdependence of prices debars us from distinguishing them and from tracing given effects to the behavior of, say, one of them. Moreover, every such sphere, however much the product of one comprehensive process acquires, when once formed, a life and mechanism of its own that enjoys many degrees of freedom. This is enough to justify our going on to work with the concept of External Factors. In particular, it is clear that we cannot from a study of economic conditions alone determine what will happen in the political sphere. On the contrary, we must deal with all the facts of each sphere as we find them—which precisely means that they are external factors for one another. For instance, it is not enough to know that—possibly—England's economic conditions and interests to some extent explain her general attitude to the United States during the Civil War. This will not explain why she came within an ace of, yet refrained from, interfering by force of arms. Even the necessity of taking account of the personal element cannot be denied. Hence, purely economic diagnosis of the type for which political action is merely a "disturbing factor" is not necessarily devoid of meaning.

In this sense the World War is for us an external factor. From the facts the above remarks were intended to cover, it seems to follow that it did not "create" any of the fundamental social features of the postwar warld, although it accentuated some and may have anticipated others. The physical destruction—including the expenditure of productive energy on that tremendous "excess in consumption"—and the loss of life in the most active age groups were made up quickly, the former with a promptness which in another social atmosphere would have been admired as a marvel of industrial efficiency. All this reduces for our purpose to two statements: first, that physical destruction, reinforced by the accumulation of omitted replacements and investments, became the source of a reconstruction demand, which accentuated the prosperities and revivals that occurred up to, roughly, the middle twenties; second, that the shift from war to peace conditions involved rearrangements that almost wholly account for the short "jolt" in 1918 and partly for the crisis of 1921, which was, however, in step with the ordinary run of cycles and was only intensified by this factor.

3. The war undoubtedly precipitated development which it is reasonable to assume would have come about without it, but would have come about more slowly and in different forms. It is in connection with these developments that foreign policies and the problems of international economic relations in general must be seen. Their history naturally divides up into three periods: the period of continuing economic—in some points even extra-economic—warfare, from the armistice to 1924 (London conference; Dawes plan); the period during which the arrangements arrived at were widely believed in and acted upon, and which lasted from the Dawes plan to roughly the end of 1927; and the period of increasing friction, ending in the midst of the world crisis in the Hoover moratorium and, later on, in the liquidation, *via facti*, of the reparations and inter-Allied debts. Since the first period coincides with German postwar inflation, which we exclude, all that need be said about it is that American business situations were for the time being little and, if anything, favorably affected by the course of international events.

As regards the second period, our statement that the arrangements arrived at were acted upon requires qualification. The world never squarely faced their fundamental consequences, the unavoidable German exports in particular, but poured American and other credits on all the unsolved problems and plastered gold currencies—most curious atavisms though they were, in a world otherwise resolved not to play the capitalist game—on essentially untenable situations. Since it is impossible to enter upon these matters and since the salient facts may be assumed to be familiar, we can for our purpose compress the comments that would be necessary into the statement that this "export of American capital" did not act as we would expect capital export to act under more normal conditions, but that for the time being it largely counteracted the disturbance that would otherwise have ensued from international political payments. Moreover, while it relieved stringencies in many countries, it did not create corresponding ones in the lending country, because America still remained a creditor on current account, even apart from the short balances which for familiar reasons continued to flow toward her. This explains the astonishing fact that those "political transfers" will not play any great role in our analysis of the processes of that period. This even applies to the third period, almost until the outbreak of the world crisis when, though partly for political reasons, short balances took fright. But the fundamental facts of the situation, accentuated as well as expressed by protectionist tendencies and the passing of the Locarno atmosphere, had begun to assert themselves before that.

If those temporary solutions of the international financial problems created by the war proved inadequate, and if their economic consequences, including their—secondary—share in the causation of the world crisis, turned out as they did, this was only because of the political environment within which they had to work, *i.e.*, our assertion of their inadequacy must be understood to be relative to the social situation previously glanced at. They were bankers' solutions, which the nations concerned were unwilling to accept and which they defeated by refusing to allow the mechanisms to work on the functioning of which the authors of those solutions relied. Looked at as business propositions, they would not, in a peaceful world accepting bourgeois standards, have been obviously absurd, and it would not in such a world have been unreasonable to expect that they would work out in the end. The well-meant proposals of all those international conferences that met to discuss the gradual removal of trade barriers look to us like strange anachronisms and certainly were as futile as proposals for disarmament must be in a world in which every nation that counts is bent on armament. But they were perfectly sound economics. Even the gold currencies were such failures only because trade barriers, fiscal policies, social and military expenditure, and insistence on higher money wages did not allow them to function and because in that hostile environment short capital was rushing about like a hunted hare. Given all these facts, it was and is indeed little short of ridiculous to trust to the remedial forces of *laisser faire*. But since they do not, any more than the war itself and Versailles, uniquely follow from the logic of our evolutionary process, it is not to the interest of clear thinking to speak of any inherent tendency of capitalism to run into such deadlocks.

4. Since the role which postwar protectionism played in the developments of the twenties and in the causation of the world

crisis has been so completely overlooked by some students of the business cycle and so obviously exaggerated by others, it will be convenient to state explicitly the view adopted for the purposes of our analysis—which, it should be borne in mind, excludes the wide aspects of the matter, such as the relation of protectionist policy to human welfare and to peace. In the first years after the war, duties, prohibitions, quotas, and other weapons from the arsenal of protectionism were, of course, elements of the general scheme of continuing economic war. But they were also something else. Adaptation of industry and trade to the new conditions above referred to, permanent and transient, was at best a difficult task, involving in many cases abrupt dislocations. This becomes obvious if we glance at the postwar figures both of commodities produced and of commodities internationally exchanged In some of these cases, protective tariffs or even prohibitions were, if not the only means, yet the most obvious means of averting sectional catastrophes, from which cumulative processes (spirals) might easily have ensued. Unequal depreciation of currencies, of course, greatly added to this class of difficulties. Many measures, such as the McKenna duties and even the Fordney-McCumber Act, must, in part at least, be interpreted in this light and on balance probably mitigated many more difficulties than they created. At the other end of our period, immediately before and during the world crisis, a similar argument applies, especially after the newly established currencies had begun to give way, although with lesser force and although a panicky policy of protection and "incapsulation" then went to obviously irrational lengths.

In the years from, roughly, 1924 to, roughly, 1928 some steps toward freer trade were actually made, some countries removing certain barriers and the tariffs of others being automatically lowered, in cases of specific duties, by depreciation not always compensated for by a gold clause. However, it is understandable that not more was accomplished: dislocations and untenable war growths continued to exist; unequal depreciation of currencies was replaced by unequal stabilization, which in some cases overvalued and in others undervalued the legal tender unit; political payments, especially but not only in the case of Germany, provided a motive for aiming at an active balance of trade entirely justifiable even from a free-trade standpoint. There was, indeed, "nationalism." Its outstanding manifestations are to be found in the policies of the majority of the newly created small states that tried to foster industrial development at any price. But that great movement of which we primarily think when speaking of modern nationalism, and which has been recognized above as allied to one of the great components of the social atmosphere of today, has really little to do with the commercial policy of the great nations—and the small ones of old standing—during those years. That policy was dominated by current vicissitudes particularly in England, America and—until the National Socialist party rose to power—in Germany.

This country's famous "refusal to accept its creditor position" still remains. In that phrase there is, no doubt, some element of truth. But since, as pointed out above, American capital export to Europe—it reached about 5 billion dollars by the end of our period—more than sufficed to service her claims, the consequences for the time being were merely to quicken reconstruction in Europe. It was not this mechanism that produced the world crisis, but the world crisis that caused its breakdown. Then, of course, the situation thus created became a major factor in the ensuing depression. But even then it is not easy to see how, had a reduction of import duties been passed instead of the Hawley-Smoot Act, this could have improved short-run conditions in Europe without aggravating them in America. Whatever the merits of free-trade sermons, they can only apply either to the course of action that might have been followed had the crisis not occurred, or else to the course of action that might have beeen followed after it had passed. With this we are not concerned. For our purpose it suffices to conclude that protectionism as such played but a minor role in the cyclical process of the postwar epoch, and to cast a glance at this country's international balance of 1928, since that is the last complete year of the "prosperity plateau."

Commodity exports to Europe were then $2,342,000,000; imports of commodities and services from Europe plus remittances of immigrants and tourists' expenditure, very roughly 2 billions. The resulting net credit of between 300 and 400 millions has to be increased by payments received on war debt account—200 millions—and net receipts from interest and dividends(?). This makes about 600 millions, which must have been mainly "paid" from additional credits, since the total of monetary gold in the United States had fallen both in 1927 and 1928. It is true that the immigration of short funds, then approaching their 1929 peak, complicated the situation. But, with due respect for the excellent motives behind many of the exaggerations of which economists of all countries were guilty in the matter of American policy—Europe's willingness to lecture was more obvious than her willingness to pay—it is presumably safe to say that a sum of that order of magnitude could not, without a crisis, itself caused by other factors, have created an unmanageable problem. In the ordinary course of things, adjustments of the commodity balance amounting to a sum of the order of 300 millions would have been possible, even in a protectionist world: exports alone could have been gradually reduced to that extent without serious repercussions on the American situation, while reinvestment could have absorbed the rest. Again, it was the crisis that prevented such adjustments, and suddenly made an insoluble problem of what otherwise was not only not beyond, but on the way to, a solution which, though in the future it might have *entailed*, did not then *presuppose* free trade.

C. Further Comments on Postwar Conditions.

1. More nearly than any other country, the United States displayed, and substantially retained until the world crisis, a frame of mind appropriate to the task of running the capitalist machine, even to the extent of reducing what was almost universally disapproved of as an "un-American radicalism" to still smaller importance than it had had before the war. Such deviations as occurred from those principles of action that are associated with the logic of the capitalist process were due, rather than to the intrusion of ideas hostile to that logic, to the failure to adapt old ideas to the new situation, as exemplified by so much as there was in the "refusal to accept the implications of this country's new creditor position" just discussed.

But apart from this and possibly monetary policies and the rate of municipal expenditure, there were no lesions inflicted on the system by action from the political sphere. On the contrary, while the nation was bending its energies to the type of tasks characteristic of a Kondratieff downgrade, the federal government was pursuing a fiscal policy eminently "sound" in the old sense. It reduced taxation, going a considerable way beyond merely eliminating the excess profits tax; it reduced the federal debt and even set about to effect some retrenchements. Up to an income of $100,000, the income tax was far below the European level. Federal expenditure, which in 1912–1913 had been 724.5 millions, moved, it is true, on a level of about 3.7 billions from 1925–1926 to 1929–1930 (including debt redemptions out of current revenue to the average amount of over 1/2 billion a year). But under general conditions so exceptionally favorable this was not a very serious matter. Local Total Gross Expenditure increased from 4,593 millions in 1923 to 6,720 millions in 1929; State Total Gross Expenditure, from 1,208 to 1,943 millions. But both states and local authorities raised, partly from a lack of consitutional powers, partly from choice, the money they spent in ways which did not substantially injure the economic machine.

Moreover, the government promptly abolished most of the wartime controls, regulations, and organizations; refrained from measures involving questions of social and economic structure at home; and successfully kept out of entanglements abroad, thereby creating the atmosphere congenial to private business and reducing the importance to the American citizen of the struggles, sufferings, and upheavals in other parts of the world to the order of importance of a football match. Economists who are passionately determined not to admit that policies answering to their social and moral vision, particularly fiscal policies of anticapitalist tendency, can possibly interfere with the working of the economic system, will no doubt hold that there was mere chance coincidence between that sociopolitical pattern and the economic results achieved in this country during the twenties, and between the different setup and the different results in England or Germany. In the fulfillment of our humble task of interpreting a given course of historical events and the behavior of given time series, we cannot, however, neglect the possible inference to the contrary. We speak of possible inference only, because in this point our argument transcends exact proof, as any argument about organic processes occasionally must, and because so many imponderable elements enter which must be a matter of personal judgment and (historical and personal) experience.

2. But the main points at issue with reference to effects of taxation as such—*i.e.*, as distinguished from those effects which a system of taxation may have if it is or is felt to be an element of a general atmosphere of hostility to capitalist success—may conveniently be mentioned here once for all. There is (comparative) agreement about the effects of indirect taxes, such as

specific taxes on the quantity produced or sold of a commodity. This agreement we owe to a fairly well elaborated theory which, though antiquated, is still widely accepted by economists and has recently been somewhat improved by borrowings from the theories of imperfect competition, of expectation, and so on. Its assumptions, however, limit its results to the case of small taxes and/or of individual commodities of small importance. The technical reason for this has an important counterpart in real life: wherever taxes are so small as to be amenable to analytical treatment by the calculus, they are also too small to affect the fundamental contours of economic behavior as reflected in the budgets of firms and households and, hence, to interfere significantly with economic processes in general and the cyclical process of evolution and its permanent results in particular. This proposition may be generalized to cover any small tax, no matter whether sectional, such as a tax on beer or on house room, or general, such as a turnover or an income tax, and extended in most cases to any tax that is small in a practical—though loose—sense and not only in the sense of the calculus. Most taxes which are not small in that wider sense, on the one hand cannot be handled by that method—further repercussions, more fundamental changes in the economic system, reactions from and through the sphere of money and credit must be then taken into account—and on the other hand, do interfere with the results of business processes, for example, with the steady rise in the standard of living of the masses *as far as it is due to the working of the capitalist machine.*

This, however, marks the point at which disagreement begins. The fiscal problem of our time does not primarily consist in the amount of revenue required by the modern state, but in the fact that, owing to the moral valuations prevailing, that amount must also be raised by heavy taxes and, moreover, by heavy taxes framed not only without a view to minimum disturbance but regardless of disturbance, in some cases even with a view to maximizing it. And the disagreement that is relevant to our purpose concerns either the reality of the effects alluded to in the last sentence of the preceding paragraph or their importance for the development of total output. We will confine ourselves to the case which is most important in this connection and consider a high and highly progressive income tax—by which, to fix ideas, we will mean an income tax which, for a significant number of taxpayers in the higher and highest brackets, surpasses 25 per cent—that so defines income as to include savings and is reinforced by a significant corporation and a high or highly progressive inheritance tax.

First, there are what we may term mechanical effects, of which the most important is the effect on the sum total of private savings and accumulations. Taxes such as those we have in mind may enforce dis-saving and even divestment, but will in general be partly paid from revenue that, in turn, would otherwise be partly saved. An obvious argument from general principles yields the result that, as a rule, this again will be partly made up for by additional saving by the same people or by those who are the ultimate recipients of the sums levied. But the net effect of high taxes on the higher incomes will be a decrease of the national total of savings as compared with what it otherwise would be. As far as this goes, therefore, our opinion on how such taxes will affect "progress" and "industrial efficiency" depends on where we stand in the controversy about the importance and the *modus operandi* of private saving, which have been fully discussed before.[1]

Second, there are the nonmechanical effects, *i.e.*, the effects through motives and attitudes. Any tax on net earnings will tend to shift the balance of choice between "to do or not to do" a given thing. If a prospective net gain of a million is just sufficient to over-balance risks and other disutilities, then that prospective million minus a tax will not be so, and this is as true of a single transaction as it is of series of transactions and of the expansion of an old or the foundation of a new firm. Business management and enterprise, being undertaken within an institutional framework of aims, ambitions, and social values fashioned to its logic, will for its maintenance depend, at least in the long run, on the actual delivery, in case of success, of the prizes which that scheme of life holds out, and, therefore, taxes beyond a percentage that greatly varies as to time and place [1] must blunt the

[1] But it should be observed that many arguments turn, not on saving in our sense, but on underspending. Taxes on idle funds may have some stimulating short-run effects if conceived as temporary measures.

[1] Moderate taxation, *i.e.*, taxation which, while making it more difficult, yet does not make it too hard to attain a given economic position, may even act as a stimulus. But however difficult it may be to determine the interval for which that is so, it is perfectly clear that since

profit motive and, especially, the motive typical of both feudal and bourgeois society, that of founding a family position. As to the profit motive in general, it must be borne in mind that a policy of taxing away gains evidently above what would be necessary to call forth the efforts of *their individual recipients* and of taxing but moderately what the community considers "adequate" returns, if it is not to affect the total amount of effort, would really have to be accompanied by an increase in the sum total of managerial and entrepreneurial income, because the presence of conspicuously high and even fantastic individual prizes is, as everyone knows, much more stimulating than the same sum would be if more equally distributed among businessmen. As to that special form of the profit motive which is embodied in the term *family position*, and is largely eliminated by inheritance taxes of the modern type, it is as reasonable to hope that high inheritance taxes, being taxes on "static" wealth, will not affect industrial "progress," *i.e.*, the creation of new wealth, as it would be to hope that a prohibitive railroad fare will not affect traffic if passengers be allowed to board the trains free of charge and the fare be collected from them after they have taken their seats.

D. Outlines of Economic History from 1919 to 1929.—A very rough sketch will be sufficient to convince the reader that all the major features of economic life during that period in fact conform closely to our idea of a Kondratieff downgrade and that none of them fights against the hypothesis which this turn of phrase implies.

1. We begin with the agrarian sphere. Both preceding Kondratieffs displayed within their negative phases prolonged agrarian depressions. In causation and symptoms they differed sufficiently, as between each other and in each case as between countries, to cast doubt on any very broad generalization about

---

the war taxation in the higher brackets goes much beyond it.—High taxation, for example in a national emergency, as long as it is considered to be temporary, may have no effect on motive or even an effect that is stimulating. What taxation is "high" and what "moderate" also depends on the prevailing margins of profits. American taxation even from 1924 to 1931 might have been high in our sense but for the ease with which the businessman rode to success. Finally, much depends on the reaction of the monetary system, for example, on whether or not taxpayers are willing and able to borrow the amounts they have to pay.

them, particularly with respect to the "necessity" or "normality" of their occurrence. Certain properties of Kondratieff downgrades, however, tend to produce depressive conditions in the agrarian world as a whole, and agricultural innovations, if any, tend to produce in sectors of that world depressive conditions that may be important enough to create a picture of general agrarian depression. Obviously, this is what we find in the postwar period and what provides the first approximation into which it is easy to fit all the other factors of agrarian situations. But the latter are, nevertheless, important and should not be neglected merely for the sake of one-factor theories and one-remedy therapeutics.

Primarily, the fall in agrarian prices was a fall not in relative but in absolute price, *i.e.*, an element of the fall in the general price level. Such a fall is part of the mechanism of cyclical downgrades—of Kondratieff downgrades, in particular. It would not, in itself, suffice to produce an agricultural crisis, although it may adversely affect the welfare of the agrarian community if the farm prices of products fall more than the retail prices of the finished products which it buys. "Crisis" may ensue, however, if the fall of the price level impinges on a debt situation that has developed from borrowing either for unproductive purposes—such as the acquisition of land—or for insufficiently productive ones—such as mere expansion. But in the United States and England agriculture had to face, as it had after the Napoleonic wars and, in this country, the Civil War, not that kind of fall in price level which is a normal element of the economic process in Kondratieff recessions and depressions, but the much more violent reaction of prices to the rise during the World War. Moreover, agriculture had been an innovating industry, or rather an industry that had innovations forced upon it which originated elsewhere, such as the internal-combustion engine, specifically agricultural machinery, electric power and appliances, new fertilizers. As we should expect, these innovations fully conquered and came to fruition in the downgrade, and they, as well as the locational shifts, which constitute the most important of agriculture's own innovations, sectionally reduced costs to a level on which large sectors were unable to compete: the food problem of humanity was, as far as the economic process was concerned, indeed definitively solved, but at the expense of the agricultural interest. Competition by other countries, development of which was accelerated by the war, harvests, conditions of demand, international barriers, and other factors have to be inserted, however, to complete the picture as it unfolded itself from year to year.

In the United States the Bureau of Agricultural Economics index of prices received for farm products rose from 1915 to 1919 by 109 per cent, while the index of commodities bought by farmers rose, until 1920, by 94 per cent. The year 1920 brought a moderate fall and 1921 a fall to 116 per cent of the prewar figure, from which the index of farm prices recovered quickly, to reach a peak of 147 per cent in 1925. Then it fluctuated on a moderately falling "trend" up to the eve of the world crisis. This development must be correlated with the development of the agricultural debt. Even in the prewar years total farm mortgages were considerable—3.3 billions in 1910. They rose to 237 per cent of that sum by 1920, quite enough to produce many untenable situations, even if we take into account the fact that incomes had risen more than farm prices, and afterward fell less than they did. But to 1925 there was a further increase to about 9.36 billions, the peak that occurred in 1928 being but insignificantly higher—9.46. Now, some part of this load probably was the result of funding short-time debts which had become irksome, and a greater part, the result of expansion and of the mechanization to be mentioned presently. But the correlation of the two periods of increase with rising land values is obvious, and the inference is unavoidable that much of this increase in debt came from purchases of land with a view to reaping not harvests but increments of value. So far, then, we conclude: there was a short and sharp crisis in agriculture in 1920–1921, which was part of the general postwar slump, though accentuated for agriculture through the burden of partly unproductive debt. In the years to 1926 there was, however unsatisfactory the situation may have been from other standpoints than ours, no general agrarian depression at all. After 1926 and to the threshold of the world crisis, the agrarian situation became increasingly unsatisfactory, but the only *general* cause of this was, again, the pressure of unproductive debt.

But this diagnosis misses, besides many minor points, a major one, *viz.*, the influence of the innovations mentioned before. Some of them, like the progress in the cultivation of citrus fruit and vegetables or in refrigeration and canning, did not spell competition of some sectors or products with others, and brought a net addition to the total of agricultural incomes. To a lesser extent this is true also of poultry and cattle and of dairying. Others, like some electrical appliances, even helped sectors that were being put out of existence by competition, especially those whose main difficulty was dear labor. But most of the improvements in the methods of agriculture, while instrumental in bringing forth agriculture's share in that rising tide of consumers' goods which, according to our schema, is a feature of Kondratieff downgrades, and even producing agricultural prosperity in wide sectors of the country,[1] tended to push certain regions below the margin of profitable production. This, of course, is wholly true of the productive success achieved on reclaimed, drained, irrigated lands and of the process by which large areas have been taken into intensive cultivation of crops and into horticulture that previously served purposes of "extensive" farming. But it is partly true also of the truck, the tractor, most of the machinery newly introduced into grain farming, and to some extent of the use of electrical power. Most of them increase the optimum size of the farming unit, some of them can be used to full advantage only under the particular conditions of the Great Plains. From 1920 to 1930 the number of motor trucks increased from 139,000 to 900,000 and the number of tractors from 246,000 to 920,000. The latter invites the combination of operations that were previously quite distinct, ploughing and the preparation of the seedbed, for instance, and thus steadily leads to ever-increasing mechanization. The use of the combine harvester, which had first been a success in California, spread and yearly sales increased nearly sevenfold in the same period. Cotton- and corn-harvesting implements must be added, but no further examples are necessary in order to establish our point. Nothing of all this was fundamentally new; all of it is typically "induced development" of the kind which on previous occasions we found to be characteristic of Kondratieff downgrades. Our old formula,

[1] That prosperity was, however, less accentuated than might have been expected, not only because profits had to be shared with the industries that were responsible for the innovations, but also because of the perfectly competitive character of agriculture, which responded to the lowering costs by a prompt reduction of the prices of products. This is what, together with the fact that the undersold units did not promptly disappear, created that impression which is sometimes conveyed by the phase "agricultural overproduction."

Depression spotted by Prosperity, fits the case as it did the others. Emigration from agriculture to industry was from the standpoint of the logic of the capitalist mechanism, a perfectly normal phenomenon of adaptation.

Other aspects of the same features and some additional features of the postwar agrarian situation will come into view if we glance for a moment at cotton and wheat in particular. Ever since the beginning of the nineties the price of cotton moved fairly well with any all-commodity index, domestic consumption of cotton—also roughly—with any index of industrial production. This on the whole remained so in our period, the chief exception being the rapid recovery of cotton consumption in 1921, right from the beginning of the year. Quantity exported was below the average of the last prewar years in 1922 to 1924, but roughly on the same level, or somewhat above, in 1924 to 1929, value rising sharply from 1921 to 1925 and receding afterward. Rayon was only one of the competing commodities that must have exerted some influence—with increasing wealth, the competition of wool increases in many lines—but owing to the emergence of new uses, such competition was of but minor importance; the standard fiber was still to come. There was the migration to lands made available by new methods of cultivation, especially to Texas and Oklahoma, partly due to the tractor and the mechanical picker (complemented by a corresponding innovation in ginning), with a consequent competitive annihilation of much of the Southeastern cotton farming.

In all this our process shows to perfection, and the process of labor being drawn away from an "old" stratum (toward the Northeastern industry) is particularly in evidence. Farmers' price of the standard quality rose from about 12-1/2 cents to about 28-1/2 cents during the war (the latter figure being of November 1918), which was perfectly normal and neither justified nor actually induced increase in acreage. Acreage harvested actually fell from its 1914—1915 peak. The ravages of the boll weevil in 1921, 1922, and 1923, however, raised it to 32 cents toward the end of the latter year, and this presumably propelled the expansion in the West, which in spite of abandonments—not all due to the boll weevil—had set in before and carried total acreage in this country from the 29.7 million acres in 1921 to about 45.8 in 1926. Acreage outside the United States at the same time increased from about 28.5 to over 42 million acres, not only, of course, in response to that price, but in consequence of the endeavor made in many countries to develop cotton growing, which date far back into prewar times and were indirectly fostered by the tariff policy of the United States. Thus there developed slowly, beneath the surface of current fluctuaations, an untenable situation which was bound to curtail the role of American cotton in the world and to explode in a major depression. The presence of overproduction in the proper sense of the term is, in this special case, as undeniable as the rationale of the argument for planned retreat. Cottonseed oil and its residues cannot be dealt with here, but their possibilities in the fields of human and animal food and of chemical products, although very considerable, would not fundamentally alter the picture.

The postwar wheat situation presents fundamentally the same features, yet differs in important respects. Before the war, United States production had indeed met increasing competition in the world's market but effects were always compensated by favorable shifts in demand. After the war, this was no longer so. Although population increased strongly, consumption per head did not. On the contrary the latter decreased considerably in response to changing tastes and habits, though the increase in the former was sufficient to increase total consumption, which at the end of our period was about 15 per cent above the average of the last five prewar years. Foreign demand rapidly fell from its war peak after the cessation of American war and emergency credits, both foreign competition and protection accounting for the sharply falling "trend" and, from 1926 on, the uninterrupted fall in quantity exported. World production, excluding Russia and China, after having decreased from 1915 to 1917, increased to 1928 by more than one-third and then moved about a level approximately 20 per cent above the last prewar years. European production alone, including Russian exports, more than recovered in strongly inverse covariation with United States exports. Interpretation of these facts must, moreover, take into account the very low elasticity of domestic demand. Some economists hold that production adapted itself to the new conditions and point to the sharp decrease in acreage harvested per head of population that occurred from 1919 to 1925. Production had, however, expanded considerably from 1915 to 1919 and though contraction followed fairly promptly upon the fall in prices, persisting excess capacity and that inelasticity of domestic demand would nevertheless account for strong effects of the fall in exports and of the variations in harvests. It does not follow that, because the price of wheat moved very much as any all-commodity index, conditions peculiar to the wheat-growing industry had nothing to do with it.

But the central fact was the technological revolution. The average yearly product during our decade of roughly 850 million bushels of wheat may not look formidable in itself. But it was not the result of harmonious expansion in all parts of the country, which it would have been possible to restrict again at proportionate and moderate sacrifice for every grower of wheat or which, in fact, would have restricted itself without catastrophe in the course of a few years of depression. It was the net result of spectacular expansion in some regions and painful elimination in others. Expansion was general up to 1919, even the East and South responding to war prices. But the really significant increase in acreage was not. That was confined to Montana, Kansas, Nebraska, Texas, and a few other states and, obviously, was not due simply to war conditions. Similarly, decrease in wheat acreage from 1919 to 1925 was general but also unequal, hardly any decrease occurring in Montana, for example. The subsequent expansion to 1929 coincided with restriction in the South and East, where acreage decreased by about one-fifth for the decade. Diagnosis of this course of events is obvious. Expansion was in the Great Plains, where the mechanized farm, the tractor and the combine thresher in particular, can be worked to full advantage and yield acceptable returns at a price of 60 cents per bushel or less. Contraction was enforced where those innovations were not profitable and a price of one dollar per bushel covers cost only on the better soils. We recognize all the features embodied in our model and especially the "competing-down process," passing sentence of economic death on perhaps half of all wheat farmers. This component of the postwar situation, in fact, originated, as it should, in the preceding Kondratieff prosperity. The great per-cent increase in Montana, Kansas, Nebraska, and Texas was from 1900 to 1915. We may even go so far as to say that this is what can be attributed to innovation per se, while the further rise to 1919—roughly, 10 million acres in the Great Plains—was a war effect. Innovation would have spread and taken full effect in the downgrade, as it always does. A depressive situation would have ensued in any case. But war prices and reaction to them accentuated it, which is all that prices or monetary factors have had to do with it.

2. Next, the postwar building booms call for comment. Of their quantitative importance in the economic processes of the period it is very difficult to give an exact idea, but very easy to give one that is approximate. If, for example, we accept the statement contained in the 1929 Census of Construction, that building will on the average (directly) give a year's full employment to one man for roughly each $5,800 spent, and if we take into account the employment created by the production and transportation of building material and in other subsidiary industries and, by way of secondary effects, in all industries, we cannot doubt that construction was the chief contributor [1] to the postwar business volume in this country. This is no more unexpected than the postwar agrarian depression. Building booms, in particular booms in residential, public, and public utility construction, occurred in the downgrades of both preceding Kondratieffs—for instance, in England in the twenties of the nineteenth century, in all three countries before 1873, in the United States from 1878 to 1894. All of them, with one exception, were stronger than any that occurred during Kondratieff prosperities.

Nor is this a mere matter of history. Taking, for brevity's sake, dwelling-house building only, we need but list the factors that would produce supernormal activity, in order to see that the general conditions prevailing in Kondratieff downgrades and revivals—more precisely, in the prosperity phases of the shorter cycles which run their course within Kondratieff downgrades and revivals—are more favorable to the occurrence of building booms than are the general conditions prevailing in prosperities. Falling rate of interest is one of them. High rate of increase in real incomes is another: from rising or constant money incomes of the middle and lower classes, accompanied by falling cost of living, new demand for better housing will naturally follow. In-

[1] As will presently become clear, this does not mean that there was a one-way relation between building and the rest of the economic organism, or that the prosperities of the period originated in the building trade. No mere appeal to the quantitative importance of construction within the total of system expenditure would have any explanatory value. In most cases it is obvious that construction rather responded to than created conditions favorable to its expansion. The latter was the case only insofar as there was innovation in the building industry itself.

novation in the building industry or its subsidiaries will work in the same direction because, like other innovations, it is likely to spread in recession. The rise in rents that occurs during Kondratieff prosperities supplies, barring a subsequent fall in money incomes—which, as we have seen, is not likely to occur—an additional stimulus. Finally, industrial evolution in general means industrial migration and, moreover, migration from the countryside to the cities, both of which create new demand for construction that is eventually provided for during recession. Of course there were, besides, other factors, unconnected with the features of the Kondratieff phase which happened to prevail. The omissions of the war period, both as to replacement and as to normal increment, constitute the most important of them.

In the United States the war did not interfere with either residential or other construction to anything like the same extent as in England or Germany, but such indications as we have leave no doubt about the fact that it was at an abnormally low level in 1917 and 1918. At least in most parts of the country, a short-lived boom set in at the end of 1918, during which building costs rose sharply—by 25 per cent or more. This was followed by a drastic fall both in building activity and costs, and from the beginning of the fourth quarter of 1923 the postwar boom in residential building definitely got under sail. There was a setback in the second and third quarters of 1924; then a peak was reached in 1925, descent from which lasted to about May 1927; another peak occurred in April 1928. After that we have decline, which though at varying rates—in 1930 there was some retardation—continued to February 1933, with 1929 and 1931 displaying the sharpest falls. In apartment-house and hotel construction the maximum occurs in 1926, but the figure for 1925 comes near it and those for 1927 and 1928 are not much below it. Expenditure on new, nonfarm, residential building, including hotels and clubs, is estimated at 34 billion dollars for the decade.

Diagnosis of that boom, which was entirely financed from private sources, presents no difficulties. At the beginning of the period there was dammed-up demand. Population, in spite of the Immigration Restriction Act of May 1921, increased from 1920 to 1929 by 15 millions, the largest absolute amount of increase per year in the history of the country. There was also considerable internal migration. Real income per head, rising strongly in all brackets, made that demand effective and added new sources. The motor was the only other "expensive" one of the items toward which the surplus turned. From 1916 to 1920 rents had risen on a national average by almost two-thirds. They fell but insignificantly, even in the crisis of 1921. Primarily the boom was a response to these conditions. Building costs rose swiftly in 1923 and after 1924 remained fairly stable on a somewhat lower level. Interest on urban mortgages was, though falling, not particularly cheap as compared with other long-term rates, except where building was financed by bond issues. But under the circumstances of that period and in the glow of its uncritical optimism neither costs nor interest charges mattered much. It seemed more important to get quickly the home one wanted—or the skyscraper the prospective rents of which in any case compared favorably with the rate on mortgage bonds—than to bother whether it would cost a few thousand dollars—or in the case of the skyscraper, a million or so—more or less, provided money was readily forthcoming at those rates. And it was. First mortgages on urban real estate represent, on the one hand, not all the loans that were made available for building and, on the other hand, also financed not only other types of building but other things than building. But it is still permissible to point to the fact that they increased from, roughly, 13 billions in 1922 to, roughly, 27 in 1929, building and loan associations contributing about 7.8, commercial banks about 5.2, mutual saving banks 5.1, life insurance companies 4.8, and mortgage bonds more than 4. This increase is out of all proportion, not only with the increase in what can in any reasonable sense be called savings, but also with the expansion of bank credit in other lines of business, and illustrates well how a cheap money policy may affect other sectors than those in which it is conspicuously successful in bringing down rates. If such a sector display a very elastic demand for the funds which that policy will drive toward it, interest in it need fall but little or not at all in order to produce all the consequences that we usually associate with "too-low" money rates.

Innovation lent its aid. The steel-skeleton structure, made cheaper by steadily increasing use of reinforced concrete and workable by the electric elevator, had created new possibilities ever since the nineties, and these possibilities had become a feature of the Kondratieff upswing. In the downgrade after the war this innovation, improved by several minor and "induced" ones, propelled by changes in the habits of life that made the apartment increasingly desirable to the American bourgeois family and by the plethora of credit, spread and conquered, much like motorcars or rayon and exactly like those innovations that carried the prosperities, and spread in the downgrades, of preceding Kondratieffs. Similarly, prefabrication, primarily made possible by the use of the new materials but also applied to stone and lumber, extended its domain far beyond the skyscraper. Excavation of basements by means of power shovels improved by the caterpillar tread and belt and bucket conveyors, the use of power hoists, of power concrete and mortar mixers, and of pneumatic riveting machines, rapidly became a matter of course for contractors in all lines of building—typical downgrade developments, all of them. Their full effect—the mass production of the perfectly standardized and mechanized cheap house—is still to come, however. During our period the ordinary family house was in the main still being built in substantially old-fashioned ways by small and inefficient firms.

But the conclusion that this essentially consequential development—in response to the omissions of the war period and increased real purchasing power of all classes, on the one hand, and in response to previous innovation, on the other—issued in overbuilding, owing to the additional stimulus imparted by the monetary factor, must not be accepted hastily, however plausible it may seem. Some types of response to those conditions, especially the ones that were linked to speculative real estate operations, were clearly of the bubble class. The Miami case may serve as an example. Nor can there be any doubt about the merits of the financial methods that were also used in less "speculative" cases—New York skyscrapers for instance—and in particular about the financial quality of the mortgage bonds, which increased from 682 millions in 1922 to 4,169 millions in 1929, and which were readily lent against by banks. Finally, everything was done to make it easy for everyone to run into debt, for the purpose of building a home as for any other purpose. It is easy to understand that such a structure would give way, not only under the impact of a serious crisis, but even in consequence of a mere failure of rosy expectations about things in general to come true. In other words, we shall readily understand why the load of debt thus lightheartedly incurred by people who foresaw nothing but booms should become a serious matter whenever incomes fell, and that construction would then contribute, directly and through the effects on the credit structure of impaired values of real estate, as much to a depression as it had contributed to the preceding booms. Nothing is so likely to produce cumulative depressive processes as such commitments of a vast number of households to an overhead financed to a great extent by commercial banks. But this does not quite amount to saying that there was overbuilding in the sense that the amount of construction was greater than it was possible to absorb without losses under the conditions then prevailing, and that this excess was an independent cause of the great depression.

Rents fell from 1924 on, but only moderately. Vacancies increased, but not more than was to be expected in a period of rapid obsolescence of existing house property. The big, old, ugly, and inconvenient house soon became difficult to sell, because of changes in tastes—some of them attributable to the automobile—and because of the increasing wages and decreasing efficiency of servants. But there is no reason to believe that the spurt of 1925 could not have settled down into an appropriate average activity and that even the results of speculative excesses could not have been liquidated without any violent crisis in building, let alone in general business. As a matter of fact, this was accomplished to a certain extent. If we accept the figures of the National Bureau of Economic Research, we arrive at the conclusion that four years of such adjustment—including local crises—actually followed upon that boom without much general disturbance being created. In the final result, expansion in this line was not so obviously greater than it was in other lines of consumption that explanation of subsequent vicissitudes could simply be given in terms of "malinvestment." And incomes had first to fall because of a general crisis, for the special crisis of building and of real estate to come about.

This analysis refers to residential building only. Results are not, however, substantially changed by including other types. One of them, commercial building, is perhaps still more than apartment houses and hotels exposed to the suspicion of speculative overdoing. Contracts awarded increased steadily to a peak in 1927 and another almost as high in 1929, and summed up for 1922 to 1929 to nearly 6.7 billions, the rate of increase over the period being substantially in excess of that of residential building. Industrial building increased at a still greater rate —contracts awarded sum up to about 4.8 billion—but there is very little reason to suspect any excess over the requirements of the general march of things. Unlike the other items, but also conforming to expectation, this moved well in the Kitchins and showed equally well the sweep of the two incomplete Juglars. Finally, more than one-third of the grand total of contracts awarded—nearly 49 billions according to the Dodge figures, which certainly understate—comes under the heading of Public, Institutional, and Utility construction. Part of this is reflected by the increase in municipal bonded debts. Alone federal expenditure on new construction, repairs, and alterations amounted, from 1920 to 1929, according to the Federal Employment Stabilization Board, to about 2.5 billions, the trend being upward all the time and 1929 displaying the highest figure (308 millions)—a fact worth mentioning in view of the prevalent talk about insufficient spending. According to the same source, the figures of which are again incomparable with those used above, the expenditure of railroads—steam and electric—and power and telephone companies on construction and maintenance moved, from 1923 to 1929, extremely steadily on a slightly rising level, summing up to 20.4 billions. But these sums were expended in ways that would not produce any material effect on the economic process beyond what is implied in the expenditure itself.

E. The "Industrial Revolution" of the Twenties.—These processes were so entirely normal in the sense of conforming to expectation from our model and so obviously repeated the history of preceding Kondratieff downgrades that no war effects or other disturbances availed to obliterate the fact, and that recalling a few familiar features suffices to establish it.

First, *we should not expect to find fundamentally new things,* but rather induced and completing development on lines chalked out before and attended by strong increase in quantities, marked improvement in qualities, "rationalization" all around, an indefinite number of individually small innovations producing a wide variety of new specialties, the phenomena which we have called conquest of new economic space. This is what we find. The electrical, chemical, and automobile industries, which together with their subsidiaries and all that directly and indirectly hinges upon them—the motorcar, for instance, is responsible for a great part of the total of postwar construction: roads, garages, gasoline stations, suburban residences—account for 90 per cent of the postwar changes in the industrial organism and for most of the increase in real income. They realized the possibilities created in the Kondratieff prosperity, continued to push ahead from the bases laid before, and *by so doing shaped things into a Kondratieff recession.*[1] So did not only those subsidiaries, such as oil and rubber, but also the minor, though still important, novelties, such as steel alloys, aluminum, rayon, large-scale retailing, and the organizational and financial complement—persistence of the merger movement, power finance and so on. There were exceptions, as there were in the two previous Kondratieff downgrades, but none of them was quantitatively significant. The most important one was air transport on a commercial scale, which may bear comparison with the role of railroads in the thirties and of electricity in the eighties of the nineteenth century.

Second, we find all the general features which analysis and historical observation have taught us to associate with Kondratieff downgrades. This will become clear beyond doubt in our discussion of time series which is to follow, but it should be clear independently of it, that those features can be accounted for in terms of the system's absorption of and reaction to the new quantities and new methods. We find prevalence of unemployment that was basically "technological." There was, though also accentuated by other circumstances, that excess capacity which is inseparable from the process of rapid reorganization of the industrial apparatus and *coexists with vigorous expansion of output*. We observe that desperate struggle of firms for outlets and against competition and the sagging of prices incident to the insertion of new quantities and capacities, which understandably creates the picture of apparently permanent "overproduction" or "overinvestment" and

[1] [Under the dating given below, Kondratieff recession gave way to Kondratieff depression in the fall of 1925, almost the middle of the period under discussion.—Ed.]

the characteristic outcry about people's inadequate power or willingness to spend. And, masked and retarded by resistance to adjustments, the competing-down process is clearly recognizable both within the relatively new and as between new and old industries, railroads and coal being conspicuous instances of the latter. All of which accounts for much of the social and business atmosphere of the period, including its economic slogans.

In the United States conformity to expectation during that period is so obvious as to make it almost superfluous to prove it, a fact the value of which is enhanced by the relatively small importance of external disturbances in our sense. That the events in the fields of electricity, motorcars, and chemistry do not constitute fundamentally new but induced and completing developments, which proceeded from bases laid in the two prewar decades, needs additional emphasis as little as does the fact that it was those developments that "carried" the economic processes of the period. We may, however, note the substantive novelty of aviation as a commercial success—1925 may serve as a date—which was perhaps the most important exception. This industry developed on its own and not, as might have been expected from standpoints other than ours, as an appendage to an older, say the automobile, industry in spite of the similarity its problems bear to those of the latter. Exactly as the telephone industry was not built up by the telegraph industry and has shown no tendency to be dominated by it, and as the rise of the automobile industry owed but little to the carriage and bicycle industries or as the moving picture industry, which we might also list among the genuine innovations of the period, did its own pioneering and was not the work, technically, financially, or commercially, of the theater interests, so aviation supplies another instance in verification of the hypothesis of New Firms and New Men (Chap. III) arising independently of the Old Firms and laying themselves alongside of them. The same often holds true of new specialties within each great line of advance, as within the field of electrical industries, partly at least, in the cases of the radio and of the refrigerator.

1. Power production increased from 38.9 billion kilowatt-hours in 1919 to over 97 in 1929, only 1921 marking a relapse of about 8 per cent. Roughly 95 per cent of this was produced by privately financed enterprise and over half of it by the General Electric,

Insull, Morgan, Mellon, Byllesby and Doherty groups and a dozen corporations jointly controlled by these. Although the more remote effects of this development on industrial activity in general were much more important factors in the cyclical variations of the period than the immediate effects of the investment in power plant, transmission lines, and distribution, yet from 1917 to 1927 balance-sheet values of power plants increased from about 3 to about 9.4 billions and more than 1.5 billions of electrical stock and bonds was issued in the yearly average between 1924 and 1930—the maximum of 2,150 millions occurred in 1927—of which perhaps something less than two-thirds was spent on new construction and extension. Gross earnings of the electric light and power industry reached 2.1 billion dollars by 1929, when household consumption was responsible for 604 millions, industrial and commercial for about 1.2 billion, street lighting and traction for the rest.

Prices differed widely, not only locally but also as between customers: in 1929 the leather industry, for instance, paid $28 for 1,000 kilowatt-hours and the chemical industry 5.9, 12.7 dollars being the average for that year as given by the census. In the average, however, they fell. The national average price of current used in households is a no less doubtful matter. The semiofficial figures are per kilowatt-hour: 16.2 cents around the turn of the century, about 9 cents for 1912, roughly 7.5 at the beginning of our period, during which it slowly but steadily fell to 6.3 in 1929, or about 3.8 cents in terms of the prewar purchasing power of the wage earners' dollar. This behavior of prices is accounted for, on the one hand, not only by the actual or potential competition of industrial—as distinguished from "public"—stations, but also by "commodity competition"—gas, nonelectrical motors—and the necessity of building up new demand: the electrification of the household and of the farm in particular was to a large extent a question of price. On the other hand, the growth of units of control and the establishment of local and sectional monopolies facilitated discrimination and went far toward eliminating price competition between those units, while their struggles were transferred to the financial sphere. That explains why the weighted average of prices did not, *within our period*, fall correspondingly to the increase in efficiency of production, and this again was why most operating companies were in a position to improve their financial status considerably and to weather the subsequent storm comparatively well. The competing-down process and its contribution to the general picture of the period, but especially to the subsequent Great Depression, took under the circumstances a form which was in many respects peculiar. It asserted itself mainly through shifts in industrial location—electrical development materially helping, for instance, in the industrialization of the South—and much less directly as, for instance, in the effect on coal.

Technological advance was much on the same lines as in Europe. Water-power development played, of course, a great role: from 1924 to 1928 it progressed at a greater rate than the capacity of steam plants, reaching an output of 29 billion kilowatt-hours by 1930 though at the end of the period steam began to gain ground relatively. The use of fuel oil and gas was an American peculiarity. Otherwise we observe the general tendencies toward larger capacity of stations—the number of plants fell by one-third between 1922 and 1929—and superpower zones. Since in extending electrical enterprise to foreign countries capital counts for almost everything, the success of American groups, especially in South America, is easy to understand. About one billion went to South America, Europe, Asia, and into what presently turned out to be so many traps.

Considering the technological nature of much that was done, mergers, partly also aiming at the control of gas concerns, were the unavoidable concomitant of this development. The financial instrument of the holding company lying ready at hand experienced a new vogue of unprecedented dimensions. Power finance definitively passed out of the hands of the manufacturing industry and coordination resulted from a struggle within the power-producing sphere, in which the groups mentioned above emerged or conquered. Since this struggle involved competitive bidding for strategic positions, such geographical and commercial rationalization as was achieved was accompanied by the growth of a huge structure of debt and share capital, which was out of proportion with the effects of that rationalization, and not only provided food for purely financial maneuvers and speculative excesses of a type suggestive of the railroad age, but also jeopardized the banking system, since power securities loomed large in its collateral and since many leading banks, among them the National City, the Chase National, the Bankers' Trust, the Guaranty Trust, associated their fortunes directly with power enterprise and in fact functioned in some cases as the agents of ultimate centralization. Without going further into this well-known matter, we will note that the great boom in power finance —and real investment—belongs to the second half of our decade. It was a feature of the fourth Juglar and clearly basic to its prosperity phase. In fact, building construction, power development—together with developments in other branches of the utility field which also fit into our general idea of the processes of a Kondratieff downgrade [1]—would in themselves suffice to account for the behavior of aggregative time series during the period.

The major instances of the propelling and dislocating effects of power developments are obvious, and description of the sum total of all the minor ones is impossible within this sketch. But it should be emphasized in view of popular dirges about lack of investment opportunity that the work of electrification—as much of it even as is technologically and commercially possible at the moment or in immediate prospect—is not nearly completed. There is enough investment opportunity from this source alone for many a cycle to come. Even industry is as yet but imperfectly electrified—perhaps to something like 75 per cent—and so are households, while but a beginning has been made in the electrification of farms and of transportation. Only the telephone and electric lighting can reasonably be said to have exhausted, *ex visu* of present technology, the bulk of their possibilities, although the automatic telephone—installation was zero in 1892 and only 1.7 per cent of the total of telephones installed in 1919, but nearly 32 per cent in 1930—which must be listed among the innovations of the period under discussion, affords a good illustration for the fact that even perfect saturation of existing demand need not call a halt of "progress."

Production of electrical equipment had, ever since 1915, increased at a greater rate than production of power and continued to do so until 1929. Its value was about 1 billion dollars in 1919

[1] Utility developments form part of the picture which we expect a Kondratieff downgrade to reveal, because they are to a large extent a function of real income and its rates of change. Accordingly, we find expansion—induced expansion—in the utility field in the two last decades of the first Kondratieff as well as in the downgrade of the second (eighties and early nineties). We find the same phenomenon in the present instance.

and nearly 2.5 billions in 1929. Examples of new industries—and the "diversifying" effect of power production—abound. The spectacular expansion of the radio and the refrigerator industries dates from 1926. The quarter of a million socket radios then in use increased to over 7 millions, the 315,000 refrigerators to 1,680,000 in 1929.[1] Though typical instances of downgrade developments, these were practically new industries with histories of their own. But they were not so independent of the older concerns in the industry of electric manufacture as, say, aviation is of the automobile industry. Generally speaking, these older concerns maintained their position well, and proved in this as in other countries successful shells of incessant innovation, especially in the heavy-current field (General Electric, Westinghouse). Dollar volume of output in electric manufacturing increased about sevenfold between 1914 and 1929, and about 26 times from 1899, the census year nearest to the beginning of the Kondratieff, to 1929.

2. The automobile industry led in every upswing and out of every downswing throughout the period and continued in the Kondratieff recession to qualify as well for the role of standard example for the processes embodied in our model as it had done in the upswing. Employment in motor-vehicle factories, not including production of parts, tires, and bodies, increased from about 253,000 in 1922 to 427,500 in 1929, the corresponding wage bill from about 396 to about 775.5 million dollars. Passenger-car registration as of Dec. 31 increased without any break from the beginning of the series (1895:4) to 1929 (23,121,589), though of course at a decreasing percentage rate, depressions affecting the latter only. Even in the world crisis and in the year of minimum registration (1933) the total automobile retail and service business, including accessories, filling stations, garages, and also retail sales by wholesalers, figures out at $4,831,800,000. Over 1.1 million persons were engaged in distri-

[1] Figures of the Edison Institute. The number of socket radios continued to increase throughout the depression to nearly 20 millions in 1935, an example for those initial spurts which are impervious to depressions. As the reader will remember, such behavior is, if anything, normal from the standpoint of our analysis, though in practice it is not the general rule. Similarly, the number of refrigerators in occupied homes kept on increasing without a break and reached the figure of 7.25 millions in 1935.

bution and servicing, among them 756,000 employees (part-time included), receiving wages and salaries amounting to 801 millions. Quantitative expansion and qualitative improvement, falling costs, prices, and rates of profit are obviously the expected as well as the actual characteristics of this industry's history during our decade. However, since there is no satisfactory way of measuring qualitative improvement, and since there was an almost uninterrupted shift from larger, heavier, and dearer to smaller, lighter, and cheaper cars even quantitative expansion becomes elusive, while indices of quoted prices, which should moreover be corrected for variations in the allowances made for old cars "traded in" and for other forms of rebates, cannot indicate more than a tendency which, of course, they understate. From 1916 on, profits of individual firms not only fell but also became more nearly equal.

The industry did not simply expand in function of the increase in real income but helped to bring it about. The former nexus, however, steadily gained in importance at the expense of the latter, as had been the case with cotton after the Napoleonic wars and with railroads from the eighties on. Innovations, increasing in number while individually decreasing in importance, are typically of the downgrade type. From 1912 on, designs became more stable. Considerable progress in the standardization of parts and in the rationalization of assembling reduced costs as did progress in subsidiary industries—tires, nitrocellulose lacquers and fast-drying solvents, and so on. Equally important or more so were the changes in organization and financing that were in part induced by the struggle for survival within the industry, in which incessant innovating and expanding into the low-price market was a matter of life and death. Competing-down went on at a rapid rate. The rise in price level after 1916 helped to keep failures and exits at a low and decreasing figure, and even the setback of 1918, when both production and wholesale value fell absolutely for the first time, cost few lives. But after 1921, when production and wholesale value again fell absolutely, exits—not necessarily failures—increased sharply *in the midst of spectacular expansion* of the industry as a whole, reaching 21 per cent in 1924. In 1923 and 1924 no less than 29 firms went out of business, 17 of them war and postwar foundations. Of the 101 plants—makers, not concerns—whose annual production of passenger cars was 5,000 or less in 1920 only 11 survived in 1930; of the 23 whose annual production was from 5,000 to 25,000, also 11; while we still find all of the 10 which produced over 25,000 in 1920. By 1918, 70 per cent of all automobiles produced in this country and Canada came from the three largest producers, by 1921 80 per cent, and by 1935 nearly 90 per cent.

Considering that the car of the masses became a reality, while the industry, which had always been monopolistically competitive, developed a typically oligopolistic situation, we cannot help being painfully aware once more of the somewhat less than realistic character of the general conclusions arrived at by the leading theorists of monopolistic competition. In fact, it should be obvious that the behavior of the motorcar industry during our decade could be described much more convincingly in terms of perfect competition working under the conditions of a new industry in the course of being absorbed by or inserted into the economic system. In the course of this development, ever since about 1916, methods of financing changed significantly. "Outside capital" began to play a greater role. We need, however, only mention the direct contact established by General Motors with the open market and its policy—followed by the other concerns—of financing the consumer. Nevertheless, owned capital accumulated from profits and retailers' and furnishers' credit remained the industry's most important sources of means, and this accounts for much which strikes the observer as particularly "sound" about it. Net tangible assets of motor-vehicle manufacturing plants reached their maximum of about 2.1 billion dollars in 1926 and then steadily fell, though up to the crisis but slowly. However unreliable any inference from this may be, it seems clear that, barring the Ford plant, the great wave of investment belongs to the third and not to the fourth Juglar.

In order to prove with quantitative precision how much of the processes of the period and of the behavior of aggregates can be explained by the motorcar developments alone, it would be necessary to go fully into what they meant for the steel, copper, and equipment industries and so on. We will, however, confine ourselves to one remark on the petroleum and another on the rubber industry. Innovations that have already been mentioned (Chap. VII) and the discovery and development of new oil fields account for the fall in gasoline prices (excluding tax) from \$0.2411 per gallon in 1919 to \$0.1557 in 1929 and—gasoline consumption did not fall until 1932—$0.1178 in 1931, which shows that the petroleum industry was not passively drawn along by the growth of demand. Yet it comes sufficiently near to this pattern to qualify as an instance. This is particularly evident at the beginning of the period. In 1920 prices of oil and gasoline rose considerably (peak of the period), so much so as to throw them out of line with those of competing fuels and as to restrict the use of fuel oil by railroads—the Great Northern, for instance, converted 70 locomotives into coal burners. This followed upon the doubling of automobile production in 1920 as compared with 1918, with which the gasoline production was then unable to keep pace. An oil boom started accordingly, which almost coincided with deep depression in other lines. Issues of oil securities were at a peak early in 1920 and again toward the end of the year and at the beginning of 1921. It is worth while to mention that the only cities in the country which experienced greater building activity in November 1920 than in November 1919 were Los Angeles, Baltimore, and New Orleans, and that the Californian cities all showed large gains in their clearing figures while these declined in the rest of the country. At the beginning of 1921 there was a large oil merger (Barnsdall Corporation). Further developments followed and crude prices reacted promptly, Midwestern prices, for instance, falling to $1 a barrel in the summer of 1921, as compared with $3 in January.

The rubber industry was, of course, also "drawn along." But its own innovations were much more in evidence. As we have seen elsewhere, beginnings date far back or at any rate to the Kondratieff prosperity (reclaiming, *e.g.*, 1899, acceleration of the vulcanizing process 1906; but commercial success of synthetic rubber came after our period), the use of various pigments in order to increase the durability of rubber compounds (1916) being the only "inventive" innovation of the twenties. It was again the "spreading" by means of discovering new and developing old industrial uses for rubber (flooring, rubber cushions, rubber linings, mountings, bumpers, and so on) which was a feature of the period under discussion. In the field of the most important article the great new thing—though also invented long ago (R. W. Thompson, patented 1845)—was, of course, the pneumatic tire (1916), which followed upon the success of the cord and may be said to have imparted immediately a significant impulse to long-distance trucking. At the same time the commercial opportunity for low-pressure tires for passenger cars manifested itself in the habit of many motorists to underinflate their tires for the sake of comfort. By 1923, 21 companies, among them practically all the leaders of the trade, were making such tires, experimentally or commercially, and several automobile manufacturers had adopted them as part of the regular equipment of their cars, while others listed them as optional. A "revolution" in tire making, the more important because it involved considerable new investment, announced itself. There was still resistance to overcome. But improvement and standardization—as to rim requirements—carried the innovation suddenly to definitive success about 1925, after one of the tire companies had taken the bold step to bring out balloon tires for all standard rims and thus to make a bid for immediate replacement of practically all tires in use. The aspect of the market changed within a few months, and the "host" followed the innovator promptly. There is no need of going into the illustrative virtues of the case or the quantitative importance of it for the fourth Juglar. With quick changes in production functions, the competing-down process asserted itself strongly. We shall interpret in this sense the symptoms of overinvestment and overproduction, observable already in 1923 and again after 1926, and expect a contribution to the picture of the subsequent crisis from this industry.

3. The heavy chemical industry had developed well before the war, but enterprise in the organic branch was entirely conditioned by the seizure of German patents and later on by protection. Prices of chemicals, which according to the B. L. S. index (1926 = 100) were at 89.4 in 1913 and which had, owing to the practical cessation of German imports, soared to 197 by 1916, testified to the vigor of entrepreneurial response to those new conditions by falling to 97.2 in 1922. Both the coal-tar group in all its stages, particularly in the production of dyes, and the aliphatic group scored a series of successes that extended over the whole of our period and throughout the subsequent depression and amounted to the creation of new industries. Investment, employment, wage bill, profits, and dollar volume of sales—about 2-1/4 billions towards the end of our decade—increased to a peak in 1929 for the chemical industry as a whole. Sales in the non-coal-tar group continued to increase without break afterward. Medicinals, solvents, perfumes, antifreezes, carbon tetrachloride, acetic anhydride, camphor, resins, nitrates (synthetic iodine and

synthetic rubber came early in the thirties) may serve as examples. Analysis of the individual cases would show little more than so many instances of the way in which innovation works.

Three points only call for additional comment. First, for the same reasons as elsewhere concentration of control and research and coordination of specialized large-scale plants were in evidence in this industry. The Dupont concern, like the J. G. Farben, expanded far beyond the chemical field. The other giant, the Allied Chemical and Dye Corporation, was the result of a merger in 1920 of five big concerns which to a large extent complemented each other. Second, new branches of industry emerged around what may be called the production of chemical fundamentals. A host of small and medium-sized firms took up the production of a truly unsurveyable variety of drugs, cosmetic articles, and so on. The results, as distinguished from the formal properties, of monopolistically competitive situations are much more in evidence in this group and within its army of retailers and advertisers than among the few big producers of the basic stuffs. For us it is important to note the quantitative importance of this trade and to account for its spectacular expansion: the unrivaled opportunity which it exploited was one of the consequences of the increase in the real income of the masses which left even the lowest income groups with a surplus that was not a priori allocated to specific purposes but ready to go wherever advertisements beckoned. The phenomenon thus fits well into our ideas about downgrade developments. Third, the chemical industry displays the (secondary) competing-down process within the innovating line much *less* than, say the automobile industry; but it displays the (primary) competition, *i.e.*, the competition with other commodities or older methods of producing the same commodities much *more* than almost any branch of economic activity. In some cases its innovations act through other spheres of production, agriculture for instance. In others they act directly and then with a promptness to the consequences of which the social fabric of capitalism may well prove unequal some day. Chemistry provides not only acceptable and cheap substitutes for things that are the basis of much employment and investment, but quite often exactly the same things —frequently in a better, especially more uniform and more reliable quality, as for instance in the case of varnishes and dyes —which had been produced by nonchemical methods before.

It does so almost always at a cost which eventually, though not as a rule immediately, falls far below the level attainable by the latter. In such cases large sectors of the economic organism may have to go out of operation at very short notice. If the consequences have so far not made themselves more strongly felt in our three countries, this is because they mostly impinged on other, on Chile for instance or India—or in the case of madder, on the countries from Southern France to Asia Minor—or Sicily (citric acid, 1927) or *pro futuro* on the rubber-producing countries. The United States, England, and Germany were, during the period under survey, not much affected in this respect, and whatever effect there was was rather favorable. But more serious dislocations may arise from such developments some of which are obviously imminent. The term revolution acquires in this connection a particular ominous meaning. Depressive influences may emanate from this line of advance by comparison with which anything that can be effected by action on monetary aggregates, central bank action included, is of negligible importance.

The rayon industry, of course, owed much to the tariff, and its great concerns owed much to their control of patents. But in all other respects the case is strikingly analogous to that of the automobile industry. We have a sharp competitive struggle at the beginning of the period, partly due to the numerous short-lived foundations after the war, from which, as has been stated elsewhere, emerged three concerns which accounted for about 90 per cent of the production of the country. In this oligopolistic setup the great expansion of consumption took place which was but little affected by the world crisis. Wholesale prices (150 denier, A grade, New York) fell from the 1918 peak to about the prewar level (1914, $1.96 per pound) in 1925, and were at $1.25 by 1929. Profits per pound of product steadily declined, although in the case of the American Viscose, which remained the leading producer throughout, they were still 58 cents in 1928. Other textiles, though not without some propelling influences—higher cotton consumption per spindle, production of cord, artificial leather, broadcloth shirting, fancy woolens and so on—behaved like the old industries they were. Quantitative expansion and qualitative improvement were considerable, and there was much rationalization in details. This does not alter the fundamental traits of the picture, which are reflected in the behavior of prices. Continuing locational shifts caused as much sectional depression as sectional prosperity. The Department of Labor's combined index of employment kept steady throughout the decade, but nevertheless marks strongly the upswing that set in during the second half of 1925.

4. As far as changes in production functions go, the iron and steel industry should really be dealt with—as should metallurgy in general—in connection with chemistry and electricity. It suffices to mention the career of light alloys, the first stage of which was run during our decade, especially from 1925. There were also technological and organizational changes of other types, such as continuous rolling or the crowding out of the merchant furnace, and of course many improvements of the rationalization kind in individual lines or concerns. Increasing use of scrap in the steelmaking as well as in the copper, aluminum, and other industries deserves particular emphasis.[1] Speaking broadly, however, the steel industry suffered in depression—especially in 1920 and 1921—and prospered in booms—the peaks in pig-iron output occur in 1923, 1925, and 1929—in consequence of the general business situations, rather than in consequence of its own enterprise. The behavior of its prices accords with this impression. Steel consumption increased strongly, however, in spite of all the steel-saving rationalizations, which were more than offset by the conquest of new uses—steel increasingly became a consumers' good—and general expansion. Per head of population it was, at the end of our period, seven times as great as it had been in 1900.

Nothing fundamentally new happened in the aluminum and copper industries. We have, however, already observed in an earlier place that the former displayed great initiative in discovering and conquering new ground. Its quantitative expansion—domestic primary production more than doubled between 1915 and 1929, while domestic consumption increased more than three-

[1] This material-saving practice, a typical downgrade development and responsible for the increasing divergence between pig-iron and steel outputs, of course, exerts a depressing influence on the production of a number of important raw materials also outside the metal field, and constitutes in each case a distinct innovation as well as a distinct industrial problem. The prices of scrap are more sensitive to the course of cyclical phases than any other commodity prices and, as has been pointed out by the Berlin Institute (*e.g.*, in 1926), the relation between scrap- and pig-iron prices is a good index, even forecaster, of business situations.

fold, secondary production accounting for the greater part of the difference—was one of the major industrial features of the period, another good instance of a downgrade development. Price behavior was in accordance with this and characteristcally different from that of finished steel. The absence, comparatively speaking, of fluctuations around the fundamental contour affords an interesting example of what "control" by one firm really means under conditions of rapid growth and of commodity competition. The domestic price of new aluminum ingot 99 per cent pure reached its war maximum by 1916 and its prewar level or, corrected by the B.L.S. index of wholesale prices, a figure nearly 30 per cent below it, by 1922. It then slowly rose to 1925, afterward fell somewhat, and was maintained at 23.3 cents through 1934. Thus it failed to fall in 1930, when it would have done so under competitive conditions. But the profits made are not in themselves sufficient to prove that in the long run prices were, given the protection, substantially above that level at which they would have moved had competitive conditions prevailed from the outset, provided we include in the latter the degree of productive efficiency compatible with the competitive scale of individual firms. Nor does it follow that, if all or most industries had been organized in the same manner, they would have still found it to their interest to adopt the same policy of price stability.

The war for obvious reasons brought a large expansion in the consumption of copper, to which the new mines and mining methods (see Chap. VII) were, however, fully equal, so much so that already in 1917 efforts were made to fix prices. They were followed by others throughout the twenties, which in fact succeeded in keeping prices fairly stable at about prewar level (12 to 15 cents) from 1921 to 1928. At the same time costs were being incessantly reduced by further development of large-scale mining methods and by new processes of smelting and refining as well as by the discovery of better deposits. There were also important horizontal combinations—among mining companies, smelters and refiners, and copper- and brass-producing concerns—and vertical ones. Thus an untenable situation developed—indicated by the fact that production kept persistently above consumption, stocks being well above prewar level throughout—under what for a decade seemed a prosperous surface: one of the weak spots that were to contribute their share to the processes of the world crisis. Secondary copper—in 1929, production of secondary copper from scrap was 40 per cent of smelter's production of new copper from domestic ore—and the output of low-cost mines in Canada, Katanga, and Northern Rhodesia did the rest. The formation of an international export cartel under the Webb-Pomerene Act (Copper Exporters, Inc., October 1926, which "controlled" 90 per cent of the world's production) only deferred the catastrophe.

We have here an extremely interesting case of an otherwise perfectly unfettered process of capitalist innovation, which was interfered with only by capitalist interests themselves and by these again only through an attempt to put out of operation a single element of the mechanism, *viz.*, the effect of "progress" on price. It is worth while to consider what the course of events might have been without such an attempt. Prices would certainly have fallen and it may well be that especially in the short run this would not have increased consumption appreciably. But this is not the point. Mines and refineries which actually were kept alive would have been eliminated in any case, though of course more of them if demand was really inelastic in the relevant range than if it was not. And this would have first eliminated waste—for it is social waste to work a mine or refinery which can be worked only at an "artificial price"—and second helped to tone down the prosperities of the twenties, to spread the work of readjustment and *pro tanto* to mitigate the subsequent crisis. If all this be possible or more than the system can stand, public regulation or ownership is, under such conditions in fact the only alternative to violent breakdowns, though not necessarily a remedy for this type of economic waste.

5. While it is believed that the above exposition suffices for our purposes it must once more be emphasized how very incomplete it is. It even leaves out some major elements—natural-gas-pipe lines (1927) have, for instance, not even been mentioned—and practically all those minor ones[1] the sum total of which is

[1] A major movement, which however resolves itself into an almost infinite number of small ones, is what may be called Taylorization. Its spread during our period is a typical consequence of the struggle for survival amidst the readjustments of downgrades. The pressure of this country's wage level adding momentum, this type of rationalization of every job was in many cases more effective in reducing costs per unit of product than fundamental innovations could have been—and in

particularly important in the downgrade of a Kondratieff. Knowledge of the full extent of the revolution which that period witnessed both in the methods of production and commerce and in the structure of the budgets of households, and an adequate analysis, in the light of it, both of the period itself and of its aftermath, would presuppose very many case studies beyond those we at present have. Nevertheless, the main features stand out unmistakably and can be further illustrated by a few facts from the Abstract of the Census of 1930. This census lists 103 industries each of which had in 1929 a Value Added of over 50 million dollars and also was independently listed in 1919. On the average (unweighted) Value Added increased between these two years by 29 and the ratio between Value Added and Pay Roll by 16 per cent.

First, however, we are interested in those industries which, while producing a Value Added of over 50 million dollars in 1929, do not independently occur in 1919, since this in itself proves a very rapid rate of growth. There are 16 of them: beverages, food preparations, millinery, motion pictures (excluding projection in theaters), paper, pulp, rayon, refrigerators, rubber tires and inner tubes, other rubber goods (excluding boots), and typewriters being the most significant ones. Besides repeating cases which we know already, this list adds a few new elements to our picture. Of particular significance is the suggestion, which underlines one feature of that phase of the long cycle, of industries which expanded simply in response to the increase of consumers' real purchasing power and without any particularly strong impulse of their own.

This suggestion grows stronger still if, second, we glance at those among the 103 industries that display an increase in Value Added of, say, more than 100 per cent. Besides aircraft and parts, which heads the list (510 per cent), electrical machinery and supplies, aluminum manufacture, motor vehicle bodies and parts, which we would expect to find, we also meet perfumes and cosmetics, signs and advertising novelties, concrete products, flavoring extracts and sirups, photo-engraving not done in printing establishments, house-furnishing goods, ice cream, printing and publishing (newspaper and periodical). Patent medicines,

---

all cases highly significant from our standpoint. It is a special case of a class of which the efforts to utilize scrap and waste are another.

soap, cigars and cigarettes, cereal preparations, bakery products, while not reaching the 100 per cent line, yet increased their Value Added by much more than the average figure so as to reinforce the evidence. Third, we will note some of those industries the Value Added of which decreased by more than 10 per cent: shipbuilding, locomotives (not made in railroad repair shops) railway cars, pianos, phonographs, leather, beet sugar (Value Added of the cane-sugar industry remained at the 1919 figure), cotton, woolen and worsted goods, flour.

We cannot expect significant correlation between per cent increase in Value Added and per cent increase in the ratio of Value Added to Pay Roll. Also, some new or relatively new industries, such as motor bodies or aluminum manufactures, understandably show very little signs of the effects of labor-saving devices on that ratio, although, of course, others, such as motorcars or aircraft, rank high, and some of the old and conspicuously noninnovating ones, such as house-furnishing goods (1 per cent decrease), rank low in this respect. It is, however, instructive to observe—and tells a great deal about the general character of the industrial processes of that time—how much labor-saving rationalization went on outside of the great lines of innovation. Thus the ratio between Value Added and Pay Roll increased by 120 per cent with cigars and cigarettes, 85 per cent with soap and with coke (excluding gashouse coke), 71 per cent with cereal preparations, 61 per cent with manufactured gas, 52 per cent with cutlery and edge tools, 52 per cent with ice cream. Even for tin cans that figure is still 33; for patent medicines, druggists' preparations, coffee roasting and grinding 32; cane-sugar refining 28; meat packing (wholesale) 26; butter 26; cement and concrete products 22; perfumes and women's clothing 17. Only in a minority of cases—printing would be one—was this due to substantive novelties that we have simply been unable to mention. In the main it was the result of that systematic effort to fight, under the pressure of a price level that tended to fall, each cost item by exploring every detail of the productive and the commercial process and by applying and developing techniques the fundamentals of which were fully established before the war, but which in many cases involved not only technological improvement in existing plant but also the erection of new, highly mechanized plant.

6. As pointed out elsewhere, it would for this country be pos-

sible to carry our count of Juglars and Kitchins through the war, which never succeeded in blotting them out completely. But we will not go beyond saying that the end of 1916 and the beginning of 1917 might, but for the war, have witnessed what would have been the beginning of the prosperity phase of the third Juglar of this Kondratieff, and that in this case the crisis of 1921 would have occurred exactly when our schema would have led us to expect it, *i.e.*, when that Juglar turned from recession into depression. Even if we wished to press this—which we do not—it would leave us all the freedom in the world to take into account the effects of war demand and war finance, of the shock imparted to the war structure by the armistice—*i.e.*, the four months of dullness or wavering rather than collapse which followed upon it—of foreign and domestic postwar demand producing the boom of 1919 and, finally, of all that partial liquidation of both war and postwar situations contributed to the slump of 1920–1921. It is necessary to add but two comments.

First, however clear it is that that slump was primarily a process of liquidation of war effects and a reaction to the boom of 1919—which in turn had little if anything to do with innovation—yet the presence, and businessmen's awareness of the presence, of an industrial situation which was new in the sense that the consequences of prewar innovations had profoundly altered the cost structure had much to do with the severe restriction in output of manufactures which first began in January and again, after a rebound, in March 1920, in the face of the facts that retail sales had throughout 1919 increased at a greater rate than had production, that the export trade as yet showed no signs of slackeniing, that *prices continued to rise*. Banks, moreover, were, by the influx of (gold imports in 1921 amounted to nearly 750 millions) and by the reduction of government debt by about 1.2 billion dollars between June 30, 1919 and June 30, 1920, enabled to increase their loans by about 1.5 billion dollars during the same time. All this puts some of the most popular theories out of court in this case. We have once more an instance of "business deflating itself" without any serious outside pressure, and we see again that this could have been prevented only by continuing government expenditure at the war level or a level still higher. The question why business deflated itself cannot be given, even in this case, without reference to our mechanism.

Second, the reaction was sharp and unimpeded and, because it was sharp and unimpeded, relatively short. Prices and wages were allowed to drop drastically, liquidation of commodity stocks and debts proceeded rapidly, elimination of firms—over 8 per cent of the manufacturing firms which were in busineses in 1919 had disappeared by 1921—was prompt, money rates fell, credit was readily available, and the situation began to stabilize itself in April 1921, the textile and clothing industries, which had expanded first in 1919 and fallen first in 1920, being among the first to revive. The resulting price relations differed greatly from those of 1913 and struck many observers as entirely abnormal. But the change was largely, though not wholly, one of adaptation to new conditions.

Though improvement slackened in October and many signs of continuing liquidation—*e.g.*, further reduction in wages—outlasted the summer of 1922, "deep depression" was over by December 1921. In April 1922 the automobile and tire industries experienced shortage of labor, while stock issues had already revived in January: it was then that the boom in public utility stocks began. Prices of steel, tires, glass, and oil rose in the fall, while those of gasoline, automobiles—the price of tractors had been reduced before by action of the Ford concern—cement and foods fell. In December 1922 the oil industry was breaking all previous records in output. The fact that such should have been the situation only one year after a major crisis and in the presence of many depressive symptoms is full of potential lessons which are as obvious as they are useless. The case also shows better than any theory could how the system pulls out of troughs under its own steam and how it succeeds in doing so while price level is still falling.

Our diagnosis then is simple: abnormally short depression phase of the Juglar, lasting from the fall of 1920 to July of 1922, owing to abnormally effective liquidation. Alternatively, we could express the same facts by saying that the depression phase lasted to the end of 1922 but that its work had so effectively been done by May 1921 that, the ground being cleared, the prosperity phase of the third Kitchin, which, as we know, still belongs to the depression phase of its Juglar, had unusual opportunities of asserting itself. In any case this Kitchin stands out unmistakably, and there is no reason why we should not so call an undoubtedly short cycle which is universally recognized—even if differently dated by students who count from trough to trough—and which completely answers expectation from our schema both as to formal characteristics and as to industrial meaning. On the other two Kitchins which within that Juglar ought to have preceded this one, we will not insist, although it would not be difficult to establish them statistically.

What followed, from either the middle or the end of 1922 on, very much looks like a normal Juglar recovery, which lasted to the autumn of 1925. Our schema would lead is to expect that it contained a setback owing to the Kitchin depression which it tells us should have occurred. It did occur. After it had run its course, recovery resumed and from August 1925 on both Kitchin and Juglar were shading off into the prosperity phases of what then would be the fourth Juglar and its first Kitchin. A few additional facts may be useful. In the first quarter of 1923 the upswing reached its peak. Unemployment was at low ebb in February. Most prices, especially those of metals and building materials, tended upward; a record year for construction was correctly foreseen. Steel—19 new steel furnaces were built in 1923—coal, and cotton txtiles expanded. Four new power stations were announced for construction. Railroads "came into their own again" and gave orders. Everything except agriculture and ship-building boomed. Wage rates rose strongly. April saw record figures but also a break in the stock market. Signs of slackening activity began to show by August, attributed as usual to external factors, and by December expectations were not very optimistic. They were borne out by the state of things during the spring and summer of 1924. More important than the uncertainties incident to the presidential campaign were the—understandable—reactions in the automobile and oil industries. Steel consumption, railroad traffic, employment, and prices fell. Nothing very serious happened, however; failures of commercial firms were but insignificantly above the 1923 figure; residential building kept up well, and so did power production, the radio industry, and other lines. The first two months of 1925 were disappointing—with employment in most industries below what it had been a year before—and a collapse of the stock market followed in March. During the second quarter business was described as steady but "spotty." New financing and other indications of imminent prosperity asserted themselves under this surface, however, and, with the help of improvement in the agrarian sphere and largely speculative land boom, the fall wore on amidst record investment, bank-clearing and construction figures, rising money rates and steel prices, stock market excesses, failures at record low.

The explanation of all this—the "ignition"—will be found on referring to the above survey of the fundamental industrial processes of the period. They clearly change during those months owing to the influence of several new impulses—while others, such as residential building, lost force—and, by conforming exactly to what we mean by a Juglar prosperity, justify our dating. So much is provable and indeed obvious. But we will for a moment trust our schema to the point of absurdity and try to "predict" the subsequent business situations on the assumptions, first, that the fourth Juglar started with the fourth quarter of 1925—although no such exactness is possible in historical analysis—second, that its duration was to be exactly 9-1/2 years—roughly the average duration of prewar Juglars—and the duration of its Kitchins exactly 38 months; third, that all the Juglar and Kitchin phases were of exactly equal length. This absurd experiment yields the following results: the Juglar depresison lasting into February 1928 should be interrupted by a Kitchin depression from May 1927 to the middle of February 1928; and the recovery of this Kitchin—to the end of November 1928—and the prosperity—to the middle of September 1929—and the recession of the second Kitchin should then run their course within the Juglar recession ending with June 1930. At that date both the Juglar and the Kitchin should enter upon their depression phases on a Kondratieff that had already entered upon its own,[1] so that the configuration of 1873 would be repeated. The reader will realize that no value attaches to, and no significance is claimed for, the exact dates. But he will also realize that the absurdity stops at the assumptions which are responsible for the exact dates. Stripped of this unwarranted exactitude and confined to essentials, the "predictions" of the schema are not absurd but on the contrary tell several important truths—and not a single untruth. It should be added that the comparative severity of the setback in 1927, which was to occur and did in fact occur within the prosperity phrase of the Juglar, does not in itself run counter to expectation: the depression of a Kitchin,

[1] It will be remembered that according to our schema Kondratieff depressions begin with Juglar prosperities. The depression phase of the current Kondratieff would, hence, date from the fall of 1925.

located as that one was after the end of the Kondratieff recession, should be well marked.[1] On the other handfi the boom of 1928–1929 was more violent than our schema leads us to expect, which in explanation has but a Kichin recovery and a Kitchin prosperity to offer. This may, however, be accounted for by certain autonomous monetary factors and the influence of the speculative mania, of which the first do not form part of our model and the second—also present in 1872–1873—is always an irregular factor.

The stock market suffered collapse in February 1926. But this is merely a normal incident of a Juglar prosperity outgrowing its initial stage. A no less regular phenomenon was, on a Kondratieff depression, the tendency of prices to sag. If business conditions began to display signs of "relaxation" already by April, when automobile concerns did not do so well as they had a year before and the cotton, silk, sugar, and other industries headed toward curtailment, and if in May there was also a decline in steel production, this is sufficiently accounted for by previous speculative excesses, in particular by the passing of the real estate boom. The stock exchange recovered by June, and almost everything was again at prosperity levels by August, motorcars and textiles included, furniture enjoying record profits. Oil developments in California, in North Texas, and on the Gulf Coast did not entail any large increase in stocks. By October, however, the 1927 setback came definitely in sight. The stock market discounted it, bank debits were running from 5 to 9 per cent below the figures of the preceding year, demand for steel dropped until operations were at 65 per cent capacity. Failures increased. Car loadings also were at the end of what nevertheless was a record year at a lower figure than they had been in 1925. Some anxiety

[1] Professor Mitchell dates one of his cycles from 1927. Since the writer naturally wishes to differ as little as possible from so outstanding an authority, he begs to emphasize that no difference in diagnosis of situations is implied in such dating, because it is simply the consequence of Professor Mitchell's principles to count from trough to trough and to recognize but a single type of cycles. The particular pattern under discussion seems well qualified for suggesting that some important elements of reality are being missed if we put troughs such as occurred in 1924 and 1927 on the same level with troughs such as occurred, say, in 1908 and 1921, and these again on the same level with the troughs of 1875 and 1932, and that the distinction of cycles of different type seems the natural way of recognizing these very real differences.

was felt about installment sales. The agrarian situation had also become more unfavorable.

Until May 1927, however, general business kept on a high level in spite of all that and even improved, several new things—the Chevrolet and Frigidaire successes, motion pictures, the North Carolina power plant, a number of smaller events—supplying impulse. In April business was prosperous. But then a definite decline set in—which we may identify as a Kitchin depression—intensified by widespread recognition of unsound practice in many fields, with retail and wholesale trade at a lower level, many failures, and cautious reserve in large-scale business. Building, the condition of which was complicated by the liquidation of the Florida boom, was a particular weak spot. The fall in automobile production was, of course, due to the reconstruction of the Ford plant.[1] The Mississippi flood, while it also explains some things about the behavior of physical indices, has in other respects to be listed as an impetus. There was no slump. Good business in the cotton, rayon, and shoe industries and a continuing stream of new things—Diesel-engined locomotives, gas-pipe lines, the refrigerator merger, development of the Kraft paper industry in the South, radios—were features throughout. By December improvement was almost general, although employment in building was still 12 per cent below that of a year before.

Railroad earnings, steel production, and gasoline markets improved in January 1928, and the "bankers' loans boom" in the stock market was getting under sail with automobile, copper, and rubber stocks leading. But the general business situation behaved until March in a manner which is in our terminology not badly rendered by the phase "conditions of Kitchin depression relieved by a Juglar prosperity." In April, however, steel was at record rates. So was tire production and by June everything—building, the automobile (contraseasonally) and the oil industry included. Symptoms of "high" prosperity then went on intensifying themselves until October, when mail-order sales broke all records. Construction of new plant, new financing—taking advantage of the stock-market boom—dividends, money rates, and so on were all in keeping with the rest of the picture. There were

[1] But the writer fails to understand how some observers could have attributed the 1927 depression wholly to that fact.

two apparently discordant elements, however. First, unemployment increased. Second, commodity markets though bouyant were not realy sellers' markets: the almost desperate efforts made by the sales organizations of big and small concerns and the fact that such increase in prices as ocurred was insignificant, while many important prices had to be reduced, indicate a certain strain in the system.

Now if the reader will remember the writer's various attempts to convey his idea of a Juglar recession, he will appreciate the warrant for expressing that state of things by saying that it was exactly what we should expect from a Juglar recession on a Kondratieff depression coupled with the two positive phases—strictly, according to our experimental schema, the recovery phase only—of a unit of the short cycle: good and expanding business accompanied by increasing unemployment and by that strain which is the consequence of the "avalanche of goods" smashing its way through the resisting framework of the existing industrial structure—this is precisely the picture which would reuslt from that particular juncture. As stated before, however, there is no doubt that the developments between April 1928 and August 1929 added to the situation many of the untenable elements which subsequently served to intensify the crisis.

October 1928 brought the first symptom of slackening activity, which was, however, to disappear temporarily by January 1929: with the exception of Ford, all automobile producers then decreased their purchases of steel. In November total building fell off more than seasonally. But barring building and production of building materials, which continued to decline, most lines of industrial and commercial activity surpassed 1928 output figures during the first six months of 1929 at falling prices but high profits. Also plant construction and financing seemed to have taken out a new lease on life. Quite a list of new things (at least of the "induced" type) were being inaugurated in June, when pig-iron production reached a maximum. Moreover, the aircraft, radio refrigerator industries prospered. So did automobiles, tires, machine tools and other implements, hardware, cotton, silk, rayon, and cigarette production. The Kettleman Hills oil field was discovered. Mail-order sales were running far above the 1928 level. Department-store sales reached a peak in September. Extra dividends were paid in the last week of August by oil, chain-store, mail-order, steel, and flour concerns. The agricultural situation became a matter of serious concern. The United States Treasury was paying 5-1/8 per cent in June; federal reserve rediscount rates rose to 6 per cent by August.

Although there is a valid objection to any such statement, we may take April to mark the peak of that (Kitchin) prosperity. But even the inadequate description presented is sufficient to show that, whatever may have been wrong in the financial sector, the great divisions of industry and commerce either expanded or contracted—steel, motorcars, building—in a perfectly orderly day during the subsequent months through September. It is, therefore, undesirable that when the stock market—not altogether unexpectedly—collapsed, this did not cause paralysis or even particularly strong pessimism in the business world. What immediately happened was in fact not much more than was foreseen, *viz.*, a drastic reduction in the demand for "luxuries," of which speculative gains in stocks had been a most important feeder. The repercussions of this were expected to induce and did induce contraction all around, but with money rates failing to rise to panic figures—as compared with their reaction in prewar crises—improvement was confidently predicted for the first half of 1930. Among characteristic reactions of "big" business we may note that Ford announced a substantial reduction in prices, that United States Steel and American Can declared extra dividends, and that prevailing opinion was strongly against a decrease in wages. The withdrawal of foreign funds, the agrarian situation, and such liquidations of concerns as occurred were —quite correctly—not considered decisive.

It is of the utmost importance to realize this: given the actual facts which it was then possible for either businessmen or economists to observe, those diagnoses—or even the prognosis that, with the existing structure of debt, those facts plus a drastic fall in price level would cause major trouble but that nothing else would—were not simply wrong. What nobody saw, though some people may have felt it, was that those fundamental data from which diagnoses and prognoses were made, were themselves in a state of flux and that they would be swamped by the torrents of a process of readjustment corresponding in magnitude to the extent of the industrial revolution of the preceding 30 years. People, for the most part, stood their ground firmly. But that ground itself was about to give way.

Chapter IX

THE WORLD CRISIS AND AFTER

A. The World Crisis and the Cyclical Schema.—We should now be able to answer the question how far the course of events from the fall of 1929 to the summer of 1938 can be described in terms of the analytic model presented in this book and how far other factors, external or internal, new or old, must be relied on for explanations. Whenever any set of propositions and observations leads us to expect a certain event, the actual occurrence of that event will always strengthen our confidence in those propositions. In such cases we are in the habit of saying—at the risk, as we have had ample opportunity of observing, of some violence to logic—that they are "verified" by that event or that they "explain" it. Now in this sense the occurrence at that time of a severe and prolonged depression in itself verifies or ratifies the application of our model, *i.e.*, warrants explanation in terms of our process. For we need only survey, in the light of our interpretation, the developments since 1898 in order to understand why such a depression should have occurred as part and parcel of that process. No claims are made for our three-cycle schema except that it is a useful descriptive or illustrative device. Using it, however, in that capacity, we in fact got (in Chap. VIII, Sec. E), *ex visu* of 1929, a "forecast" of a serious depression embodied in the formula: coincidence of depression phases of all three cycles. For reasons we know, capitalist evolution spells disturbance. We also know that it spells simultaneous disturbances of different order of importance and different range in time. Junctures therefore occur in which the symptoms incident to scrapping and rearranging dominate the scene. Among these junctures there are some in which adjustments to long-range and more fundamental, and adjustments to short-range and less fundamental industrial changes do not occur at the same time, and there are others in which they do. In the first case, symptoms will be mitigated; in the second, intensified—or, to return to the schema, in the first case the depressive phases of one or two cycles will hit a "floor" provided by the nondepressive phases of the other or the two others; in the second case there is no such floor and hence a more serious and especially broader trough—all of which could easily be translated into terms of hard business fact.

In VIII, E we went a step further by making the—absurd—assumption of strict periodicity of all the cycles and equal duration of all their phases. Counting on in the same manner, we should get a Juglar depression—on the Kondratieff depression which dates from the fall of 1925—from July 1930 to the middle of November 1932, which should be severe, to be followed by a Juglar recovery to March 1935, which we should expect to be, owing to its position within the Kondratieff, slow and weak. That depression would contain three Kitchin phases, a depression to the middle of April 1931, a revival to January 1932, and a prosperity to the middle of November 1932; and the latter two should assert themselves mainly (not wholly) by decrease in rates of decrease. *This* schema has none except illustrative significance and no value attaches to the dates. It is, however, important to stress the common sense of the broad diagnosis thus invested with a spurious precision as to details. Realizing from historical observation the extent of the revolution that had occurred in the industrial structure and was in the act of upsetting its system of values, shall we be surprised at the emergence of a situation in which perhaps three-quarters of all businesses in the United States (including farms) had to face the necessity of an adaptation that threatened them with economic death? And is there really much to object to in the statement that this situation was the fundamental fact about the world crisis, compared with which all other factors, however important, were after all but mitigating or accentuating accessories?

Before proceeding to qualify and to elaborate, we will advert to a consequence which follows if that diagnosis can be established. Capitalism and its civilization may be decaying, shading off into something else, or tottering toward a violent death. The writer personally thinks they are. But the world crisis does not prove it and has, in fact, nothing to do with it. It was not a symptom of a weakening or a failure of the system. If anything, it was a proof of the vigor of capitalist evolution to which it was—substantially—the temporary reaction. And in any case it was—again, substantially—no novel occurrence, no unprecedented catastrophe expressive of the emergence of new factors, but only a recurrence of what at similar junctures had occurred before.

The first qualification is that, so far, the above argument covers only the course of events down to the bottom of the depression, which, as we shall see, occurred in the second half of 1932. Subsequent events raise problems concerning recovery policies, which bar any statement at this point.

Second, it should be recalled that we never undertook to explain everything about any crisis or even depression. There was, in particular, the important class of "understandable but nonessential incidents." In this instance they may be exemplified by the activities of, say, Hatry or Kreuger and so on; even German experience might have been somewhat different but for the impulsive personality of the leading man of the Darmstädter und Nationalbank. An example of more important elements of this class of phenomena is the violence—though not simply the occurrence—of the boom and the crash in the stock market of the United States, which forms no part of the essentials of our process, yet powerfully influenced it. But the boundaries of this class should not be extended too far. The building booms and their slackening from about 1928 on, for instance, or the bulk of the difficulties in the agrarian sectors do not belong here but were perfectly normal elements of that process.

The American debt situation and the American bank epidemics—there were three of them—are in a class by themselves. Given the way in which both firms and households had run into debt during the twenties, the accumulated load—in many cases, though not in all, very sensitive to a fall in price level—was instrumental in precipitating depression. In particular, it set into motion a vicious spiral within which everybody's efforts to reduce that load for a time only availed to increase it. There is thus no objection to the debt-deflation theory of the American crisis, provided it does not mean more than this. The element it stresses is part of the mechanism of any serious depression. But increase of total indebtedness at the rate at which it had occurred in this country is neither a normal element of the mechanism of Kondratieff downgrades nor in itself an "understandable" incident, like speculative excesses and the debts induced by these. It must be attributed to the humor of the times, to cheap money policies, and to the practices of concerns eager to push their sales; and it enters the class of understandable incidents only if we include specifically American conditions among our data. Similarly, bank failures are of course very regular (though still not essential) occurrences in the course of any major crisis and invariably an important cause of secondary phenomena, in particular, again, of downward cumulative processes. Those epidemics cannot, however, be considered as wholly explained by the ordinary mechanism of crises or by that mechanism plus the fact of excessive indebtedness all round or even by all that plus the stock exchange crash. The American epidemics become fully understandable only if account be taken of the weaknesses peculiar to the American banking structure, which made it succumb as no European system would have succumbed under similar circumstances—in particular, the presence, fostered by legislation and public opinion, of a large number of small and inefficient banks and the absence of anything like the English tradition.

Third, there were the external factors. In noticing them in Chap. VII, Sec. C, we found that their importance, *so far as the causation of the world crisis is concerned*, may easily be overestimated. In particular, it would be unwarranted to attribute any of the major features of the American depression to a "flood of imports." Imports, on the contrary, fell rapidly at the critical time; they totaled $4.4 billions in 1929, little over 3 in 1930, little over 2 in 1931, and about 1.3 in 1932.

It is true that the indirect influence of policies, certainly in the case of Germany and possibly also in the case of England, on short capital movements had much to do especially with what in a narrower and perhaps more proper sense should be called the *crisis*. And the provisional solution that had been arrived at for the problem of international payments was bound to break down in any major depression and, before doing so, to accentuate its difficulties. We do not even wish to palliate the influence of such monetary disorders as occurred before the depression had the chance of tearing up the flimsy tissue of pseudo gold currencies. The South American, especially the Argentinian, disorders and the fall of the price of silver have undoubtedly played some role. But all this looms so large because a depression occurred for other reasons. As a man may suffer from many ills and yet for an indefinite time lead a vigorous life without being seriously inconvenienced by them until, when his general vitality has ebbed away, those ills or any one of them may suddenly acquire what to the specialists' eye will seem paramount or even fatal importance; so the economic organism always does bleed from many wounds which it bears lightly in three out of the four cyclical phases, and which spell discomfort when one cycle, distress when two, catastrophe when all the cycles are in the depression phase. No doubt, external injuries were of unusually great importance in this case,[1] but explanation cannot be derived from them.

B. 1930.— The businessmen and forecasters, who in the fall of 1929 had made up their minds that nothing worse was ahead than a "recession" not much more serious than that of, say, 1924, cannot have been very disappointed by the general look of things during the first half of 1930. At the beginning, stock prices rallied strongly, security issues were large, signs of improvement showed in many spots, money was easy. All that, except the easy money, passed quickly, it is true, and proved to have been a meaningless flurry, due perhaps to the confidence that was so widely felt or to the organized effort to make a stand that prompted some additional spending. But until about the end of June business moved along on a but slowly falling level not much below the figures of 1929 in practically all lines.

The second half of the year presents a wholly different picture. What was generally recognized as liquidation all round was the outstanding feature. Rates of contraction quickened and comparison with 1929 figures became increasingly melancholy.

[1] It should not be forgotten, however, that the crisis was nowhere else anything like so severe as in the United States, the country most nearly free from injury by external factors.

People felt that the ground under their feet was giving way. There was, however, no panic or even alarm until, late in the year, distress signals showed in the banking sphere, the failure of the Bank of the United States (December) attracting particular attention abroad. And not only totals for the year but also figures for the end of the year were far from being catastrophic. Total corporate issues were $5.473 billions—slightly above the level of 1926, though only about 55 per cent of the 1929 figure—or, exclusive of refunding issues, 4.5 billions, slightly below the level of 1926. Outside debits (133 cities) with 137.5 billions were only a little below 1926 and about 14 per cent below 1929, though contraction was severe from the beginning of July to the beginning of September. Outside net demand deposits, as already pointed out in the preceding chapter, neither were appreciably lower for the year nor fell appreciably within the second half of the year—July, 8.117 billions; December, 7.911 billions. But *All Other Loans had already shrunk sharply* from November 1929 to May 1930 and then continued to decline. Some hoarding demand for money, increasing "money in circulation" and total federal reserve credit outstanding, showed in December. Number of banks suspended (1,345) was in fact more than double the yearly average 1921–1929 (627), but 1,158 of them were nonmembers. Excepting July and August, there was net influx of gold in every month which, together with the issue of additional national bank notes, brought excess reserves of member banks to about $475 millions by the middle of November—a position of the banking system as a whole that was technically anything but weak, authough the value of collateral was already seriously impaired.

There was nothing abnormal under the circumstances in the quickening decline of prices of finished products, which within the year fell by about 10 per cent. The wholesale price index was pulled down by the fall in the prices of semifinished goods and especially of raw materials—the December average of the latter was over 20 per cent below the January average. Money rate of wages fell considerably in agriculture, but was (see below) substantially maintained in industry. In the fourth quarter, however, reductions in individual industries were sufficiently important to affect the general index, though they still left real hourly earnings at a level higher than that of 1929. Weekly money earnings decreased even for the first quarter, and weekly real earnings eventually fell to 90 per cent above the prewar level. Wage bill continued its descent from the peak of the third quarter of 1929. In New York State, for instance, factory pay rolls declined by about 25 per cent from January to December.

Total monetary labor income for the year was, however, only 7.9 per cent and total monetary income produced only 15.1 per cent below 1929. But net earnings of all corporations (excluding tax-exempt ones and life insurance companies) before deduction of income taxes were by over 78 per cent below the 1929 figure, printing and publishing, foods, beverages, tobacco products, chemicals, metal and metal products, paper, pulp and its products doing comparatively well, textiles particularly badly. The most serious features of the picture are displayed by the indices of industrial production and of employment. Output of equipment and durable goods in general, as reflected, for example, in steel ingot production, fell sharply after May. Motor-vehicle factory sales were less than 2.8, as against 4.6 billions. The Harvard Society's index of volume of manufactures declined by over 22, the Federal Reserve Board's index of employment by over 16.2 per cent within the year, whereby the former almost reached the trough figures of 1921 and the latter slightly fell below them.

Mining did somewhat better than manufactures, and power production was in the first six months above, and in the last six months not much below, the 1929 level. Total construction as measured by contracts was over 20 per cent below 1929 and would have been still lower if publicly and semipublicly financed building had not kept up or even somewhat increased. But public utilities increased their expenditure on construction ($644 millions as against 473 in 1929) and residential building did not decline much. It was, as we should expect, industrial and commercial building which caused the fall in the total.

The brightest features of the picture are to be found in the sphere of consumption, the surprisingly good showing of which has not always received the attention it merits. Sales by department stores, while consistently and increasingly below those of 1929, were still 102 per cent of the 1923 to 1925 average and their December holiday trade in the New York district—containing, however, one more selling day than in 1929—was only 4.5 per cent under that of the previous year. Considering the fall in prices there obviously cannot have been decline in physical volume. This is borne out by the behavior of carloadings of the l.c.l. category, which in contrast to total carloadings declined but moderately. Consumption of a number of articles, such as cigarettes and gasoline, electric current for domestic use, telephones, radio sets, and refrigerators, increased or declined but insignificantly. The number of business failures, consistently and increasingly above that of 1929, was as yet far from alarming: about 2,000 a month, which is less than the average number of failures from October 1921 to June 1922.

An attempt to answer the question how far these facts can be trusted to reflect the working of our model (including "understandable non-essentials") naturally divides up into two tasks. On the one hand, we have to ask whether expectations from our model are adequately borne out. This is obviously the case. Even disregarding the exact coincidence of dates with our experimental count, we readily see not only that the history of that year as a whole is not badly rendered by the formula "a recession sliding off into deep depression," but also that the economic physiognomies of the two halves of the year, differing as they do characteristically from each other, conform to our idea of such a situation in every single symptom excepting the short-lived rally at the beginning. The reader should have no difficulty in verifying this proposition as to general contours—the behavior of price level, output, interest rates, deposits, clearings, incomes, employment, and so on—and it will be sufficient to draw attention to a few points.

That rally at the beginning was due to organized effort, but too much importance should not be attributed to that effort, because expectation would in any case have been for fairly sustained business at that time. In particular, it is perfectly in keeping with our schema that industrial money wages did not during the first half of the year fall to any significant extent—there is no reason to expect wages to fall in recession and no inference about subsequent disturbance can be drawn from their failure to do so. The ease in the money market was also normal under the circumstances and a simple consequence of "business deflating itself." It does not call for explanation by Federal Reserve Board policy, although the latter no doubt contributed to it. Not less true to form were the effects of that ease: as normally happens in recession, it helped to keep up residential construction and to induce certain types of investment, for example, by utilities, which, however, acted also under another stimulus. The unequal—in the case of some, especially of new, commodities negative—rates of restriction, the severe slump in the second half of the year in the sales of "postponables," and the behavior of consumption should be particularly noticed.

Hence, although our methods do not enable us to formulate our expectations numerically and although it is impossible to say whether our series exactly behaved as they should have done according to our theory, it is possible to say that they did so as far as we can make out. Facts would not refute us even if we made bold to say that nothing but our process had acted on the economic system, and they certainly bear us out if we conclude that that process constituted the dominant factor.

On the other hand, we must consider the possibility that other factors influenced the course of things in such a way as to produce a spurious verification. Attempts to influence the process have not been entirely absent and must be taken into account even if we discard the possibility that influences from abroad might have significantly affected the American situation in other ways than through the stock exchange. There were, first, measures in aid of agriculture and an appeal to the household remedy of the party in power, the Hawley-Smoot tariff. The effects of the former, though certainly not negligible, failed even in the agrarian sector to modify conditions sufficiently to make them diverge from expectation and cannot a fortiori have been very important for the system as a whole. The effects of the latter, partly counteracted by reprisals, may under the circumstances be equated to zero.

Second, there was the President's hortatory action, which was, by staving off reductions in wages and by stimulating investment, "to make certain that the fundamental business of the country shall continue as usual." The interest for us of this and similar attempts consists mainly in testing those theories that see in depressions nothing else but the result of businessmen's moods, which, themselves ultimate data, shape business situations by means of the cumulations and accelerations induced by individual acts. In this case conditions were quite exceptionally favorable to success. The American business world was, as has been pointed out, by no means overpessimistic at that time. It was in the habit of looking for a lead to the heads of a relatively small number of concerns, which, moreover, were big enough to be able to influence the situation "mechanically" by their own action. Expansion would have been eminently to their interest and certainly was what they actually wished to see. Receiving themselves a lead from a political agent that was in no way antipathetic to them and being, many of them, imbued with high-wage theories, they, in fact, made an effort both by refraining from lowering wages or from doing anything else that would have been suggestive of depression, and by launching out into investment—the utilities and railroads in particular responded to the appeal and even borrowed for the purpose, so that the "principle of acceleration" had plenty to work with. Nor was the result simply nil. The case shows to perfection what can and what cannot be achieved—and explained—in this way. We have above noticed the "flurry" at the beginning of the year, which may, though only in part, be attributed to that effort.

Third, we have seen that public expenditure was kept going and even increased, especially by means of public construction. It has been estimated that net federal income-generating expenditure for the year was 251 and for the second half alone $450 millions. This is not negligible. But it may well be doubted whether that part of the total which may be reasonably assumed to have become fully effective during the year can have influenced events materially. The Federal Reserve System, finally, followed a policy of easy money—which policy, as we have seen, but ratified the situation—thus giving business all the rein and all the encouragement it could possibly have wished for. As soon as it had become obvious that business was in for a "recession" and before any vicious spiral had developed, the reserve system resorted to what the public and many economists had by then come to believe in as *the* remedy, open-market purchases on a large scale. From October 1929 to December 1930, it bought government securities to the amount of 560 millions or, more precisely, its holdings of government securities rose from 136 millions on Oct. 23, 1929, to 533 millions on Dec. 18, 1929, then fell to 477 in January 1930 to rise again to 602 by the end of August. After that date, purchases were reduced to insignificant amounts. For this there were two excellent reasons. First, those purchases which it was thought had been so effective in stimulating activity in 1924 and 1927, at this time did not seem to have any effect at all. Members reacted primarily, although they also increased their investments, by paying off rediscounts, and were obviously much more troubled about finding customers for their funds than about finding funds for their customers: to anyone at all open to argument and evidence on the subject, any further steps in that direction would have seemed altogether futile. Later on, in the second place, the gold influx provided another reason for discontinuing that policy. We may, hence, conclude that the behavior of the reserve system, while it favored cheap money and expansion and certainly exerted no depressing effects, yet was no major factor in shaping the business situation—our process seems, as far as that goes, in fact to have worked all but undisturbed.

C. 1931 and 1932.—While it was necessary to have the facts of 1930 firmly planted in the reader's mind, it seems possible to confine discussion of the two years which span the real "catastrophe" to a number of comments that can easily be worked up into a connected survey.

1. *Physical Production.*—The fundamental point to emphasize is again that there is nothing in the fact that severely depressive symptoms continued to dominate the picture to require additional explanation from our standpoint—nothing has to be explained away, and that fact fully conforms to expectation from our model. That picture reflects ever since, roughly speaking, the middle of 1930 an element not in evidence before—the "vicious spiral" which for nearly two years would by itself suffice to describe the surface of what was going on. But the process thus designated is to a greater or lesser extent a feature of any depression. It is, in fact, largely responsible for turning the "normal liquidation" of recession into the "abnormal liquidation" of depression (Chap. IV). *At that stage,* the phenomena expressed by the "principle of cumulation or acceleration" and by the "debt-deflation" theory become part of the cyclical mechanism, a particularly important part when all three cycles are in the phases most favorable to them.[1] But since we also know that the work-

[1] Hence, it would not constitute valid objection to say that the events of these years do not require explanation by the theory of innovation but are adequately explained by the vicious spiral or by the principle of aceleration. The one and the others do not stand on the same plane of argument and cannot be pitted against each other. Believing he has made this abundantly clear throughout this book, the writer wishes to add only two minor points. First, the word *acceleration* seems to suggest increasing rates of change; this would, however, even if the word were to be taken at face value, not contradict the expecta-

ing of the spiral is erratic ("internally irregular") and extremely sensitive to incidents, accidents, and external factors, and that the troughs it creates are intrinsically unreliable, we must, especially in the face of the various recovery policies that were taking shape in those two years, recognize the limitations of any attempt at verification beyond that fundamental fact. Barring crises and panics, which may occur at any time and the occurrence and effects of which have simply to be registered, we expect a depression to display shrinkage at decreasing rates until it shades off into recovery, in the case of the Kondratieff on a very broad bottom and in the case of the Juglar on a bottom of about a year, while the Kitchin phases should show in what statisticians call surface movements in series corrected for seasonals. Even without attaching weight to the dates yielded by our experimental count (see above, Sec. A) we will note that since a Juglar depression must contain positive Kitchin phases—and, if we trust our schema to that extent, end up with a Kitchin prosperity—it should display an observable, though possibly weak and short, upturn at the bottom, which again is nothing else but our way of expressing a familiar fact of business experience.

What are the facts? A preliminary answer may be derived from the behavior of industrial production: nothing else qualifies equally well for the role of an indicator of the objective state of the system in the later part of depression and during recovery. We will look first for the lower turning point, or rather, remembering our view about troughs, for the lowest segment of our graphs. In almost all countries, however different their structures and general conditions, particularly in Austria, Belgium, France, Germany, Hungary, Italy, Poland, and Sweden, it occurs in (the middle of) 1932. In the Canadian index the trough comes in February 1933. Japan was an exception all along, in fact, the standard instance for advocates of inflationary policies, who have only to be reminded that the case is a special one in that this policy found all the conditions ready at hand for a rapid

tion to be presently met with in the text, because that word refers only to a component and the expectation to a resultant. Second, it might be held that, the facts covered by the term Vicious Spiral being the outstanding feature of those years, we may stop at that and discuss the theoretical and practical problems of the situation without going beyond those facts. This is not so. It is not indifferent, for either diagnosis or therapy, what starts the spiral.

industrialization of the country. In the English case there is some doubt, but our chart displays a well-marked trough in the summer of 1932. So it does for this country. The relapse in the spring of 1933, which carried the American index back to about its previous low, while not in itself astonishing—that after a depression of such severity relapses should occur in the first stages of recovery is perfectly understandable on common-sense grounds, even without appeal to the course of Kitchin phases—was serious enough to suggest the presence of disturbing factors. But since the advent of a new administration pledged to pursue an active policy and the third epidemic among banks readily supply the explanation, it seems reasonable to accept the 1932 trough as the "true" one, although according to some indices—not, however, that of the Federal Reserve Board—the trough in March 1933 is somewhat deeper still. For both manufactures and minerals, also for steel, lumber, petroleum refining, coke (by-product), foods (the descent of which, however, was hardly perceptible) textiles, automobiles, and construction (values) taken separately, decline came to a stop by roughly the middle of 1932. Only for cement, rubber products, and power production, possibly also tobacco, the halt does not come before the spring of 1933, while leather and leather products turned up by the end of 1931. The behavior of carloadings and imports (current values) bear out the general picture and so did business failures, which fell sharply after reaching their peak in the summer of 1932. The Federal Reserve Board's index of department-store sales declined until the spring of 1933, but this was due to the continued fall in prices.

Thus it seems that, so far as physical production is concerned, the location of the bottom of the depression answers well to our idea as to where it should have occurred. American industrial production declined for 1932 as a whole very much less than it did in 1931 and, owing to the upturn at the end, the average rate of change within the year would also be smaller. But the contraction at the beginning of 1932 was (in percentage rate) the most serious of all, and whether the decline of 1931 was milder than that in the second half of 1930 is a matter of index construction. These irregularities may, however, be partly accounted for by the specifically American difficulties in the sphere of credit and banking.

One fact which sheds much light on the nature of the process cannot be passed by, *viz.*, that the depression acted as an efficiency expert. This is particularly in evidence in the United States. Output per man-hour, which may be roughly said to have increased by 22 per cent from 1923 to 1929, surpassed in 1932 the 1929 figure by an amount that will greatly vary according to the indices entering into the computation, but may plausibly be put in the neighborhood of 20 per cent. This was, of course, not only due to rationalization under duress in the concerns that continued operations, but also to the shutting down or permanent elimination of others, which may as a broad rule be assumed to have been less efficient. The second component, however, enters our model no less than the first. More rigorous selection of the workmen employed or to be employed may also have had some, the mere underutilization of fixed factors cannot have had significant effect—the latter factor is likely, under the conditions of modern industry, to have worked the other way, at least in many cases.

For most countries total industrial as well as manufacturing production experienced a beginning of recovery, as small as we should expect, in the second half of 1932, which slackened toward the end of the year, when, as we would say, the last Kitchin of the Juglar turned into recession. Such a relapse at that juncture is in itself no problem. In the United States production of manufactures and mining as measured by the seasonally adjusted index of the Federal Reserve Board increased substantially during August and September—from the July low of 58 per cent of the 1923 to 1925 average to 66 per cent—and went on at that level in October; then, after a slight setback, regained it in December. It is important to note that it was the activity of cotton, woolen, silk, rayon mills, shoe factories, and the like which was responsible for the increase in August, while automobile production still declined and steel and lumber industries did not show even seasonal advance. In September, though the steel industry expanded a little—it then reached 20 per cent of capacity during the first three weeks of October—the same general features characterize the situation. In October, automobile production increased, but there was still little activity in investment industries. This is in accordance with the usual pattern. We know that in a four-phase cycle recovery from the lower turning point does not typically start either by innovations or, more generally, investment, or by firms' borrowing but exclusively by moves, from an indefinite number of points and within the existing framework of plant, equipment, and balances, toward a neighborhood of equilibrium.

2. *Incidents, Accidents, and Policy in the United States.*—In this country the principles of a recovery policy began to take shape as soon as the plateau on which business moved during the first half of 1931 gave way. This new dive in the third quarter of 1931, which was deeper than we should have expected, was but to a minor extent due to the unpleasant experiences this country had had in the role of a creditor nation. Losses from defaults of foreign debtors on long-term loans and from the depreciation or worse of other long-term investments, however considerable, were small relatively to the size of the organism. More important embarrassments followed from the freezing or worse of short credits to foreign banks, because this paralyzed the first line of defense against the withdrawals of foreign balances. But until September 1931 there was hardly any sign that serious difficulties would arise on that score. Repatriation of part of those balances was to be expected, because there was little to do for them here. Throughout the summer this was, however, more than compensated by movements in the opposite direction and by the middle of September the figure for total monetary gold stock stood at a maximum of 5,015 million dollars: the golden armor of the United States currency seemed to grow stronger as the Federal Reserve System serenely sailed through those troubled months.

For the withdrawals which began on Sept. 20, the day on which the Bank of England suspended gold payments, the writer has no other explanation to offer but that this event suddenly convinced the world that no currency was to be trusted and that it thereupon discovered weaknesses and inflationary possibilities in the American position, among other things the possibility of a domestic run and the comparatively small amount of gold that was "free" within the American definition. With this the fact accords well that it was in the first instance the European central banks which made haste to convert their holdings of American exchange into gold. The gold exports to France, Belgium, the Netherlands, and Switzerland which ensued had not under these circumstances the classical but exactly the opposite effect: there was a "crisis of the dollar" during which forward dollars in Paris fell to a discount of from 5 to 10 per cent, President Hoover's Second Plan (Oct. 6) becoming another argument, although perhaps no *reason,* for feeling pessimistic about the dollar. But on Oct. 22 Mr. Laval arrived in New York. And the fact that his and Mr. Hoover's *professio fidei* sufficed to stop the efflux and even to reverse it proves the comparative innocuousness of the intermezzo. In (February and) May and June 1932 a similar wave of withdrawals occurred, though on a smaller scale. Reversal in the second half of the year this time left the country's total monetary gold stock slightly increased—release from earmark and domestic production, etc., more than balancing exports—while it had decreased, though only by 133.4 million dollars in 1931.

With due respect to "psychology," no major feature of the conditions in this country can possibly be ascribed to either those gold movements themselves or such effect as they had on the structure of interest rates. But another element asserted itself more and more as 1931 wore on, *viz.*, the debt and especially the mortgage situation. Its importance is not adequately measured by the number of bank suspensions, although it was formidable: in 1931 2,298 banks had to pull down their shutters or, more significantly, 1,702 from September 1931 to January 1932, the period of the second epidemic, which was, of course, a major factor in the general slump of the first half of 1932 and the then soaring figure of business failures. Nor is it adequately measured by the losses incurred by banks and other creditors on bad debts. Certain classes of the latter, debts from installment sales for instance, behaved remarkably well. But the strain and drain of the repayments that were successfully made—Professor Fisher's debt-deflation—and the general awareness of the fact that the value of collateral was impaired and the net worth of so many people negative, partly enforced and partly suggested restriction of operations all round, pressed on prices, decreased employment. There is nothing astonishing in the fact that this situation did not assert itself fully until about a year after the setting in of depression in our sense. It takes time (and an altogether abnormal burden of debt incurred) for it to develop and for people to realize it and to cease to act on the hope of speedy recovery. And it will then—this is not the only case of its kind as an analysis of 1875–1876 would show—cause dents and slumps in the interval in which deep depression should be giving way to more gentle descent.

This being the diagnosis of the nature of American "incidents and accidents," how far were their effects plus the fundamental processes of depression influenced by recovery policy or anything else government and federal reserve banks did? That policy must, again, be defined in terms of actual measures and not in terms of disconnected, often contradictory, always inadequate pronouncements. What strikes us first is the handling of the international situation by the coordinated efforts of the government and the reserve system with a view, (*a*) to avoiding or mitigating breakdown of foreign credit structures by direct help or by refraining from pressing American claims; (*b*) to relaxing tension by the moratorium of political payments; and (*c*) to minimizing repercussions on the domestic money market. As regards the last point, the aim was achieved to a greater extent than is generally believed. We have seen that prompt action had, soon after the crash of 1929, reduced money-market conditions to a state of ease which—for "natural" reasons—prevailed through 1930 and still more so in the first part of 1931. The rate of the Federal Reserve Bank of New York went down to 1.5 per cent on May 7. Nevertheless, the reserve system bought from June to August another 130 millions of governments, with the result not only that member banks in the main centers accumulated considerable excess reserves and that bond yields were forced down, but also that new financing revived.[1] But the efflux of short balances after Sept. 20 put member banks into debt again and also forced many of them to sell bonds. And until the Glass-Steagall Bill (signed February 1932) removed the obstacle to their borrowing from reserve banks, which lay in the scarcity of eligible paper, by permitting loans on hitherto noneligible collateral, and the obstacle to further open-market purchases of the reserve system by permitting governments to be used as collateral for Federal reserve notes, that is, through 5 months, there was indeed that "deflationary pressure" of which so much has been made by some students of the depression. But this pressure was altogether unequal to the inferences that have been drawn from it.

Although the rediscount rate of the Federal Reserve Bank of

[1] While this was going on, however, production and employment, from June on, decreased strongly. Once more, such an experience, while not in itself sufficient to dispose of certain theories about the efficacy of either rates or open-market operations, should not be lightly brushed aside. In this case it cannot be urged that the power of the spiral was unbreakable. For 5 months had preceded during which business had been "looking up."

New York was, in obedience to the rules of financial tradition, raised to 2.5 per cent on Oct. 9 and to 3.5 on Oct. 15 and kept there to Feb. 26, when it was reduced to 3 per cent, rates charged by member banks to customers, which had reached a monthly minimum of 3.93 per cent for September 1931, increased to a monthly maximum of but 4.72 for March 1932. This is the real test of the severity of the pressure exerted, and on the strength of the most common experience it disposes of the idea that there was discouragement of industrial and commercial business. Immediately, however, after the president's signature had been affixed to the Glass-Steagall Act, the reserve system embarked upon the biggest open-market operation in its history, buying $1.11 billion governments from March to August, driving down rates all round and piling up excess reserves, more than balancing the effect of the gold efflux in May and June which this policy produced.

The National Credit Corporation (articles filed Oct. 13, 1937), the Home Loan Banks (bill signed July 22, 1932) and the Reconstruction Finance Corporation (the original bill signed Jan. 22, the extension, Emergency Relief and Construction bill, July 21) represent the attempts made to mend what, in fact, were the most important consequences of domestic "accidents and incidents," the removal of which would allow the system to recover. The inadequacy of the first measure to improve materially the banking situation is obvious, as are the limitations of the second, which, however, within its limits did something toward improving things in one sector of the mortgage embroglio. Both were far surpassed in importance by the third, which, especially as extended by the Emergency Relief and Construction Act, pegged a number of tottering structures, thus stopping up some sources of infection from which cumulative disorders would otherwise have spread, especially among banks and trust companies, railroads, building and loan associations, insurance companies, and mortgage loan companies. By Sept. 30, 1932, the grand total actually advanced—not merely authorized—amounted to nearly 1.2 billion dollars, of which 185 millions had then been already repaid, and the corporation had issued 750 million dollars of 3.5 per cent notes, 600 of which were taken by the Treasury. These few data suffice to indicate the aims and financial nature of the measure during the first 8 months of the Corporation's life and to appraise the kind and extent of the influence it can have exerted on the economic processes around the lower turning point of the index of production. Primarily intended as a support to banks and cognate institutions, and as an agency to carry part of the burden of loans that were non-eligible in the sense of the reserve bank legislation, its scope naturally included the only type of big business that was seriously threatened, railroads. The rationale of this is as obvious as are the results: additional disasters were averted, but not much positive impulse was imparted by it.

Also something was done under this scheme, especially in its extended edition, for agricultural credit institutions—new regional agricultural credit corporations were created, for instance —for financing the carrying and marketing of farm products and so on, and this worked in with institutions and policies previously established for the benefit of the agrarian interest. But as compared with the plight of a large part of the agrarian sector, all that was done during those two years was surprisingly inadequate. Since 1929 the index of farm products at the farm had fallen by over 60 per cent. Total figures of gross revenue from agricultural production—which, according to the estimates of the Department of Agriculture, was about 9.4 billion dollars in 1930, somewhat less than 7 in 1931, and about 5 in 1932—and nation-wide indices of land values—as of Mar. 1, that index was 115 in 1930, 106 in 1931, 89 in 1932 (1912 to 1914 = 100, maximum of 170 occurring in 1920)—do not tell the whole tale. For a minority, but a nonnegligible one, net income must have been negative, and for a considerable minority net worth of the farm must have been zero or less. Foreclosures increased rapidly and so did the proportion of forced sales that were due to tax delinquency. Hence, it is clear that the process of depression was in the agrarian sector allowed to go on even in directions in which it would have been most easy and for a conservative government, one would think, most imperative to stop it.

The Emergency Relief and Construction Act (Sec. 1, Title I) marks a new departure in authorizing expenditure for relief and work relief, a little more than two years after such a measure was indicated according to our schema, or a little more than one year after the plateau of 1931 had crumbled. No measurable effects can, however, have emanated from the 35.5 million dollars which were made available and the 14.2 millions which were actually spent for that purpose to the end of September 1932. The mentality which had such difficulty in reconciling itself to this—anything but novel or radical—course of action and the persistence of which is as curious as the violence of the reaction it produced, also asserted itself in the incessant appeals of the chief executive for retrenchment of public expenditure and increase of taxation (*e.g.*, messages and pronouncements of Dec. 1, 1931, of Jan. 8, of Mar. 8, of Apr. 4, and of May 5, 1932.) In some cases there were special reasons for this, *e.g.*, the weakness of the dollar exchange in March and at the beginning of May 1932. But in all cases account must be taken of the fact that that mentality was, until it changed into its opposite, a datum of the situation which it was hardly possible to modify to just the extent that would have seemed rational. Under these circumstances a "budget crisis" was no matter of indifference. And adherence in principle to what were considered sound methods of finance was not unlikely to help recovery as well as to facilitate fiscal normalization after the depression, provided it went not beyond what was necessary to convince everybody that the budget would automatically be balanced *in future* while for the time being expenditure was allowed to unbalance it. This is precisely what the administration actually tried to do. Owing to the insuperable prejudice that defeated the sales tax (Mar. 24), little came of the first part of the program, and the tax bill signed June 6 and the omnibus economy bill signed June 30, 1932, cannot have had any but reassuring "psychological" effects. But the second part was all the more fully carried into effect. According to an estimate used before, the net Federal income-generating expenditure amounted to 1,748 million in 1931 and 1,646 million in 1932 (calendar years). There cannot be any doubt that this was the most directly effective part of the government's policy—the real Emergency Relief—which only gained in effectiveness by being coupled with official emphasis on those "sound" principles that at first sight appear to be at variance with it. The inference is that it prevented much potential disaster. Yet since that expenditure—to which, of course, a very low multiplier would have to be applied—did not stop the shrinkage in total outside debits, which fell throughout the year, the inference seems reasonable that, although by partly compensating the influence of Incidents and Accidents it facilitated the turning of the tide, it did not turn it.

We will finally glance at the third epidemic among banks,

which belongs—as a belated installment—in the nexus of events we are now surveying, although it ran its course entirely within incipient recovery, lending it for a month or two all the colors of deep depression. It started in November—the banking holiday in Nevada declared on the first of that month may be taken as the starting point—gathered momentum in January and February and was cut short by emergency legislation on Mar. 9, 1933. The suspensions and holidays spread from Feb. 14 on until on Mar. 5, almost complete stoppage of banking having greeted the new president on his inauguration, they had to be ratified by Congress. This time agricultural distress, more precisely the agricultural mortgage situation, was not merely a contributory cause but the main one, as is seen from the fact that the hurricane started in the agrarian states of the middle and farther West and then moved to the East, thus collecting the fine for the neglect of the agrarian plight. This suffices to insert that panic into our picture. Its features are well known. Distrust in banks, to some extent coupled with a distrust in the currency, led to indiscriminate withdrawals of deposits and forced the banks in turn to withdraw currency from reserve banks—member banks (in the official sense) withdrew over 1.7 billions between Feb. 8 and Mar. 3—and from New York correspondents who lost almost 800 millions in this way. On Mar. 2 and 3 alone, money "in circulation" increased by nearly 700 millions, federal reserve credit outstanding by nearly 730. Loss of reserves and increase of notes outstanding reduced excess gold reserves of the reserve banks by 1.1 billion dollars to 400 millions. Domestic difficulties were increased by a simultaneous efflux of gold from the country which amounted to over 270 millions in February and March. The New York Reserve Bank had to rediscount with and to sell governments to other reserve banks. After the banking holiday and under the pressure of the Emergency Banking Act of Mar. 9 (amended by the Act of Mar. 24) gold coins and certificates speedily flowed back, over 600 millions returning to the reserve banks before the end of March, so that their excess gold reserves were, thereby and by the reduction of the amount required to be held against notes outstanding, increased to 1,172 millions. In spite of the restrictions to which gold movements had been subjected, the international position of the dollar was remarkably strong at the end of March. Member banks (in the official sense) holding about 90 per cent of all member bank deposits were reopened by license on Mar. 15. By the middle of 1933 the number of All Banks (including private banks under state supervision and mutual and stock saving banks) operating under license—no doubt many very weak ones among them—was 14,530.

The immediate consequences of that panic, the new spiral it set in motion, do not call for additional comment; but its ulterior consequences cannot be too strongly emphasized. It completely demoralized all classes and, by doing so, fundamentally changed the problem before the incoming administration. Without it—and it was certainly an avoidable incident—recovery policy would have been confronted with an entirely different situation. As it was, the psychic framework of society, which till then had borne up well, was at last giving way. Nobody for the time being foresaw anything but continuing disaster, and everybody was resolved not to put up with it any longer. The talk about impending revolution presumably was nonsense; but it characterizes well the prevailing state of the public mind, which, bewildered and exasperated to the utmost, clamored for political action in redress of what every group in its own way felt to be some grievous wrong. Politicians and "intellectuals," suddenly moved into a position of saviors and judges, had a rich keyboard to play on. But the mentality of the country, the traditions of the victorious party, the nature of the catastrophe that had to be dealt with immediately, and the strength of the inflationist interests united the majority of them on monetary expansion.

4. We now return to the question whether other time series confirm the location of the bottom of the fourth Juglar which above has been determined mainly from the behavior of physical output. That they otherwise behaved as we should expect, taking account of the incidents and accidents just discussed, is obvious. Money rates in particular do not seem to require additional comment—in this country the third banking epidemic failed to produce panic rates and only interrupted the downward course for a short time, as the gold panic of September-October 1931 had done: bankers' acceptance rate for 90 days' unindorsed bills was 1-1/8 per cent on Feb. 28 and only 2 per cent on Mar. 31, 1933, other rates moving correspondingly.

The index of prices of all listed stocks clearly indicates the trough for June–July 1932 and reacts well to the incipient recovery throughout the third quarter of that year. But outside bank debits (and dollar volume of department-store sales) continued their downward course, with but an insignificant upward movement in the last (department-store sales in the third) quarter, right into 1933, and thus at first sight seem to cast doubt on our location of the trough. Considering, however, the persistence of the fall in price level and the fact that bank debits were, of course, particularly sensitive to the banking calamity, this does not mean much. Moreover, incipient recovery is compatible with some further shrinkage of total dollar volume of business operations. It would be compatible even with some further increase in failures—although in this case maximum of failures actually occurred at the trough. These and other symptoms may be likened to those symptoms of disease which often show most markedly in convalescence. The real question arises with respect to employment and prices.

As noticed before and as we should expect, the number of workmen employed throughout fell less and increased[1] less than production, and also lagged behind it. The annual minimum, of course, occurs for 1932. More important than this, employment in manufacturing industries began to increase, slightly at first, in the second half of July. The Federal Reserve Board's index then records some more than seasonal net increase for August, though there was decrease in the automobile and allied, as well as in the machinery, industries. Increase spread in September and persisted to the middle of November—when employment in the automobile industry increased considerably—after which there was more than seasonal decline in December and January. Unemployment behaved accordingly. As in Germany, however, a new low point occurred in the first quarter of 1933, which in this case is amply accounted for by the banking crisis.

But price levels declined unequivocally through 1932 and for some time after in all countries that remained on the gold standard and in some that did not, and the failure of other series to display trough and recovery in 1932 is primarily due to this fact. Since this might prove disturbing to the reader who has followed so far but still holds on to his habit of associating cyclical phases

[1] It will be recalled that this is due not only to statistical causes and to the fact that workmen are not promptly discharged, so that at the beginning production increases simply in function of decreasing short-time or underutilization, but also to the changes in production functions (rationalizations).

primarily and even causally with movements of the price level, it is necessary to remind him that the processes of recovery do not require that price level should first rise or even cease to fall. It will be useful to recall how we should expect it to behave at such a juncture, *i.e.*, at the beginning of the recovery of a Juglar (preceded by a Kitchin prosperity) which lies within a Kondratieff depression. On the one hand, although there may be belated price reductions—in some cases induced precisely by producers realizing that, paralysis being over, reductions may now have some effect in stimulating demand—the bulk of wholesale prices will, in fact, recover from panic lows. But, on the other hand, such "correctional" movements are superimposed on a fundamental tendency that works against their effect on the index. The price level should in every neighborhood of equilibrium be at a lower figure than in the preceding neighborhood, and in a Juglar within a Kondratieff depression this tendency may result in its recovery phase ending up with a price level below that of the lower turning point. Owing to the violence of the break in prices during the preceding Juglar depression, this would not have been likely to happen in this case even without the subsequent efforts to raise prices by political action. But that any rise in prices that may have been due in reaction to depressive excesses was slow in coming about and even that the fall in wholesale prices and in cost of living persisted for several months after the turning point of the cyclical process is neither surprising nor a reason to question our dating, let alone to date the cyclical trough February 1933. It should be observed that this argument is independent of the fact that for this country the bank holidays and the events that led up to them provide a special and, according to our diagnosis, an "accidental" cause for that trough, and therefore suffice to rule out that dating; for although this is true, the fall in price-level graphs also went on in other countries.

Particulars of price movements would merit discussion. We must limit ourselves to the following remarks. First, barring the effects of monetary changes, the fall in price level and in cost of living was remarkably uniform. When all qualifications on the score of comparability have been made, it is still significant to note, for example, that the American and German indices of wholesale prices yield, if 1929 is taken as base year, practically coincident curves and that cost of living fell from 1929 to 1932 by about 22 per cent in both countries. And this is not merely due to the influence of the international prices which enter the indices.

Second, it follows from the argument of this book as a whole and more particularly from what has been said in the preceding chapter that that fall is not adequately characterized by being called an unforeseen disaster or a catastrophe of the price structure wantonly wrought by monetary factors or the vicious spiral—debt deflation, in particular—and the like. No doubt these and other elements contributed to the violence and, in many individual cases of raw materials and semifinished products, to the extent of the drop from, say, the middle of 1931 on, when wholesale prices had fallen by about 22 per cent of the 1929 average. But it has been shown that a price level markedly below that of 1913 was what would certainly have prevailed without the war and what, even with the war, was bound to emerge in time as a result of the evolutionary mechanism and as a consequence of the industrial revolution of the age.

Third, it has often been pointed out how differently different groups of commodities were affected and how rigorously the price system was changed thereby. The difference between the behavior of prices of raw materials and the behavior of prices of manufactured products has attracted particular attention and been held to have not only reflected but also intensified the growing disequilibrium. All this is true to some extent, but it does not tell the whole story either as to facts or as to inference. The minimum of the B.L.S. index wholesale prices (February 1933) was 62 per cent of its value for July 1929. The National Bureau's index of physical volume of total production gives for the minimum *year* almost exactly 62 per cent of the annual figure for 1929. But one component, construction, contracted to 31.5 per cent, while the index of building material prices was still 75.9 per cent, and the hourly wage rate about 80 per cent of their 1929 values at the trough in February. Here we have an obvious case of maladjustment. On the other hand, agricultural raw products show no influence of the depression on output for 1931 and at most a small one for 1932: "the farmer accepts the cut" both because he works under conditions of competition and because of the technological peculiarities of his production. The opposite reasons do not, however, wholly explain the fact that output of mineral raw materials contracted a little more than total output; for there were, in addition, elements of prime costs which failed to fall correspondingly, especially wages. These elements—selling charges among them—acquire, of course, increasing importance for manufacturing industry as we proceed toward the finished article of consumption, and there is, hence, little to be surprised at in the February figure of the price index for processed nonfood consumers' goods (73.2 per cent of that of July 29). But many manufacturing industries also "took the cut," for instance, petroleum refining, food, tobacco, and leather product industries, paper and printing, clothing, and house furnishing. Equipment industries did so to a much lesser extent or not at all. But precisely in their case, reduction of prices would hardly have stimulated demand.

These observations as in keeping with the view previously arrived at on the subject of price rigidities. They are also relevant to the question of the nature and consequences of the disruption by the depressive process of the preexisting structure of (relative) prices. Our model does lead us to expect dispersions—because of rigidities as well as for other reasons—which spell disequilibrium. But it does not follow that every change wrought by depression in the price system necessarily falls into that category or that return to equilibrium necessarily requires the reconstruction of the preceding system of relative prices. The contrary may well be the case—an example is the price of copper, which the opening of new sources of supply had turned into an untenable maladjustment that would simply be conserved by uncritical attempts to restore either price or income parities. Nor does it follow that every change in the price system which does fall into that category necessarily impedes recovery. It may facilitate it or be harmless. An example of the first possibility is afforded by any panicky and temporary drop in foreign-produced raw materials; an example of the second, by the short-term rigidity of prices of equipment goods, for recovery does not typically start from expansion of real investment.

Adjusted demand deposits of reporting member banks in reserve cities outside New York, after keeping up to almost the middle of 1931 fell sharply to May 1932, after which there was a small increase that was just about wiped out in the first quarter of 1933. "Country banks" taken separately displayed but a decreased rate of decrease in the second half of 1932. Net demand deposits of reporting member banks outside New York City fell after the middle of 1931, first at an increasing then at a decreasing rate, the curve flattening out and then slightly rising in 1932. This is not exactly what we should expect but is accounted for by the changes in the investment item, which increased strongly through 1930 and the first third of 1931, then fell to the beginning of 1932 and increased again to almost the end of the year, while All Other Loans fell strongly and almost continuously throughout and beyond. The index of rate of turnover of demand deposits in principal cities declined at a decreasing rate near the end of 1932, when it began to rise again.

National Income produced, evaluated at 1929 prices, fell from 1930 to 1931 by a larger amount than it had fallen from 1929 to 1930, and from 1931 to 1932, the minimum, by a larger amount than from 1930 to 1931. Net corporate income became negative to the amount of 2,850 millions in 1931, and for 1932 displays the maximum loss of 5,200 millions. The number of corporations reporting loss was greater than the number reporting positive revenue as early as 1930; in 1931 the relation was 284:176; in 1932 it was 366:80. Still more significant are the figures of corporate accumulation, though the limited value of such accounting items must again be borne in mind. Already in 1930 it was negative to the amount of 4,110 millions. It was minus 6,040 millions in 1931, minus 6,550 millions in 1932, and minus 3,060 millions for 1933. "Business Savings" as measured by the Department of Commerce were minus 4,903 millions in 1930, minus 8,052 millions in 1931, minus 8,942 millions in 1932, and only in 1935 reached a modest positive value for which year Professor Kuznets' "net savings of enterprises" are still at minus 3,252 millions. The fact that the minima mostly (not for national income measured in current dollars, however,) occur for 1932 is valueless for us, because there can be little doubt that government action in 1933 is responsible for that.

For the moment the situation that faced the incoming administration looked untenable. The unpopular necessity of refinancing corporate business becomes particularly obvious if, accepting again the National Bureau's method of correcting corporate accumulation by subtracting the difference between depreciation on a cost basis and depreciation on the basis of current prices we realize that the sum total of those accumulations for the period from 1919 to 1933 turns out to be minus 7,110 millions. This does not mean that the sum total of cash items fell spectacularly. On the contrary, cash was precisely the item that actually shrank least as compared with 1929—from about 7.5 to about 6.1 billions in 1932—although omission of current revaluation formally also kept up others; needless to repeat that this phenomenon was wholly consequential and merely reflected but did not cause the spiral. Nor does that mean that dividends fell as much as earnings which were minus 0.6 per cent in 1931 and minus 2.8 in 1932, only utilities, foods, beverages, tobacco products, chemical and allied products, and printing and publishing, staying on the positive side throughout. Not only stockholders in many corporations but, if considered as a class, *all* stockholders were to a considerable extent allowed to live on their capital. Thus already for 1930 negative accumulation ensued from the payment of a total of net cash dividends amounting to nearly 5.7 billions, while all the net income that remained after tax payments was less than 1.3. And in 1931 4.2 billions of dividends compare with a net deficit plus taxes of over 3.2. While we shall think about the long-run effect of this according to the theory of accumulation or saving that we make our own, we cannot differ about the remedial or contraspiral effects such a behavior must have had in the short run—however much they may have been overcompensated by other factors—particularly since it preceded the setting in of deep depression. Flotations of new securities accord with those contours. Corporate issues, foreign included, were still 1,736 millions in 1931 but only 325 millions in 1932, while municipal borrowing was active and the Federal government borrowed over 3 billions net.

Industrial pay rolls fell, of course, more strongly than employment and arrived, in the middle of 1932, at about 40 per cent of the 1923 to 1925 averages. Per cent fall, less steep in 1931 than it had been in 1930, then came to a halt. After declining substantially from the middle of June to the middle of July, practically in all manufacturing industries and many others, aggregate factory wage payments increased though subseasonally in August and more significantly in September and October, after which they dipped again to a new low point in February–March 1933. Real wage bill (pay roll by cost-of-living index) fell considerably. Average per capita weekly earnings in the United States, as per monthly data of the Bureau of Labor Statistics, declined from 1929 to 1932 by about one-third in manufacturing, only insignificantly with public utilities and only by 12.5 per cent in retail and wholesale trade. The fall came about at a percentage rate that increased to 1932 and continued in 1933 but at a decreasing rate, the total reduction in the end amounting to about 36 per cent in money and about 16 per cent in real terms.

Hourly rates fell, to the middle of 1933, but very much less—in some industries, such as anthracite coal mining, not at all. In manufacturing they declined from 59 cents in 1929 to 50 in 1932 and 49 in 1933. This would yield a gain in real terms, and so would to a lesser extent the course of money wages of unskilled labor as recorded by the Bureau of Public Roads. But no estimate which aims at a single figure of nation-wide significance can possibly yield a *fall* in real rates.

Now two things are obvious from this behavior of hourly rates. First, they cannot have been a factor in starting the depression, whatever the theory we may entertain on the subject: their fall cannot, because they kept up well at first and only reacted to a depression already in full swing; their previous rise cannot, because it was altogether inadequate to produce that result. Second, if there is anything at all in the view that the long-run level of American money wage rates, as distinguished from their cyclical variations, was "too high" in the sense that it was partly responsible for the unemployment of the twenties, then it is clear that the fall which occurred during the depression was inadequate to correct that level, although the latter might have been corrected by a subsequent rise in prices occurring without an increase in wage rates.

But it is more difficult to say whether wage rates, by behaving as they did, intensified or alleviated the depression. Since the dominating factor in the short-run situations, especially of "deep" depression, is the downward shift of individual firms' "demand curves" for labor, and since many of them no doubt become less elastic in the process of shifting downward, it is not only likely that actual reductions failed, for the time being, to call forth additional demand for labor sufficient to raise the total wage bill above what it otherwise would have been, and that greater reductions would have still more completely failed to do so, but there must also have been cases in which reductions of rates simply resulted in a decrease of total output and employment.

This argument progressively loses force as the system approaches the recovery point and beyond it the opposite conclusion suggests itself. Then our question admits of a much more definite answer. We still have the same classes of cases before us. But their relative importance changes when "demand curves" for labor tend to shift upward and to become more elastic. Resumption or expansion of operations begins, as we know, in individual spots. It certainly did so begin in the case before us, so that the effect on prime costs of individual firms is all that has to be taken into account. Firms try to resume or to expand operations in a situation which, while no longer discouraging, yet does not offer those enticements—profits in our sense or any of those gains which are induced by the emergence of profits—that later in the cycle may make moderate variations of wage rates a matter of indifference. They are likely to calculate closely. Even in the short run they have, particularly if starting afresh after a shutdown, some latitude as to the combination of factors that they are going to adopt. The prevailing cheapness of money will give them a slant toward mechanization, which may be intensified by an increase and counteracted by the previous decrease in wage rates. Hence pay rolls are likely to increase faster in the absence than in the presence of an increase in wage rates, as long as there is abnormal unemployment. Thus it seems permissible to infer, not only that such fall in rates as occurred facilitated inception of recovery, but also that a stronger fall would, at least in the American case, have facilitated it still more.

D. Recovery and Recovery Policy in the United States from 1933 to 1935.—What, according to our schema, should have been a Juglar recovery covers the period from the autumn of 1932 to the first months of 1935.[1] Separate treatment is necessary, not only because of the difference in phase, but because of the presence of another difference which while, strictly speaking, but one of degree is so important as to amount to one in kind: while, as we have seen, recovery policy was a distinctly minor factor in 1931 and not of decisive importance in 1932,

[1] More precisely, our experimental count gives from the middle of November 1932 to March 1935 inclusive, and within this period a Kitchin recession to the end of August 1933, a Kitchin depression to the middle of June 1934, and a Kitchin revival covering the remaining months. Again, this is not intended even as a reference schema but merely as an illustration. But it should be observed that, properly understood, it is not out of step with actual events.

it thenceforth dominates the scene. This is so obvious as to raise the question whether there is any sense at all in going on speaking of cyclical phases and trying to date them, or to relate actual business situations to our process. Many economists would not hesitate to answer in the negative. Theories have, in fact, been offered which are explicitly or implicitly based on the hypothesis that either from 1914 or from 1929—the beginning according to some writers of a series of completely new vicissitudes of capitalism that are unheard of in the sense that previous history does not present anything at all comparable—or, finally, from 1933, a new economic pattern has more or less suddenly emerged which superseded the previous one for good and calls for a new analytic model and fundamentally new assumptions as to both data and mechanisms, especially with respect to the investment process.

We are not concerned with the methodology underlying those theories and with their intrinsic merits or demerits. We are face to face not with a question of principle but with a question of fact. The only principle involved is the one which has been stressed throughout this book and which rests on the *certainty* that the economic process of capitalist society will eventually turn into something fundamentally different and on the ever-present *possibility* that our process be temporarily blotted out by the action of more powerful factors, such as, for instance, ruled events in Germany 1914 to 1923. As to the facts, we not only know that all the essential features of the postwar period up to the world crisis, but also those of the world crisis itself answer perfectly to expectation from our model, *i.e.*, from past experience. Moreover, we know something else that sweeps from our path what otherwise would be an extremely thorny problem: we need not ask whether the system "could have" recovered without political action stimulating it out of a state of prostration. For it did.[1]

[1] The author, who so often is painfully aware of the fact that his argument has to contend against a powerful aversion to its real or supposed implications, thoroughly enjoys the psychological vantage ground over which he is traveling at this point. For any aversion of readers against accepting the writer's opinion will be much mitigated by the only alternative open to them, which to many would be no less distasteful: whoever refuses to believe that the recovery in 1932 occurred in the ordinary course of the working of the system will have to believe instead, that Mr. Hoover turned the tide. That his ad-

This being so, affirmative answer to our question is unavoidable: there is not only point in going on to relate the course of events to our process—in the sense that we assume every one of the successive situations to have been the resultant of the working of this process and of the effects of government action, both, of course, not only superimposing themselves on but also influencing each other—but there is no choice but to do so. For it would be contrary to all experience and common sense, though of course no logical impossibility, that a process, which can be strictly proved to have been running its course since at least the sixteenth century and right to the end of 1932, should have come to a stop suddenly on Mar. 4, 1933. It should be observed, however, how severely our task restricts the scope of our discussion of the policies of the period. What are their most important aspects to many—to those in particular, who welcome them as the dawn of an epoch of social reconstruction—must, if we are to focus our attention on the mere effects of those policies on the process which is the subject of this book, be excluded to the point of exposing the writer to the indictment that he is completely lacking in social vision and in the grasp of the broad social issues involved. While nothing can be done about this, it is hoped that enough has been done to protect the argument that is to follow from the different, though cognate, misunderstanding which may result from our speaking of recovery policy as an external factor acting on our process. It has been pointed out not only that economic—or any—policy grows out of and is, though not uniquely, shaped by the economic situation with which it attempts to deal, but also that in the case before us the short-run situation in the spring of 1933 was such as to force any but the strongest hands irrespectively of prevailing preferences for or aversions to "planning."

1. Thus narrowed down, our task may be further simplified by excluding a number of measures which cannot have had major effects on successive business situations or which cannot have had them before 1935. Nobody will, for example, attribute major consequences to the Federal Economy Act of Mar. 20, 1933, or to the revision of veterans' claims (Sec. 20 of Inde-

---

ministration would, but for the whim of the political calendar, have come out with flying colors and admist a universal clapping of hands is, for reasons of political psychology, very plausible in any case.

pendent Offices Appropriation Act of June 16, 1933) or—though some *stimulating* effect, extending beyond the industries directly affected, is of course beyond doubt in this case—to the modification and the subsequent repeal of prohibition. Most of the more than 80 acts passed by the Seventy-third Congress up to June 16, 1933, may for our purpose be dismissed as both uncontroversial and unimportant, although the sum total of them, no doubt, influenced—mainly steadied—the existing situation. The only measure of this class for which this may be and actually has been called into question is the Securities Act of May 27, 1933. The writer would have passed it by, thinking that it was not only the kind of thing that has, ever since South Sea Bubbles days, often been done after abnormally severe breakdowns revealing reckless financial practice, but also a sober and well-drafted piece of legislation, from which no depressive influence could emanate. But it caused a flutter, and not only in interested quarters, the main point attacked being the construction of the liabilities imposed on issuing houses and security dealers. These, however, do not seem to amount to more than responsibility for what one "knows or ought to know" or to enforce more than the care habitually taken by any decent firm. Much more plausible reasons than this act are available in order to explain the stagnation in nonpublic issues at that time.

Recovery was substantially facilitated by the Emergency Banking Act of Mar. 9, 1933, which provided machinery for the reopening of closed banks, by the Banking Act of June 16, 1933, which introduced a number of important reforms—the most important refer to strengthening the Federal Reserve System's power over members, particularly with a view to regulating extension of credit for speculative purposes; to holding company and security affiliates; to stricter centralization of open-market operations; to branch banking, and, for us most important of all, to deposit "insurance"—and by Title II of the Emergency Farm Relief Act of May 12, 1933, which dealt with the agricultural credit and especially with the refinancing problem. The Farm Mortgage Corporation Act of Jan. 31, 1934, and the Home Owners' Loan Acts of June 13, 1933, and April 27, 1934, were similarly to cope with another thoroughly frozen part of the credit structure and thus also to relieve the banking situation—they look quite conservative with the homage they pay to "local thrift." We will add further examples of measures of this type:

the extension in various directions (insurance companies especially) of the scope of the Reconstruction Finance Corporation's assistance by the Acts of June 10 and 14, 1933; the Emergency Railroad Transportation Act providing facilities for consolidations, rationalizations, and reorganizations; and the United States Employment Service Act of June 6, 1933.

These and similar measures did not make recovery. They helped to provide conditions, rather than stimuli, for the process of recovery to resume quickly after the catastrophe of the spring of 1933, by solving individual problems, removing impediments and potential storm centers, constructing safeguards, allaying fears, and, on balance, improving the general atmosphere—all of which would otherwise have been the source of prolonged difficulties and waste. In these respects the combined effect of the recovery measures of this type must be rated high, although, if they had stood alone, we should have no hesitation in speaking of a process of recovery propelled by the forces embodied in our model.

2. We shall arrive at no very different conclusion as regards the two towering monuments of early New Deal policy, the AAA and the NRA. All the great and small questions of principle that surround them and all the ultimate effects they had or eventually would have had on the institutional framework of the economic process of this country and on this economic process itself being excluded from our discussion, we easily arrive —discarding for the moment the provisions on money inserted into the act creating the one and the labor provisions contained in the other act—at the result that, on balance, both of them promoted recovery of the usual type without replacing it by a recovery that would have to be explained on different principles. They certainly paralyzed, and replaced by others, certain parts of the ordinary capitalist machine but, taking the national organism as a whole, in a way and to an extent which was corrective rather than constructive.

This is especially clear in the case of the agricultural adjustment policy. It was to deal, unlike NRA, not with an emergency simply but with an emergency in which a long development creating fundamentally untenable conditions had suddenly come to a head. Wholesale liquidation of farms, impinging on an industrial unemployment which itself was unmanageable for the moment and which had set into motion a current of remigration to the land, would have been the "automatic" method of restoring equilibrium. The alternative to this—what we have called "orderly retreat"—precisely implied temporary or even permanent preservation of disequilibrium in the agrarian sector to be unavoidably financed by the (normal) surplus of the industrial sector. To do this would, *ipso facto,* facilitate general recovery. It would reestablish something like the previous processes in the agrarian sector and the previous relations of the agrarian to the industrial sector. Thus it would also relieve the debt and banking situation and thereby stop up a source of actual and possible cumulative depressive effects. At the same time it could not, the relative financial strength of the two sectors being what it is, exert pressure on the nonagricultural sector severe enough to open up another such source instead. This argument applies a fortiori in case the means transferred were to be created *ad hoc* or taken from sources other than that part of nonagrarian incomes which was being currently spent. But it should be observed that it would also apply if nonagrarian consumers' expenditure had been reduced by an equal amount, *i.e.,* if the agrarian Paul had really only received consumers' dollars taken from the industrial Peter. The problem thus being perfectly clear and soluble, a very simple program suggests itself of refinancing bona fide farmers threatened by foreclosure, of nationalizing the marketing of, and particularly the export trade in, agricultural products, and of strictly planning production—into which program measures of more fundamental adjustment and of further rationalization could have been inserted at will. Most of this being out of the question under the Constitution and owing to the unpreparedness of public opinion, the well-known devious route was chosen (Title I of the Emergency Farm Relief Act of May 12, 1933), which raises a long string of problems peculiar to it, incidence and other effects of processing taxes among them.

But provided we agree that the net effect was to increase farm revenue considerably, we need not go into those problems since then the rest, *i.e.,* the proposition that a contribution was made to general recovery, automatically follows. It is not necessary for us either to accept palpable exaggerations of the role that the farmers' plight played in the general depression, such as a prominent authority has been guilty of in stating that 60 per cent of all the unemployed "lost their jobs because of the reductions in rural buying power"; or to share the opinion of fervent advocates about the effects of agricultural recovery on general recovery, some of whom went so far as to call the advantages accruing to agriculture a mere "incident" of a general benefit conferred on the nation; or to fall back upon doubtful theories about effects through an incident decrease in savings or, somewhat less incorrectly, nonspending; or, finally, to overlook the role of the droughts, of the depreciation of the dollar, and of general recovery itself. Net results, which are all we have, are at best difficult to interpret, and the panegyrics of the administration of the agricultural adjustment act on its own activities no doubt bear discounting. If, for example, we read in its first report that in rural communities delinquent taxes were being paid, debts owing to banks discharged, schools reopened, orders placed for clothing, furnishings, implements, automobiles and parts, all because of AAA, we cannot help feeling that a sound case is being spoiled by overstatement. It is, moreover, not easy to determine how much of the results actually attained is attributable to the basic idea, restriction of production—"paying for not producing"—and how much to other devices that were not, or not necessarily, bound up with it, such as marketing agreements and semimonopolistic export practices. The energetic tobacco program supported by the Kerr-Smith Act scored the most striking success, in fact, considerably beyond the goal envisaged, owing to particularly favorable conditions of demand. In dairying where, because of a relatively sound fundamental situation, there was much less need for action, restriction (purchase of dairy cattle) was secondary, and market agreements mainly did, not always successfully, what there was to be done. Leaving aside the somewhat equivocal results of the corn-hog action and other items, we will recall that the effect of the wheat program, whatever it might have been, was largely absorbed by the dominant effects of four successive bad harvests—1933 to 1936—so that, disregarding various supplementary measures of minor importance, the actual benefit to wheat farmers from AAA substantially reduced—except perhaps for 1934—to the benefit payments financed by the processing tax which for the three years during which the arrangement was in force, amounted to $326 million and may be likened to a simple subsidy.

The cotton program was but to a minor degree interfered with by adverse natural conditions. Participation was extensive from the outset and became still more so under the pressure of the Bankhead Act and of various privileges (seed loans, loans of the Commodity Credit Corporation) that were confined to participants. This actually did for cotton what nature did for wheat. Curtailment of acreage for 1934 and 1935 was made more effective by destruction of roughly 25 per cent of the 1933 crop. (Annual) prices to growers for 1934 were nearly double the (annual) prices for 1932—which were depressed, however, by the government holdings of over 3 million bales resulting from the operations of the Federal Farm Board 1929 to 1931, to the point of reconquering foreign markets lost (partly) through the price-pegging policy of those years—and revenue of growers rose from 483 millions to (inclusive of benefit payments) 880 millions in 1933 and 893 millions in 1934. This was not even all. For without the program, the crop of 1933 would have been one of the largest on record. In this case, of course, monetary policy also counted for more (see below) owing to the relative importance of the export interest.

Net costs and losses to the Treasury (including reduction of the import duty on sugar) were about 900 millions, which may roughly be said to constitute additional expenditure within the system. Apart from this, such additional expenditure was involved in the running of the scheme though it was originally intended to be self-supporting. Whatever we may think about technique, details, aims professed, or arguments used, the success of the policy in removing a major obstacle from the road of recovery and in reviving shriveled tissues in the economic organism is beyond reasonable doubt.

3. Title I of the National Industrial Recovery Act of June 16, 1933, as embodied in the codes of fair competition, introduced a type of state-supervised industrial self-government the gist of which was legal recognition and official encouragement, amounting to compulsion, of a modified form of the German cartel which, quite independently of this legislation, tended to grow out of the activities of trade associations. Thus it is not easy to understand the enthusiasm with which some "liberal" economists greeted a measure which associated Planning with that very restriction and price rigidity that are usually debited, as its greatest blemishes, to the account of Big Business. But it is all the easier to understand how it helped recovery: exactly as the German cartel, it pegged weak spots within industries, stopped spirals in many places, mended disorganized markets, especially

in cases of inelastic demand and of that "overproduction" which is incident to the process of underselling the obsolete. There is little doubt about its effectiveness in paralyzing, in some instances, the process of industrial transformation that was going on: the failure to see that there was such a process at all or, in fact, anything else but breakdown and deadlock was part of the philosophy of the time. There is as little doubt about its effectiveness in improving, in other instances, situations in which lack of organization really wrought wanton destruction as in the cases of oil and bituminous coal and others to which a less sweeping and spectacular measure could have confined itself.

Immediate results for the general business situation were, however, only the stronger because of the range over which this policy was indiscriminately applied and so were its purely psychological effects, which *in a situation of that kind* we have a right to consider an important factor—even Blue Eagles do count for something when, objective conditions for revival being given, it is broken morale that is the matter. Invalidation by the Supreme Court (June 1935) came when the end had been achieved and was for the administration a blessing in disguise. But aftereffects were not entirely eliminated thereby. Business had learned a lesson. The "chiseler" continued to be frowned upon. And we shall have to bear in mind that there is here a possible, if only partial, explanation of the fact that output figures failed to come up to expectation in the subsequent prosperity phase, which precisely for this reason most economists preferred to call imperfect recovery.

The *quid pro quo* which the Act and the Codes offered to possible opposition from the ranks of labor and to possible criticism of what might easily have been called antisocial tendencies, were the labor provisions. Many an objector was reconciled by the clauses on child labor, hours, and minimum wages which all codes (including the blanket code) contained, or gratified by the protection extended in Sec. 7*a* to collective bargaining, to organizing activity, and so on, which went far beyond the Norris-LaGuardia Anti-Injunction Act of 1932. The larger aspects of the progress thereby achieved in social legislation being once more beyond our scope, our only question concerns the effect on recovery of general labor policy and of wage policy in particular. As to the first, the present writer is confident that no inhibiting effect can be proved for the period under consideration.[1] As to the second, it follows from previous argument that, under the conditions of this country and of the prevailing cyclical phase, the persistent official efforts to raise the whole structure of wage rates must on balance have had an adverse effect both on the expansion of output and on employment per unit of output. While this effect was probably small during the first great upward rush in 1933, the further development of output, pay rolls, and especially employment, which can hardly be said to come up to expectation, substantiates the presence of this brake. The reader will realize that this is perfectly compatible with an opposite result in many individual cases; with such truth as there is in antisaving arguments; and with recognition of the facts that the rise in price level partly absorbed and government spending partly counteracted [2] that effect. Again, and notwithstanding the rise in price level, labor was made expensive relatively to real capital. Coupled with a cheap money policy, a high-wage-rate policy was, under the circumstances of phase and country, the very recipe for the production of a maximum of unemployment. While dampening recovery, however, this would not necessarily affect the general character and the duration of the phase.

So far we have before us the following elements of the situation in 1933. There was first incipient recovery dating from about the middle of 1932. This incipient recovery, second, had been interrupted by the banking catastrophe in the spring of 1933 and was weighed down, independently of that, by the conditions in the agrarian sector, by the results and remains of a

[1] In other words, the mere recognition of the right of collective bargaining and the elimination of the yellow-dog contract cannot in themselves have worked against recovery. It does not follow that an organized drive, facilitated by the newly acquired opportunities for action, or further legislation on the same lines might have done so. But no such drive or legislation occurred during the two years during which the NRA regulations of wages and hours, paralleled by regulations by other federal agencies and state governments were in force. The question will hence have to be touched upon again in the next section.

[2] Since government spending was in part a function of the amount of unemployment, it can even be said that any unemployment created (relatively to what unemployment there would otherwise have been) by that wage policy may possibly have induced a net increase of total expenditure in the system. It will be seen, however, that this does not invalidate our argument.

preceding state of overindebtedness in general, and by depressive factors special to certain individual industries. Third, on this pattern impinged the series of measures mentioned, all of which, with the exception of the high-wage-rate policy, were on balance remedial in effect, *i.e.*, not only devised in order to remove those millstones but actually effective in achieving this. Nothing more than these three groups of facts is necessary for us to expect a strong and even violent rebound of the system, more than compensating for the subnormal revival during the preceding six months, to be interrupted, however, by the setting in of a Kitchin depression late in the year.

This may be expressed by means of terms which have been so uncritically used as to elicit, when used now, little else but contempt: *natural* and *sound* recovery. To the former term we assign the meaning of recovery coming about in the course of the cyclical process by virtue of its mechanism. The latter term we define as a recovery that is brought about by factors which do not carry an inherent tendency to reproduce the same difficulties as, or to produce other difficulties in place of, those that they have been instrumental in overcoming: relapse is the most obvious instance of the first type, and undoing of such work of readjustment as may result from the processes of depression is an instance of the second. Natural and sound recovery are not synonymous. Whether "natural" recovery is always "sound" depends on whether we exclude all those "understandable nonessentials" which may easily land the system in an untenable situation. But inasmuch as depression itself is a pathological process, sound recovery need not be natural. In our case the recovery we now envisage would—whatever might have been the *ultimate* effects of NRA—have been substantially sound. And a natural recovery was at the bottom of it. But the midwife role of public authority was so important that it would not do to draw laissez-faire conclusions.

It is not implied that Congress or the administration "should" or "could" have stopped at the measures so far mentioned. The prevailing unemployment would in itself suffice to refute any such implication. But it is implied as a matter of diagnosis that to a greater extent than is commonly realized the recovery of 1933 can be accounted for irrespectively of the monetary and spending policies inaugurated at that time. For this proposition there is, it is true, no such proof as the constellation of facts enabled us to give for the cognate proposition that recovery started "of itself" and not simply in response to recovery policy. But there is a prima-facie case which is much strengthened by the fact that during the critical second and third quarters of 1933 the new spending program, being still in the incubating stage, cannot have had major, at least mechanical, effects[1] on the economic process. That substantially the same holds true of the monetary policy will be evident from the cursory discussion to which we now turn.

4. When banks reopened after the "holiday" in March 1933, they were estopped from paying out gold except by special Treasury permission, but only an insignificant fall in the international value of the dollar occurred. On the afternoon of Apr. 19, *i.e.*, immediately after the declaration of the (partial) embargo on gold, dollars were internationally traded in at a discount of about 9 per cent and during the following eight days at a discount which fluctuated between 8 and 12 per cent. There was no panic such as had occurred in the English case. This is highly significant. It shows, on the one hand, that international speculation did not believe in a substantial depreciation of the dollar —in spite of the fact that a bill was introduced on Apr. 20 which contained the main provisions that were later embodied in the Thomas amendment—and on the other hand, that in the absence of such speculative anticipation there was no reason why the dollar, if left to itself, should fall at all. There was, thus, a complete absence of parallelism between the fate of the dollar and the fate of the English pound. The dollar was not under economic pressure either in a short-run or in a long-run sense, either from abroad or at home. We recall in particular that it had weathered the preceding storm, the third through which it had had to sail during the depression: the reserve system had the situation well in hand, and in less than three weeks after the bank holiday over half of the amount was repaid which had previously been borrowed from reserve banks in order to meet loss of gold and withdrawals of notes from all centers and

[1] According to Mr. Currie's and Mr. Villard's figures, net federal income-generating expenditure for the year was 1,856 millions, only 210 millions more than in 1932. If the effect was more than proportionately greater than this, it can only have been due to the difference in cyclical phase.

of bankers' balances from New York. And almost all the losses of reserves suffered by reserve banks were made good.

What pressure there was, was entirely political, and it was not until the world became convinced of the imminence of "inflation" that the dollar really gave way. This conviction was the result of the passing of Title III of the Agricultural Adjustment Act of May 12, which was even officially referred to as Emergency Relief *and Inflation* Act. Although there cannot be any doubt that the interests, the exponents of which swapped votes in order to insure the passage of that act, aimed at inflation in every conceivable sense of the term, the act itself was the result of a compromise that yielded less ground to them than it seemed to yield and than almost everyone pretended to believe. Its provisions, besides being only enabling and not mandatory, offered plenty of opportunity, subsequently extended, to defeat any kind of inflation at will, and effective use was made of it up to 1937. It was clear enough, however, that at least devaluation would be unavoidable. Even so, the dollar manifested its natural strength by the hesitancy with which it fell. Therefore, when in the autumn recovery dimmed and NRA and AAA enthusiasms cooled, when, moreover, the announcement by the Reconstruction Finance Corporation of its willingness to lend to banks up to a billion for the purpose of relending failed, as it naturally would, to produce results, the administration encountered the consequent inflationist onslaught by resorting in October to a method which would bring down the dollar *without* "inflation," *viz.*, the gold-buying policy,[1] and by speedily investing the political capital thus gained in putting a stop, for the time being at least, to this type of "experiment" by the Gold Reserve (De-

[1] Inflation of the German type would, of course, automatically send down the dollar. It was to association with such inflation (though not necessarily with exactly that dose of it) that part of the support of the policy of depreciation and devaluation was due. What this group of "inflationists" overlooked was the possbiility of having the token without the substance. Although facilitating future inflation, reduction of the gold value of the dollar by the gold-buying policy was really (whatever the intention) a means of avoiding it. Its tactical virtue consisted in the fact that, in spite of being a device to avoid inflation, it would satisfy certain inflationary interests, *e.g.*, exporters and speculators, who were particularly vocal and supplied the motive power of much of the inflationary propaganda. Hence, it would break the inflationary phalanx.

valuation) Act. And still the dollar resisted: a torrent of gold turned toward this country. We will but glance at the movements in its gold stock during the February following upon the presidential proclamation of Jan. 31, which raised the price of the fine ounce from $20.67 to $35 and the value of the monetary gold stock to 7.03 billions. No less than 381 millions—a record—were imported during the month (213 of which from England) chiefly in response to the new price, banks at home and abroad taking advantage of the undervaluation of the dollar. There was also some release (8.6 millions) from earmark.

In order to appraise the effects of this policy on the economic process, it is first of all necessary to realize how much or how little it had to do with easy money. There is no doubt, of course, that the influx of gold, which already in February 1934 carried excess reserves of all member banks to the new peak of above 1 billion, was then and later the chief factor responsible for what, at least from the spring of 1935 on, will strike us as abnormally low rates. With government expenditure what it was and reviving business, for example prime bankers' acceptances (90 days) could hardly have reached 1/8 of 1 per cent by November 1934 and stayed there, nor prime commercial paper 3/4 to 1 per cent by June and fallen to 3/4 after that. But if such lows were beyond expectation from our model, prevalence of very low rates was not, and it is not very obvious that, if, for instance, New York City customers' rates steadily fell from their modest "panic peak" of 4.88 for March 1933, to 2.64 for March 1935, this was substantially more than we should have expected to find without the gold movements induced by devaluation. In other words, the latter did not *create* the conditions of monetary ease. The commercial paper rate was down to 2 per cent by the autumn of 1931 and, in spite of the subsequent rise, to less than that by the autumn of 1932, and there is nothing in the processes of incipient recovery to enforce an upturn. As far as this goes, devaluation did not lift any weight from the economic process, as is indeed obvious from the behavior above described of the dollar in 1933. Moreover, such pressure on rates as there was during that year was due not only to the depreciation but also to the open-market purchases of the Federal reserve banks, which in response to the greenback threat contained in the Inflation Act acquired 570 millions of governments from May to November and then stopped because this only served to swell excess reserves. But that step would have been possible without going off gold. Its ineffectiveness finally—a last verification of our views on the subject—goes far toward establishing the proposition that, whatever influence on rates and credit facilities was exerted by whatever external factor, the influence of these on the economic process was next to nothing.

Devaluation must, in the second place, be considered in relation to the policy of public expenditure. It has, in fact, been held that the meaning of the former primarily consists in its implementing the latter, which was what really produced results. There is, of course, some truth in this view, which is at any rate much superior to the naïve belief that redefining the gold content of the dollar would per se change the price level in the same proportion—a curious survival from the days of the commodity theory of money. For although increase in price level neither is, as a matter of principle, nor has been, as a matter of fact in this instance, the main effect of antidepression public expenditure, it is true that devaluation can, with the qualification to be mentioned presently, only act on prices if it either induces or facilitates increase in expenditure. Therefore, if public expenditure that would not otherwise have been technically possible had been made so by devaluation, we should have to list the latter among the major factors influencing the recovery process. But public expenditure perfectly adequate to produce the results that actually were produced would have been possible with the dollar at the old gold par. Devaluation may have facilitated it by removing all concern about monetary limitations, but this is all.

There remain, in the third place, direct effects. We will mention two. The year 1933 was one of monetary disorder and of widespread apprehensions about impending inflation. An impulse was thereby given to speculation in securities and commodities, which was very obvious on stock and produce exchanges. Stock prices (and prices of second-class bonds), in particular, reacted visibly and until September consistently to every drop of the international value of the dollar. The only question is how far this effect extended beyond speculation in a wide sense of the term. We have seen that the response of productive business to monetary policy is, to say the least, equivocal. The notable instances of 1896 and 1878 should suffice to show that anticipation of monetary expansion is not necessarily a propelling, and anticipation of "sound" money not necessarily a depressing influence. Nor is this at all astonishing. Hence, although the anticipations induced by going off gold certainly contributed to the hectic rise of the wholesale price index which occurred from March to July 1933, and although this spurt in turn no doubt had *some* effect on productive operations, we shall not weight that component very highly, especially in view of the fact that strong revival would in any case be understandable without it.

The other immediate effect of depreciation and devaluation is on foreign trade. The changes during our period in raw figures of either values or quantities—which are not impressive—do not in themselves prove much. As to export of United States merchandise, they are compatible with the opinion that the motorcar and machinery industries benefited somewhat. Since, however, industrial exports are in any case not importing enough to matter greatly, we need not enter into the nice questions surrounding any effort to isolate the influence of devaluation. The official index of quantity of agricultural products exported continued its downward course throughout the period, the annual figure for 1935 being a little less than 58 per cent of that for 1932. Some benefit to wheat and especially to cotton farming is, nevertheless, beyond doubt. In the latter case it also served to counteract the effect of the depreciation of the rupee, the Egyptian pound, and the milreis. However, this instance only strengthens the case for the broad proposition that, with qualifications which need not be repeated, public spending was the only positively propelling measure acting on our process—as distinguished from the measures previously discussed, which mainly removed obstacles and thus helped in what may be termed a *negative* way.

5. Prima-facie federal income-generating expenditure actually was from about December 1933 to about the middle of 1937 the dominant factor in the increase of net national income (current dollars).

We will not go into the methods and agencies by which the spending program was put into effect and which were in an incessant process of change from the time that foundations were laid by the Unemployment Relief Act of Mar. 31, 1933 (forestation, prevention of soil erosion, plant disease, and so on), the Emergency Relief Act of May 12, 1933 (revision of powers of the Reconstruction Finance Corporation, creation of the Federal Relief Administration, grants to states for the purpose of direct unemployment relief) and titles II and III of the National Recovery Act of June 16 (Public Works Program, grants to states for highway construction, appropriation of 3.3 billions). Methods and objects are not indifferent either for the recovery or any other aspect. Even for the immediate effect on the economic process it is by no means indifferent whether a given sum be spent on direct relief or on purchase, from stock, of materials the proceeds of which are used by recipients for repaying debts: there is, according to the way of spending, a continuous variety of effects which range from increasing system expenditure by several times the amount spent down to not much more than refinancing. Nevertheless, we will merely note that net national income increased by about 8.6 billions in 1934 and by about 5.2 billions in 1935 (and by 8.8 billions in 1936), which compares with federal net income-generating expenditure of 1,856 millions for 1933, of 3,238 millions in 1934, and of 3,154 millions in 1935 (and 4,025 millions in 1936).

As measured by those and other figures—for instance, of employment—effects may well seem surprisingly small. They have, in fact, been felt to be so even by those economists who simply attribute the whole of the observed increase in national income to federal income generation. But obviously we cannot do this, for to hold that income generation alone has been responsible for that increase involves either circular reasoning or else the theory that in the absence of it the economic process would have gone on shrinking or would have dragged along indefinitely at the minimum level. There is no warrant for believing this. On the contrary, there is, as we have seen, reason to believe that there would have been recovery in any case—a recovery strong enough to produce by itself most of the increases, especially in output, that actually occurred and more. It follows that by taking account of the cyclical phases on which federal income generation impinged, our expectations as to its effects can be only raised and not lowered. We will restate these expectations under four heads.

First, government expenditure will improve *any* business situation, even if it increase the national income of the year only by the amount spent or by less than that or even, in a limiting case, by nothing at all, through helping the public to build up depleted balances and to repay debts. If firms repay bank loans by means of money which the spending government raised from existing but idle deposits, improvement may even be accompanied by a decline in total or total demand deposits which may thus be a favorable symptom. As a rule, only a moderate amount of unfreezing is left for the early stages of the recovery phase. But owing to the extent of the preceding catastrophe and of the continuing state of overindebtedness, it is reasonable to assume that in this case "consolidation" was one of the major remedial effects of the spending policy.[1] Though acting in the monetary sphere, it would, however, primarily show outside of it.

Second, there were what we will call the *direct* results of handling the government's money as far as it was not absorbed by the replenishing of balances and the repayment of debts: the unemployed man spending his dole, the man who has been reemployed in order to fill a government order spending his wages, at the retailer's shop, the retailer thereupon placing additional orders, and so on. Separate evaluation of this effect, which was no doubt considerable, is impossible in the present state of our information, since among other things we do not know the value of that income efficiency of money by which the relevant part of government-created income would have to be multiplied.

Third, firms—particularly in recovery—will react not only directly to government orders or to purchase by the first recipients of government funds but also *indirectly* by expanding operations in anticipation of those orders or purchases and by otherwise "magnifying" the immediate effects of government disbursements. Under the conditions prevailing in the early stages of recovery, however, new investment cannot be expected to be much in evidence. If in this instance it had been, this would before 1935 have introduced an entirely abnormal feature. This is not, of course, to deny that stimulation of investment is en-

[1] If we call the effect *remedial*—and the same term could be applied to the effects to be noticed under the remaining heads—we do not thereby "justify" the spending policy. A drug may be "remedial" with respect to headache but "injurious" to the heart. The writer entertains no doubt but that public income generation outside of "deep" depression (roughly from the middle of 1930 to the middle of 1931) impairs the efficiency of the capitalist process for reasons that should be familiar by now. They apply especially to public income generation during the later stages of recovery and the first stages of prosperity. The difference in the effects of public and entrepreneurial expenditure, the latter involving, the former not involving, change in production functions, should particularly be borne in mind.

titled to a prominent place in a general theory of governmental income generation. In and after 1935 some such stimulation may have been present. In depression and recovery, however, it is current operations in and near the consumers' sphere that need to be and, as a matter of fact, have been stimulated.

Fourth, irrespectively of reactions of the type noticed under the preceding heading, there will be *ulterior* effects on economic activity. The relief in the debt structure, the steadying of prices, the improvement in the sectors immediately affected by government disbursements, the general feeling that a floor is being provided will remove inhibitions and invite advance all round. This class of effects should have been particularly strong in a situation in which not only the stage was set for recovery but in which a recovery that had already begun had been interrupted by an experience so trying to business nerves as an epidemic among banks.

Federal income generation must also have given an impulse to consumers' credit by making many households "credit worthy" which had previously ceased to be so. 1934, in fact, displays much higher figures than 1933 for the credits outstanding of intermediary and cash-lending agencies and also for the receivables of retail merchants. This was much facilitated by the fact that this type of financing afforded at that time the most obvious chance for banks to respond to the incessant appeals to "liberalize" lending. Since the above analysis applies, with but little modification, to income generation by consumers' credit as well as to income generation by government expenditure, it is easy to realize that the former reinforced the effects of the latter.

This analysis evidently harbors no tendency to underrate the potentialities of pump priming which, as the war experience shows, may even turn depression into a state displaying all surface characteristics of prosperity. In some points we do not share the disappointment felt alike by advocates of governmental income generation and by its opponents. We were not, for instance, disappointed on the ground that private investment was not more strongly stimulated in 1934. Nor did we consider that application of government-created funds to the replenishing of balances and to the repayment of debt constituted *pro tanto* defeat of the spending policy. Observed results were, nevertheless, no better than they could have been expected to be had that policy been the only component to act. Since we are not at liberty to disregard the other component, which also was adequate to produce those results, we are driven to the conclusion—to be verified in the next section—that other factors weakened the combined effects of both.

Since so many economists accept the quantitative adequacy of the injection of purchasing power to produce observed results as an *ipso facto* proof that there cannot have been any contribution from the economic process itself—or that there was a negative one—it will be well to retrace our steps, in order to state explicitly the case for alternative possibilities. That part of net income-generating expenditure which increased national income only by its own amount or less will, as long as we do not know its amount, obviously be credited with more than its share if expansion unconnected with it should occur at the same time—financed, let us say, from existing deposits—and if, on the strength of a plausible quantitative relation between total income-generating expenditure and total increase in national income, the one be connected with the other. The state of overindebtedness, on the one hand, and the cyclical phase on the other, combine to make it a practical certainty that this coincidence was of some importance in shaping the statistical picture.

Again, if government funds swell business deposits, as of course they did, they will then finance the subsequent transactions of the recipient firms, whether those transactions are induced by the act of expenditure or not. It does not follow that every expansion of operations by these firms must, therefore, be causally related to those receipts and that without them they would not have expanded operations at all. In this case it is indeed still more obvious than it is in the other how government expenditure propelled recovery. But since resumption or expansion is, for that cyclical juncture, independently motivated, it will not do to attribute all that was financed by money originally inserted by government disbursements to the impulse imparted by them: it cannot be inferred that government carried business as Aeneas carried Anchises. To some extent at least, financing by receipts simply replaced financing by borrowing.

It should not be replied that this is a case of speculation about possibilities *vs.* hard statistical fact. It is a case of common sense *vs.* a type of monetary theories. What we *see* is the income-generating expenditure and certain developments. The relation between them we do not see. Our interpretation of it is not more but less hypothetical or speculative than the one which exclusively relies on mechanical relations between the two, because it assumes and asserts much less.

Finally, no account has been taken of the possibility that government spending might have interfered with business expansion (excepting, of course, the expansion of bank loans). Some of the arguments adduced for this possibility fully merit the shrugging of shoulders with which they are usually met, for instance the argument that the unbalanced budget destroyed confidence. Others do not. But the net effect of the spending policy, *taken by itself and considered only with reference to the general complexion of short-run business situations,* seems to the writer to have been so clearly positive as to justify him in disregarding, for the purpose in hand, any possibilities of that kind.

6. We will now glance at the statistical picture. It should be recalled that we need not lean too much on "inflationary" anticipations or on speculation in general when explaining the boom of 1933, which culminated in July. Nor need we call it simply an affair of restocking (inventory boom). Though all these and other factors no doubt materially helped, that boom is fundamentally understandable as a belated and hence more violent reaction to the ravages of the spiral, the intensity of which it may reasonably be said to measure. Nor is it necessary to emphasize the element of reaction to excess which undoubtedly intensified the sharp slump in the third, and the almost level movements of the fourth quarter: a relapse was quite within ordinary regularity (Kitchin depression). But public spending no doubt shortened the relapse and accentuated the upswing—which came in December—as well as the strong expansion in the first half of 1934. There was but moderate relaxation in the third quarter of 1934, and expansion resumed in the fourth quarter. It went on at a much increased rate in the first quarter of 1935. Outside debits express the fundamental contour very well from month to month. For the years in question, monthly averages (which were at a maximum of 27.66 billions in 1929; at 23 billions for 1930; at 12.87 billions in 1932) struck their low point of 12.2 billions in 1933 (mainly in consequence of the banking troubles) and rose to but 13.83 billions for 1934 (to 15.85 billions for 1935). In the absence of government income generation we should have called this conforming to ex-

pectation. As it was, the smallness of the increase becomes a problem.

Profits fell from the fourth quarter of 1932 to the first quarter of 1933, if allowance be made for seasonal behavior, and recovered strongly in the second quarter, but less than uncorrected figures suggest. Then they relapsed again but made a showing much beyond expectation from our model in 1934, the quarterly average for that year (Federal Reserve Bank of New York) being about 75 per cent above that of 1933—roughly speaking, the writer would attribute three-quarters of this increase to government spending and the NRA. Stock prices copy this contour fairly closely. They merely continued, however, the upswing of the third quarter of 1932. The monthly average of new corporate capital issues (maximum 1929: 666.8 millions) touched its low of 13.8 millions in 1933 and increased to but 14.8 millions in 1934. This is even less than we should have expected on the strength of the proposition that recovery does not typically or necessarily start from real investment and still less from capital issues. Government disbursements in part supplied the funds which it would otherwise have been necessary to raise by issues or to borrow from banks. Also, the proceeds of the issues of 1929 were still largely unused.

Some idea of the extent to which government disbursements replaced bank credit by enabling firms to finance from receipts can be gathered from the behavior of All Other Loans of reporting member banks. Those loans did not increase in the incipient recovery of 1932—which conforms to expectation—but went on falling and ended their downward course by a sharp drop in the first quarter of 1933. Then they did rise moderately until the beginning of the fourth quarter, when they decreased again. So far there was nothing abnormal. But they did not at all participate in the upswing of the first half of 1934, while United States securities held increased by about 1 billion in the first quarter and by another half toward the end of the second. Increase in the third was weak and short-lived and more than compensated by the fall to the end of the year, and no increase accompanied the strong upswing of the first quarter of 1935: firms did not go to banks for what they got from government.

Outside net demand deposits had increased during the second half of 1932. After the understandable slump of the following spring—which brought them to a low that is spurious in our sense—they increased more than All Other Loans to July 1933, mainly, of course, because of the increase in members' investment incident to federal reserve banks' open-market purchases. Their rate of turnover also increased at the same time. Then they fell and rose along with outside debits until the middle of 1934, investment again taking the place of loans in creating them. But they continued to increase after that, in response to investment that did *not* take the place of loans which would otherwise have emerged, until the end of the period: government by selling deficiency bills acquired deposits which, when used, produced other deposits: the old method of war finance. Transfer of surplus funds to centers and influx of gold also swelled net demand deposits. There is no problem in any of these movements or in the growth of excess reserves.

We have noticed how interest rates behaved under the monetary regime that obtained, and will only add that bond yields fell (monthly average) from 6.27 per cent in 1932 to 5.92 per cent in 1933 and 4.86 per cent in 1934, and were 4.78 per cent for March 1935. The B.L.S. index of wholesale prices, excluding foods and farm products, rose from its minimum of 65.3 in April 1933, to not more than a monthly average of 78.4 for 1934 (75 for 1931), the greater part of the rise occurring before 1933 was out, *i.e.*, before the spending program had had time to produce its full mechanical effects. This is within the limits of what might have been expected as the result of a rebound from panic lows. Besides the presence of underutilized resources, the weight of incessantly increased productive efficiency is mainly responsible for the failure of prices to respond more strongly to the price-raising policy of the administration. The latter was more "successful" with respect to the prices of foods and farm products. Prices received by farmers increased by 84 per cent between March 1933 and December 1934. The B.L.S. index for farm products rose, however, from 40.9 for February 1933, to 78.3 at the end of our period, *viz.*, for March 1935, *i.e.*, by over 91 per cent of its minimum.

Average hourly money wage rates behaved very differently in different sectors—in anthracite coal mining they increased very little, in bituminous coal very much, for instance, which again illustrates the lack of realism incident to speaking of a wage level. On the whole, however, these different rates of increase seem to have worked in the direction of a more balanced wage structure. For manufacturing industries as a whole an increase of over 22 per cent occurred between June (the minimum) and December 1933. After that there was no relapse—though there was one in the wages paid by the wholesale and retail trade—but an increase at a much slower rate, which was, nevertheless sufficient to produce an increase in real rates of about 6 per cent by March 1936. The annual average of the hourly rates of skilled and semiskilled labor in manufacturing industries was 55 cents for 1933 and a little over 64 in 1934. This is clearly contrary to expectation from our model. Excepting, perhaps, a fraction of the increase in 1933 which might have resulted in any case from the general reaction to panic lows, it must be attributed to government policies which are the only available factors to explain how the upward shift of the demand "curve" for labor could have produced such rates in spite of the prevailing unemployment.

Both factory pay rolls and employment started on their upward course before monetary wage rates. In fact, they began to increase in the third quarter of 1932 and the increase which occurred from March to September 1933 was but a continuation and not a break. Monthly averages of factory pay rolls were for 1933 about 6 per cent above 1932, for 1934 nearly 21 per cent above 1933, and for 1935 a little over 13 per cent above 1934, while the corresponding increases in employment averages were 10, 13, and a little over 4 per cent, the latter figure being suggestive of inhibitions. Particulars of incidence of unemployment or reemployment were as we should expect and need not be discussed here.

Output of manufacturing and mining, as measured by the Federal Reserve Board's index and as reflected in production of electric power—which, even if corrected for "trend," increased by 19 per cent from March to July—and in carloadings, also behaved according to expectation for our model modified by the political factor. Building contracts, for example, were, of course, affected by the public works program and would not otherwise have increased much in 1933—private building was indeed below expectation, if anything. The sharp increase in steel-ingot production in the second quarter of 1933 was from a very low level, but even so surprisingly great—over 300 per cent in 4 months, thereby reaching the 1923 to 1925 average—so that the subsequent reaction of over 50 per cent was very understandable.

Neither its rise nor its fall, however, meant what they used to mean of old, when steel satisfactorily represented equipment. But it should be observed that from any reserve capacity which may have existed in 1929 and which was obviously greatly increased by the shrinkage of the subsequent years, a substantial deduction must be made on the score of wear and tear and of obsolescence.

Although machine tool orders rose to a fairly high level at the end of the period, steel output was, during 1933 and 1934, primarily associated with durable consumers' goods. Output of automobiles nearly reached 3 million units in 1934.[1] Refrigerators, air-conditioning installations, and other members of the class of "depressionless industries," such as gasoline, cigarettes, rayon, and some chemicals, showed considerable gains.

In the behavior of output three points must be noticed. First, short fluctuations do not quite correspond to our idea of what they should have been. The increase of 66 per cent from March to July 1933, which carried it to the 1923 to 1925 average and the subsequent decline are at least *timed* according to expectation. But the increase in the first half of 1934 came 6 months earlier than we should have expected—relapse in fact followed—and for the decline and stagnation in the first half of 1935 we have only political influences (?) to offer. Second, the index did not, even before the decline early in 1935 and excepting the 1933 peak, reach the level of 1925–1926, the preceding neighborhood of equilibrium, while it should have surpassed it. We attribute this to the severity of the depression and may recall that the recovery after 1873 also was not satisfactory in every way. Nevertheless, effects of the NRA policy may be partly responsible. Third, we must supplement the case for an adverse effect of the increase in wage rates on employment by noting the striking difference between the latter and the corresponding output. To that 66 per cent increase in output corresponds an increase of only 33 per cent in factory employment. This is in part due to underutilization of the working force employed around the bottom of the depression—average hours worked per week, which may be taken as an indicator, in fact, increased by nearly 5 per

[1] This was not simply "rebound." Much had changed in the industry during depression years, and part of that increase must be attributed to its own impulse. There is a kernel of truth in the exaggeration that "motors led us out of depression."

cent from 1932 to 1933—and in part simply the consequence of labor-saving rationalization which had been going on through the depression. But it is impossible to overlook the premium that the wage policy set on this rationalization.

To sum up: The reader will have no difficulty in listing the symptoms by which the effects of governmental income generation unmistakably show. In spite of them, however, the statistical picture presented does not differ fundamentally from what we should have expected to see in the absence of that factor. Since it would have been possible for such a picture to emerge, public expenditure notwithstanding, under the sole influence of the normal recovery process, the conclusion seems to suggest itself that—barring minor deviations caused by it, such as we observed in the behavior of deposits—that expenditure took no effect. This conclusion we do not draw. If we did, we should, in fact, be committing the very same error which those economists commit who simply attribute to government spending everything that happened. But we do draw two other conclusions: first, that attributing all observed developments to the normal recovery process would, though wrong, not be more so—or more "speculative"—than the opposite opinion; and that the prima-facie impression with which we started in 5 is misleading.

E. The Disappointing Juglar.—If past experience be a guide and our schema a roughly correct expression of it, then the rise of a new Juglar—the fifth of the Kondratieff—was due for the spring of 1935, however little meaning we may attach to the precise date yielded by our experimental count (beginning of April). Though facts did not entirely fail, for a time just about equal to the duration of an average Juglar prosperity, to bear out the expectation which would follow from that, the difference is great indeed between such upswing as there was and what happened in the last comparable instance, 1879–1880. Conditions external to this country which then produced an agricultural boom may no doubt be invoked in partial explanation. But government policy largely did for agriculture now what European demand had done for it then, and if we take account of government expenditure in general, agrarian and other, the picture becomes still more disappointing. This was, in fact, universally felt. People never spoke of more than recovery and an unsatisfactory one at that. It would not, however, help us much if we did the same; for the real trouble with expectation from our model is not in the weakness of that "prosperity" but in the fact that it was followed, instead of by a recession in our sense, by a break which landed the system, within a few months and at a rate surpassing everything witnessed during the years from 1930 to 1932, in a state displaying all the phenomena of deep depression. This would be still more unexpected—from the standpoint of our model as such—as a sequel to a recovery than it is as a sequel to a prosperity phase. Does it mean that the capitalist process has spent its force, that private investment opportunity has vanished to the point of making it dependent on government expenditure for motive power or in such a way that the system must collapse as soon as government expenditure is withdrawn, like one of those children's balloons that shrivel as soon as one ceases to blow air into them?

Reasons for believing that this is unlikely have been offered in the introduction to the preceding section. But there seems to be evidence for it of an almost experimental nature. The figures of federal income-generating expenditure for 1935 and 1936 have been mentioned. It was, prima facie, quite sufficient to justify the statement that it induced such prosperity as there was during those two years, and if we take into account deferred effects, also during the first half of 1937. Though there were developments that seem to be beyond the range of its consequences, it might still be said without absurdity that the spending policy then "took effect at last." After that it was discontinued. On cash account the Treasury got out of the red.[1] A slump ensued in due course. Moreover, the writer entertains no doubt not only that that slump will give way to recovery as the new spending program within the 4 billion deficit budgeted for 1938 unfolds during the fall of 1938, but also that tapering off will again be attended by the symptoms of—according to the way in which it is effected—recession or depression.[1] This should make us both

[1] The figure of income-generating expenditure for 1937, $900 million, must be interpreted with due regard to the fact that this sum was almost entirely spent in the first seven months of the year.

[1] That sentence has been left standing as it was written in July or August 1938. It may be useful to add the following comments (May 1939).

Marked improvement in fact showed in the third and fourth quarters of 1938, especially in the indices of manufacturing output construc-

envious and thankful: envious because fellow economists will be able to enjoy so delightful a verification of their views, thankful because in other fields—medicine, for instance—people do not reason like that, or else we should all of us be morphinists by now.

1. In order to see more precisely what there is to explain, we will begin by a survey of time-series contours. 1935 was the third year to show almost consistently higher levels of annual figures than its predecessor. Monthly figures, however, were not consistently higher. The weekly operating rate of the steel industry may serve as an example. Excepting the first two months, it was at or below the 1934 level until nearly the end of June; only in the second half of the year did it rise above that. By end of September it was 50 per cent—in itself sufficient proof of the weakness of that upswing, though 90 per cent was eventually reached (March–April 1937). Moreover, there were other irregularities, among them two setbacks in which leading series behaved in a somewhat discordant manner: during the first half of the year it was the index of production of manufactures and minerals and allied indices, such as carloadings, that sagged, while outside debits steadily increased;[2] the little relapse in the autumn shows primarily in outside debits, while production was hardly affected

---

tion, carloadings, department-store sales, employment, though, conforming to expectation, prices continued to decline. These facts obviously bear out the first part of the statement in our text.

But the relapse during the first quarter of 1939, which continued during April, does not illustrate the second part. There was indeed, a considerably increase in Traesury deposits during February, due to the sale of savings bonds and of securities issued on behalf of various public credit agencies, which for a few weeks raised government cash receipts above government disbursements. This, however, was hardly adequate to produce the observed results, and beyond this there was nothing but talk. We are still within the rising tide of spending, and if effects do not show more visibly, this is due, apart from the presence of depressing extrasystematic factors, to the cyclical phase. If the reader refer to our schema he will see that, barring possible reactions to the abnormal slump of 1937-1938, there is little reason to expect from the mechanism of our process any very strong upturn for several years to come.

[2] That in the beginning of the prosperity phase money volume of transactions should increase more than physical output is not in itself an irregularity; but output fell, especially in steel, cotton and silk textiles, and bituminous coal.

at all. These relapses and discordances were—though on a very small scale—repeated in 1936,[3] which otherwise is the year of the strongest and most nearly uninterrupted increase all round. At its end the 1929 peak of the Federal Reserve Board's index of production of manufacturing and mining was almost reached (with 120 per cent of the 1923 to 1925 average; from May 1935 to May 1936 the index increased by 16 points, and the value in current dollars of national income produced (63.8 billions) was almost 80 per cent of the 1929 figure. Aggregate profits of 700 industrial and mercantile companies, which had in 1935 been about 80 per cent above 1934, further increased by about 50 per cent in 1936, aviation heading the list and steel, automobiles, tires, petroleum, chemicals and drugs, machinery and tools showing up particularly well. Only 6.4 per cent of those companies reported net losses.

As stated above, a Juglar recession *in our sense* was due for 1937 (the middle of August in the experimental count). But what actually happened was very different. After a drop in January, outside debits recovered through May—not, however, to the figure of the preceding December—then hovered on a horizontal level until August—so far conforming to expectation—and after that shrank rapidly. In the first half of 1938 they continued to decline—not merely in function of falling prices—but at a decreasing rate. By June they seemed to have reached an even level. Output of manufacturing and mining behaved irregularly from the first, and more irregularly than debits in the second half of 1937; instead of the increase that we should expect, we find that it declined in January and recovered only to May, after which it fell by about one-third until the middle of 1938, at a rate that decreased from November until a floor was apparently reached in June. Durable goods, especially equipment goods, for which demand temporarily ceased altogether, of course, suffered most.

Profits behaved similarly and, hence, until the last quarter of 1937, conform better to expectation. As far as data of quarterly reporting concerns allow us to judge, profits were larger by one-half in the first quarter of 1937, and lower by about one-third in the fourth, than they had been in the corresponding quarters of 1936. For the year as a whole they were higher by about 7

[3] But recalling our experimental count we shall not, as we must for 1935, consider the occurrence of those setbacks as abnormal.

per cent. Of the 700 concerns 9.6 per cent reported net loss. Substantial gains on 1936 figures were shown by steel, railroad equipment, machinery, agricultural implements, electrical equipment, oil, metal, and mining including copper and copper products, the automobile industry being among the chief mourners.

Factory employment rose and fell much less than output all along. In the monthly average of 1935 it was but little over 4 per cent above the level of 1934, then increased at a somewhat greater rate in 1936 and reached its maximum, a little over the 1923 to 1925 average, in the second quarter of 1937. From July to December it fell by 14 per cent. But it was still 84 per cent of that average early in 1938 and 79 per cent for April. Subsequent changes in most lines were small, but decreases in the steel, machinery, motorcar, and men's clothing industries still further reduced the index through May. Pay rolls, of course, rose —also to about the 1923 to 1925 average in the first half of 1937 —and fell, by 23 per cent from July to December, more than employment. But the rise above and the fall below proportionality reflect not only advances or reductions in rates but also increased or decreased employment in industries paying higher than average wages and decrease or increase of part-time employment, here and there even overtime—but since this was largely due to the reduction in hours, it was but another form of increase in rates—and its elimination.

Money wage rates gained less in 1935 than they had gained in 1934. Then they scored further gains. Average hourly rates for skilled and semiskilled males in manufacturing (64 cents in 1934) were about 66 cents in 1935 and about 69 cents in 1936. Unskilled males did worse, and women suffered a small loss in reaction to the particularly strong increase which had previously occurred in their case. In 1937 rates were increased by another 10 per cent, reaching a level substantially above that of 1929, while real rates then surpassed the latter more than 25 per cent.[1] Labor cost per unit of product also rose. Again, it follows from previous argument that this must have been a major factor in the industrial situation which it tended to make more sensitive to depressive influences, and a major reason why unemployment, in

[1] Real rates were, after their rise in 1933, substantially constant during 1934, 1935, and 1936. They rose by about 6 per cent in 1937, as they should in recession. There was further increase in the first half of 1938.

spite of a substantial decline in 1936 remained at a high figure. Besides forcing the pace of labor-saving rationalization, it may in spots even have interfered with expansion of output while prosperity lasted. Construction may serve as an example.

The strong increase in contracts awarded in the fourth quarter of 1935 was not repeated in 1936, although both total and privately financed construction gained considerably over the year. In 1937 publicly financed construction (a little over 1 billion) declined by over 15 per cent, but privately financed contracts for building and engineering work (about 1.8 billions in the 37 States) showed an increase of almost 40 per cent over 1936, to which public utilities contributed considerably. The index advanced at the end of the year and into January 1938. In February there was a sharp fall in nonresidential construction—though this was partly made up for in March—and privately financed contracts for the quarter were 30 percent below the first quarter of 1936. But even before the slump, the showing was again, as in the recovery, below what we should expect considering possibilities and monetary conditions. Building costs, which rose to the 1929 level in 1936—they increased further by nearly 20 per cent in 1937—and the role of wage rates in them obviously supply the explanation. However, it must be emphasized once more that such increase in hourly rates as occurred from the spring of 1935 to the last quarter of 1936 is not only quite within expectation, a rise of money wage rates being a normal element of prosperity,[1] but also that this rise cannot be thought of as a cause of the slump. Not even the total rise from the depression low can, except as an element of a complex pattern.

2. Conditions of extreme monetary ease prevailed throughout. Prime commercial paper, for instance, was at 3/4 of 1 per cent until March 1937. Then it managed to climb to 1 per cent, but relapsed to the old figure by June 1938. Rates on customers' loans, which on May 31, 1935, had been 1.83, fell to 1.67, and, after an excursion to 1.71, to 1.63 by May 1938. In spite of the heavy treasury financing, the yield of treasury bonds declined, after a slight rise in the third quarter of 1935, to a little over

[1] It cannot be objected that this is speaking from a model which does not include the possibility of abnormal unemployment in prosperity. It does; for if the labor market be imperfect, unemployment will not prevent a rise in wage rates.

2.2, and the yield of AAA corporate bonds almost without interruption to 4.5 at the end of 1935 and to a little over 3 per cent at the end 1936. Then there was an increase through April, but decline to new lows in May 1937, mortgage rates keeping again a much higher level all along. This behavior of short rates and yields obviously calls for explanation other than can be gleaned from our model. We cannot even see a trace of the expected effect in the slight increase that occurred late in the upswing, since that resulted from measures of monetary management. But the irregularity should not be exaggerated.

It must also be emphasized again that the financing of 1929 still exerted effects which should also go some way toward mitigating surprise at the low figures of domestic corporate issues. The monthly average of 378 millions in 1936 measures well up to the 1925 to 1929 average, but most of those issues were for refunding. Only the second quarter of 1937 surpasses, with 140 millions per month, the modest figure of 1931 for new capital issues. But under the circumstances full time at machine and machine tool shops was perfectly compatible with that. As far as this goes, the common saying that private investment did not really revive during the upswing must be modified. Other Loans behaved, in fact, more nearly according to expectation and the shift in bank assets that is characteristic of prosperities did not altogether fail to show: other loans of reporting member banks started to increase from the end of 1935, continued to do so up to the last quarter of 1937, and then fell, while investments, partly at least in connection with this, fell from about the middle of 1936 and began to increase again in the last quarter of 1937 and at the beginning of 1938. Variations in deposits were too much under the influence of monetary policy and government action in general to be trusted to reflect the pulse of our process, except perhaps in the second half of 1936.

All that need be said about stock prices is that they continued to copy fairly faithfully the course of profits, to the point of disregarding the lowering of margin requirements that came into effect on Nov. 1, 1937, and the relaxation of the rules about margin trading in December.

If wholesale prices may be said, according to the guess we ventured to make in an earlier place, to have in 1933 made up for as much of their fall as was due to the preceding spiral, they should then have resumed their downward course. They would, in fact, have done so but for the rise that was forced upon farm products and foods: the index of the prices of other commodities declined until the second quarter of 1935. The slow and hesitating increase in the latter, which then began and after a setback continued until October 1936, was exactly what we should have expected for the prosperity phase of a Juglar located as this one is within the Kondratieff: we know why in this particular pattern—compare the eighties—prices offer a strong resistance to any forces that strive to raise them, to the internal ones which originate in the mechanism of prosperity, as well as to any external ones, political or other.

But precisely because of this we cannot agree with those observers who hailed the violent rise which occurred in the fourth quarter of 1936, as the sign that prosperity—let alone "recovery" —had come at last. From the standpoint of our process that was, on the contrary, abnormal and calls for external explanation, which, of course, is not far to seek. That rise of prices heralded not prosperity but "inflation." The gears of the engine composed of public spending and newly created facilities for credit expansion began to mesh. The case illustrates, as regards the former, the proposition that income-generating expenditure may raise the price level in the presence of underutilized resources and, as regards the latter, the proposition that increasing the lending power of the banking system does next to nothing in the depression which it is intended to remedy, and very little in recovery, but takes effect when it is not intended to do so, *viz.*, in prosperity. It equally illustrates the mechanism that works by two levers, anticipations on the one hand and, what is more important, a race between prices and wages on the other. Of course, only fractional use was actually made of the powers of the deposit-manufacturing machine, but this is no objection to that diagnosis. And it is significant to observe how much of it went into financing of households' expenditure. Banks, trying to find outlets for their idle cash and responding to the incessant appeals, underlined by threats, that they should lend more freely, sometimes went to the length of inviting applications for personal loans by newspaper advertisements, but more commonly financed intermediate lending agencies and retailers' receivables, from installment paper to open accounts. Cash lending by other types of lenders also increased. Thus, consumers' credit which had been reduced by depression rose again to the 1930 figure or nearly so. We are not going to reopen the theoretical problem of consumers' credit. It is enough to point to the fact, its relation to prices, and its importance in any relapse, which it may be sufficient, long before any great percentage of households default, to turn into a vicious spiral.

The powers of credit creation being what they were, that process could not only have gone on indefinitely but also at a pace beyond the possibilities of expanding physical output. We cannot, therefore, completely rely on the automatism of our process for full explanation of the precipitous fall of prices in the last quarter that rapidly tapered off in the first half of 1938. But expectation from our model is for a fall during recession phases, and the recession of a Juglar that runs its course on a Kondratieff downgrade should end up with a price level lower than that of the neighborhood from which the Juglar rose. If the fall that actually occurred was from a higher level and hence steeper than can be explained by our process, the eventual result was not so different from what it should have been if anything else had contributed to it. We should even have expected a decline to below the figure of the second quarter of 1935. No group save farm products, foods, and textiles fell as much as that, and the index of commodities other than farm products and foods never returned even to its annual figure for 1935. There is a strong presumption that, barring monetary management and other price-raising policies—policies, that is, which are price raising in effect, whatever the intentions and phraseologies—price level would continue to fall, though gently, for more than another decade.

Of the 784 commodities which enter into the B.L.S. all-commodity index, the 189 items that fell most from 1926 to 1933 (when their prices ranged from 5.4 to 42.9 per cent of the 1926 figures) were at the end of 1937 on the average at about 60 per cent. Of these all but 10 belong in the categories of extractive raw material, agricultural products, and little-processed staples. The 190 which fell least (and in 1933 stood at between 78.1 and 118.3 per cent of their 1926 prices) were at the end of 1937 on the average at about 100 per cent. Highly finished articles form the bulk of this group, such as chemicals, agricultural implements, and so on. The implications of this are in many cases weakened, in some reversed, by taking account of changes in quality. In others, special conditions explain the "rigidity." In no case is it possible to infer from these facts alone anything about lack of balance in the price system or about lack of flexibility in prices per service unit. The relative fall in raw-material prices foreshadows, and is a condition of, a new equilibrium at vastly increased figures of output.

3. There is thus some justification for going on to speak of Juglar phases. Our main reason for doing so lies, however, in the nature of the industrial processes of the period. This becomes apparent if we ask ourselves what we should have expected to happen. We may think, for example, of our experience with the railroad Juglars of the nineteenth century. They all had a family likeness and were quantitatively dominated by railroad construction not only as long as this was the fundamentally new thing but also for a time of completing development. Historical record does not lead us to expect that innovations of the first magnitude —in a financial sense—will turn up in Kondratieff downgrades: every railroad Juglar had, besides marking a step in the evolution of the railroad system, its own contribution of novelties to make; but quantitatively they were of minor immediate importance compared with the innovation that made the railroad Kondratieff. We know what made the current one and are thus in a position to form a definite "forecast" in order to compare it with the actual course of things. We also know that downgrades are characterized by very numerous small and induced innovations. To these it is impossible to do justice. But the great lines are simple enough to list.

In doing so we do not on the whole meet with disappointment at the first step. This is, first and foremost, the Kondratieff of electricity. The current Juglar should have carried on the work of its predecessors at least as much as the fifth Juglar of the second Kondratieff carried on the railroad work of the four that went before it, *at least* because investment opportunity seems even greater in this case, considering the work to be done within the range of present technical and economic vision.[1] The production of, and the innovations in, electrotechnical manufacturing, in fact, come fully up to expectations, so obviously that we

[1] In 1935 only 800,000 of the 6,800,000 farms were supplied with electricity. Urban domestic consumption was 673 kilowatt-hours per home, whereas according to Mr. Samuel Ferguson it might be 8,400 kilowatt-hours (?). It increased by 50 per cent between 1929 and 1936.

need not stay to prove it. Kilowatt-hours produced passed the 1929 mark in 1935. Power developments have consisted chiefly in progress with the great public ventures: Boulder Dam, Bonneville, Grand Coulee, Fort Peck, and Muscle Shoals, which are to increase capacity installed by over 4 billion kilowatts, and in the smaller projects sponsored under the Rural Electrification Act of 1936, mainly by rural cooperatives. But the amount of construction done by privately owned public utilities is indeed disappointing. We should have expected vigorous expansion in power plants, substations, and transmission lines, and the pecuniary investment corresponding to this and to the incident expansion of equipment should have contributed decisively to the process of prosperity. Whether or not the failure of the actual development (which was, however, not negligible) to bear out those expectations is to be recorded against the principles that yield them depends on whether or not it is adequately accounted for by some inhibiting factor external to the industrial organism. This will be touched upon later.

In the second place, this is the Kondratieff of the automobile. No such development as that of the motorcar industry has ever broken off suddenly. Therefore the current Juglar should include another automobile wave. We are again not disappointed in this expectation. Such prosperity as there was clearly centered in the motor industry and its satellites, such as tires and inner tubes, plate glass, steel, by-product coke, and gasoline, and this accounts for the characteristic inequality of the upswing as between industries which was evident even in 1936 when improvement had become general. Automobiles recrossed the 4 million unit line in 1935 and the 5 million unit line in 1937, when production was higher than in any previous year excepting 1929, or, if we take account of the decline in the number produced for export and merely consider production for domestic consumption, about 94 per cent of the 1929 figure. It is true that owing to the slump in the second half of the year part of this output merely went into dealers' stocks, but on the other hand, part of the increase in the motorization of the country occurred in rural communities, the demand from which was to two-thirds satisfied by second-hand cars. The essential point, however, is that the industry was not simply "drawn along" by environmental growth or improvement (roads) and that it not merely grew into existing, but also created new economic space. The changes in the product were not merely routine changes in design and so on, such as occur in operating any textile mill, but included also a number of, if individually minor, innovations—33,721 patents were issued in this field since 1934—such as the turret top (all-steel frame), automobile radios, knee-action suspension, nonfading finishes, and others, among them still "incubating" ones as, for instance, the pancake motor.

Moreover, the industry reached out into neighboring fields and became responsible for innovations in these—the Diesel-engine division of General Motors (new plants in La Grange and Detroit), which had much to do with the increase in speed of trains during the period, and the same concern's activities in the fields of refrigeration, air conditioning, small-scale light and power production, and aviation (Delco Frigidaire and Conditioning Division, Delco Radio Division, Delco Electric Light and Power Plants, Bendix Aviation Corporation, North American Aviation) may be cited as examples. Considerable outlay for current developments, as well as for new and improved plant capacity, attended this development. The "competing-down" process is evidenced by the increasing share in production of the three leading concerns. Behavior of stock prices, wages, and prices of product conform to our general idea of an industry that was still innovating and expanding under the impulse of innovations. Average hourly rate excluding increase in payment for overtime increased, for example, by nearly 20 per cent in 1937 and was then over 28 per cent above the 1929 level. As to price, there is the usual difficulty about quality. Retail sales value in 1937 was roughly 3.85 billions as compared with about 4.77 billions in 1929.

The allied industries all display, though to a varying degree, the same characteristics. For the rubber industry, in particular, every one of the above statements could be paralleled. Innovation was of a similar type ("supertwist" again, the tractor and implement tire, output of which in 1936 was 1,775 per cent above that of 1933, activities in rubber and even in cotton growing and cotton milling), but price and effect on output must be corrected for the increased amount of service units contained in a modern tire of good quality—according to estimate by the industry on an average 31,446 miles in 1937 as compared with 18,546 in 1929, which would make a fall in price per mile of something like 38 per cent. Wage rates also make a similar showing.

Improved quality and more economical use progressively deprive steel output of its value as a cyclical thermometer. Only if this is taken into account, do the 33.4 million tons of ingots produced in 1935 or the 46.9 millions produced in 1936 acquire their true significance and some comparability with the figures of the preceding Juglar prosperity, and only then is it possible to recognize the output of the first five months of 1937 as truly indicative of Juglar high tide. The relative importance of the lighter steel products, steel sheets, strip wire, tin plate, and so on which, though they enter into farm implements and machinery in general, may be said to be more nearly consumers' goods material was, of course, greater than at any previous time —absolute output was also at record figures in 1936 and during the first three quarters of 1937—but its variations yet indicate the course of cyclical subphases: lighter products were 47 per cent of the total in 1935, only 42.5 per cent in 1936 when prosperity had got into its stride, and about 43 per cent in the first half of 1937 when it was tapering off. The new advance in rolling ("continuous mills"), foreshadowed at the threshold of the depression, constituted the most conspicuous innovation, but there was a large number of smaller ones, principally in the field of alloys and other specialties (flat-rolled steel), but also in others, some of which, such as the progress in welding, were effective in creating new markets. The amounts reported as spent by the industry on new construction and equipment, a little less than 700 millions for 1935 to 1937, do not indicate more than that there was non-negligible investment, for that figure, on the one hand, includes some replacements and mere extensions while, on the other hand, additional allowance should be made for improvements financed under other headings. New blast furnaces—three in 1937, two of them replacing, though of course with improvements, dismantled ones—coke ovens for a million tons beyond replacement, open-hearth furnaces, electric furnaces, and then the new rolling mills mentioned constitute the main items. Behavior of prices, employment, and wages also conforms to expectation. Composite price of steel, which was $67.71 per ton for 1923 and $47.41 for 1933, increased to $56.85 in 1937, average hourly rates were respectively 59.6, 52.4, and (from Mar. 16, 1937) about 83 cents, well above the industrial average and above 1929. Employment (number of wage earners; not man-hours) increased in spite of the labor-saving nature of some of the innovations, and was about 30 per cent above the 1929 level in the summer of 1937.

In appraising steel developments and prospects, armament and construction demand must be taken into account.[1] The latter comes in as a negative item, *i.e.*, the cyclical significance of steel production must be interpreted in the light of the fact that this component failed to contribute as much as we should have expected. We have noticed the fact and one of its causes, but an additional remark suggests itself. We would not per se have expected a particularly high wave of residential building during a prosperity phase, although this is more likely to occur—as it did occur in 1925 and 1926—in the downgrade than in the upgrade of a Kondratieff. But we miss enterprise which in this case there were particular reasons to expect.

The chemical industry does not disappoint us. Expansion, innovation, and investment were on a considerable scale—advance in the fields of "synthetic organics," of refrigerants, of protective coatings (which also gave an impulse to the paper industry), or of plastics may indicate a type of improvements which sum up to a very substantial item—both within and without the two big concerns. The rayon industry outstripped previous records partly by conquering new uses or markets and partly by technological progress, which included a major innovation. The standard fiber did not even begin to show its possibilities—and threats. New in our sense was air conditioning. Although installations started in 1919, they reached a maximum value of but 17 millions in 1930. The industry was still in the experimental stage. It was only in the prosperity of the current Juglar that it rose to the modest heights of 35 millions in 1935, of 53 in 1936, and about 85 in 1937. Aviation may be said to have reached

[1] It is, presumably, also necessary to take account of the fact that the demand for railroad equipment, which materially contributed in 1934 and after, was greater than was warranted by the results and prospects of the railroad business, which continued throughout recovery and prosperity to illustrate our competing-down process. Operating revenue from freight of Class I railroads, which at its maximum of 1929 was only 10 per cent above 1920, fell to below 60 per cent in 1932 (minimum) and was not quite 75 per cent at the end of 1936. Revenue from transportation of passengers fell all along except in 1923, reached 30 per cent of 1920 in 1932, was still lower in 1933 and only very little over 30 per cent at the end of 1936 (below 30 per cent for the year).

about that stage in which railroads were in the thirties of the nineteenth century. Aircraft making enjoyed a great boom every year, setting a new record, mainly, however, because of military demand, which accounted for about 60 per cent of 1937 sales. Even so, the decisive technological advance achieved hardly began to unfold its effects, and total sales (109 millions in 1937) and profits of the eight major concerns were distinctly modest. Still more so was the progress, in everything but equipment and quality of service, of the three great operating companies, whose operating revenue for 1937 did not exceed 25 millions, spelling deficit in all three cases. Two-thirds of their total investments of about 120 millions would *ex visu* of that year have to be considered as lost. Many reasons besides the peculiar difficulties incident to this industry (and the series of disasters) account for this. But since its lack of quantitative significance for the current Juglar is obvious, we need not touch upon its problems.

4. Having thus satisfied ourselves that the processes which in the past used to carry prosperities have not been absent in the present instances, we have established a right to speak of a Juglar prosperity and to infer from experience that it would have asserted itself without any external impulse being imparted to the system by government expenditure or any other factor. In particular, there is nothing to indicate that objective opportunities were smaller or capitalist motivation weaker than they had been, say, in 1925. The problem why that prosperity was so weak, and why it should have been followed by so severe a slump now emerges in its proper setting.

At the outset we dismiss the possibility—which, in fact, has not been sponsored, so far as the writer knows, by any economist —that the steps taken toward freer trade (the Reciprocal Trade Agreements Act of June 12, 1934) can have materially dampened prosperity or intensified depression. Of the 17 agreements actually entered into up to March 1938, only those with Cuba and Canada can possibly have exerted nonnegligible effects in spots, and from what depressive effects they did exert it would be necessary to deduct gains in other sectors. There may even have been a net contribution to recovery and prosperity. If so, it cannot have been significant, however. Exports, which in 1929 had amounted to 5,241 millions, rose from the 1932 figure of 1,611 only to—in millions of full-weight (or devaluated) dollars —1,280 (2,133) in 1934 and to 1,370 (2,283), 1,474 (2,456), and 1,977 (3295) in the subsequent years. And the effects of general improvement in the world, of devaluation, and of armament demand account for the bulk of that.

The momentous changes in the sphere of money and credit, which have been the subject of so much controversy, did not, except by facilitating government expenditure, decisively influence economic processes during the years under survey. We have indeed noticed the effects on money rates, on price level, and on consumers' credit. But the lessons administered by an experience extending over a century and a half and the scarcity of acceptable applications for credit—admitted, in the end, even by fact-finding agencies set up for the purpose of convicting banks of restiveness—prevented excesses which in fact were not at the time encouraged by the federal reserve authorities. The Banking Act of Aug. 23, 1935, codified and made permanent the chief innovations previously introduced, but in doing so it emphasized the restrictive rather than the expansive element in them. Following upon the removal of the restrictions previously imposed upon transactions in foreign exchange (Nov. 12, 1934) it was widely understood in that sense, in spite of the criticism it met from "sound-money" quarters. Later on, it was proved that brakes of the engine were not mere window dressing. The only problem relevant to our subject, therefore, concerns the use which was made of them and which many people held responsible for the occurrence or the severity of the slump.

Faced with an influx of gold, as persistent as it was natural—since any commodity will go to where it is being overpaid—and perhaps somewhat concerned about the violent rise in prices, the Treasury and the Federal Reserve Board took action. The Treasury, not prepared to go back upon devaluation, entered at the time of the French devaluation (Sept. 28, 1936) into the Tripartite Agreement with England and France, undisclosed operations under which helped to control the gold movement temporarily. Moreover, in December 1936, it inaugurated the gold sterilization plan: by directly acquiring and impounding newly received gold it prevented, up to September 1937, any effects of the influx on bank reserves and deposits, the increase in monetary gold stock and treasury cash going into an Inactive Gold Account—an important, if negative, measure.

The Board, using its new powers, directly operated upon the incubus of excess reserves by raising reserve requirements, first by 50 per cent (effective Aug. 16, 1936) and then again by 16-2/3 and 4-2/7 per cent (effective Mar. 1 and May 1, 1937). Total and excess reserves had been rising steadily from the beginning of 1933 for all other, and from the beginning of 1934 also for New York City member banks, thus absorbing much of the flood and once more illustrating the value of the theory that banks are always "loaned up." Great as was the gold influx in 1934, it was surpassed in 1935 by more than 50 per cent (total net gold imports roughly 1.75 billions, over half of them from France). Together with various smaller items which need not concern us, this spelled an increase of nearly 1.9 billions in the monetary gold stock—an increase of about 350 millions in money "in circulation" and an increase of about 1.5 billions in members' reserves, or of about 1 billion in their excess reserves. Influx continued, though with abated force and significant intermissions, throughout 1936: the monetary gold stock rose by more than 1 billion and members' reserves by almost as much, the loss to circulation being almost wholly compensated by the reduction of federal balances at reserve banks. In 1937 the tide swelled again, 1.3 billions producing an increase in monetary gold stocks of 1.5 billions, in spite of the reversal of the movement in November and December. But owing to the sterilization policy this did not go into bank reserves, which continued, however, through 1937 to move at the high level attained toward the end of 1936, not far from 7 billions for all member banks. The increase in adjusted demand deposits of about 2.5 billions in 1935 and of about 1.7 in 1936 substantially reflects government disbursements and, until May 1936 investments, thereafter other loans. They began to fall at the end of the first quarter of 1937 and went on falling almost uninterruptedly, though more in New York than Outside, throughout that year. The first part of this development until about the middle of 1936 does not call for additional comment; the second part brings us back to our problem.

In our survey of time-series contours it has been observed that prosperity did not bring about that stiffening of money rates which, even in a prosperity within a Kondratieff depression, we should have expected. The facts we have just glanced at—excess reserves, in particular—amply explain this. It has also been pointed out that, given these conditions, the microscopic rise of some rates that occurred in 1936, and the somewhat more perceptible though still insignificant increases that occurred in 1937 also in bond yields, cannot primarily be explained by the modest increase in business borrowing but was due mainly to monetary management. It was, in fact, a reaction to the increase in reserve requirements—under conditions of imperfect competition curtailment of even an unsalable excess of supply can have effect on price. But while monetary management produced this effect, it certainly did not, via the rate of interest, produce any other; for no business calculation can in practice be affected by so minute an increase.

But altogether with the increase in all other loans, the increase in reserve requirements by 50 per cent was the signal for member banks to start reducing their investments. The effectiveness of this signal can, however, have been due only to the fact that member banks had for other reasons already begun to feel uneasy about their portfolios. For no reaction was in itself enforced by that measure, which only reduced excess reserves from about 2.9 billions (July 15) to 1.8 (Aug 19), because almost simultaneously treasury disbursements absorbed the effect to the extent of about 360 millions. It is true that application of this weapon, as shaped, will unavoidably create some difficulties unless the reserve positions of all members are exactly equal. But these difficulties were negligible in this case, and very few members had to borrow small amounts form reserve banks at the critical time. Even withdrawals of funds from New York correspondents did not amount to much, nor did the sales of investments between the middle of July and Aug. 19 (160 millions) and in November. Adjusted demand deposits declined but slightly in August and then increased vigorously again.

It is a question of some interest why the Board did not leave things at that. The prospective reduction in federal income-generating expenditure was, after all, no secret, and *pro futuro* the gold influx was being taken care of by the sterilization policy. The revival of business borrowing which kept up total earning assets of members and even increased outside deposits, and the strong increase in money in "circulation" were no reasons for further action, considering the phase of the industrial process. Mechanistic views about the Supply of Money seem once more to have carried more than their due weight. But even so, the announcement on Jan. 30 of a further increase in reserve requirements of 33-1/3 per cent cannot be held responsible for any depressive symptoms and, especially, for the rapid fall of corporate security issues in the third and fourth quarters of 1937. In case the behavior of interest rates should not be considered sufficient proof, we will observe how well the market stood the experiment. Some management was indeed necessary, especially at the second step, and transition was then not quite so easy as it had been with the 50 per cent increase. In April, banks prepared themselves for that second step, which, as it seemed at the time of the announcement, should have reduced excess reserves to 500 millions, but reduced them only to about 850, owing to an increase in total reserves, the decline in deposits, and government disbursements. The reserve system also helped by an open-market purchase (96 millions), and all this raised excess reserves to 1.6 billions toward the end of April. Thus prepared, the market went through the treasury financing and the quarterly tax payments of June without any difficulty. Not even New York banks (which one would think should have displayed some symptoms of strain) had to borrow from the reserve bank. Bill dealers reduced rates on bank acceptances on June 22 after 200 millions of treasury bills had on June 17 and 18 been repaid without replacement. There was some interbank borrowing, but to a very small extent. It is true that members liquidated investments to the amount of about 2 billions, counting from the peak in 1936 to the end of September 1937 and that this naturally weakened the market of governments. But this was, as our narrative amply shows, not due to strain, nor did it cause any. It was, moreover, what happens in every prosperity without producing any depression.

In deference to the prevailing belief in the *gratia efficiens* of the supply of money, those steps toward normalization of money-market conditions were retraced precipitously. Both Board and Treasury went to entirely unnecessary lengths in the opposite direction when the slump had developed. While it is not correct to say that what monetary management has proved itself able to learn was how to create slumps, it is correct to accept that panicky retreat as an indication of the practical value of brakes, the application of which so quickly results in excess of speed. The Treasury first desterilized 300 millions of gold in September, then reduced the sterilization policy to a shadow by the decree of Feb. 14, 1938, and finally reversed it by releasing on Apr. 14, 1938, the whole of the 1.4 billions of gold in the inactive account, *i.e.*, practically by transferring the equivalent to the Treasury account with federal reserve banks. Thereupon, the Board, which had already authorized further open-market operations and reduced margin requirements on security transactions in November, also reduced reserve requirements by 13.25 per cent on Apr. 15, 1938. Members' total reserves having risen toward the end of 1937 because of that release of those 300 millions of gold, the increase in monetary silver, the open-market operations, and later also because of some purchases of gold, excess reserves were more rapidly built up again. They were 2.5 billions by Apr. 20, 1938; 2.75 for June; and went to 3.15 in July.

Treasury redemption bills—which was the chief use so far made of the formerly inactive gold—sent their yields to practically zero. Adjusted demand deposits moved in the opposite direction to total loans plus investment, increasing by 768 millions, while the latter fell by 250 in the second quarter of 1938 and cash piled up. These measures were more recently supplemented by advance on the other line of expansionist policy, *viz.*, by new rules for the lending practice of member banks, calculated to "liberalize" it. Thus we have before us, untouched by previous experience but implemented by much more powerful tools, the main ideas of the policies of 1933–1934. No doubt, argument based on the logic of *post hoc ergo propter hoc* will be heard and read very soon. It should be noticed, moreover, that some of the steps taken cannot be retraced, that the rest can be retraced only with difficulty, and that such a policy, while ineffective in depression, tends to become viciously effective afterward. Monetary policy per se may, hence, become a major factor in the near future; but it had but little to do with the prosperity of 1935 to 1937, and nothing with the subsequent slump.

Finally, we will return to income generation by means of government expenditure and try to appraise the effects of its cessation in 1937. Our historical survey (Chaps. VI and VII) has supplied us with instances of crises that occurred near the upper turning point of a Juglar. Although recession is not depression, the transition from prosperity to recession, implying as it does a difficult reorientation, always creates some danger of breakdown. It is true that severe slumps at or near that point are without exception associated, not simply with excesses of speculation, but with excesses of speculation induced by a supernormally rapid pace of industrial development, conditions which were conspicuously absent in the case before us. But the idea suggests itself nevertheless, that government expenditure may have played the role which in the past belonged to the expenditure by innovating firms and that, considering its quantitative importance, its cessation acted in much the same manner as the cessation of the latter did in previous cases. The elements of truth in this argument are no more obvious than its limitations.

There can be no doubt not only that income generation by government must always create problems of adaptation, but also that in this case its timing was singularly infelicitous.[1] Its high-water mark came exactly at the time when the economic process could most easily have done without it and its cessation exactly at the time when the economic process was in its most sensitive phase. Reference to our experimental count will illustrate this drastically. The widespread opinion that the cessation of that income generation was the "cause" of the slump thus derives some support from our analysis,[2] although it should be superfluous to add that no argument for permanent deficits follows from that.

But the explanatory value of the shock thus imparted to the system should not be exaggerated. Since no excessive expansion or speculation had been called forth by the preceding spending policy—any more than by such "natural" prosperity as there was —and since there was, as we have seen, no monetary strain, the usual starters of downward spirals were not operative. The injections were not suddenly discontinued but tapered off gradually. Hence, the analogy with previous crises that occurred around

[1] So was the disposal of the amount spent. Sums were thrown about in the country almost at random, without systematic regard to existing structures and probable developments, thus creating industrial and commercial positions that rested on nothing but this temporary flood of money and were bound to die off when it ebbed.

[2] Since the payments under the Social Security Act materially helped in (slightly more than) balancing the combined federal cash account, it is even true to say, as has been said by some economists, that those payments had for the time being a "deflationary effect." As a long-run proposition this would, of course, not be true. Another point should be noticed in passing. The downturn of 1937, following upon that of 1930, impinged upon a business community which for the time being was supernormally "crisis conscious." Moreover, many concerns may have harbored vivid recollections of what the "stand" they had made in 1930 had cost them.

the upper turning point fails after all. The obvious inference is that the collapse induced by the cessation of income generation was so severe, and that the jolt which it would in any case have been natural to expect turned into a slump, because under the surface watered by income generation the processes characteristic of recession in our sense (see Chap. IV) failed to work as they always had worked before. The parachute refused to unfold.

5. *a.* This view, which implies the presence of an additional and more fundamental problem, is hardly controversial and, in fact, shared by very many fellow economists who offer in explanation the theory of vanishing investment opportunity. The vogue that this theory enjoys in this country is obviously due to the occurrence of that slump after what is universally recognized as an abnormally weak prosperity (or "recovery"). Since in order to understand the economic situation of our time it is essential to realize fully why that explanation cannot be accepted, we will restate the case against it at the risk of repetition.

The validity of that theory is not denied on the ground that its basic proposition is wrong. This proposition can in terms of our analysis be rendered as follows. Capitalism is essentially a process of (endogenous) economic change. Without that change or, more precisely, that kind of change which we have called evolution, capitalist society cannot exist, because the economic functions and, with the functions, the economic bases of its leading strata—of the strata which work the capitalist engine—would crumble if it ceased: without innovations, no entrepreneurs; without entrepreneurial achievement, no capitalist returns and no capitalist propulsion. The atmosphere of industrial revolutions —of "progress"—is the only one in which capitalism can survive. Hence the capitalist organism cannot, in case opportunities for innovations give out, settle down into a stationary stage without being vitally affected, as it could if "changes in production functions" were an incident to its life process and not the essence of it. In this sense stabilized capitalism is a contradiction in terms. Moreover, this kind of stabilization would produce a class of abnormalities and instabilities of its own. There would be increasing reluctance to invest or even reinvest, a tendency to "live on capital," to hold on to balances, to recreate vanishing returns by all the shifts open to a class which, though by then economically functionless, yet would, like its feudal predecessor, for a time retain the powers acquired by and associated with the functions previously filled. Maladjustments, unemployment and underutilization of resources—though now of a different nature—and neutral, unstable, and subnormal equilibria might hence well stay with a nonexpanding world.[1]

The colors of this picture will fade if proper account be taken of the fact that transition to a stationary state would not be sudden but would necessarily come about by slow degrees (see below). Also, it must be borne in mind that the proposition in question is not as a rule formulated in that way. Some writers try to demonstrate it by means of models which assume unchanging production functions or "methods of production" and thus exclude the pivot on which it turns. Most writers unduly stress the mere mechanics of the saving-investment process. But as far as the result is concerned, there is nevertheless affinity between their view and the one submitted in this book. We may even admit that one of the difficulties of that transition may proceed from people wanting to invest and getting ready to invest, while they are not able to do so at rates of returns acceptable to them (see below). It will, therefore, be convenient to accept the current slogan for the purposes of the argument in hand. The connecting link which allows us to do so is the fact that innovation is, directly and indirectly, the great source of investment opportunity.

Nor do we take issue with the companion proposition that investment opportunity in this sense may, and in fact is likely to, vanish sometime in the future. The reasons usually offered for this are old acquaintances of ours. For instance, although we hold that the conquest of the air may, entrepreneurially speaking, be as important as or more important than the conquest of India and that, from the standpoint of our analysis, the two are exactly the same kind of thing, we shall not deny that opportunities of the latter type are being, or ultimately will be, exhausted. Or, although we hold that nothing at all reliable can be predicted about it, we do not deny the possibility that technological innovations may some day give out, either "objectively" or be-

[1] Such a world would not display cycles in our sense: a cycle in a nonexpanding world is also a contradiction in terms. But fluctuations of the type which we have called waves of adaptation (Chap. IV) would continue for some time. And the circumstances alluded to in the text may, while transition lasts, also cause fluctuations of yet another type.

cause people do not care to proceed with the available ones. We have even an element of our own to add. The mechanization of "progress" (Chap. III) may for entrepreneurs, capitalists, and capitalist returns produce effects similar to those which cessation of technological progress would have. Even now, the private entrepreneur is not nearly so important a figure as he has been in the past. We have, moreover, noticed the implications of chemical and other developments which *may* result in making innovation capital saving or at least less capital absorbing than, say, it has been in the railroad age. Also, it may well be true that an increasing proportion of the "things still to be done" will lend itself to public rather than private enterprise, although this would per se not mean more than the addition of another component to a tendency toward public enterprise which exists independently of it.

Finally, we do not even exclude the possibility that investment opportunity might vanish through saturation. The argument from declining birth rates, in particular, loses but little by the fact that it is often inadequately formulated. Reduced "need" for expanding capital equipment in a society in which population increases at a decreasing rate—still more in a society in which it is stationary or declining—is not the point. It does not matter whether the purposes to be served by an expansion or reorientation of the productive apparatus strike the observer as particularly "necessary" or not—whether it is radio sets or cradles that are in demand. And so long as the majority of people in the civilized, let alone uncivilized, nations are as far from anything like saturation [1] as they are now, no shrinkage of total investment

[1] Once more we meet that overemphasis on the possibilities of expansion within existing lines which we repeatedly met before. But it should be observed that even these are important enough to negative any idea of deadlock from that source for quite a time. Another argument may be noticed here. It has been held that the process of providing "capitalist" equipment for the population—the stock of producers' goods necessary for the Boehm-Bawerkian "roundaboutness"—was a historically unique and uniquely capital-absorbing task, which has been performed once for all in the nineteenth century. This seems not only to assume that, within the production functions that existed at any time, capital equipment has been carried to saturation point, but also to overlook that the insertion of new production functions in many cases, not to say typically, annihilates the old equipment economically, so that that task has to be periodically repeated and, as experience abundantly shows, repeated by means of new savings and new credit

opportunity will result from the saturation of a particular want—even if we disregard the temporary, but for the time being very important, effect of the changing age distribution. But there is a more fundamental objection which at this state of our analysis should be familiar to the reader: "needs," whatever they may be, are never more than conditioning factors, and in many cases mere products of entrepreneurial action; it is not they that set the capitalist engine into motion, as the old household examples (China and so on) show; and economic development (capital consumption included) has *never* been conspicuous in the countries which to the observer seem to be most lavishly supplied with needs. However, the argument may be upheld, at least to some extent, in another way: as has been pointed out, provision for an indefinite family future is of central importance in the scheme of bourgeois motivation, and much power may be eliminated by childlessness.

b. But we do take issue with the third proposition, which asserts the relevance of those considerations for the diagnosis of the situation of 1938. Obviously, we have been speaking of longest-run tendencies just now. Opportunities for technological or organizational or commercial innovation cannot be thought of as vanishing (if they are vanishing) except very gradually. If there actually be a general tendency toward decline in capital absorption, it can assert itself only in time, though shocks to individual industries may be both sudden and serious. The rate of increase in population declines imperceptibly per year. The call of entrepreneurial adventure is too deep-seated to cease dramatically *of itself*. And so on. Such tendencies, even if well established as some of them undoubtedly are, qualify but ill for the task of explaining the peculiarities of a particular Juglar. They may affect contour lines over time and bend them downward. But they cannot explain the weakness, relatively to its predecessor, of any given prosperity, and they look absurd in the role of explaining factors of a sudden slump. If it be held, nevertheless, that one or all of them suddenly acquired dominating importance at any given historical juncture, such an assertion requires, in order to be taken seriously, proof not only

creation. Long-distance transportation by motorcar, "replacing" long-distance transportation by railroads, is surely not financed from the depreciation accounts of the latter.

of a secular tendency or "trend" but of the presence of circumstances adequate to account for so improbable an occurrence as sudden action would be.

The essentially gradual *modus operandi* of those tendencies must enter into any speculations about the phenomena to be expected from vanishing investment opportunities. For instance, there is no warrant for the assumption which has been made the basis of far-reaching conclusions, that in the face of them people will go on saving at a rate sufficient to produce difficulties. Owing to the persistence of habits, this could conceivably be so in the short run of a depression phase, though we have seen plenty of reasons to doubt it. But in the short run investment opportunity cannot decline perceptibly. And in the long run there is no reason to suppose that savings—and both things and psyches in general—will not adapt themselves. Moreover, it is obvious not only that declining rates of savings will accompany declining birth rates because both phenomena flow from the same sociopsychological source, but also that there is a causal connection between the two.

But reasons less general than that estop us from accepting the theory in question. Whatever may be thought about those "trends" and the way in which they operate, none of them has in this country advanced far enough to bear it out. We have seen in some detail that "objective" opportunities are not lacking. We are less than ten years removed from as vigorous a prosperity as was ever witnessed and from a depression provably due, in the main, to the pace of preceding "progress." It has been argued that that prosperity differed in character from previous ones by the prominence of (durable) consumers' goods production, and hence indicated that a fundamental change had, already then, occurred in the cyclical process. Of course that prosperity differed from the Juglar prosperities of the Kondratieff upgrade. But it did not differ in character from the comparable Juglar prosperities of the preceding Kondratieff downgrades, and therefore does not indicate any fundamental change in the working of the capitalist organism. Expansion of production of consumers' goods, including expansion in the fields of utilities and of public works, was, proportions guarded, no less prominent a feature in the developments of the twenties, thirties, seventies, and eighties of the nineteenth century. Nor can it be urged that fundamentally new opportunities of first-rate magnitude are not in prospect. Barring the question whether that is so, it is sufficient to reply that in the eighteen-twenties hardly anybody can have foreseen the impending railroad revolution or, in the eighteen-seventies, electrical developments and the motorcar. No less an authority than John St. Mill compromised himself by holding in 1870 that the possibilities of capitalist enterprise were substantially exhausted. *Vestigia terreant.*

As applied to the American situation of today and to the abnormalities of the current Juglar, the theory that the capitalist process is stagnating from internal causes inherent to its logic and that income generation by government is nothing but the self-defense of a shriveling organism, is therefore a complete misfit—at best a mistaken interpretation of certain aftereffects of the world depression, at worst the product of wishful thinking on the part of all those who crave for a presentable basis for policies they approve. It still retains two merits, however. The one consists in the many elements of truth which, as we have seen, enter into its arguments as distinguished from its application. The other consists in the recognition, by implication at least, of the fact that, as any social system depends for its functioning and survival on the actual delivery of the premia it holds out, so capitalism depends for its functioning and survival on the actual delivery of the returns, anticipation of which provides its motive power.[1] For this is, after all, what the stressing of investment opportunity amounts to. Slightly extending and modifying the meaning of that phrase, we may hence continue to use it ourselves and *agree* that it is vanishing investment opportunity which is the matter with present-day capitalism—anything can, in fact, be put into that form, the structural principles of the capitalist process being what they are. And our task then reduces to substituting for unconvincing reasons why investment opportunity should be vanishing, a more convincing one.

c. The analysis of Chap. VIII, Sec. B supplies it: capitalism produces by its mere working a social atmosphere—a moral code,

[1] This would in the times of intact capitalism have been taken for granted. In our time, however, the attempt to run capitalism in an anticapitalistic way has given rise to arguments which came near to denying it. Hence the recognition by the theory of vanishing investment opportunity of that rather obvious point may well be recorded to its credit.

if the reader prefer—that is hostile to it, and this atmosphere, in turn, produces policies which do not allow it to function. There is no equilibrating apparatus to guarantee that this atmosphere or these policies should develop in such a way as to prevail in the fullness of time, *i.e.*, when the capitalist process will have really spent its force or be spending it. Whenever they prevail sooner, there is danger of a deadlock, by which we mean a situation in which neither capitalism nor its possible alternatives are workable. This is what, to a certain extent and presumably not yet for good, has happened in this country.

It might be replied that anticapitalist attitudes are also, like the tendencies adduced by the theory of vanishing investment opportunity in its usual acceptance, a matter of slow growth and, hence, similarly open to one of the objections raised against that theory above. But we are able to do in this case what cannot be done for those tendencies, *viz.*, to show that, and how, that attitude came *suddenly* to a head and suddenly acquired dominating importance. And anticapitalist policies, unlike attitudes, may be dated.[1] The coincidence in time between them and disappointing performance of the economic engine is indeed striking. We will survey them under the headings of Fiscal, Labor, and—for want of a better expression—Industrial policies.

At least since 1932 the burden of direct taxation imposed upon that part of the national revenue which goes to the higher and highest brackets was undoubtedly high enough to affect "subjective" investment opportunity or, as we have previously expressed it, to shift the watershed between "to do and not to do." No other than direct or mechanical effects need, however,

[1] It should be observed at once that, anticapitalist measures being, of necessity, measures hostile to private investment opportunity, the accredited exponents of the theory of vanishing investment opporttunity must perforce agree with the argument that is to follow; for the consequences of inadequate investment opportunity are obviously independent of its causes. They will be the same whether these causes are internal or external, *i.e.*, whether the process itself, by virtue of the law of its life, produces inadequate margins, or these margins, if produced, are or would be taken from recipients, or, finally, the anticipation of them is in other ways prevented from having its normal effect. Hence, those economists will in any case, even if unconvinced by our argument against their explanation of vanishing investment opportunity, at least have to insert ours into their schema. If they do insert it in a place appropriate to the importance of its constituent elements, there will not be much room left for difference of opinion.

be attributed to this burden until roughly 1933–1934, because the increase in taxation was then accepted as a sacrifice to be made in a national emergency, as it had been during the war. But from the revenue act of 1934 on, this was no longer so. Permanence of the burden for reasons unconnected with emergency, involving a transfer or redistribution of wealth which in the highest brackets amounted to the socialization of the bulk of private income, and in some cases taxation for taxation's sake and regardless of insignificance of results for the Treasury,[1] then became part of an established policy, the general drift of which was not reversed in 1938. Aspects other than effects on the process of economic evolution are irrelevant to our purpose. The quantitative importance of the change to the interests concerned is unquestionable and unquestioned. Hence, we need not go into details or follow up the successive steps embodied in the revenue acts from 1934 to 1937, but can confine ourselves to the following comments.

As the above suggests, the writer is inclined to stress the importance of the income, corporation, and estate taxes at the expense of others which, being novelties, have been more widely discussed. The facts that the limit of exemption from the income tax is very high, the flat rate very low, and the surtax distinctly moderate up to an income of $30,000, are irrelevant to the argument. It is above that range, principally within a group of not more than 30,000 or 40,000 taxpayers that those taxes, raised within a few years to their present figures, exert a serious influence on "capital supply" [2] and business behavior, which, of

[1] The insignificance of financial results is very likely in the case of the estimates—which are what is relevant as regards purpose—of additional revenue from the revenue act of 1935. The increases of the surtax were, for example, to yield 45 millions more, the graduated income tax 37 millions, the excess profits tax 10 millions, the increase of the estate tax plus the gift tax 101 millions—the nibbling of a mouse at the mountain of the deficit. The arguments that this was a matter of that budget and that in future booms much higher yields could be expected are not to the point. The latter, moreover, begs the fundamental question.

[2] The writer does not wish to stress, under the circumstances of the past years, short-run effects on quantity of monetary capital and its rate of increase. As far as these go, that fiscal policy may even have had a net result favorable to prosperity and unfavorable to depression through enforcing an increase in total expenditure. That element is primarily stressed in their interesting study on Economic Consequences

course, is greatly intensified by the failure of legislation to permit the carrying forward of business losses,[1] by the new treatment of personal holding companies and by other inroads into actual or potential capital.

The so-called capital gains tax has been held responsible for having accentuated, if not caused, the slump. The writer is, however, unable to see that it can have had much to do with the processes of the current Juglar except by way of damping speculative ardors and thereby making issues of stock more difficult than they would have been. The financing of the positive phase cannot, considering the abundance of cheap money, have been seriously interfered with by this; the subsequent slump should, if anything, have been mitigated by it. Other points, in particular the effect it exerts by enforcing dis-saving, though relevant to a prognosis of the results to be expected in the future from the capitalist engine and not substantially affected by the modifications introduced by the revenue act of 1938, need not concern us here.

The antisaving theories and the *ressentiments* of the day found a very characteristic expression in the special surtax on undistributed corporate income (undivided profits tax), which ranged from 7 to 27 per cent. Discarding again the question of the long-run effects which the measure might have had if it had been allowed to remain on the statute book, we may split immediate effects into those of a further increase in the burden on corporate income and those of the specific penalty imposed on corporate accumulation, and confine ourselves to the latter. It possibly resulted in an absolute and relative increase in distributed income which is neither certain nor easy to evaluate because there were also other reasons for the increase that actu-

---

of Recent American Tax Policy, Supplement I to *Social Research,* by Professors Colm and Lehmann, who attempt quantitative evaluation of the difference made to the supply of capital. But to the writer supply in the sense of "willingness to sell," that is to say in this case, willingness to invest, seems to have been the more immediately important thing affected.

[1] That feature, for which no rational argument has ever been offered to the writer's knowledge, is more important than it seems. A loss which can be carried forward without penalty is one thing, a loss which cannot, quite another thing. A risk which it may be rational to take in the first case will frequently have to be refused in the latter. This would not, of course, apply to "small" or even moderate taxes.

ally occurred, but which presumably increased, or helped to counteract the decrease of, system expenditure. Nevertheless, the measure may well have had a paralyzing influence on enterprise and investment in general. The actual presence of accumulated "reserves," and the possibility of accumulating them quickly, strengthens the position of a concern with respect to the risks and chances of innovation and expansion which it confronts. One of the causes of the efficiency of private business is that, unlike the politician or public officer, it has to pay for its mistakes. But the consequences if having to do so are very different according to whether it risks owned or borrowed "funds," or whether a loss will only reduce surpluses or directly impinge upon original capital. Adequate book reserves are as necessary a requisite as adequate stocks of raw material, and in their absence, or with reduced facilities of acquiring or replenishing them, an entirely different and much more cautious business policy would impose itself. In prosperity, investment opportunities would be seen in a perspective of reduced proportions; in depression, firms would have to bow more readily to the storm. In the latter case in particular, the important class of considerations—pure business considerations among them—that used to induce many firms "to make a stand" for some time, even at considerable immediate loss, would tend to vanish from the businessman's mind. All this, it is true, vanishes from the economist's mind as soon as he buries himself in the mechanics of aggregative theory. But many industries, which are among the chief economic assets of the nation and of which the automobile industry is the standard instance, would under a regime of undivided profits taxes never have developed as they did. And as regards the current Juglar, the actual course of events both during prosperity and during the slump is compatible with the opinion that this attack on the foundation of corporate finance weakened the former and intensified the latter.

This is a matter of value of assets and not of liquidity, which under the conditions prevailing in this country since 1931 was never a problem for a concern of unimpaired standing. Similarly, the argument that accumulations make it easier for a concern to live in depression and to "cushion" the effects of depression on the economic process by keeping up dividend and wage payments cannot be met by pointing out that only a part of total accumulations is held in cash or near-cash and that the rest cannot be "paid out." It is true that from the standpoint of the individual management liquidity constitutes an advantage. The ease with which the bulk of American large-scale industry steered through the vicissitudes of 1931 and 1932 was to a considerable extent due to it. It is also true that accumulations which are held in a liquid form tend to work in an anticyclical sense. But this must not be confused with the point which the writer is trying to make and which, in this case, is entirely independent of cash considerations, though it would not be so for other times and countries.

The effect on the combined federal cash account of the method chosen for financing the social security program has been mentioned before. No further attention need be paid to the money-market and expenditure aspects of the payments into the Old Age Reserve Account and the Unemployment Trust Fund. Independently of this, the tax on pay rolls levied on firms was of course an element in the increase of the total fiscal burden which occurred in 1937.[1] The question of effects raises difficult problems in transference. In a situation in which wage rates are firmly upheld and prices of the products of "big business" not allowed to rise, increase of the tax to the full amount ultimately contemplated may not only produce additional unemployment, but also be sufficient, as comparison with corporate net earnings shows, to cause paralysis in some industries, such as would, for example, enforce the creation of another and much more stringent NRA. But for the time being no major effect can be attributed to this tax taken by itself.

Labor policies reduced investment opportunity—besides employment per unit of output—mainly by forcing up wage rates. Not all of the increase which actually occurred can be attributed to those policies; and precisely because rising rates were to a considerable extent met by labor-saving rationalization, the effect on investment opportunity was presumably not very great. Costs incident to employing labor were also increased in other ways. And it is here necessary to define investment opportunity widely and to take account of the less measurable effects of increasing

[1] The steel industry, for instance, paid for 1937 156.6 millions in federal, state, and local taxes, or about 40 per cent of net earnings or 15 per cent of pay rolls, or about 60 per cent more than in the preceding year. About 37 of the 60 per cent are accounted for by the increase in the pay roll tax.

difficulties in operating plants which the growth of a new body of administrative law entails. A major measure of this kind, the National Labor Relations Act (July 5, 1937) was placed on the statute book in the period under survey. As the reader knows, more vigorous use was immediately made of the facilities created by it than is suggested by its actual contents, which keep within the most ordinary lines of labor policy in modern democracies and only develop the principles of earlier legislation, such as the labor clauses of railroad acts, the Clayton Act, certain acts passed during the war, Sec. 7*a* of the recovery act, and other enactments. Official support given to the campaign of the Committee for Industrial Organization and lending to the act a color not naturally its own, must be listed independently. But after the fullest allowance for these and other elements of the case, we shall still be left with the result that labor policies—more precisely, what has actually been done in the field of labor policy—were not, *taken by themselves,* of decisive importance in shaping the business situations of those years.

As regards what we have called industrial policies unfavorable to investment opportunity, two instances will sufficiently illustrate what we mean. First, we have seen reasons to expect that developments in the field of public utilities would be a leading feature of the current, as they had been in the preceding Juglar. We have also seen that, barring federal enterprise, that expectation was not fulfilled. Existing investment opportunity was prevented from having its normal effect, not so much by what was actually done, but by the blanket threat behind it. Expected competition from federal or municipal power plants was a factor in some sectors. The Public Utilities Holding Company Act endangered the American solution of the fundamental problem of power finance. But the decisive element of the situation was that indefinite threat: executives and investors would have had to be completely blind to the political forces that were being marshaled against them, if they had been prepared to take the responsibility for new investment on a large scale. The case thus serves to show not only how unrealistic any theory of investment opportunity is which leaves the political factor out of account, but also how easily the latter may acquire an importance compared with which that of any decline of investment opportunity from reasons inherent to the capitalist process would be negligible, even if it did occur at a significant rate per year.

Second, there is nothing surprising in the fact that under the circumstances the no less old hostility against "monopoly power" should have asserted itself all over the industrial field. But "monopoly" really means any large-scale business. And since economic "progress" in this country is largely the result of work done within a number of concerns at no time much greater than 300 or 400, any serious threat to the functioning of these will spread paralysis in the economic organism to a much greater degree than a similar threat to the corresponding number of concerns would in any other country. No compensation was afforded by the federal government's extreme anxiety not to show hostility to private business in general or to do anything that could have aroused the cry of Government in Business, because the contributions of the favored strata to "progress" and their investments are not only comparatively small but also, to a large extent, induced by what happens in the world of big business. That hostility propelled or facilitated the fiscal and labor policies which we have glanced at above. Beyond these very little was actually done; but much was foreshadowed at various times, even before the monopoly investigation, recently instituted. This may have meant nothing or everything, according to whether or not the threats were taken seriously by those whose decisions they could have influenced. But it should be observed how very much like "liquidity preference owing to vanishing investment opportunity" the behavior would look which would result if they were.

d. None of all the *measures* mentioned under our three headings can, if considered individually, be reasonably held to have played a dominant role in shaping the current Juglar. An easy road thus seems to lead toward the conclusion that no explanation can on these lines be derived for the lack of vitality displayed by the economic process during the period under survey, and that investment opportunities must, hence, be vanishing from causes internal to that process, in spite of all we have adduced to the contrary. The following considerations, however, greatly strengthen the case for the adequacy of that explanation.

First, the combined effect of a series of measures unfavorable to investment opportunity can evidently not be evaluated by adding up the effects which each of them would have had in the absence of the others. We might make even larger concessions than the writer would be prepared to justify, to the prevalent tendency to underestimate the effects of any or all the individual measures we have glanced at, and nevertheless have to conclude that their combined effects were adequate to produce the observed result. The individual measures obviously tended to reinforce each other. "Objectively"—*i.e.*, irrespectively of intentions harbored by any individuals—they amounted to systematic attack on investment opportunity all round: it was frontally attacked by direct reduction of net revenues through taxation, which would have been only the more effective if there really had been also an inherent tendency for investment opportunity to shrink; simultaneously, it was attacked in the rear by increasing costs; and both attacks were supplemented by a third—the attack on those traditional methods of management, pricing, and financing in the sphere of "big business" which were associated with the latter's emergence and successes. No doubt, opinions still may in all fairness differ as to the importance both of these combined attacks and of the precise points in the industrial structure that were being attacked. But difference of opinion is not possible about the relevance of the principle of interpretation which the writer is trying to stress.

Second, the mistake involved in trying to arrive at an estimate of combined effects by that process of addition is not more serious than the mistake of confining attention, in evaluating either isolated or combined effects, to the wording of enactments, congressional declarations of policy, and statements of the chief executive. Economists who pride themselves on the practical bent of their researches could really be expected to know that the personnel and methods by which and the spirit in which a measure or set of measures is administered, are much more important than anything contained in any enactment. The events surrounding the National Labor Relations Act will serve to illustrate that simple truth, particularly if we compare American with English experience in that field: it should be obvious that in the one case effects on investment opportunity may result which it would be absurd to expect in the other. This already covers part of what we designate by the term Social Atmosphere.

But, third, this atmosphere should also be listed independently as an additional factor in its own right. Behavior in human societies differs from behavior in animal societies or in physical systems, in that it not simply reacts to "disturbances" but to interpretative and anticipative—correct or false—diagnoses of them. Real or supposed drifts and trends may count as much as or more than facts, threats as much as actions, indefinite threats more than specific ones, in creating the psychic environment in which the nation's work has to be done. *We* know that behind those measures, administrative acts, and anticipations there is something much more fundamental, *viz.*, an attitude hostile to the industrial bourgeoisie which is no ephemeral composite of individual circumstances and political exigencies of the day but the product of the same social process that created that bourgeoisie. Businessmen presumably do not hold that theory. But they need not hold any in order to realize that there is in those measures and programs more than there would have been in similar measures and programs 30 years ago. They *are* not only, but they *feel* threatened. They realize that they are on trial before judges who have the verdict in their pocket beforehand, that an increasing part of public opinion is impervious to their point of view, and that any particular indictment will, if successfully met, at once be replaced by another. Again, we may differ in our estimates of the importance both of this factor and of the functions it tends to paralyze, but it should not be overlooked.

Fourth, the effects of all that on investment opportunity—if the reader prefer, on what to the businessman appears as an investment opportunity of a given degree of attractiveness—were greatly enhanced by the suddenness of the change of scene. Any major change in the relations between the individual and the state, including any major shift in favor of the latter of the shares in total private revenue earned, involves changes in the fundamental habits of mind, the attitudes to life, and the valuations at least of those who are immediately concerned. Such changes usually come about by small installments and as the result of a slow process of education, which must be far advanced for codification of principles into a new body of law to be a success. We observe, in fact, that the modern principles of English taxation took about 30 years to develop and "sink in," and that the beginning of the modern system of English social policies dates back to at least the eighties of the nineteenth century, when the ideas of Chamberlain and Dilke spread dismay among their colleagues in Gladstone's second administration. The English bourgeoisie was thus given time to acclimatize.

But in this country there was no such preparation; hence, there was a different reaction. Barring the war intermezzo, there was nothing except the feeling against "monopolies" and utilities to indicate any resentment, and that was of the middle-class type only and easy to keep in hand. On the whole, the businessman's moral world was the nation's moral world right up to the crisis. And for nearly two years the Democratic administration, though doing many things which were felt to be "unorthodox" by its friends as well as by its foes, in no way displayed the attitude that we are discussing now but, on the contrary, signs of a thoroughly bourgeois attitude. The change in policy dates only from 1934–1935. It therefore followed rather than preceded the radicalization of the public mind, which in consequence of the crisis had occurred between 1930 and 1933 as radicalization in countries in which authority is associated with military values will occur in consequence of military defeat.

The analogy with the German breakdown in 1918 suggested by the last remark indicates the line on which we should explain how and why a secular process, after having failed to assert itself to any practically significant extent for fully forty years after the closing of the frontier, then suddenly became the dominant factor of the political situation. In doing so, we should no doubt have to go into many circumstances peculiar to the American environment in general and to American politics in particular, in order to understand the details of the change in attitude and of the resulting political pattern. But the fact, the broad causes, and the effects on business behavior are sufficiently obvious to establish our point without any analysis of details.[1] There are, however, two aspects which cannot be passed by.

On the one hand, we have insisted above on the importance of personnel and of methods of administration. New measures as well as new attitudes must be implemented by a skilled civil service. In any case they set a difficult task to even the most

[1] Some of the economic causes of the sudden change of scene have, however, been pointed out previously, among them the agrarian situation, the last epidemic among banks, the stock exchange crash, unemployment. The main factors which are and must remain absent from our sketch are the structure and technique of American politics and the role played by the "intellectuals." A complete analysis would also have to take account of random configurations, of which one has been mentioned, *viz.*, the fact that a presidential election occurred, a few months after the lower turning point, exactly at the time at which the sociopsychological "hangover" of the depression should be at its maximum.

experienced bureaucracy. As a rule, however, reforming governments enjoy at least the advantage of having that indispensable tool ready at hand—in most historical instances it grew up along with the tendencies which they represent. This happened, for example, in England, while in Germany the regime of 1918 was able to take over from its predecessor both an excellent civil service and a state-broken public. In this country a new bureaucracy had suddenly to be created. However good part of the material on which it was necessary to draw, and however creditable, considering the circumstances, the performance of a great many individuals and groups may have been, there was no experience, no *esprit de corps*, no clear idea even of what civil service is and what it can and cannot do. No less inexperienced—to the point of not seeing the fundamental administrative problems at all—were the men in whose hands that unwieldly apparatus was put. The tact, the reserve, the *savoir-faire* which are second nature to a seasoned bureaucracy were alike absent. Enthusiastic individuals and groups developed their own policies and tried to push them with Congress and the public, scornfully refusing counsels of self-denial and patience. In consequence, that sense of indefinite threat was immeasurably increased. English policies may be felt to be equally or more oppressive, but they are never aggressive: spectacular manifestations of aggressiveness proceed only from quarters that are firmly held in check, and never from members of the public service. The methods of the latter may be likened to deerstalking and tend to minimize trouble and disturbance caused by any given measure. Administrative methods in this country tend to maximize them and are more like those of the fox hunt—and this makes a lot of difference.

On the other hand, sudden change, unless of the Russian type, is of necessity imperfect change. It impinges upon a set of economic and political conditions which are very unequally ripe. This puts advocates and opponents of new departures in false positions, adulterates arguments, and makes it impossible to face issues squarely. In England the question of the employment of nonunionized labor, for instance, having been allowed to mature, is now one of secondary importance. In this country it cannot even be frankly put, yet it is at the bottom of much strategy and struggle which, precisely because the issue is not ripe for decision, must be expected to remain for some time a source of difficulties and losses to all parties concerned. But the standard instance is the policy followed with respect to public utilities. Here, if anywhere, there was an all but united public opinion, united at least in its hostility to the private interests involved. Moreover, European experience suggestively pointed toward nationalization of power production and transmission, which could have been carried without any shock to "business confidence" if the interests of investors had been fully safeguarded, and with but a sharp and short one if they had been sacrificed—always provided that there were no clenched fists or indeterminate threats of other nationalizations to follow. Yet it was not even attempted. The clenched fists and indeterminate threats were all the more in evidence, however, and the result was, as we have seen, to paralyze one force without substituting another. This will always result from raising issues before they can be effectively dealt with and illustrates what above has been described as deadlock. To deny that this impairs the efficiency of the economic engine or, if we retain the slogan, reduces investment opportunity, would seem to the writer unreasonable.

If the above considerations are given their proper weight, there should not be left much doubt as to the adequacy of the factors external to our process [1] to account both for the dis-

[1] Let us add, however, for the last time, "in the narrow sense adopted for the purposes of this book." In a wider sense those factors and the mentality or moral code behind them are not external to the process of economic evolution but part of it, a part as essential and unavoidable as any other and, in particular, as any "objective" shrinkage of investment opportunity could be. The above argument would, hence, be completely misunderstood if it were taken to imply that, "only" politics or humors being the matter, pristine vigor of the capitalist process could easily be restored at the next swing of the electoral pendulum. As far as that goes, the practical implications of our diagnosis do not differ much from those of the theory of vanishing investment opportunity in its usual acceptance. Even government spending as a permanent policy could be rationally defended on our diagnosis: the pattern resulting from the action of inhibiting factors would in all respects be similar to the pattern envisaged by the saving-investment theory; it would display the same lack of resilience and the same tendency toward subnormal quasi-equilibria; in particular, it would always produce or reproduce extensive unemployment. Therefore, government spending would, given the general will to conserve those inhibiting factors, always suggest itself as a remedy for shortrun difficulties each application of which would impose, under penalty of breakdown, the application of the next dose. Fear of such breakdowns

appointing features in the current Juglar and for the weakness of the response of the system to government expenditure, in particular for the failure of the latter to affect investment and employment more than it did. It cannot be proved in the sense in which a mathematical theorem can, that the balloon shriveled, not from causes inherent to its structure, but because the air was being sucked out of it. It is, however, highly plausible and, after all, only what, if we clear our minds of cant, we should expect to occur in transitional stages. Prognosis would, in this country more than in any other, have to take account of the likelihood that there will be intermissions or even reversals; of the effects of "acclimatization"; and of the fact that, if our schema is to be trusted, recovery and prosperity phases should be more, and recession and depression phases less strongly marked during the next three decades than they have been in the last two. But the sociological drift cannot be expected to change.

---

may in the end become the dominant motive even among those who on principle are most strongly opposed to spending policies.

SUMMARY OF SCHUMPETER'S THEORY OF THE BUSINESS CYCLE

by

Rendigs Fels

When in discussing the theory or history of business cycles it becomes necessary to refer to the late Professor Schumpeter's treatise,[1] an embarrassing dilemma presents itself. Either one must summarize briefly a theory too elaborate and rich in detail to lend itself to such treatment, or one must assume the reader has an intimate knowledge of the theory such as few who have not read his book recently are able to retain. This makes his treatise less useful than its merit warrants; even the historical portions are difficult to utilize directly because they contain so many allusions to details of the theoretical model. In my own work, I have felt the need of a compact summary not only to use myself but also to refer the reader to.[2] These are the reasons for the summary which follows. My aim is neither to criticize nor to "interpret" but merely to reproduce as faithfully as another mind can what Schumpeter actually said.

The Fundamental Question

To Schumpeter the fundamental question of business cycles was causation. In causation, he explicitly recognized the importance of external factors. "In fact, it would be possible to write, without any glaring absurdity, a history of business fluctuations exclusively in terms of external factors, and such a history would probably miss a smaller amount of relevant fact than one which attempts to do without them." [3] Likewise, it would be possible to frame a theory entirely in terms of external events, saying that depression occurs whenever an unfavorable event occurs. But this would leave unanswered the question as to whether the economic process in itself tends to produce booms and depressions. It is all very well to say that men die from a varicty of causes, but there is still sense to asking whether they would die "in the absence of all lesions, by virtue of the working of the human organism . . ." [4] ". . . the presence or absence of a fluctuation *inherent* to the economic process in time is practically and scientifically the fundamental problem . . . In order to make headway with it, we shall proceed as physical sciences do in those cases in which it is impossible actually to isolate a phenomenon by producing it in a laboratory: from our historic and everyday knowledge of economic behavior we shall construct a 'model' of the economic process over time, see whether it is likely to work in a wave-like way, and compare the result with observed fact." [5]

The Entrepreneur

Innovation plays the central role in Schumpeter's theory. He defined it "as the setting up of a new production function. This covers the case of a new commodity, as well as those of a new form of organization such as a merger, of the opening up of new markets, and so on." [6] Innovation is different from invention, which provides the raw material, so to speak, for innovation. The individuals who introduce new production functions as distinct from reproducing old ones and altering the proportions and quantities of factors within old ones [7] are called entrepreneurs.[8] Innovation is more difficult than the ordinary running of a business for it involves a choice not between the tried and the tried but between the tried and the untried. But once the way has been shown it becomes easier for others (1) to do the same thing, (2) to improve upon it, and (3) "to do similar things in similar lines"; the latter two categories represent what Schumpeter called "induced innovation," though the first presumably is not innovation at all. This provides the explanation for the observed facts that innovations are not evenly distributed over time but come in clusters and that they "are not at any time distributed over the whole economic system at random, but tend to concentrate in certain sectors and their surroundings." [9] Contrary to Kuznets' impression in his review, the fact of comparative rarity of innovating genius is not called upon to explain why innovations cluster during the prosperity phase of the business cycle.

Schumpeter assumed that innovations are carried out by new men and new firms. Innovation enables the new firm to make profits for a time, but eventually they are competed away, and the firm goes into decay.[10] There are exceptions, cases of giant companies which are just shells for changing personnel carrying out a succession of innovations. This Schumpeter called trustified capitalism, to distinguish it from competitive capitalism. At the time Schumpeter wrote the exceptions were not yet great enough to invalidate the model.[11] Sometimes the competing-away of profits is almost instantaneous, leading to the possibility of what Schumpeter called "Profitless Prosperities." [12]

Innovations usually require the building of new plant and equipment (or the rebuilding of old), involving time and expenditure.[13] The money comes ultimately from credit creation even though the bulk of current credit finances current transactions and has so lost its original contact with innovation that the financing of innovation has become almost the last thing a banker may properly do.[14] Saving [15] comes mainly from profits which in turn (including much that appears to be windfalls) mostly come from innovation; savings therefore in a logical sense ultimately come from credit creation too. Saving is defined as "the earmarking, by a household, of an element of its current receipts—as distinguished from 'capital gains'—for the acquisition of titles to income or for the repayment of debt." [16] Accumulation is the same thing done by firms (though Schumpeter sometimes used the word *saving* to include accumulation). Saving and accumulation are distinguished from non-spending and hoarding; saving in Schumpeter's sense can never be the cause of crisis. "The carrying into effect of the decision to acquire titles to income we shall call Investment."[17] For households, this means buying shares, bonds, and land and buildings for business use. For firms, it includes also "spending on all kinds of producers' goods beyond replacement," [18] which is called "Real Investment." Thus saving and investment are distinct events and are not necessarily equal. But they are subject to an equilibrating mechanism; if the rate of interest falls to zero, so does saving.

Equilibrium

The concept of equilibrium plays an important part in the model. As a matter of common sense, the boom year of 1872 and the crisis year of 1873 in the United States both appear unbalanced, though in very different ways, whereas 1897 represents a comparatively balanced state of affairs.[19] More explicitly,

Schumpeter used equilibrium in the Walrasian sense of every firm, industry and household having no incentive to do anything but what they are already doing.[20] The importance of the Walrasian system lies not so much in the counting of equations and unknowns to show that they are equal in number but in the tendency, which can be observed in real life, for the economy to move towards it.[21]

Real life of course does not fulfill the requirements of the Walrasian system, but this does not destroy its value.[22] Some of the exceptions are important for business cycles. In particular, equilibrium is compatible with a considerable amount of employment (estimated for England at 3.3 per cent prior to 1914), which Professor Schumpeter called normal unemployment.[23] It may arise from inappropriate wage rates, from elasticity in the concept of what constitutes an unemployable, and from familiarity with the contours of economic evolution which leads labor to hang around investment goods industries to meet peak loads.[24] Thus, even at equilibrium, the economy can expand output, an elasticity which is increased by the possibility of overtime. There are other imperfections too so that it is more appropriate to think of the real economy as passing through neighborhoods rather than points of equilibrium.[25] Equilibrium involves saving and real investment due to (population) growth and deepening of capital but no innovation.[26]

First Approximation

Schumpeter started the description of his model with many simplifications which he later dropped—perfect competition, perfect equilibrium, no saving, constant population.[27] The first approximation, therefore, is a long way from historical fact.[28] In this simplified economy, mere increase in knowledge plus the profit motive induce an entrepreneur to undertake something new and unfamiliar, borrowing money to build his plant and equipment. "Then other entrepreneurs follow, after them still others in increasing number, in the path of innovation, which becomes progressively smoothed for successors by accumulating experience and vanishing obstacles."[29] Under the simplifying assumptions used at this stage of the argument, no increase in output is possible while the first entrepreneur is building his plant; indeed, output of consumers goods declines as entrepreneurs bid factors away from them with their newly created bank balances. (Later it will be seen that output in fact increases during the innovating period because employment rises above normal.) This upsets the partial equilibria of firms and industries throughout the economy, spelling losses for some and gains for others; but at this stage the non-innovating firms in the aggregate increase profits (which had been zero), because they pay out only part of the increase in incomes but in the second round, before the new products come to market, receive all of them.[30]

When the products of the entrepreneurs at length come to market, total output of the economy is increased more than it formerly was reduced.[31] Old firms now face a new source of disequilibrium, but whereas formerly the difficulties of adaptation were tempered, even for those firms which had to undergo losses, by the increase in expenditure, the new disequilibrium requires more difficult readjustments. Nevertheless, some firms find their demand increased and make windfalls.[32] Moreover, the adverse effects may be overcompensated as long as entrepreneurial activity persists.[33]

Entrepreneurial activity eventually slackens and stops. "In actual life so many accidents and incidents combine to produce this result that we are never lacking plausible reasons with which to explain that stoppage in any given case. But this obscures the question of principle with which we are now concerned—whether the mechanism described would in the absence of such incidents and accidents run on forever (on a 'prosperity plateau') or come to a stop from reasons inherent in it and by virtue of its own effects and of the business situations it creates."[34] It *would* stop apart from accidents and incidents, first, because in any instance its possibilities are limited and eventually it results in the competing-away of profits, by which time the innovating impulse will have spent itself; and, second, because innovation upsets equilibrium, meaning "fluctuations and successive attempts at adaptation to changing temporary situations" and "the impossibility of calculating costs in a satisfactory way."[35]

Cessation of entrepreneurial activity brings new borrowing to an end (still under simplified conditions), tending to depress the price level and bringing discomfiture to many firms. But in addition "auto-daflation"—repayment of (bank) debts by entrepreneurs, destroying balances—accentuates the effects.[36] The process which now takes place—"adaptation to the new things created, including the elimination of what is incapable of adaptation, resorption of the results of innovation into the system, reorganization of economic life so as to make it conform to the data as altered by enterprise, remodeling of the system of value, liquidation of indebtedness . . . under our assumptions and with but minor qualifications . . . leads up to a new neighborhood of equilibrium . . ." The stage is now set for innovation to begin again.[37]

The above sequence of events corresponds to what are generally known as prosperity and recession.[38] But the usual welfare connotations of those terms are absent. This is partly because certain facts have not yet been introduced into the model. Nevertheless, the model in its present form brings out some essential points: prosperity is a period of abstaining from consumption for the sake of investment; recession is a period of reaping the harvest.[39]

Second Approximation — the Secondary Wave

In the prosperity phase, investment from innovating activity increases consumers spending almost as quickly as producers spending. ". . . old firms will react to this situation and . . . many of them will 'speculate' on this situation. A new factory in a village, for example, means better business for the local grocers, who will accordingly place bigger orders with wholesalers, who in turn will do the same with manufacturers, and these will expand production or try to do so, and so on. But in doing this many people will act on the assumption that the rates of change they observe will continue indefinitely, and enter into transactions which will result in losses as soon as facts fail to verify that assumption . . . New borrowing will then no longer be confined to entrepreneurs, and 'deposits' will be created to finance general expansion, each loan tending to induce another loan, each rise in prices another rise." In a footnote, Schumpeter added, "While, as we have seen, no such rise is, on principle, necessary to call forth innovations and while they are, in the Pure Model, profitable without it, there may and generally will be some which show profit only if rising prices are anticipated. These belong here and not to the igniting mechanism." This is the well-known cumulative process Schumpeter called "the secondary wave."[40] In it is included the clusters of errors, waves of optimism, and over-indebtedness which play such a large part in other theories.[41] It is quantitatively so important that it obscures the phenomena of the primary wave.[42]

"The break in secondary prosperity is similarly induced by the turn of the underlying process."[43] The reckless, fraudulent, speculative or otherwise unsuccessful enterprise of the secondary wave means much more liquidation than the primary wave implies. "All this does not necessarily amount to panic or crisis . . . but it easily induces panics or crises."[44] It leads to the "vicious spiral" which is defined by two effects: (1) "any fall in values which enforces liquidation, induces quite mechanically another fall in values;" and (2) pessimism may enter as a causal role as people realize how much there is to liquidate or even get hysterical about it.[45] As a result the process is likely to overrun the neighborhood of equilibrium toward which it is moving and enter another phase—depression—which is characterized by "Abnormal Liquidation, that is to say, by a downward revision of values and a shrinkage of operations that reduce them, often quite erratically, below their equilibrium amounts. While in recession a mechanism is at work to draw the system toward equilibrium, new disequilibrium develops now: the system again draws away from a neighborhood of equilibrium as it did during prosperity, but under the influence of a different impulse . . . But when depression has run its course . . . the system starts to feel its way back to a new neighborhood of equilibrium."[46] This constitutes the fourth phase, called recovery or revival. ". . . while recession and—if depression occurs—revival are necessary parts of the cyclical process of economic evolution, depression itself is not . . . Whether it occurs or not is a question of fact and depends on accidental circumstances, such as the mentality and temper of the business community and the public, the prevalence of get-rich-quick morals, the way . . . in which credit is handled in prosperity, the ability of the public to form an opinion about the merits of propositions, the degree to which it is given to belief in phrases about prosperity plateaus and the wonders of monetary management and so on."[47]

It is conceivable that the depression phase might go on indefinitely, but buffers in the economy tend to limit it. Closing down of a factory may force a grocery out of business, but the grocer's market does not entirely disappear; and while some of the factory's creditors may be forced into bankruptcy, others will be able to stand the strain.[48] Moreover, "total income fluctuates less than total output, the item wages plus salaries less than total income, expenditure on consumers' goods less than wages plus salaries" partly because of the dilution of effects just described but partly because there are incomes little affected by depression.[49] On the other hand, the spiral is often accentuated by external factors.[50] The depression phase is longer than the spiral.[51] Once depression stops, revival to a neighborhood of equilibrium follows as a matter of course. To assert the contrary is to claim that business men will deliberately incur losses or forego profits.[52] Once equilibrium has been reached, conditions are sufficiently stable to induce another burst of innovating. Then the cycle repeats itself.

If depressive forces can gather mometum so that the economy outruns equilibrium into the depression phase, why cannot revival similarly gather momentum and outrun equilibrium into prosperity without benefit of innovation? This is less likely because there is nothing in revival analogous to the breakdown of the secondary wave during recession. But even if excess optimism lifted the economy above equilibrium, it would soon relapse in the absence of innovation (though perhaps with a damped fluctuation around equilibrium.[53]

At this point Schumpeter relaxed the restrictive assumptions with which he started. First, "each neighborhood [of equilibrium] contains undigested elements of previous prosperities and depressions, innovations not yet completely worked out, results of faulty or otherwise imperfect adaptations, and so on." [54] In particular, as noted above in the discussion of the concept of equilibrium, firms and workers in cyclical industries learn to provide for peak loads, so that in equilibrium there is capacity to expand output.[55] Second, Schumpeter dropped the assumption of perfect competition. "In fact, evolution in our sense is the most powerful influence in creating such imperfections all around.[56] This complicates the analysis of reality, makes proofs less stringent, gives rise to zones of indeterminateness, inserts buffers into the mechanism, lengthens the lags in sequences of events, and otherwise makes life difficult for the economist but nothing more.[57] One important consequence, however, is that full employment is no longer associated with equilibrium but, because imperfections create unemployment, indicates a particular type of disequilibrium.[58]

Third Approximation — Many Simultaneous Cycles

So far, the model has been discussed as if there were only one wave-like motion. Actually, there are three reasons for expecting the simultaneous operation of many different waves.

First, "The periods of gestation and of absorption of effects by the economic system will not, in general, be equal for all the innovations that are undertaken at any time. There will be innovations of relatively long span, and along with them others will be undertaken which run their course, on the back of the wave created by the former, in shorter periods." [59]

Second, "Major innovations hardly ever emerge in their final form or cover in one throw the whole field that will ultimately be their own . . . One railroad or a few lines may be all, and more than all, that can be successfully built in a given environment at a given time . . . In such cases, innovation is carried out in steps each of which constitutes a cycle. But these cycles may display a family likeness, and a relation to one another which is easy to understand and which tends to weld them into a higher unit that will stand out as a historical individual. The case is entirely different from the previous one. There we had a multiplicity of cycles each of which was an independent entity. Here we have a sequence of cycles of one type only, and the cycle of higher order is but a product or composite of these and has no existence of its own." [60]

Third, there may be a cumulation of effects from all the commercial and industrial processes of an epoch which take the form of a long cycle. "Railroadization may again serve as example. Expenditure on, and the opening of, a new line has some immediate effects on business in general, on competing means of transport, and on the relative position of centers of production. It requires more time to bring into use the opportunities of production newly created by the railroad and to annihilate others. And it takes still longer for population to shift, new cities to develop, other cities to decay, and, generally, the new face of the country to take shape that is adapted to the environment as altered by the railroadization." [61]

Strictly speaking, we should expect an indefinite number of cycles. For analytic *convenience*, however, Schumpeter in his historical outline used a three-cycle schema: the forty-month or Kitchin cycle, the ten-year or Juglar cycle, and the 60-year or

Kondratieff cycle.[62] The first Kondratieff cycle was that of the industrial revolution, from the 1780's to 1842; the second that of steam and steel, from 1842 to 1897; the third that of electricity, chemistry, and motors, from 1898 on.[63] There is nothing either in the model or reality which requires three cycles. More, however, would be cumbersome, less would be inadequate to illustrate the three reasons given above.[64]

At this point, Schumpeter postulates "that each Kondratieff should contain an integral number of Juglars and each Juglar an integral number of Kitchins. The warrant for this is in the nature of the circumstances which give rise to multiplicity. If waves of innovations of shorter span play around a wave of a similar character but of longer span, the sequence of the phases of the latter will so determine the conditions under which the former rise and break as to make a higher unit out of them, even if the innovations which create them are entirely independent of the innovations which carry the longer wave. There will be a relation between the phases of each of the two movements which will tend to keep the shorter ones within the longer span." [65]

All cycles are generated by innovation (though Schumpeter on page 172 expressed some doubts about Kitchins, which may be "waves of adaptations" and have either two or four phases, depression and revival not being a necessary part of the schema.[66] However, in the historical outlines there are no examples of 2-phase cycles. Since the three cycles interfere with each other, nothing is known *a priori* about the net result, other than the presumption that when all three are in the same phase, particularly if it is depression, the movement will be of unusual intensity.[67] By way of illustration—but nothing more—Schumpeter presented a chart [68] showing three sine curves and the result of adding them. In history, Schumpeter found three Kitchins to each Juglar, and six Juglars to each Kondratieff, though there is nothing in his model which would lead him to expect such regularity. There are some exceptions, however, due to external events.[69] The chart accordingly shows three of the smallest sine curves for each intermediate-sized curve, and six of the intermediates for one large sine curve. The result of adding the three is a curve of considerable irregularity.

One more point. "Since, of course, shorter waves must in most cases rise from a situation which is not a neighborhood of equi-

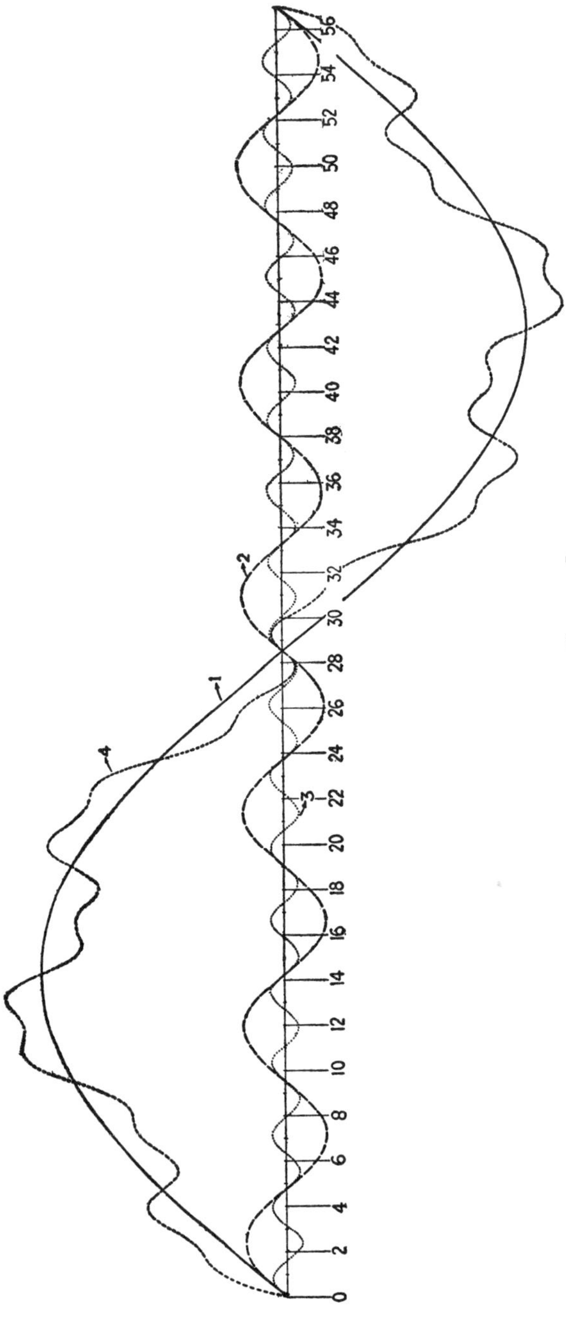
1
2
3
4
0
2
4
6
8
10
12
14
16
18
20
22
24
26
28
30
32
34
36
38
40
42
44
46
48
50
52
54
56

CHART I

librium but disturbed by the effects of the longer waves in progress at this time, we must now modify our previous proposition that the process of innovation starts from such neighborhoods only, as well as our concept of neighborhood of equilibrium itself. From the standpoint of the transactions which carry a fluctuation of short span, the sweep of the longer waves constitutes the long-time conditions of doing business, although full equilibrium could, even theoretically, exist only in the points in which all cycles pass their normals." [70]

Other Fluctuations

Cycles of crop production belong, according to Schumpeter, in the category of "special cycles." Although in a closed economy increased spending by farmers as a result of favorable crop situations is in general offset by reduced spending elsewhere, "Expecting bigger receipts, farmers will borrow and spend promptly, beyond the requirements of harvesting and moving the crops (which if the harvest be supernormal will also, though not proportionately, be supernormal). We observe, in fact, increased banking activity in this country's agricultural districts in such cases. This, then, my enliven business all round. Moreover, many industries will on their own initiative prepare for meeting farmers' demand, and also borrow and expand, before any compensating fall in demand from other sectors has had time to show, which therefore may not show at all." [71] Schumpeter considered that such fluctuations superimpose themselves (though not additively) upon the cycles of his model.

He knew of no other cases of special cycles. In particular, "We have seen in the instance of building that what strongly looks like a very special movement can yet be brought within the schema of cyclical events and understood as a consequence of conditions which, in turn, can be traced to our process." [72] Apparently, this sentence refers back to a discussion on pages 159–160 of the relation between building cycles and cycles of interest rates generated by his model: "In prewar Germany, for instance, apartment-house building—significantly enough, *not* factory building—could have been represented with satisfactory approximation as a function of the mortgage rate alone. And something of the kind is suggested by the fact that residential building in the United States precedes the Harvard barometer's curve *B* by a few months—which makes it in the short run roughly inverse to the money curve C. This is somewhat more significant than it looks because, apart from the influence of interest, we should, if anything, expect a lag." It is likely, however, that Schumpeter when claiming his model accounts for the building cycle also had in mind the effect of innovations (*e.g.*, railroads) in opening up investment opportunities in building.

Schumpeter criticized Kalecki's model of the business cycle for omitting the equilibrating mechanism of the interest rate, inclusion of which would cause Kalecki's wave to die down unless new disturbances occur. This observation, however, "affords the opportunity to recognize the contribution of Mr. Kalecki's construction: it adds one more item to the list of possible waves of adaptation or of the reasons to expect wavelikeness of contours within the cycle." [73]

Implications

Schumpeter's theory implies that the output of consumers' goods increases most in recessions and revival.[74] "We shall . . . expect the facts to conform best to the above expectation in the case of the Kondratieff, less so in the case of the Juglar, least of all in the Kitchin cycle." [75] Output of producers' goods should increase in revival and prosperity and decrease, or increase less, in recession and depression.[76] Consequently, "total output will increase through all phases of the cycle, 'deep' depression alone excepted . . . the exception hardly ever extending over the whole of the depressive phase, since it is due to panics and vicious spirals, which as a rule do not last more than one year." [77]

In principle, the price level should mean the prices in the market for consumers' goods.[78] In this sense, "Price level should rise in prosperity . . . and fall in recession . . . *more than it had risen in the preceding prosperity*." [79] The continued fall of prices in depression tends to be corrected in recovery, but because output continues to increase in recovery, the correction is not complete.[80] "In the long swing of the Kondratieff, in particular, short-run fluctuations such as are caused by panics and spirals play so small a role that there is not the same reason to expect a rise in price level—at least in its absolute values as distinguished from rates of change—during a Kondratieff recovery as there is to expect it for the recovery phases of shorter cycles." [81]

"[E]xpectation as to the cyclical behavior of interest . . . will be for a lagged rise in prosperity and a similarly lagged fall in recession . . . further fall will, in general, occur in depression as a consequence of abnormal restriction of volume of business. But as in all other cases, it must be remembered that the processes of depression are erratic, even apart from the effects of panics on the rate of interest which are peculiar to it. Uncertainty extends, in consequence, to its behavior in revival, which should bring it back to neighborhood [equilibrium] value." [82]

"Obviously, it is not unreasonable to expect that employment will increase at a slackening rate during prosperity, that it will decrease at an accelerating rate during recession, that the rate of decrease will be at a maximum when the system embarks upon depression and that employment will then go on decreasing at a rate which gradually decreases until recovery point is reached, after which it will increase, haltingly at first and then more and more decidedly as the processes of recovery get the upper hand, until equilibrium is reached. All this is highly schematized, of course, and very far from being the picture of any actual process, but it is not absurd. [83]

Expenditure rises in revival and prosperity and diminishes in depression, "but for recession it is necessary to recall that owing to the facts, first, that entrepreneurs' repayments do not actually go to the length of eliminating their debts and, second, that other borrowing partly, wholly, or more than wholly replaces entrepreneurs' borrowing, our expectation loses its definiteness. All we can say is that system expenditure will increase in prosperity more and in recession less than total output, although we may also hazard the guess that it will increase in the recession of every cycle at a smaller rate than—due attention being paid to the simultaneous phases of the other cycles—in the preceding prosperity." [84]

"In a cyclical movement fashioned according to our pure model expectation would, if that movement were confined to one country and if the economic process in the others were stationary or merely growing (in our sense), be for decrease of exports and increase of imports in the positive phase, and for the opposite behavior of both in the negative phase. We cannot hope to find this, of course. But traces of it show in many instances . . ." [85]

Because the stock market is freer from friction than almost

any other market, "it is natural to expect that upward movements on the stock exchange will, in general and in the absence of unfavorable external factors, set in earlier and gather force more quickly than the corresponding upward movements in business, *i.e.*, often come about already in the later stages of revival when things are beginning to look better every day, with new possibilities showing themselves. Similarly, it is to be expected that stock prices will turn before other indicators, *i.e.*, when in the later stages of prosperity limitations and difficulties emerge and it becomes clear that possible achievements have been fully discounted." [86]

It is not easy to crystallize a clear-cut summary from Schumpeter's discussion of how he expected wages to behave.[87] The wage bill (*i.e.*, total payrolls) he expected to rise most strongly during prosperity,[88] with money wage rates displaying a lagged rise (owing to existence of unemployment in equilibrium) in prosperity and a lagged fall on the downgrade.[89] Neither the wage bill nor money wage rates need, however, decline in recession nor even in depression.[90] Real wages increase more in recession, depression and revival phases, especially of the Kondratieff, than in prosperity.[91]

During prosperity, costs will increasingly encroach upon profits, and recession brings real trouble for many firms.[92]

All of these expectations are subject to interference from external factors. Any given failure of facts to conform to expectations need not count against the theory provided external events can be found which account for the deviation.

FOOTNOTES TO SUMMARY

[1] Joseph A. Schumpeter, *Business Cycles*: *A Theoretical, Historical, and Statistical Analysis of the Capitalist Process,* New York, 1939, 2 vols.

[2] An excellent summary is, however, available in Richard V. Clemence and Francis S. Doody, *The Schumpeterian System,* Cambridge, 1950, Part II. See the reviews by Simon S. Kuznets (*American Economic Review,* June 1940, pp. 257-71), Oscar Lange (*Review of Economic Statistics,* November 1941, pp. 190-93), Jacob Marshak (*Journal of Political Economy,* December 1940, pp. 889-94), and E. Rothbarth (*Economic Journal,* 1942, pp. 233-9). See also Joseph A. Schumpeter, *The Theory of Economic Development,* (tr. by Redvers Opie), Cambridge, Mass., 1934, Ch. 6 (a version which does not include Professor Schumpeter's later thinking), and Joseph A. Schumpeter, "The Analysis of Ecoonmic Change," *Review of Economic Statistics,* May 1935, pp. 2-10, reprinted in *Readings in Business Cycle Theory,* Philadelphia, 1944, pp. 1-19 (a version which omits many details).

[3] I, p. 12. (References not otherwise specified are to *Business Cycles.*)

[4] I, p. 34.

[5] *Readings,* p. 3.

[6] I, p. 87.

[7] I, pp. 87-89 and 94.

[8] I, p. 102.

[9] I, pp. 99-101.

[10] I, pp. 94-96.

[11] I, pp. 96-97.

[12] I, p. 105.

[13] I, p. 93.

[14] I, pp. 110-11, and 114.

[15] I, pp. 75-84.

[16] I, p. 75.

[17] I, p. 76.

[18] *Ibid.*

[19] *Readings,* p. 5.

[20] I, pp. 42-43.

[21] I, p. 47.

[22] *Ibid.*

[23] II, pp. 511-13.

[24] II, p. 511.

[25] I, p. 71.

[26] I, pp. 79 and 83-84.

[27] I, p. 130.

[28] I, p. 137.

[29] I, p. 131.

[30] I, pp. 131-132.

[31] I, p. 133.

[32] I, p. 134.

[33] I, pp. 134-135.

[34] I, p. 135.
[35] *Ibid.*
[36] I, p. 136.
[37] I, p. 137.
[38] I, p. 138.
[39] I, pp. 142-143.
[40] I, p. 145.
[41] I, pp. 140 and 146.
[42] I, p. 146.
[43] I, p. 148.
[44] *Ibid.*
[45] *Ibid.*
[46] I, p. 149.
[47] I, p. 150.
[48] I, p. 153.
[49] I, p. 155.
[50] I, p. 153.
[51] I, p. 154.
[52] I, p. 152.
[53] I, p. 157, note 1.
[54] I, p. 157.
[55] I, p. 158.
[56] I, p. 160.
[57] *Ibid.*
[58] I, p. 161.
[59] I, pp. 166-167.
[60] I, pp. 167-168.
[61] I, p. 168.
[62] I, p. 169.
[63] I, p. 170.
[64] I, pp. 169-70. According to note 1 on page 170, the second and third reasons bear mainly on the Kondratieff cycle. Whether the first reason serves mainly to distinguish Kitchins from Juglars or applies equally well to distinguishing Juglars from Kondratieffs is not made clear.
[65] I, p. 172.
[66] I, p. 172.
[67] I, p. 173.
[68] I, p. 213. See Chart I, to which I have added such dates of the cycles as I have found in *Business Cycles*, though Schumpeter himself regarded the dates as merely suggestive.
[69] I, pp. 173-174.
[70] I, p. 173.
[71] I, p. 178.
[72] I, p. 179.
[73] I, p. 188.
[74] II, pp. 502-503. What he meant to say beyond this is not altogether clear. According to my interpretation, there is normally some increase in prosperity; whether it decreases or increases in depression depends on whether there are or are not spirals or panics; if output falls in depression, then output increases more rapidly in revival than recession.

[75] II, p. 503.

[76] II, p. 501. This expectation is shaped partly by growth (especially in the Kondratieff) and by the circumstance that "the demand for equipment that is *induced* by entrepreneurial activity not only does not cease, but actually concentrates in recession and revival . . ." (Schumpeter's italics.) See also II, pp. 593-594.

[77] II, pp. 500-501.

[78] II, p. 458 and preceding.

[79] II, p. 462. (Schumpeter's italics.)

[80] II, pp. 462-463.

[81] II, p. 463.

[82] II, p. 628.

[83] I, p. 209.

[84] II, p. 553. For a similar statement concerning money national income, see II, p. 562; for bank balances, II, p. 581. "Clearings [taken to represent expenditure] should . . . rise more in prosperity and fall more in depression than balances do." II, p. 585.

[85] II, p. 666.

[86] II, p. 685. See also p. 689 on new stock issues and foundation of new firms.

[87] See II, pp. 568-577.

[88] II, pp. 568 and 571.

[89] II, p. 572.

[90] II, p. 573.

[91] II, pp. 576-577.

[92] II, pp. 481 and 685.

INDEX

C

G

H

I

S

T

U

V

W

Y